A NATURAL HISTORY OF PRA

Joan Richardson provides a fascinating and compelling account of the emergence of the quintessential American philosophy: pragmatism. She demonstrates pragmatism's engagement with various branches of the natural sciences and traces the development of Jamesian Pragmatism from the late nineteenth century through modernism, following its pointings into the present. Richardson combines strands from America's religious experience with scientific information to offer interpretations that break new ground in literary and cultural history. This book exemplifies the value of interdisciplinary approaches to producing literary criticism. In a series of highly original readings of Edwards, Emerson, William and Henry James, Stevens, and Stein, *A Natural History of Pragmatism* tracks the interplay of religious motive, scientific speculation, and literature in shaping an American aesthetic. Wide-ranging and bold, this groundbreaking book will be essential reading for all students and scholars of American literature.

JOAN RICHARDSON is Professor of English, Comparative Literature, and American Studies at The Graduate Center, City University of New York (CUNY). She is the author of the two-volume critical biography, *Wallace Stevens: The Early Years, 1879–1923* (1986) and *Wallace Stevens: The Later Years, 1923–1955* (1988) and co-editor, with Frank Kermode, of The Library of America edition *Wallace Stevens: Collected Poetry and Prose* (1997). She has been the recipient of a Senior Fellowship from the National Endowment for the Humanities, a Mellon Arts and Society Fellowship, a Woodrow Wilson Fellowship, Huntington Library Research Fellowships, and several research awards from the Professional Staff Congress of CUNY.

Recent books in this series

152 JOAN RICHARDSON
    A Natural History of Pragmatism: The Fact of Feeling from Jonathan
    Edwards to Gertrude Stein
151 EZRA F. TAWIL
    The Making of Racial Sentiment: Slavery and the Birth of the Frontier
    Romance
150 ARTHUR RISS
    Race, Slavery and Liberalism in Nineteenth-Century American Literature
149 JENNIFER ASHTON
    From Modernism to Postmodernism: American Poetry and Theory in the
    Twentieth Century
148 MAURICE S. LEE
    Slavery, Philosophy, and American Literature, 1830–1860
147 CINDY WEINSTEIN
    Family, Kinship and Sympathy in Nineteenth-Century American Literature
146 ELIZABETH HEWITT
    Correspondence and American Literature, 1770–1865
145 ANNA BRICKHOUSE
    Transamerican Literary Relations and the Nineteenth-Century Public Sphere
144 ELIZA RICHARDS
    Gender and the Poetics of Reception in Poe's Circle

A NATURAL HISTORY OF PRAGMATISM

The Fact of Feeling from Jonathan Edwards to Gertrude Stein

JOAN RICHARDSON

The Graduate Center
The City University of New York

CAMBRIDGE
UNIVERSITY PRESS

CAMBRIDGE UNIVERSITY PRESS
Cambridge, New York, Melbourne, Madrid, Cape Town, Singapore, São Paulo

Cambridge University Press
The Edinburgh Building, Cambridge CB2 2RU, UK

Published in the United States of America by Cambridge University Press, New York

www.cambridge.org
Information on this title: www.cambridge.org/9780521694506

First published 2007

Printed in the United Kingdom at the University Press, Cambridge

A catalogue record for this publication is available from the British Library

ISBN-13 978-0-521-83748-4 hardback
ISBN-10 0-521-83748-0 hardback

ISBN-13 978-0-521-69450-6 paperback
ISBN-10 0-521-69450-7 paperback

For Raf, Anno, and Marina

Contents

Preface   *page* ix
List of abbreviations   xvii

1   Introduction: frontier instances   1

2   In Jonathan Edwards's room of the idea   24

3   Emerson's moving pictures   62

4   William James's feeling of *if*   98

5   Henry James's more than rational distortion   137

6   Wallace Stevens's radiant and productive atmosphere   179

7   Gertrude Stein, James's Melancthon/a   232

Notes   253
Bibliography   303
Index   316

Preface

The chapters here follow the moves in the American language game that comes to be known as Pragmatism, specifically, the method of thinking described by William James in his 1907 volume. My argument opens by tracing the conceptual framing of America's native philosophy out of an earlier form of thinking brought to the New World by seventeenth-century Puritan ministers, beginning its adaptation in conditions belonging to what William Bradford called "a hideous and desolate wilderness, full of wild beasts and wild men." The impelling theological motive to build "a city upon a hill" was informed and sustained at its deepest level by the practice of typology, the manner of reading the Old Testament as prefiguring the New, extended naturally, as it were, in a strange and frightening landscape, to reading all facts, all things, as signs of continuing Divine Providence. The settlers recorded their notations in journals, sermons, and poems. What happened to the idea of Providence thus construed represents the first stirring of the mind's life in America as it pursued its Reformation project. Being lost amidst signs, in a native and naive semiotic experiment, was prerequisite to reform, if not reform itself. Spiritual conversion was to be amazed by grace and performative utterance its testimony. Truth as what happens to an idea was lived experience in this new world long before being inscribed in its philosophical method.

My subjects are figures whose work most clearly evidences the development of this thinking language that announces itself as Pragmatism: Jonathan Edwards, Ralph Waldo Emerson, William James, Henry James, Gertrude Stein, and Wallace Stevens. The argument is grounded in the premise that both thinking and language are life forms, subject to the same laws as other life forms; indeed, as we know, and as will be discussed in Chapter 3, it was language theory that provided Charles Darwin the model for what would become evolutionary theory. Evolution, as we now know as well, proceeds by imperfect replication, the ongoing result of the spiralling alignments of matching and mismatching protein strands, repetition with variation; detailing the relation of this process to what happens in language will begin in Chapter 2. Each of the writers I consider perceived language not only as matter but as all that matters in interpreting what Stevens called the "exquisite environment of fact."

For the introductory chapter I borrow from Francis Bacon, by way of Darwin's *Notebooks*, the term "frontier instances" – "cases in which we are enabled to trace that general law which seems to pervade all nature – the law, as it is termed, of continuity"– to describe the works under discussion because they illustrate their authors' realization of language as an organic form, an instance of "that general law." Of course, when "that general law" began to be recognized and eventually theorized and named as "evolution" during the extended period covered in the scope of this volume, something happened not only to the idea of truth, but to what has been called by W. V. O. Quine and Richard Rorty following him, expanding the notion, the "'idea' idea." Alfred North Whitehead described this shift as well somewhat earlier when he underlined the signal contribution made by William James in applying the Darwinian information to thinking about thinking and language. Not only did James and each of the other writers examined here understand language to be an evolving form, but each experimented with it, like the pigeon breeders described by Darwin in *On the Origin of Species*, who, having observed chance variations, natural selection, chose specific traits to propagate.

The multifariousness of the New World situation, where so many forms of animal and vegetable life, ranges of geological scale, extremes of climate and weather had no names or categories in existing systems of classification, demanded of those intent on survival, of themselves and of the idea of spiritual community informing their continuing errand, acute attention to the double task of preserving in the texts they wove enough of what was familiar from the past to provide continuity with it while at the same time providing a map of the exotic physical and spiritual terrain: the result, "old wine in new bottles"– familiar words set spinning and hissing in sentential ratios, patterns of repetition, grammatical inversions, varieties of paradox, semantic expansions, evasions of predication, and contextual oxymorons stretching the inherited language to describe the new facts and to accommodate the fact of feeling in meeting them. The traits selected to be bred into America's linguistic strain by the writers who are my subjects were to preserve the habit of religious experience and expression while braiding into it the most accurate representations possible of the natural world insofar as it came to be understood in their moments. Each one, a self-appointed priest of the invisible, diligently read in current natural historical and scientific literature and tried in varying syntactic, grammatical, and logical arrangements to mimic what Emerson called "the method of nature."

Darwin, as we know, revised *Origin* five times and attempted to rid his sentences of the idea of teleology, of design, trying to transform the inherited language of intention that his discoveries had disturbed. Similarly, Edwards, Emerson, William and Henry James, Stein, and Stevens repeatedly performed the reflexive gesture of looking back at the forms of language in use and at earlier forms they used, aligned those forms against newly imagined projections of the shape and movement of the cosmos that came more and more to replace the idea of heaven, and transcribed these imaginings into their verbal stock. The recombinant forms of their visions and revisions produced vigorous hybrids that reflect continuing, asymptotic adjustments of what Emerson described as the "axis of vision" to things as they are in the "flying Perfect." At the same time, these hybrid forms offer linguistic analogues of the experience of being lost amidst signs. These analogues describe not only the fact of the experience but the "fact of feeling" inseparable from it. "Amazing grace" for the audiences of these texts was and is an exercise in Pragmatist thinking where readers/listeners devised and devise manners of reading and interpretation, *conversions* to new ways of seeing and understanding that save them from confusion.

The chapters here point to the informing texts in natural history, language theory, and science read by my subjects and discuss the ways in which what they learned inflected their ministerial mission to fashion an instrument more adequate to describe the situation in which they found themselves, stranded on the edge of a new world of physical and spiritual experience, like the Doctor of Geneva at the end of Stevens's eponymously titled poem, without words. The solutions these writers found to fill the anguished space, the expanding void opened by the gradual disappearance of God, were, in the most primary sense, aesthetic, expressions of the feelings earlier embodied in purely religious forms, prayers, and rituals. As these latter forms decayed, their practitioners, left without the ballast of belief the forms provided, were set off-balance; the writers discussed in the pages to follow sought to restore balance by adjusting the "axis of vision" to the laws of nature. We know from biology and work extending from it into cybernetics that all organisms, from the cellular level to complex systems, depend on the self-regulating feedback process called homeostasis to maintain the internal balance necessary to life. The homeostatic function of the life of the mind is the work of the aesthetic. Recent research in neurobiology, cognitive science, and neuropsychology – that of Gerald M. Edelman, Antonio Damasio, Oliver Sacks, Jean-Pierre Changeux, John

Tooby, and Leda Cosmides, among others (all acknowledging their debt to William James) – maps the contours of the aesthetic understood in this way; importantly, the descriptions offered by these researchers counter reductive adaptationist explanations. The aesthetic choices made by the subjects of this volume, choices shaped from attending to, in William James's phrasing, "real fact in the making," instance what he would describe as the method of Pragmatism, projecting imaginative structures, informed by feeling, which provide, again in his words, "resting-places" for thinking to go on. That these choices derived for these writers from their observing aspects of nature, in the desire to offer, in Stevens's words, a new "vulgate of experience" to those still searching for something in which to believe, gave actual survival value to the hybrid forms they conceived.

The present work began years ago as I set out searching for the elements that combined to shape what Stevens called his "rude aesthetic." Appropriately, I borrow his phrase "the fact of feeling" for my title. Following his pointings, persistently looking for the "true subject" twined and twinned in the "poetry of the subject"– the two things he described as always happening at once in poetry – brought me to the "frontier instances" I map in these chapters. Reading and rereading through Emerson's essays and lectures has unsettled not only the way I read words on pages but everything around me, making the ordinary extraordinary, an ongoing secular conversion. Reading Edwards's astonishing contributions has made me feel the urgency of America's "errand into the wilderness," an errand which continues ever more pressingly as we find ourselves bewildered by the perversion of the nation's spiritual aspirations. My deepening reading of William James, in the context of Edwards and Emerson before him and those, considered here, following him, has transformed my habit of mind, his work serving for me as the scripture through which I interpret the fact of feeling thinking. In this I am one more in a growing congregation whose membership includes individuals one is sometimes surprised at first to meet among the brethren.*

---

* David Milch, for example, creator of *Deadwood* and chief writer for earlier successful television series (*Hill Street Blues*, *NYPD Blue*), attributes his noted ability for characterization to what he learned from William James about both the "physiology of thought" and "spiritual experience" as a "gradual unfolding" determined to the greatest extent by environmental factors – *Deadwood*, the latest "frontier instance," being an illustration of these aspects. Milch, once a student of R. W. B. Lewis, had at one point conceived a twelve-part television series about the James family on which he collaborated with Lewis. Though it did not materialize, Lewis went on to write *The Jameses: A Family Narrative* and opened his acknowledgments with a paragraph expressing "a very large debt of gratitude" to Milch from whom, as he indicates, he drew "many ideas, feelings and emphases originating in [their] discussions and dry runs."

A preliminary version of a section of my first chapter appeared as "The Fact of Feeling: American Aesthetics" in *REAL: Yearbook of Research in English and American Literature,* vol. XV, pragmatism and literary studies, ed. Winfried Fluck (Tübingen: Gunter Narr Verlag, 1999); a portion of the Stevens chapter appeared as "Music is Thinking, Then, Sound: An Aesthetic Exercise" in *"Never Again Would Birds' Song Be The Same": Essays on Early Modern and Modern Poetry,* ed. Jennifer Lewin (New Haven: Beinecke Library, University Press of New England, 2002). A version of the second half of the Emerson chapter was presented as a lecture, "Emerson's Moving Pictures," at the European Association for American Studies Biennial Conference (Graz, Austria, April 2000). Portions of the William James chapter were presented at meetings of the Society for Literature, Science and the Arts (Paris, 2004; Chicago, 2005).

Readers will notice throughout my indebtedness to those who through their work have helped me learn how to read, what to do: put my ear to the ground of language to listen for shifting rhythms, halts, swerves in direction that signal movements of mind. Indispensable have been the directions offered by Stanley Cavell and by Richard Poirier, who examine, as well as exemplify in their own styles, the performative aspects of language and thinking; the acute attention to the music of words charged with the energy of particular times and places demonstrated by John Hollander; the manner of relating scientific fact to developing fiction epitomized by Gillian Beer. My attempt is to honor their models in my manner and to practice the self-reflexive method of Pragmatism, incorporating into my sentences and paragraphs phrases, echoes, passages that provided and continue to provide the materials for the "room of the idea" in which I have been able to imagine how this variety of intellectual experience came to be in the ongoing American experiment. These materials are the facts to which my feeling, my sense of the thing – *pragma* – is attached. My hope is that both the content and form of my offering will not only illustrate the naturalization of the spiritual aspect of the life of the mind as it becomes Pragmatism – complementing Louis Menand's indispensable historical tracing in *The Metaphysical Club* – but will, at the same time, help in clarifying what we mean by the "aesthetic" or "aesthetics" by looking at its evolution in a specific environment, thereby naturalizing it as well. My motive in attempting these ends, my own experiment, is to open the fields of literary and cultural history to broader consideration of what constitutes critical reading by taking fully into account, as did William James, the Darwinian information. Taking this information into account does not mean reading as a reductive exercise in evolutionary criticism.

On the contrary, following James's lead, reading as it is considered and exemplified in these chapters underscores the stochastic amplification of human experience attendant on using language in reciprocal relation to thinking. Indeed, James's project was to continue Emerson's effort and restore to what we understand as "thinking" its sense in Greek where the word for thought, *stochasmos*, embodies the activity of aiming for a target, *stochos*.

My offering here would not have been possible without, in addition to the contributions made by those mentioned above, the vast body of scholarship surrounding each of my subjects. This scholarship has provided material for discussions in the graduate seminars in American Aesthetics that I have been conducting for the last few years, in and out of which my thinking has developed. My references point only to a small portion of the work of these others who have nourished me. Equally important has been my reading in philosophy, in natural history and natural philosophy, in science (including current work in evolutionary theory and neuroscience), in semiotics, in aesthetics. It has been a privilege to have been able to do my work, voice my part, and I would like now to acknowledge the personal and institutional support that most immediately provided its occasion.

Particular thanks to Luke Menand who, a few years ago, in a gesture typical of his generous collegiality, suggested to Heinz Ickstadt and Winfried Fluck of the John F. Kennedy Institute at the Free University in Berlin, who had invited him to give a talk on pragmatism at an upcoming conference, that, as he would be unable to attend, they invite me instead. The talk I gave, the core of what would become my chapter on Edwards, was heard by Ross Posnock, who afterwards asked me who was "doing the book." Heinz Ickstadt, in turn, then President of the European Association of American Studies, invited me to propose a paper for the following year's EAAS conference; the paper I proposed is a portion of what developed into my Emerson chapter. Luke Menand has consistently, since we conducted seminars jointly (and once as a troika with John Patrick Diggins) at The Graduate Center of CUNY, urged me on in pursuing my "take" on pragmatism and supported my efforts in doing so, as have Stanley Cavell and Richard Poirier in response to reading early draft sections of chapters. These Emersonian encouragements to do my work have been essential to it, as has, since the beginning of my career, that of John Hollander who, during the years he was himself at The Graduate Center, served as my adviser as I completed a dissertation on Stevens. Without John's introducing me, by way of my work, to Richard Poirier, I would not have learned to write, as well as to read, "in slow motion."

My experience in respect to these relationships is paralleled more recently by that with another who has become indispensable to me as interlocutor in the ongoing conversation surrounding Jamesian Pragmatism, as well as in so many others – Steven Meyer, like me indebted to John Hollander and Richard Poirier for their inspired mentoring. Indeed, his thanks to them in the preface to *Irresistible Dictation: Gertrude Stein and the Correlations of Writing and Science* could, with the substitution of "Stevens" for "Stein" serve as my own. The comments Steven Meyer made as reader of a complete draft of this volume, as well as the additions he suggested, exemplify the kinds of illuminations attendant on reading in slow motion and illustrate premises we share, voiced in his preface as well: "that texts exist in relation to other texts or they do not exist at all, and that it is in uncovering these relations that the activity of reading proceeds"; "that the practice of reading is never restricted to any particular field, and always occurs between fields." I am immensely grateful to him. I am no less grateful to Ross Posnock whose responses to my work all along the way have been truly thrilling and all the more valuable for me as he is, and notes himself, laconic by temperament. It is he who is most directly responsible for making this volume possible. I am grateful for his insight, his trust, his help, our conversations. I had not anticipated such wonderful new friendships to be among the pleasures of working on this book.

I am most fortunate, as well, in enjoying old friendships that have richly nourished me. Ann Lauterbach's intellectual vigilance and rigor, her linguistic acuity and vitality have persistently stimulated my thinking. Our long talks over the years about Emerson, Stevens, Stein, William James, and sometimes just about this word or that have been as valuable as her comments about the sections of the book she read as it was being written. William Kelly, with whom I have been in conversation about the contours and particularities of American literature, religion, and history since we were appointed to the faculty of The Graduate Center in 1986, has been a constant source of motivation for me in that I have had to meet his insistent demands for grounding as I have tried to persuade him, the most formidable of devil's advocates, of the central significance of Emerson and William James to thinking about thinking. His meticulous reading of the entire typescript produced suggestions which directed me precisely to the points in the argument needing further elaboration. Further, he, as President of the Center, together with Steven Kruger, Executive Officer of the Program in English, and the Research Foundation of the Professional Staff Congress of CUNY have provided the institutional support without which I could not have completed my work. I am grateful, as well, to my students and colleagues, my dear friends at the Center who, in response to lectures and seminars I have given have offered comments and insights that have refined my thinking, and particularly to: Morris Dickstein, Richard McCoy, Joseph Wittreich, Jennifer Bernstein, Andrea Knutson, Devin Zuber, Sharon Lattig, Maggie Nelson, Matthew Gold. I also want to acknowledge, in memory, Alfred Kazin, my colleague for a while at the Center. I was privileged in having been able to talk with him often about the writers and texts he so loved. We one day walked back and forth across the Brooklyn Bridge as he recited Whitman, punctuating lines with comments describing his ever new astonishment at the power of his words. I remain enormously indebted to Alfred's spirit. He was one of my wonderful friends.

In the years I have been writing these chapters my son has grown from uncertain and sometimes chaotic adolescence into manhood and become another of the friends on whom I depend. His reading over my shoulder, especially during this last year, produced conversations that made me rethink and rephrase many passages. Similarly, Leslie Miller, my friend for ever so long, while not a specialist in American literature but, as a publisher of seminal contemporary offerings, familiar with the general terrain, has, through her response to this volume, encouraged me that its resonance will extend beyond the academy. I am grateful for these different kinds of close readings. I am grateful, as well, to Renée Simon for her constant and invaluable support. Finally, I thank Ken Gill for providing the sacred space in which I was able to bring this work to fruition.

I am greatly indebted to Ray Ryan and the Syndics at Cambridge University Press, who, following Ross Posnock's suggestion that I submit to them my proposal and sample chapters, read and responded with enthusiasm and with confidence in what was to come. It is an honor to be included in the Cambridge list of authors. To Maartje Scheltens, Elizabeth Davey, Leigh Mueller, and the staff responsible for seeing the book through production I extend particular thanks. Maartje's genial guidance and easy efficiency in these last stages of realization, exemplifying the very best in editorial capability, have added to my good fortune in being affiliated with Cambridge University Press.

Abbreviations

The following works have been abbreviated for convenience. Quotations from them are identified by abbreviated title and page number. Complete citations can be found in the Bibliography, pp. 303–15.

A	Henry James, *The Ambassadors*
ABT	Gertrude Stein, *The Autobiography of Alice B. Toklas*
Auto	Henry James, *Autobiography*
BC	William James, *Psychology: Briefer Course*
CDN	*Charles Darwin's Notebooks, 1836–1844*
CPP	Wallace Stevens, *Collected Poetry and Prose*
Crystals	Donna Jeanne Haraway, *Crystals, Fabrics, and Fields*
CWJ 1	*Correspondence of William James*, vol. I: *William and Henry, 1861–1884*
CWJ 2	*Correspondence of William James*, vol. II: *William and Henry, 1885–1896*
CWJ 3	*Correspondence of William James*, vol. III: *William and Henry, 1897–1910*
CWJ 4	*Correspondence of William James*, vol. IV: *1856–1877*
EL	Ralph Waldo Emerson, *Essays and Lectures*
GBV	Richard Powers, *The Gold Bug Variations*
GHA	Gertrude Stein, *The Geographical History of America*
HJPT	Richard Hocks, *Henry James and Pragmatist Thought*
HWR	Jonathan Edwards, *Works*, vol. IX: *A History of the Work of Redemption*
ID	Steven Meyer, *Irresistible Dictation: Gertrude Stein and the Correlations of Writing and Science*
JER	John E. Smith, Harry S. Stout, and Kenneth P. Minkema, eds., *A Jonathan Edwards Reader*
LIA	Gertrude Stein, *Lectures in America*

LR	Ulla E. Dydo with William Rice, *Gertrude Stein: The Language That Rises, 1923–1934*
LWS	*Letters of Wallace Stevens*
MA	Gertrude Stein, *The Making of Americans*
NHJ	*The Complete Notebooks of Henry James*
NOW	Dennis L. Sepper, *Newton's Optical Writings*
OF	Gillian Beer, *Open Fields: Studies in Cultural Encounter*
P	William James, *Pragmatism*
PN	Jonathan Edwards, *Personal Narrative*, in *JER*
PP	William James, *The Principles of Psychology*
PR	Alfred North Whitehead, *Process and Reality*
Sermons 1720–3	Jonathan Edwards, *Works*, vol. X: *Sermons and Discourses, 1720–1723*
SMW	Alfred North Whitehead, *Science and the Modern World*
SP	Jonathan Edwards, *Scientific and Philosophical Writings*
SR	Paul Jerome Croce, *Science and Religion in the Era of William James*
TL	Gertrude Stein, *Three Lives*
V	William James, *The Varieties of Religious Experience*

CHAPTER ONE

Introduction: frontier instances

Every science must devise its own instruments. The tool required for philosophy is language. Thus philosophy redesigns language in the same way that, in a physical science, pre-existing appliances are redesigned. It is exactly at this point that the appeal to facts is a difficult operation. This appeal is not solely to the expression of the facts in current verbal statements. The adequacy of such sentences is the main question at issue. It is true that the general agreement of mankind as to experienced facts is best expressed in language. But the language of literature breaks down precisely at the task of expressing in explicit form the larger generalities which metaphysics seeks to express.

Alfred North Whitehead, *Process and Reality*

THUS, IN THE BEGINNING, ALL THE WORLD WAS AMERICA[1]

Each of the chapters to follow focuses on an aspect of the life of the mind in America as it develops the habit we know as Pragmatism, specifically, the method of thinking described by William James and inflected by radical empiricism.[2] My subjects are figures whose works serve as what Charles Darwin in his *N Notebook* called, noting his borrowing from Francis Bacon, "frontier instances": "cases in which we are enabled to trace that general law which seems to pervade all nature – the law, as it is termed, of continuity."[3] The argument proceeds by amplification, a gesture mimetic of Pragmatism itself, each essay illustrating what happened over time to a form of thinking brought by the Puritans to the New World. Under the pressure of conditions on the American strand, this form of thinking began its evolution, by way of aesthetic adaptations I shall map, into Pragmatism.

The signal, if implicit, motive of Pragmatism is the realization of thinking as a life form, subject to the same processes of growth and change as all other life forms.[4] Regarding thinking in this way makes perfect sense given the centrality of *On the Origin of Species* to the work of Charles Sanders

Peirce, who first read *Origin* just after his graduation from Harvard in 1859, and to William James, who, in *The Principles of Psychology* (1890) works out the implications of the Darwinian information for the understanding of consciousness, of thought; as Darwin indicated: "– we can thus trace causation of thought.– . . . obeys same laws as other parts of structure."[5] This sense is deepened by taking a step back and recalling that the model for evolution, or development theory as it was first called, came from the study of language, a primary material embodiment of thinking.[6] Thus Pragmatism's identifying notion that truth happens to an idea did not spring fully formed and ready to do intellectual battle from the head of Peirce or James, but germinated and grew in a particular environment of fact. As Wallace Stevens reminds us, "[H]is soil is man's intelligence."[7]

A persistently disturbing element of this environment, observed repeatedly and variously by astute recorders of the American experiment, beginning with the diligent journal-keeping Puritans and running through to the poets of high modernism, was/is the incommensurability of nature, its unavailability to the categories of description embedded in the language of the settlers.[8] Nature literally amazed them. Words failed in "this new, yet unapproachable America."[9] The insistent conditions of American nature invited, and more often demanded, scrutiny of the relation between fact and feeling. These conditions had been announced from the moment of first arrival. John Winthrop's journals, Anne Bradstreet's poetry, Cotton Mather's sermons, to note only a few examples, offer abundant evidence of the effects of what William Bradford described as a "desolate and howling wilderness" on the sensibilities of those following their errand to build the "city upon a hill."

The strangeness of the New World environment to European perception, its immense scale, extremes of climate, the habits of its natives, seen through the Puritan typological scrim, made of those tracking their experience, in preparation to hear the call to election, "inquisitorial botanist[s]."[10] Under the charge to make the invisible visible, not content simply to list what they saw and heard, they felt compelled to translate these facts into signs. They made wind, thunder, and hail into lines of text which they interwove with lines from Paul, Matthew, and Mark in their attempt to find types that would provide at least a virtual reality where their spirits could find temporary rest. Francis Bacon's directive to read the Book of Nature as the Book of God was nowhere more assiduously followed than in seventeenth-century New England. In much the same way that Shakespeare's language is characterized by the counterpointing of high and low rhetorical forms mimicking the experiential diversity of the Elizabethan world,[11] the language of sermons, journals, conversion and captivity narratives, and the poetry of the seventeenth-century colonists registers the perplexing juxtapositions of their world, stretched between the residual security offered by their foundational text, the Bible, and the actualities of the threatening landscape. Instances of these occasions are myriad. This recording of existence on simultaneous planes, the supernatural or sacred and the natural or profane, like treble and bass staffs on which notations were made, would find full expression in Emerson's style, especially after "The Divinity School Address" and *Nature* (1836).

The responses of the first settlers were strong and inflected by two strains: the feeling of the theological impulse that to the greatest extent determined the shape of the polity, and the fact of stone age nature that gradually came to be tamed somewhat in descriptions informed by increasingly specific scientific information. Left with the feeling of what happens,[12] thrown into the paradoxical situation of being both inside and outside their language at once, forced to live in the world but outside of existing conceptions of it, the most attentive and concerned seventeenth-century doers of the word were to devise solutions that were in the purest sense "aesthetic," before the term itself had become established as a category of experience. By the end of the eighteenth century, the pressure on the classical episteme, as we know from Michel Foucault, was extreme. "Aesthetics" emerged as a distinct term on the intellectual horizon at roughly the same time as different "sciences" were emerging from natural philosophy. They became the containers for what theology once held, the excess of experience described by "more than rational distortion."[13] The coincidence is not in itself surprising, but the way these categories came to function and to be understood in the evolution of American thinking is central to the argument of these chapters and to the selection of the figures who are my subjects: Jonathan Edwards, Ralph Waldo Emerson, William James, Henry James, Wallace Stevens, and Gertrude Stein. Each of these writers built an aesthetic outpost in an endeavor that was at the same time Lucretian, in taking into account the order of things insofar as it could be known, and ministerial, in performing in language the ritual responses requisite to keeping a community together, an aspect distinguishing this line of American literary experiment.

The accumulating information about American nature from the time of discovery and well into the nineteenth century came to those collecting such data in the Old World precisely as that, data *about* what they could only imagine and which they attempted to fit into a system to the greatest extent still dominated by an Aristotelian scheme dependent on the subject–predicate, substance–quality distinction. This scheme continued to ground experience and reflections on it, even though, as Alfred North Whitehead pointed out, Descartes had already unsettled the scheme, though without realizing it, as Locke and Hume would also fail to realize in their extensions of Cartesian perceptions into empiricism and sensationalist philosophy.[14] Indeed, it should be noted in connection with Locke's thinking that whenever, in presenting his argument in *An Essay concerning Human Understanding*, he arrived at points where the logic issuing from the substance–quality basis failed him in descriptive power, he used analogy to communicate the glimmering of a new idea.[15] This intrusion of what to him would have belonged more properly to literary rather than to philosophical discourse was something that *happened to the idea* of how philosophical thinking goes on. This seemingly incidental breakdown of what was showing itself to be an outworn form was to whisper its knowledge into the ear of Jonathan Edwards.

Edwards's hungry reading of Locke was sensitive to nuances of syntax, grammar, and logic in large part as a result of his ministerial training but equally because of his lifelong habit of closely observing natural phenomena, especially the relation of physical structures and processes to the accidents of environment. His natural historian's eye is particularly instanced by his study of spiders and light. Edwards gave words and sentences the same kind of attention Darwin would just over a century later. While Darwin would rewrite *Origin* five times, persistently attempting to escape the prison of sentences expressing the very idea of design he was trying to overturn, Edwards simultaneously theorized and performed stylistic experiments that opened up spaces in his language for the play of imagination with and around what Stevens would later describe, in drawing a distinction between "the poetry of the subject" and the "true subject" out of which the former develops, as "the irrational element," the welter of feelings out of which the framing propositions of the larger containing sentences and paragraphs emerge.[16] In each "room of the idea," Edwards's term for such a conceptual/linguistic space, was the "furniture," in Locke's terms,[17] that made it a pleasing habitation for the mind in its constant searching for places of rest.[18] These "rooms," sites of rhetorical expansion, interrupt and deflect the trajectory of linear logical argument. It was as though Edwards added to the form of thought he had inherited a third dimension that altered its formal presentation in language in much the same way that the addition of perspective altered the conceptual ground of Renaissance painting. The instruments permitting this conceptual deepening, over time, would, out of their scopic possibilities, generate useful distortions of things as they were: Mercator projections, for example. Other instances are the extraordinary anamorphic depictions of the sixteenth century where two scenes, one sacred, the other profane, are rendered on the same panel, the profane scene enfolded in the perspectival stretching of the sacred scene and perceptible only from a particular oblique point of view, or through a keyhole – as a voyeur or child curious to view the forbidden scene might glimpse – or with the aid of a cylindrical mirror.[19] Thus, two registers of perception could be presented simultaneously, the "true subject" resting within the "poetry of the subject," within the "room of the idea."

Of course, by the time Edwards came to reflect on language and experience, a mass of evidence of telescopic and microscopic accounting had accumulated in the records of the generations before him, as well as in those of his contemporaries, all examining their souls for signs of election.[20] But Edwards was the first New World representative to regard these records, as well as those recounting his own spiritual journey, as material for philosophical examination. While it is impossible to know all the reasons for his self-appointment to this office, it does seem that it was in large part Locke's *Essay*, together with Newton's *Opticks*, coming to Yale (rather than to Harvard, say) in the gift of Jeremiah Dummer to the library in 1717/18 (which year is in question), that catalyzed the various elements of his perception and precipitated his becoming America's first, if retrospectively acknowledged, philosopher.

Intensely aware of what it felt like to be overwhelmed by what could not be understood, and compelled, at the same time, as a minister in a time of spiritual degeneracy, to attempt the translation of this condition for himself and his community into an experience of being amazed by grace, Edwards found himself in a situation common to innovators in thinking and perception, that is, using techniques of persuasion as much as, if not more than, reasoned argument to effect his intention. As Paul Feyerabend observes:

One should rather expect that catastrophic changes in the physical environment, wars, the breakdown of encompassing systems of morality, political revolutions, will transform adult reaction patterns as well, including important patterns of argumentation. Such a transformation may again be an entirely natural process and the only function of a rational argument may lie in the fact that it increases the mental tension that preceded *and caused* the behavioural outburst.
. . . Even the most puritanical rationalist will then be found to stop reasoning and to use *propaganda* and *coercion*, not because some of his *reasons* ceased to be valid, but because the *psychological* conditions which make them effective, and capable of influencing others, have disappeared. And what is the use of an argument that leaves people un noved?[21]

The most extreme and public instance of this kind in the American settlement before Edwards and the Great Awakening was the Antinomian
Crisis, when the rhetorical distortions so masterfully deployed by John
Cotton in his sermons were taken up and extended experientially by Anne
Hutchinson in the gatherings she convened to explore precisely those psychological conditions which made Cotton's words effective.[22] But, as a
woman, Hutchinson lacked the canonic language and familiarity with the
containing forms of argument; her discourse was all, so to speak, free play,
consisting solely of the "distortions" and so was perceived as an unsheathed
threat to the body politic. While her experience epitomized what was happening to the idea on which the errand into the wilderness was premised,
it was necessary that this experience be represented not as a primary process, but subtly, as an adaptation or transmutation within and of traditional
forms. It was in this redactive expression that Edwards succeeded. It cannot
be stressed strongly enough, keeping in mind Whitehead's (note 14) and
Feyerabend's observations concerning the constitution of the self in relation to environmental strangeness, that the psychological conditions of the
New World experiment were such that the subject–predicate breakdown
was being *felt* as terror by the "stranded" Americans.

It is important to keep in mind the continuity of successful forms of
expression in the evolution of thinking, and more particularly to consider
this feature in the context of language as an organic form as well, as natural
and necessary to the survival of human beings as the honeycomb to bees,
the structure in and by which transformations essential to the life of the
community are made. Appetite and sustenance determine the one as much
as the other. This realization about language has, of course, begun to emerge
with some degree of clarity only recently in the period following Darwin's
contribution.[23] Darwin's recurrent reminders in his published work, and
even more persistently made to himself in his notebooks, of the primacy
of pleasure in and for all organic forms extended to language. He struggled
to make *Origin* a text that would survive. In order to accomplish this end,
Darwin knew, he had to fashion his language so that it would satisfy the
dual requirement of preserving a residual form to ensure continuity with the
past while introducing within that form the adaptations mimicking what he
had come to understand about the laws of chance and accident operating
throughout nature.[24] His considerations in shaping his text were in the
deepest sense of the term, as I hope to have begun to suggest, *aesthetic*.[25]

"Pleasure," the word Darwin chose to return attention to "that first,
foremost law,"[26] would become William James's "interest," while Freud,
pursuing the permutations of the same law, held on to the more piquant

original. Whitehead, taking direction from and continuing the work James had taken on in *Principles* – to provide in academically acceptable form an explanation of the human experience of life on the planet – chose "appetition" and "satisfaction" to describe pleasure's two-step process.[27] While we may delight in Roland Barthes's lubricious suggestions concerning the "pleasure of the text," it is more useful to turn to Whitehead for help in making clear the connections of this natural law to language, particularly because of his acknowledged debt to James. Whitehead's dry terms serve the purpose for which he designed them, to analyze the "actual entities," his term for any temporal forms subject to process.[28] In the case of language, then, to return to Darwin's concern, and to the argument of these essays, it is necessary to ask how appetition and satisfaction function.

William James in "The Stream of Thought" chapter of *Principles* offers the following observations which open up the aspect of appetition for consideration; the emphases are James's:

> If there be such things as feelings at all, *then so surely as relations between objects exist in rerum natura, and more surely, do feelings exist to which these relations are known.* There is not a conjunction or a preposition, and hardly an adverbial phrase, syntactic form, or inflection of voice, in human speech, that does not express some shading or other of relation which we at some moment actually feel to exist between the larger objects of our thought. If we speak objectively, it is the real relations that appear revealed; if we speak subjectively, it is the stream of consciousness that matches each of them by an inward coloring of its own. In either case the relations are numberless, and no existing language is capable of doing justice to all their shades.
>
> We ought to say a feeling of *and*, a feeling of *if*, a feeling of *but*, and a feeling of *by*, quite as readily as we say a feeling of *blue*, a feeling of *cold*. Yet we do not so inveterate has our habit become of recognizing the substantive parts alone, that language almost refuses to lend itself to any other use . . . All *dumb* or anonymous psychic states have, owing to this error, been cooly suppressed; or, if recognized at all, have been named after the substantive perception they led to, as thoughts "about" this object or "about" that, the stolid word *about* engulfing all their delicate idiosyncrasies in its monotonous sound. Thus the greater and greater accentuation and isolation of the substantive parts have continually gone on.[29]

We recall that James begins his chapter by suggesting the imprecision of using "he thinks" or "I think" by noting, "If we could say in English 'it thinks,' as we say 'it rains' or 'it blows,' we should be stating the fact most simply and with the minimum of assumption. As we cannot, we must simply say that *thought goes on*."[30] Buried as it is, announcing the subject of the ninth chapter in a 1,400-page text, this opening seems a mild-mannered gambit, yet James would accomplish with this move the revolutionary change in the language game that, as Whitehead observed, Descartes, and Locke and Hume following him, did not realize to be implicit in the subject–predicate, substance–quality shift he had initiated. This change does not seem revolutionary to us any longer as we have already been conditioned by the new habits James suggests be taken on, most specifically in this chapter and in different ways throughout his work, habits more recently, and, to the American market mentality, more stylishly theorized in various foreign modes of Marxist, neo-Marxist, structuralist, deconstructionist, multicultural discourse, all charging us to put the cart before the horse and realize our condition of being locked in the prison-house of language.[31] But James recognized that Emerson – "Every sentence is a prison" – had heralded this news long before:

It is very unhappy, but too late to be helped, the discovery we have made, that we exist. That discovery is called the Fall of Man. Ever afterwards, we suspect our instruments. We have learned that we do not see directly, but mediately, and that we have no means of correcting these colored and distorted lenses which we are, or of computing the amount of their errors. Perhaps these subject-lenses have a creative power; perhaps there are no objects. Once we lived in what we saw; now the rapaciousness of this new power, which threatens to absorb all things, engages us. Nature, art, persons, letters, religions, – objects successively tumble in, and God is but one of its ideas.[32]

As I demonstrate in the chapters following, Emerson, and Edwards before him, had been enabled, no less than Darwin, by the New World experience of nature, to realize the actuality of Locke's perception concerning the effect of words and simple ideas.

The appetition of language for new forms of expression is described concisely in the passage from James quoted above – "We ought to say a feeling of *and*, a feeling of *if*, a feeling of *but*, and a feeling of *by*." James learned from Darwin and from Emerson to consider not only language but thinking, too, as a life form constantly undergoing adaptation and mutation. In his essays and lectures Emerson showed what sentences and paragraphs that mimic thinking as process look like, as natural facts subject to the same evolutionary process Darwin would theorize and exemplify in *Origin*. (As I shall detail in Chapter 3, the coincidence of Emerson's and Darwin's approximately simultaneous realizations of this process was also prepared – in addition to their experiences in New World nature – by their responses to a body of common texts.)[33] Emerson's stylistic practice significantly incorporated the prime features of nature's process as Darwin would describe: the profligacy of forms necessary to ensure the possibility of adaptation or fit to constantly changing conditions; and the physical responsiveness of an organism, in this case language, to its accidental environment – but to return to Edwards, who began the recalibration of the instrument of language that Emerson reminds us to suspect.

The unsettling of the subject–predicate, substance–quality distinction that Descartes had unknowingly instigated and that Locke had begun to exemplify in his slips into analogy, for Jonathan Edwards became the actual, if shifting, ground of experience. In sharp contrast to the Old World where traditional linguistic forms continued to reflect, for the greatest number of language users, the situation of subjects still subject to predication in social orders preserving residual feudal and/or religious ties, the New World experience, in fact, physically effected the revolution into "the modern" instanced by the collapse of the subject–object distinction. The colonists pursuing their errand were indeed accomplishing the fate signaled by the Reformation as, from the margins of their being, they regarded themselves as objects and made notations. Edwards found in Locke the sketch for a template his experience inscribed. The American situation provided him the occasion to convert Locke's perception into actuality.[35]

What Locke had begun to conceptualize as an abstraction in the mental space opened by his thinking *about* the relation between words and perception, Edwards experienced as fact. His subjectivity decentered, he regarded it/himself as the object of alien feelings. Whitehead makes the point again and again, implicitly acknowledging his debt to Darwin and William James, that it is through the body that reality is processed. In the context of the New World experiment, it is crucial to recall an observation astutely drawn by Perry Miller in his discussion of Edwards's realization about the power of words:

Edwards works his way from the Lockean theory of language to his distinction between the "understanding of the head" and the "understanding of the heart." This is not, as in Coleridge's distinction of Understanding and Reason, a division into separate faculties. In Edwards' "sense of the heart" there is nothing transcendental; it is rather a sensuous apprehension of the total situation important for man, as the idea taken alone can never be. What makes it in that context something more than an inert impression on passive clay, is man's apprehension that for him it augurs good or evil. It is, in short, something to be saluted by the emotions as well as the intellect. *When a man is threatened, when his life is endangered, the whole man is alerted; the word then becomes one with the thing* [a natural incarnation, as it were], *becomes in that crisis a signal for positive action.* (Emphasis mine)[36]

As Whitehead concisely states in his systemizing of how propositions function: "The primary mode of realization of a proposition in an actual entity is not by judgment, but by entertainment. A proposition is entertained when it is admitted into feeling. Horror, relief, purpose, are primarily feelings involving the entertainment of propositions."[37] Following Whitehead's formulation clarifies what I have been pointing to as the aesthetic function in language: distortions in syntax and grammar are mimetic of feelings entertained, animal responses to what exists as matter of fact, whether the facts be features of the natural environment or, as Locke had begun to inflect, the realization of language itself as fact.

It is, then, exceptional only in the sense of accidental that in America the combined threat of nature and the fragility of the body politic provided the *occasion* whereby propositions implicit in the Lockean theory of language and mind became what Whitehead calls *lures for feeling*:[38] in this setting, for feeling the anomie attendant on the breakdown of the old order of things. The kind of statement that evolved was characterized by an *appetition* for forms where questions and questing reflexively undermined predication: for forms of paradox; for a preponderance of analogy; for repetitions imitating ritual and prayer; for paratactic listings of experiences and phenomena not encountered before. These features, evident in American writing beginning with the colonial period, resolve in Edwards into a self-conscious style that, moreover, and most significantly, deploys structures adopted from his close attention to natural processes. As Whitehead observes, it is the translation of the welter of emotional experience in the face of "stubborn fact" – a term he borrowed from William James and deployed persistently throughout his work – into a private, self-conscious form that marks the aesthetic. In the case of the American experience, the imported theological framework inappropriately structures this aesthetic translation, and thus distinguishes the American from the British and European aesthetic. By the nineteenth century, writers of the American Renaissance themselves began noticing this difference: Hawthorne's contrasts, for example, in *The Scarlet Letter*, between Elizabethan style, as represented by Pearl, and the colonial "plain style."[39] After Edwards, the next move in the American language game is made by Emerson who, like Edwards, was doubly prompted by theological and natural cues and thereby found in the reading of key European texts a call, "a signal for positive action." This "positive action" was his translation, his recombination in the alembic shaped of his time and place, of the word into thing, *pragma*, an incarnation: "Cut these words and they would bleed."[40] This was a ministerial performance, albeit for Emerson, from the time of *Nature* (1836), a secular one, but nonetheless a performance that repeats in a naturalized context the inciting gesture of the Reformation, turning words that had been still ciphers, impenetrable, perplexing, into ecstatic messengers trumpeting meaning.

For Edwards, for Emerson, and for the other figures who are the subjects here, it is as though theaters or stages are set up within their sentences so that we end up with periods containing within themselves not only images, tropes, and analogies to make the idea clear but, in addition, stage directions for the performance of utterance, even if only to ourselves, as speakers/readers engaging in a kind of prayer. These performances provide the signals for positive action, or, at the very least, the taking on of a particular attitude in relation to the fact described or idea presented. In the remaining pages of this chapter I shall preview the features of the performances within the texts of the leading actors who transform the elements of the American aesthetic into Pragmatism.

Within this preview the reasons for selecting the figures I have named will become apparent. It is of course the case that the aesthetic choices made by these individuals were also made by others and, in many instances, prompted by some of the same readings and similar experiences. It could not be otherwise since what I am tracing is a "law of continuity" in a particular environment of fact. The mark distinguishing the writers under discussion here is the expressed self-consciousness of their ministerial office, a stated desire, as Emerson put it in "The Method of Nature," "to annul that adulterous divorce which the superstition of many ages has effected between the intellect and holiness," and this to be achieved through "discovery and performance."[41] It is to be especially noted as well, in clarifying what I mean by ministerial office, that while the figures who are my subjects understood the role of the American writer to be a religious one, it was with a sense of religion naturalized and at the same time returned to its purest etymological meaning as "binding together" – in this case, binding perception to the order of things. For all of these writers this sense meant taking into full account and translating into their stylistic practices as accurate a representation as possible, within a linguistic system, of the structure of the natural world as it was known in their moments. All actively sought out and studied timely scientific descriptions in order to be able to imagine the moving structure in which they lived. This structure for all of them replaced or was identical with the idea of God, and preserved, as well, in realigning the axis of perception, the function, in secular dress, of justification, now preparing them and those instructed by them for the reception of grace understood as fact informed by feeling.

I have not, therefore, included either Hawthorne or Melville because each was, by his own account, still too haunted by the idea of an "unnaturalized" Calvinist deity to shed the feeling of a mind inhabited by guilt to be able to put on a new habit, the feeling of what happens to a mind enjoying "an original relation to the universe."[42] The attitude prompted by the stage directions in Hawthorne's and Melville's sentences indeed sentences us, even now, to feel, in spite of our secular moment, the fear incited by America's outworn religious dispensation. While being able to experience this attitude has value, it is a wholly different value from that derived from rehearsing an attitude learned from reading lines composed by those whose idea of God, if not replaced by Nature, has, continuing the work of the Reformation, replaced the image conceived as icon, static, the "'idea' idea,"[43] with moving pictures of an ongoing process.

I have also not included Whitman because, while he was impassioned with the idea of nature and of the human being and language as fully animal and animate aspects of nature, and shared as well in a secularized ministerial mission, his preparation did not include systematic reading in natural history and science. On the other hand, Poe, who did read in natural history and science, and who was, in turn, read by Peirce, did not express ministerial purpose. In contrast, Dickinson is not included because, while she shared with the other figures who are my subjects both spiritual ambition and the attempt to reshape language so that it would, at least, question, following her own reading in natural history, the idea of a world unfolding teleological design, her work was unavailable to the development of the aesthetic into Pragmatism. For a quite different reason I have not included Thoreau, who, indeed, belongs fully in the category of "frontier instances." The groundbreaking work done by Stanley Cavell in *The Senses of Walden*, leading so clearly to the work of these chapters and to recent studies and editions underlining Thoreau's involvement with natural history and science, obviates the need for further elaboration in the trajectory I map. Similarly, in the case of Robert Frost, Richard Poirier's exemplary articulation of what he calls the "Emersonian-pragmatist idea about language"[44] embodied in William James's work and performed by Frost in his poetry provided another of the starting points for the thinking continued in these pages. My chapters are responsive additions to these earlier essential studies.

EXPERIENCE IS IN MUTATION . . .[45]

The facts or natural models imaginatively adopted by Edwards and Emerson were, of course, different, reflecting both what they had each come to know through direct observation and experience and what they had read. Similarly, the conceptual innovations of William James, of Henry James (especially in his late work), of Wallace Stevens and Gertrude Stein – throughout the bodies of their work – reflect "the exquisite environment of fact"[46] as it had come to be registered for them on their more and more finely tuned instruments, calibrated by their own reading and experience.

For Edwards, as mentioned earlier, the two natural phenomena that most tenaciously held his attention were spiders and light. His fascination began when he was a boy. Revealingly, as he describes in his *Personal Narrative*, his adventures in the woods were combined with shaping habitations for prayer:

I used to pray five times a day in secret, and to spend much time in religious talk with other boys; and used to meet with them to pray together. I experienced I know not what kind of delight in religion. My mind was much engaged in it, and had much self-righteous pleasure; and it was my delight to abound in religious duties. I, with some of my schoolmates joined together, and built a booth in a swamp, in a very secret and retired place, for a place of prayer. And, besides, I had particular secret places of my own in the woods, where I used to retire by myself; and used to be from time to time much affected.[47]

Suzanne Langer, a student of Whitehead's, drawing on nineteenth-century language theorists read by Darwin and Emerson, persuasively illustrates that the inciting characteristic of human language is not social intercourse but aesthetic expression:

What we should look for is *the first indication of symbolic behavior*, which is not likely to be anything as specialized, conscious, or rational as the *use* of a semantic. Language is a very high form of symbolism; presentational forms are much lower than discursive, and the appreciation of meaning probably earlier than its expression. The earliest manifestation of any symbol-making tendency, therefore, is likely to be a mere *sense of significance* attached to certain objects, certain forms or sounds, a vague emotional arrest of the mind by something that is neither dangerous nor useful in reality . . . Aesthetic attraction, mysterious fear, are probably the first manifestations of that mental function which in man becomes a "peculiar tendency to see reality symbolically," and which issues in the *power of conception*, and the life-long habit of speech. [Emphases Langer's][48]

She goes on to discuss how, under the pressure of new natural conditions, new linguistic forms emerge. Edwards's faithful recording in linguistic forms mimetic of the conditions under which his perceptions developed provides invaluable documentation of a mind coming to know itself in a new relation to an environment.

While Edwards's curiosity about light might have been sparked by his early excursions into the woods, it was, as noted above, a text, Newton's *Opticks*, as important to him as Locke's *Essay*, which nourished his interest. What he learned from his study of Newton was like light itself, the invisible thing making things visible, the unity underlying particularity, a mode of apprehension. His manner of deploying what he came to understand about light is paradigmatically exemplified in his *Personal Narrative* where the appearance of "light" in word play, and most often in "delight," is repeated throughout like beams of sunlight coming through trees in a wood, variously illuminating shades of meaning in surrounding words and phrases. Similarly, what he had learned from spiders suggested a symbolic form. Watching spiders, dropping from branch to branch, or carried this way and that by wind, and finding, by the combination of necessity and chance conditions, the points that would determine the shape of their webs, suggested a model for translating the movement of his mind as it shaped itself into a flexible and resilient linguistic form suspended to catch and hold the feelings that feed thinking.

While Emerson's secular conversion after his famous 1833 visit to the Jardin des Plantes, when he vowed to himself to become "a naturalist," has been richly discussed, as has his reading of the work of late-eighteenth- and early- to mid-nineteenth-century natural philosophers, geologists, and botanists such as John Herschel, Humphry Davy, Michael Faraday, Charles Lyell, Richard Owen, Alexander von Humboldt, Charles Bell, and Augustin de Candolle, these experiences have not been sufficiently considered in connection with the dramatic effects of his style.[49] More particularly, his reading of Emanuel Swedenborg has not been investigated in this light. Reading the work of each of these "scientists"– as they came to be named in his time – was for Emerson an active exercise of the imagination, an example of an "appetition," in Whitehead's terms, a search for what would suffice, resting places for his mind in its yearning for the satisfaction that, in the absence of God, he would call "good," the adjustment of his "axis of vision"[50] to things as they were coming to be known.

Emerson transferred into his essays and lectures significant elements from the work of the scientists he studied and read, rarely as cited quotations but rather in the form of paraphrases, examples, and references woven into the texture of his sentences and paragraphs. Reading Emerson with the texts from which he borrowed alongside reveals his mode of composing sentences to be a linguistic analogue of the process of speciation he had observed in the adjoining parterres at the Jardin des Plantes, where, as a consequence of the propinquity of the plant beds, cross-pollination had created, in the spaces between, modified forms of parent stocks. While he did not have the conceptual vocabulary of evolutionary change, his own writing – and, later, in an even more apparent way, his manner of indexing and re-indexing observations and passages from his journals, essays, and lectures – evidences how deeply he had internalized into his perceptual framework, derived from his close observation (in the same way Edwards's observation of spiders and light affected his style), "the method of nature," which, in the essay so titled, he described as "ecstasy."[51] Emerson's recursive method of transcribing and interpolating these elements of natural histor- ical description into his writing, moreover, is also an analogue of what we now know to be the manner in which DNA information is transferred along and between chromosome strands. Emerson's imaginative work changed the idea of imagination itself, representing in the formal characteristics of his writing the process of imperfect replication, or mutation, that is the engine of evolutionary change. (Discussion of "imperfect replication" and its relation to the "modern evolutionary synthesis" in genetics will be intro- duced in Chapter 2.) In this way, Emerson's "poetry of the subject," the aesthetic choices he made intuitively, prompted by his "appetition" to see, to understand, created, in Whitehead's terms, a "vision" of the "true subject," which he could not have named since there did not yet exist categories for such precise description: "The second [supplemental] stage [of an actual occasion] is governed by the private ideal, gradually shaped in the process itself, whereby the many feelings, derivatively felt as alien, are transformed into a unity of aesthetic appreciation immediately felt as private. This is the incoming of 'appetition,' which in its higher exemplifications we term 'vision.'"[52] It is important to bear in mind, while considering Emerson's self- imposed charge to provide in his work a "natural history of the intellect," his ministerial inheritance, his preparation to make the invisible visible. This inheritance, combined with his variously expressed commitment not to be bound by inherited ideas, permitted him the freedom of voice necessary to announce his vision.

Following Emerson, William James offers the next "frontier instance" in the evolution of Pragmatism. It is, of course, impossible to discuss James and Pragmatism without taking into account the work of Peirce, and, indeed, Peirce's contributions inform the chapter on James. Peirce has not been chosen as a "frontier instance," however, because, while he certainly did describe throughout his writing the effects of Darwin's theory on the process of thinking, on the refashioning of logic, on perceptual categories, his concern was not that his texts themselves serve as the corrective lenses through which this new universe of chance could be perceived. James, in contrast, following through on his stated motive to make available for study, in a form suitable to the academy, the Darwinian information as it affected the understanding of the mind, produced in *Principles* a text mimetic of the evolutionary process Darwin described and evidenced in the style of *Origin*. The salient feature of both *Origin* and *Principles* is the overabundance of examples used to illustrate each of the aspects of the process. This manner of presentation follows the "profligate" method of nature as described by Darwin, producing several variations optimizing the possibility of survival of species, forms. In the case of texts intended to have maximal survival value – and James no less than Darwin expressed such an intention – providing a profusion of instances was a way of ensuring a fit between the theory being presented and the greatest number of imaginative and experiential niches of reception both in the present and over time. As James notes in closing his preface:

I have therefore treated our passing thoughts as integers, and regarded the mere laws of their coexistence with brain-states as the ultimate laws of our science. The reader will in vain seek for any closed system in the book. It is mainly a mass of descriptive details, running into queries which only a metaphysics alive to the weight of her task can hope successfully to deal with. That will perhaps be centuries hence; and meanwhile the best mark of health that a science can show is this unfinished-seeming front.[53]

He even went so far as to indicate the same principle of variety by suggesting that *Principles* be approached differently by different readers:

The man must indeed be sanguine who, in this crowded age, can hope to have many readers for fourteen hundred continuous pages from his pen. But *wer vieles bringt, wird manchem etwas bringen* [who brings much brings something to many]; and, by judiciously skipping according to their several needs, I am sure that many sorts of readers, even those who are just beginning the study of the subject, will find my book of use. Since the beginners are most in need of guidance, I suggest for their behoof that they omit altogether on a first reading chapters 6, 7, 8, 10 (from page 314 to page 350), 12, 13, 15, 17, 20, 21, and 28. The better to awaken the neophyte's interest, it is possible that the wise order would be to pass directly from chapter 4 to chapters 23, 24, 25, and 26, and thence to return to the first volume again. Chapter 20, on Space-perception, is a terrible thing, which, unless written with all that detail, could not be fairly treated at all. An abridgment of it, called "The Spatial Quale," which appeared in the *Journal of Speculative Philosophy*, vol. XIII, p. 64, may be found by some persons a useful substitute for the entire chapter.[54]

While in our post-post-modern moment we have become comfortable deploying random access modes in our habits of mind, James's offering to an 1890 audience remains a stunningly prescient achievement, marking him as one of the priests of the invisible following in the line of Edwards and Emerson.

The chapter on William James will detail his inclusions among the "mass of descriptive details" what he learned about the method of nature and its intrinsic relation to the processes of thinking not only from Emerson and Darwin but also, here following Emerson's interest, from Emanuel Swedenborg, especially in his imaginative projection of crystallography into his angelology; from Hermann von Helmholtz in his extension of Faraday's electrical contribution into the physiology of human perception, most particularly focusing, for James, on the dual properties of light as particles and waves (from which his expressed intention in *Principles*, "the reinstatement of the vague to its proper place in intellectual life"[55] in considering perception, cannot be separated, playing, as he did, on the French *vague* for "wave"); from the investigations, as well, of others of his generation, Chauncey Wright, for instance. The development of what was laid out in the extravagantly prolific text of *Principles* is traced into its branchings in *The Varieties of Religious Experience* to "re-crystallize"[56] in *Pragmatism*.

A consideration of Henry James's *The Ambassadors* is offered in the following chapter, examining the many points of coincidence in the interests and perceptions of Henry and William James, each equally motivated to provide in the varieties of their work as accurate a representation as possible of what they had come to understand about the nature of human nature both from their common intellectual inheritance and from their ongoing lifelong interchange. One of Henry James's particular turns on the scientific information to which he, no less than his brother, was privileged involves the registration of visual data and the ways in which this registration affects other sensorial/perceptual categories. Investigations of light and optics, of course, had advanced greatly during the nineteenth century; these investigations compelled the attention of both James brothers. Repeatedly noted in Henry's accounts of the observational acuity he developed in early childhood, as recorded in his *Autobiography* as well as in letters and journals, is his sensitivity to and curiosity about the manners in which images impressed in watching translate into verbal representations, and, most importantly, how these images, through time, transform with the accretion of additional associative information. In pursuing this exploration, richly illustrated in the prefaces to the New York edition (1907–9) of his novels, Henry James provides an experiential description of what, from the late nineteenth century and until Einstein's momentous discoveries, was coming to be disclosed concerning the relation between time and perception. In these retrospective analyses of the various motives prompting the development of the elements forming the main corpus of his work, James exemplified, albeit without naming his examination as such, the effect of taking into account, in the description of experience, the dimension of time in the complex architecture of being. A new horizon revealed itself as a frontier instance in the ongoing process of knowing. It was not, then, out of the pique of filial rivalry that Henry, on the occasion of having read William James's *Pragmatism*, commented in a letter to his brother that he realized from it that all his life he himself had "unconsciously pragmatised."

Indeed, putting ideas to work in the service of sharpening the instrument of thought was something all the James children had been prepared to do from early childhood, when Henry James Sr. encouraged his offspring to debate vociferously around the dinner table by throwing out some newly offered fact or opinion as fodder for discussion. Henry James Sr. delighted in instigating arguments among his children, hoping to teach them early on to cultivate the rhetorical strategies necessary to negotiate the new world of change he had come to know as a consequence both of his forebears' accidental experience on this side of the great "ocean-stream" and of his own intellectual explorations in reading and imagining.[57] Again, the actual geographical openness of the American frontier, providing as it did an imaginative landscape for prospecting, cannot be gainsaid in this context. We know from Darwinian theory the significance of the integral, incremental steps provided by individual change to speciation. In the cases of William and Henry James, the effects of their individual variations continue to be traceable in their relational affinities, as, of course, is true also of Darwin, of Emerson, of Edwards, for the purposes of the conversations opened here, or of Newton, Milton, Augustine, Plato, among many others, for the more ancient conversations prompting these later ones. The underlying principle informing the American "frontier instances" and those generating them, is the same: that at particular accidental moments in time and place, or, in the modern vocabulary, in spacetime, the intruding features of as yet unaccountable phenomena, instances of being, interrupt an old logic to produce new habits of mind, new species of thinking, motives for metaphor.

It was and was not accidental that Henry James recognized in pictorial anamorphosis a vehicle which he had himself used as a stylistic device to communicate an essential feature of New World experience. Anamorphic distortion in painting was a Renaissance discovery, so too America. Lambert Strether, the protagonist of *The Ambassadors*, is a character stretched while tethered by the crossing experiences of Old World and New.

The novel had remained untitled until James sent the finished manuscript to his agent in July 1901. It was only after the rehanging and re-titling of Holbein's panel as *The Ambassadors*, the first Holbein acquired by London's National Gallery, that the novel found its naming device.[58] While there are obvious thematic connections between different aspects of the painting and the novel, as noted by Adeline Tintner – the role of Strether as ambassador, the importance of what French culture represents, the significance of the *memento mori* device – these are surface details, facets of *the poetry of* James's *subject*, the face of the novel viewed head-on, so to speak. But, from a point of view permitting the distortion of James's style to be considered, what is revealed is a simultaneous *true subject*, in the manner of the double representations of the Renaissance panels described earlier. Being able to see from this additional point of view depends on reading obliquely, as a voyeur of sorts, peeping through the keyhole of James's "hidden," though available, references, somewhat in the way of Poe's purloined letter, seeing what was always seen but never seen before. The disclosure of this simultaneous plane is the subject of the chapter on James's *Ambassadors*, a disclosure that reads the novel against the central borrowing from Swedenborg's seeming mysticism coded into James's text through the perception of his protagonist, named after a character in a novel by Balzac whose immersion in Swedenborg determines his fate.

James ministered to the actualities of the American scene at the turn of the twentieth century in taking fully into account the occulting properties of language, presented through the signaling of syntactic and grammatical distortions superpositioned on a story unfolding, in the same way that the distortion of the death's head in Holbein's *Ambassadors* is suspended in the center of the pictorial rendering of its ambassadorial representation. From the time of the Puritans' first settlement, the inadequacy of their inherited language to the task of describing where they found themselves generated an anxiety which manifested itself in a self-conscious awareness of an inescapable split between rhetoric and the possibility of accurate representation. While his brother had in *Principles* pointed to the necessity of shifting attention away from the substantive-based language brought with the first settlers and toward the dream of an imagined language animated by a predominance of transitives, the *in-between* words and phrases where the facts of feeling are contained, Henry James began the actual experiments in this kind of language, deploying lexical and syntactic adaptations to stretch into new psychological territory. His most immediate and direct heir was Gertrude Stein, who, as we know, had been directly involved in psychological experiments with William James and Hugo Munsterberg having to do with language and perception. While the chapter on Stein closes this volume, its outline is presented here, before that of the Stevens chapter, because of the transitional position her early work – translating the Jamesian project into her strange demotic – occupies in the development of America's high modernism during the years in which Stevens began to publish.

While *The Making of Americans* is the most extended example of Stein's adaptations to a new linguistic environment, it is *Three Lives* that first describes the latest dispensation of America's continuing Reformation project. Specifically, the "Melanctha" section is read as Stein's self-recognized sign of election in having taken on the role of Melancthon to William James's Luther. Considered as the central panel of a triptych celebrating America's linguistic diversity, "Melanctha" focuses on the tensive interplay between thinking and feeling, in the characters of Jefferson Campbell and Melanctha, that is at the heart of the American experience and which provides the occasion of the discussions collected in this volume. "Jefferson" Campbell speaks the thought-language of the eighteenth century paradigmatically represented by his eponymous forebear. In Jefferson Campbell, genetic inheritor of a group in fact more congenial to the native environment of American nature, the oxymoronic aspect of taking on the habit of mind fashioned from centuries of Old World experience displays itself most poignantly and painfully: until his contact with Melanctha, he is unable to feel outside the parameters allowed by his rational, Enlightenment-educated sensibility. Henry James somewhere observed that attempting to express emotion in English is like trying to do a quadrille in a sentry box; Jefferson Campbell offers a prime example of this difficulty. Melanctha, in contrast, is a creature fully in touch with the fact of feeling, the animal motive of change, and confronts Campbell repeatedly with the accusation that he is "always too much thinking." The trajectory of the problems they encounter maps the situation of America at the beginning of the twentieth century, a situation foregrounded by vexed eugenicist discussions resulting from the accumulating evidence of human declension, together with other mammals, from "a hairy quadruped furnished with a tail and pointed ears, probably arboreal in his habits."[59]

Additionally informative, in connection with the development of American modernism and its affiliations to Pragmatist thinking, is the fact that *Three Lives*, together with Stein's portraits of Picasso, Matisse, and Cézanne, constituted part of the required reading of those belonging to what is informally known as the "Arensberg Circle." Walter Arensberg, heir to one of America's Gilded Age fortunes, had been a classmate of Wallace Stevens at

Harvard, editor of the *Harvard Crimson* while Stevens edited the *Advocate*. Arensberg, who lived in New York City from 1914 until 1919, came to be known as "The Father of New York Dada" in consequence of the salon he established as a weekly meeting place in his spacious studio apartment on West 67th Street, where, together with his wife, Louise, he invited the then *avant-garde* of the *avant-garde*: Stevens, William Carlos Williams, Mina Loy, Edgard Varèse, Carl Van Vechten, Marcel Duchamp (who was for a while in residence in an adjoining apartment provided by Arensberg) were among the regular guests. All the *salonistes* were participants in a contemporary version of an experiment Arensberg modeled after one Francis Bacon fictionally described in *The New Atlantis*, where the best minds in all fields were gathered to speculate and exchange ideas. In the Arensberg Circle speculation was generated in various ways: by participants' responses to various texts selected for discussion – in addition to Stein's work, Freud's *Interpretation of Dreams* and Arensberg's own work on the "coding" of Dante's *Divine Comedy* were among the readings; by the presentation of new work – many of Stevens's poems were in this way first broadcast, for example; by members solving chess problems or uncovering a pun or puns in the latest Rousseau canvas acquired by Arensberg.[60] The significance of Stein's work, emphasizing as it does the fact of feeling in relation to a particular time and place, was not lost on the members of the circle.

Stevens's mock-epic, "The Comedian as the Letter C," begins with the assertion that "Man is the intelligence of his soil." Half-way through this imagined adventure, a turn-around offers instead, "his soil is man's intelligence," a counter-assertion that will serve as platform for the poet's later elaborations of the relation between an individual and his moment. Like Emerson, whose collected works were presented to the young Stevens by his mother on the occasion of his Christmas visit back home from Harvard in 1898, Stevens believed that it was incumbent on the poet to study and come to understand as much as possible about the structure of nature insofar as it had come to be known in his time. And, like the earlier figures discussed in the chapters in this volume, Stevens considered language to be a phenomenon equally as subject to the laws of change as any other part of nature *and* to be a constituent of changing nature, in his words, "Part of the res itself and not about it."[61] In his work the translation of the aesthetic into Pragmatism, "not ideas about the thing, but the thing itself,"[62] achieves one of its most available demonstrations.

Intent on translating what he, like Emerson and William and Henry James before him, believed to be the inextricable connection between thinking and the evolving content of information that, indeed, *informs* how and what is thought, Stevens throughout his *oeuvre* – conceived by him, following Mallarmé, as being a body, a *corpus*, in the fullest sense, subject to its gathering of facts, and possible mutations, through its time – provided a made thing, a "fiction" in his terms, a verbal analogue of all he had come to understand about the structure of "things as they are"[63] in his lifetime of experience and reading. Stretching between 1916 and 1955, his poems record, in their changing grammatical and syntactical usages, his attempts at registering the new, accumulating facts about the structure of nature. Hence, his poems, progressing on their surface in seeming regularity, reveal on closer scrutiny disturbing effects: category errors, "Dry Birds Fluttering Through Blue Leaves"; one stanza, among several others all of the same number of lines, with one line short; sentences extending into apparent periodic closure yet without predication. These effects repeated with variations throughout the body of work serve as punctuating realizations of altered relations between subject and object as he tracks his movement over the course of his lifetime as a point on a planet circling the sun, source of all life on this sphere, his appropriately preponderant image.

Stevens came into his maturity as a poet in the years just following Einstein's discoveries. The impact of these revolutionary descriptions together with the later developments in quantum theory and mechanics persistently engaged his imagination. Particularly taken by the challenges to perception that the work of Max Planck, Niels Bohr, Werner Heisenberg, and other quantum theorists presented, Stevens explored the possibility of describing this invisible universe in sentential relationships. Woven into the texture of his poems are experiments mimicking an uncertain universe in uncertainties of predication and meaning. Within the seemingly stable grammatical structures, semantic equivocations, not apparent at first, create storms of decision: either a sentence is read attending to its structure or attending to structure is suspended to allow semantic resonance and ambiguity. Readers sensitized to these permutations are, in consequence, called on to perform the paradigmatic Pragmatist act, to choose a way of reading that will make "truth happen" to the shimmering ideas offered, to reach at least temporary closure. The effect of these repeated disturbances on careful readers of Stevens is break-down, a quizzing of all sounds, all words, all everything in the search for a momentary resting-place, a perch, specious, "a fiction," to catch onto. This "catching on," this "apprehension," is, in Stevens's perfect phrase, "momentary existence on an exquisite plane," the aesthetic platform, the "stay against the violence without" which provides an organism with the temporary homeostatic balance essential to its being able to go on, to continue.[64] Stevens's aphorisms, "Poetry is a health,"

"Poetry is a cure of the mind,"[65] were not inscribed as sentimental dicta, but anchored with the full weight of all he had realized from imagining the moving new worlds described by the scientists of his time, as well as what he had internalized from his ministerial forebears. The chapter on Stevens offers a response to his invitation to participate in the ongoing dance of understanding our "bond to all that dust."[66]

The discussions of Stevens's and Stein's linguistic experiments will redirect attention to the beginnings of America's philosophical project in Edwards, spinning words into webs where we might catch real fact in the making.

CHAPTER TWO

In Jonathan Edwards's room of the idea

External and internal sensations are the only passages that I can find of knowledge to the understanding. These alone, as far as I can discover, are the windows by which light is let into this dark room. For, methinks, the understanding is not much unlike a closet wholly shut from light, with only some little opening left . . . to let in external visible resemblances, or some ideas of things without; would the pictures coming into such a dark room but stay there and lie so orderly as to be found upon occasion it would very much resemble the understanding of a man.

John Locke, *An Essay concerning Human Understanding*

THE MIND FEELS WHEN IT THINKS[1]

In 1948 Perry Miller published an essay entitled "Jonathan Edwards on 'The Sense of the Heart'" around the text of one of Edwards's "Miscellanies," no. 782, which bears the multiple title, "Ideas. Sense of the Heart. Spiritual Knowledge or Conviction. Faith."[2] In his essay, Miller stresses the importance of John Locke's concept of sensation for Edwards's development of his "sense of the heart," and, indeed, as further scholarship has elaborated, Edwards's reading of Locke did provide one of the fundamental sets against which he would stage his thinking.[3] Another set, equally significant but not yet sufficiently investigated in connection with the movement of Edwards's mind as it contemplated the origin and course of mind as itself one more, if not the greatest, of divine things, is his reading of Newton's *Opticks* and the impact of what he learned there about the nature and behavior of light.[4] Edwards composed, or, better, noted down "Ideas. Sense of the Heart. Spiritual Knowledge or Conviction. Faith" during the winter of 1738–9 in Northampton,[5] twenty years after his first readings of Locke and Newton, both texts having been part of the library of Jeremiah Dummer, given to Yale in 1717/18, but which Edwards probably would not have read before

1719.[6] It was this same period, 1738–9, during which he composed and delivered the three extended series of sermons that marked the transformation of his preaching style, about which more will be said further on. By this time the key concepts, terms, embedded metaphors, and analogies deployed by Locke and Newton to communicate their new world views had become part of Edwards's basic vocabulary in the language he found himself devising as he attempted to persuade his increasingly alienated congregations of the need for "attention of the mind in thinking" in order to be able "to excite the actual ideas" evidencing the direct "influence of the Spirit of God assisting the faculty of human nature."[7] Providing directions for creating "actual ideas" in the "room of the idea" was Edwards's stated purpose in entry no. 782. He braided Locke's concept of perception – of ideas conveyed "from without to their Audience in the Brain, the mind's Presence-room (as I may so call it)"[8] – with what he learned of light from Newton.[9]

In tracing the evolution of Edwards's intellectual method and ministerial purpose, it should not be forgotten that from early adolescence it had become his habit to observe and record details of nature and to make isolated, swampy redoubts, where he watched rays of sunlight variously penetrate the surrounding forest, places of meditation and prayer. His direction, in entry no. 782, to find a way and place to "excite" the "sensible" apprehension of an "idea" in order to experience it as "actual" should not be separated from this early and repeated formative experience if we are ourselves to apprehend the distinction between "speculative" and "sensible" knowledge Edwards was at pains to draw in describing the salvific grace of the "sense of the heart." The imaginative exercise detailed in this entry *depends* – in the sense Edwards uses this verb here and elsewhere – to the fullest extent on attentive auditors/readers experimenting, searching, to locate the "sensible" correlatives in their own experience that might serve, for each, as the "room of the idea" in which the divine can be divined, *felt*, like heat *excited* by light.[10] Astutely aware and respectful of the infinite variety of natural forms, including minds, Edwards understood that true conversion could only be an individual, idiosyncratic experience, *dependent*, like the myriad varieties, shades, hues and tones of color perceived, on the accidental composition of each being. His was, in other words, a *naturalized* version of election.[11] The "room of the idea" out of which this understanding emerged was fashioned for Edwards by his reading of Newton's *Opticks*, in which "rooms" of different kinds, admitting light through apertures and prisms of varying dimensions and shapes, constituted the crucial experimental device.

As Dennis Sepper in his study of Newton's optical writings discusses, Newton described as "crucial" the particular experiment, several steps down the line from his first, by which he discovered "that *Light* consists of *Rays differently refrangible*, which without any respect to a difference in their incidence, were according to their degrees of refrangibility, transmitted towards divers parts of the wall." Newton's conclusion was that light is not a uniform thing, but rather is composed of diverse kinds of light: "Since there are no discontinuities in the spectrum, for each value of the sine proportion between the extremes there corresponds a kind of light refracted according to that proportion. Since there is no limit to possible intermediate values between any two sine proportions, there may be no limit to the number of intermediate kinds of light." Sepper notes that this experiment was special because all the previous experiments had served to refute hypotheses, while this one was designed to allow a "true and invariant property of light" to be recognized:

Newton does not present the crucial experiment to confirm a hypothesis: no hypothesis has been enunciated. The crucial experiment is not deduced by logic from premises. It is not an inductive generalization, though one might argue that Newton is trying to develop a new variety of induction. Induction is ordinarily a process in which one examines a large number of cases of one kind or, where possible, all possible cases in order to arrive at a true generalization. Here there is just a single experiment to justify the conclusion. But in Newton's eyes this is a very special experiment, an experimentum crucis – an experiment made at a crossing point – which, by producing a striking phenomenon, is supposed to prove a theory, a way of seeing things truly.

In the second part of the *New Organon* Francis Bacon (1561–1626) explained how experience could be employed to arrive at a true assessment of the forms and natures of things, and he provided a classification of different kinds of experiences and instances according to how they contributed to understanding. One of these was the *instantia crucis*, the instance of the crossing. The name plays on the images of the intersection of two or more roads: some experiences or instances are designed to place one at the crux of several possibilities, and the outcome can definitively rule out one or more of them as unviable and perhaps even point to a single one as the correct way.[12]

"Crucial experiment" had also been used by Robert Hooke in the *Micrographia* in a section dedicated to the investigation of light.[13] This first step in understanding the infinity of wave frequencies constituting light, which Newton further theorized based on his continuing experiments, was "crucial" in the same sense for Edwards in his understanding of God as Light.

Before going on to measure the imaginative dimensions of the room of the idea that Newton's descriptions of light and its behavior helped

Edwards construct, two preliminary observations will give a sense necessary to realizing Edwards's particular sensitivity to language and habit of mind. One concerns his relation to texts and the other a distinctive feature of his style. Repetition and variation of different kinds are central to both these aspects.

First, it is important to keep in mind the practice of typological reading and thinking in the training of Puritan ministers. The effect of this training for Edwards is abundantly evident in all he wrote. While the manner of interpreting Old Testament texts as prefiguring what would be recorded and revealed in the New is a defining technique of the Puritan sermon and belongs no less to Edwards, what is unusual is that for him the habit extended to almost everything in his perceptual field, so that even the homeliest intimate detail, like "clothes put off in sleep," one of the every-day actions he interprets in *Images or Shadows of Divine Things*, became a sign prompting a reflective search through the texts that had become the scrim through which he regarded the world and himself.[14] It is impossible for lay readers today, even specialist academic readers who have internalized major portions of poetry, to know what this kind of textual experience would have been: indeed, in Stevens's later phrasing, "Part of the res itself and not about it."[15] Glimmerings of this sort of involvement are offered by those moments in our thinking when phrases or lines from texts in which we have become more or less fluent appear, somewhat miraculously – immemorial gesturings pointing the way to the working out of some syntactic/linguistic/grammatical solution to an idea we have trembling in mind which we are attempting to fix for a moment, to mount like a specimen, to communicate. Closer to Edwards's kind of experience is that of mathematicians and scientists who see the aspect of the universe they are investigating through the sets of equations and formulae they have learned and continue to manipulate, where, in the case of discovery, the shape or movement of the searched-for object or process exists in possibility, in faith, as it were, before it is found in fact, as what Edwards would have called "an actual idea"; the feeling of faith might be said to be, or to derive from, the balancing of the equations, the ground of their being described as pleasure and beauty by those employing them. The uppourings prompting these plottings are instances of intuition – "hypotheses" in scientific terms. The more complete and complex the fund derived from earlier tuition in the texts or language belonging to a discipline, the greater the possibility of finding "an actual idea" that will confirm the instigating intuition.

Fluency in any language comes from constant repetition, a process that begins with conscious reflection. A thought word, phrase, eventually a line, in one's first language is directed toward the other medium, the language to be acquired; the word or line is bounced back, more or less reflecting the sense of the directed thought, the second language still an opaque medium. The more fluent one becomes in a language, the more transparent the medium of that language becomes, the directed lines then becoming refracted through its surface, the angles of meaning changed, colored, in and by the composition of the medium. One no longer thinks *about* the language, but *in* it, the light of one's thinking contained in, though varied, slanted by and through it, a prism permitting, as well, the analysis of what constitutes that light, an analysis which would not have been available without the experimentation with the second language. Such, somewhat, was the effect of typological tuition. In the case of Edwards, the immersion in texts most significantly extended from the Book of God, the Bible, to the Book of Nature, the latter through his own native interests and through the books he read which opened into his room of the idea.

A child of his time, born into the extended present of the Scientific Revolution and the Enlightenment, Edwards became as fluent in the languages of Locke and Newton as he was in that of the prophets and apostles, reading and rereading their texts until memory and reflection on them were replaced by perception through them. In this way, the particular hang of his habit of mind *depended* on the prisms these texts provided. As Perry Miller observed, "Holding himself by brute will power within the forms of ancient Calvinism, he filled those forms with a new and throbbing spirit. Beneath the dogmas of the old theology he discovered a different cosmos from that of the seventeenth century, a dynamic world, filled with the presence of God, quickened with divine life, pervaded with joy and ecstasy."[16] In addition, it should be noted that Edwards first read Newton's *Opticks* in Samuel Clarke's 1706 Latin translation, the edition that was part of Dummer's gift.[17] Research in mapping cognition, beginning with William James's descriptions in *The Principles of Psychology*, reveals that the process of internalizing this kind of new information in an acquired language would have been doubly intensified in the neuronal pathways set down by Edwards's studying and learning during this early period from 1718 through 1721 when, as Wallace Anderson observed, "it is clear that he enthusiastically devoted himself to scientific works."[18] Describing the process by which new neuronal paths are established in the cortex – the existence of which, James reminds his readers, is the result of this kind of activity – he explains memorization as a bypassing of "normal paths," which are "only paths of least resistance" – the paths of one's native language, for example – to establish "paths formerly more resistant," the new paths being set down in the repeated practicing of a second language or in learning new ideas:

The normal paths are only paths of least resistance. If they get blocked [as in diverting the sense of a word or phrase from the first language into one being learned] or cut, paths formerly more resistant become the least resistant paths under the changed conditions. It must never be forgotten that a current that runs in has got to run out *somewhere*; [James opened this paragraph noting that "the brain is essentially a place of currents, which run in organized paths"] and if it only once succeeds by accident in striking into its old place of exit again, the thrill of satisfaction which the consciousness connected with the whole residual brain then receives will reinforce and fix the paths of that moment and make them more likely to be struck again. The resultant feeling that the old habitual act is at last successfully back again [in effecting the translation and linking the senses of the first and new languages], becomes itself a new stimulus which stamps all the existing currents in. It is matter of experience that such feelings of successful achievement do tend to fix in our memory whatever processes have led to them and Memory is only a matter of paths.[19]

Furthermore, as James observed in particularizing additional details of brain activity, following experimental work begun by J. S. Lombard in 1867, *"Brain-activity seems accompanied by a local disengagement of heat"* (emphasis James's). As a result of over 60,000 observations, Lombard found, from thermometers and electric piles placed on the scalp, "that any intellectual effort, such as computing, composing, reciting poetry silently or aloud, and especially that emotional excitement such as an anger fit, caused a general rise in temperature." Moreover, this rise in heat was found to be much greater in mentally reciting poetry or repeating something silently than in reading or saying it aloud. James concludes "that the surplus of heat in recitation to one's self is due to inhibitory processes which are absent when we recite aloud . . . the *simple* central process is to *speak* when we think; to think silently involves a check in addition" (emphases James's).[20] Edwards's process, then, of following and coming to be able to project imaginatively Newton's delineations in Latin of light's properties would have both stimulated "the thrill of satisfaction" accompanying the activation of the earlier paths set down from his having learned Latin and provided the "feelings of successful achievement" attendant on his increasing fluency in Newton's language of description. Following Lombard and James, the "heat" excited by Edwards's silent practice in this doubly reinforced "attention to the mind in thinking" in *fact* grounded his "sense of the heart" in the "room of the idea" of light, the most excellent language and being of God.

In connection with Edwards's internalizing scientific information into the language of the divine, Janice Knight has observed:

Jonathan Edwards claimed that meaningful divine types overflow . . . biblical boundaries. He described typology as a "certain sort of Language, as it were, in which God is wont to speak to us." [Jonathan Edwards, "Notebooks on the Types," manuscript, Andover Collection, cited in Lowance, *Language of Canaan*, p. 198, as noted by Knight.]

Edwards contended, moreover, that God's extrascriptural communications are neither serendipitous nor occasional. Instead, they are part of a divinely instituted system of symbols that continuously prefigure and communicate the divine presence in nature and in history. God displays his will through a wide variety of types: "Thus God glorifies Himself and instructs the minds that He has made." In harmony with this emphasis on God's benevolent tutorship, Edwards identified sainthood with a new sense or knowledge of divine things. Grace endows the believer with a capacity to perceive God's presence in his own heart and in the wider world. With new eyes to see and new ears to hear, the true Christian can read sermons in stones and portents in the rituals of daily life.[21]

Important to note in connection with Edwards's extension of reading typologically is how the habit of contemplating the nature and being of God necessarily expands imaginative possibility. Indeed, what it means to inhabit a mind occupied by God is not an experience available to the secular. As Knight notes,

For Edwards, God's disposition to communicate himself inspired and sanctified all human idioms, so that even the vocabulary of science became theologically resonant. Thus, he described God as "that being who has the most of being, or the greatest share of universal existence" – the entity of greatest possible mass. Inherent in the mass of entities was an attractive force, an emanation of energy . . . Edwards identified being and its communication as God's Glory . . . the "emanation, exhibition or communication of this internal glory." Edwards derived this meaning of glory from his translation of the Hebrew word *kavod*, which he rendered as "heaviness, greatness, and abundance." Converting ancient faith into modern metaphors, Edwards took the next step to translate *kavod* as gravity, to signify both the degree of being and of emanation inherent in the glory of God.[22]

Edwards's capacity for understanding the properties and behavior not only of gravity, but of light, which Knight and others have not examined, belonged to this cultivated potential which was itself a fundamental aspect of his faith and, more concretely, a consequence attendant on the will informed by grace which translated into the ability to focus close "attention of the mind . . . to excite the actual ideas," the evidence of the "influence of the Spirit of God." Edwards's perception of divine types found in nature "overflowing" biblical boundaries, to which Knight calls attention, should also be considered in the context of learning described by James in *Principles*, specifically to the "inhibitory process" of brain-activity belonging to silent intellectual exertions and its intrinsic connection with will. The "inhibitory process" of silent repetition, which demands, or, better, is identical with an exercise of will, sends the instigating impulse to speak what is thought either back along the same channel followed from its source of firing during its initial discharge or back to that source along a parallel channel which is reinforced as many times as the thought word, phrase, or sentence is not spoken. This recursive brain-activity produces, in effect, an actual "overflow" of the channel carrying the information blocked from issuance in speech, a form of feedback loop.

Quite remarkably, the pattern of this naturally recuperative activity while learning is recorded and extended in Edwards's writing to map the varying associations that inevitably accrue in the combined working of perception – which admits these associations while sorting through past experience in encountering a new subject – and will, which keeps attention fixed on the informing impulse that is the subject of a particular intellectual exercise. Edwards's deliberate manner of recording the process of formation of the "actual ideas" that focused his attention belonged to his interest in studying what he called, variously, "The Natural History of the Mental World, or of the Internal World" or, more simply, "The Mind." His precision in setting down as closely as possible the process by and through which he perceived testifies to how much he had learned about the importance of such meticulousness in recording from his reading of Newton. In his writing, moreover, following the variations of the words and phrases that focused his attention through the syntactic permutations taken on as his understanding progressed, we observe a movement akin to an aspect of the children's game "Giant Steps," where the most common commands of the designated leader take the form of "Take x number of baby or giant steps back and x number of giant/baby steps forward." This pattern of backtracking in Edwards to retrieve the salient element, which with each return is somewhat qualified with either additions or modifications, is a form of spiralling, a manner of progression identified, significantly, with the fugue in music, most notably in Bach's "Art of Fugue,"[23] and, mathematically, with the Fibonacci Series, the progress of which depends on the internalization of an earlier pattern projected onto what will come next, a pattern which, in fact, describes in its spiralling a pattern we now know to be integral to the information exchange between the generative DNA and messenger-RNA molecules and which has been observed to be at work, as well, in phyllotaxis (maximizing the exposure of leaves to light), in the formation of galaxies, crystals, snowflakes, and other inorganic forms. That Edwards would have intuitively recognized this pattern to be an effective manner both of recording his perceptions and of delivering his sermons is not surprising when his close attention to the mind in thinking and his equally close attention to what he learned about natural phenomena from his reading and from his observation are taken fully into account.[24] We shall have the opportunity, shortly, to consider a passage from his writing where this recursive manner is abundantly apparent.

In addition to the intellectual and imaginative nourishment provided Edwards by his study of Newton's and other natural philosophical/historical texts, it is also important to keep in mind, on a more mundane level, in terms of the New World environment, the excitement that would have been occasioned simply by being able to access these new texts;[25] the intellectual stimulation occasioned by these precisely described worlds within worlds rivaled his native curiosity about nature itself. The effects of perceiving through the typological scrim, combined with observing and recording details of nature and of human nature in its new environment, produced in Edwards's writing aspects that would become distinctive features of American style, an "aesthetic," in later terms, determined as much by the sensations wild and open spaces prompted as by the anchorages of thought, the texts returned to again and again, his style a spiritual hybrid of the New World experiment. Light, in all its senses, would be the element most desired. Specifically, the idea of light fortuitously offered to Edwards through Newton provided the perfect analogue for a "real" ontological model of conversion, one that could displace the model of conversion by justification that had been weakening the fabric of spiritual life in the Connecticut Valley during the first quarter of the eighteenth century.[26] Perry Miller beautifully described this context in the passage quoted here earlier (p. 9), the context in which Edwards's "sense of the heart" was felt as the addition necessary to experience saving grace: "When a man is threatened, when his life is endangered, the whole man is alerted; the word then becomes one with the thing, becomes in that crisis a signal for positive action."

Light, of course, is the central figure signaling revelation, salvation, source, and power not only for Reformed Christianity but for almost all Western and Eastern religions; in the eighteenth century especially, after the publication of Newton's *Opticks*, as Marjorie Nicolson has illustrated, light was "everywhere in the poetry of the second quarter-century."[27] More recently, George Marsden in his expansive biography of Edwards, commenting on light as his "favorite metaphor," observes: "No one looked more intensely at the biblical meaning of light for his day than did Edwards. For him, light was the most powerful image of how God communicated his love to his creation. *Regeneration* meant to be given eyes to see the light of Christ in hearts that had been hopelessly darkened by sin."[28] The particularity of Edwards's use of the figure, however, not remarked by earlier readers, is in the deployment of it, following his understanding of Newton's analyses, as the cosmic model for and source of the human experience of the "sense of the heart." Without indicating a link to Newton, Wilson Kimnach has remarked on the connection between light and heat, the head and the heart in Edwards:

There [in his ordination sermon on John 5:35, *The True Excellency of a Minister of the Gospel* (1744)], he insists that a minister must be "both a burning and a shining light"; that "his heart burn with love to Christ, and fervent desires of the advancement of his kingdom and glory," and that "his instructions [be] clear and plain, accommodated to the capacity of his hearers, and tending to convey light to their understandings." This peculiar combination of head and heart, he insists, is absolutely necessary to the success of a preacher.

Further, Kimnach adds, "in the full context of the sermon and through the extensive use of light imagery, he [Edwards] suggests a standard of transcendent dedication and nearly mystical fervor which is rare in any age."[29] In Edwards's terms, the "sense of the heart" was thus a type of "divine and supernatural light." Light, ever-present, the invisible element making all else visible, unaffected by anything humans might do, provided the perfect figure for the ontological model of conversion. In this context, Anderson has noted:

Edwards was particularly stimulated by the Queries that Newton added at the end of the *Optics*. He was interested in the variety of unusual and experimentally dis-covered phenomena that Newton mentioned there, and jotted notes upon several of them with his own proposals about their correct explanation. His hypothe-ses reflect his excitement over one of Newton's main suggestions in the Queries, that many phenomena cannot be explained by mere mechanical collisions among particles of matter, but must arise from attractive and repulsive forces by which the particles act upon each other without surface contact . . . [H]e seems from the outset to have had unique appreciation of [Newton's] theory's revolutionary implications for the fundamental framework of concepts that had traditionally been used to interpret the intelligible order of the world.[30]

Anderson further observes that Edwards was predisposed to apprehend Newtonian physics, especially his concept of force, because of his having been, like Newton, affected by his reading of the Cambridge Platonist Henry More.[31] Edwards's arguments in "Of Atoms" and the opening paragraphs of "Of Being," Anderson notes, incorporate conceptions of matter, space, and time that are described by More in *An Antidote against Atheisme* and *The Immortality of the Soul*, and Edwards's "line of demonstration" is quite like that of More. In a striking parallel to the way that in the following century readings common to Ralph Waldo Emerson and Charles Darwin at almost the same early moments in their intellectual development predisposed both to evolutionary ways of thinking,[32] Newton's and Edwards's common reception of More's refutation of metaphysical materialism helped set the stage for possibilities of imagining that would eventually transform their perceptual syntax. The main conclusions for both men, "that matter neither exists nor acts by itself, but depends immediately on the immaterial," which they understood as and through the activity of light and which they, preserving their faith, identified with "divine Being," together shaped the axis around which their thinking continued to hiss and spin. For all practical purposes, light, for Newton and for Edwards, was God, that which could explain and expose the "inner constitution of matter . . . uncover nature's most deeply hidden mysteries."[33] Indeed, for Edwards, God as light was no longer a figure of theological speech but "an actual idea," which functioned both to "prove," to verify in the manner of a "crucial experiment" as Newton described, the truth of Revelation, of the "actual ideas" embodied in Scripture, and to literalize, to ground, religious affections in the natural world. As he carefully explained in *Religious Affections*, in a passage where the recursive spiralling of "new" attached to "spiritual sense," "dispositions," "faculties," "principle/s of nature," "foundation laid in . . . nature," "kind of exercises," inflecting the progress of his understanding as syntactic transformation, can be easily plotted:

This new spiritual sense, and the new dispositions that attend it, are no new faculties, but are new principles of nature. I use the word "principles," for want of a word of a more determinate signification. By a principle of nature in this place, I mean that foundation which is laid in nature, either old or new, for any particular manner or kind of exercise of the faculties of the soul; or a natural habit or foundation for action, giving a person ability and disposition to exert the faculties in exercises of such a certain kind; so that to exert the faculties in that kind of exercises, may be said to be his nature. So this new spiritual sense is not a new faculty of understanding, but it is a new foundation laid in the nature of the soul, for a new kind of exercises of the same faculty of understanding. So that new holy disposition of heart that attends this new sense, is not a new faculty of will, but a foundation laid in the nature of the soul, for a new kind of exercises of the same faculty of will.[34]

The spaces opened by what Edwards knew theologically syntactically drew, as by gravitation, his sensed feeling in words, perhaps most paradigmatically in his *Personal Narrative* where the use of "delight" enacts a literal drawing into himself of light, *de-light*, repeating the word rhythmically throughout. It became natural for him, as he records in the *Narrative*, "to sing or chant forth my meditations; to speak my thoughts in soliloquies, and to speak with a singing voice."[35]

It is important in attempting to create for ourselves a room of the idea in which to project the activity of Edwards's thinking to imagine the effect of his reading, in the first paragraph of the *Opticks*, Newton's description of the stage he, as a 22-year-old experimenter, set up: "having darkened my chamber, and made a small hole in my window-shuts, to let in a convenient quantity of the Sun's light, I placed my Prisme at his entrance." By using the prism in place of a spherical lens in his homely *camera obscura*, Newton was able to "isolate the behavior of a part of the light that goes into the formation of a larger image without the complication and overlap produced by the simultaneous refraction of all the other parts of the light at different angles because of the curvature of the lens."[36] Further, by varying the shape and thickness of the prism, Newton was able to select out particular rays for scrutiny. In his "dark Room" the experiments following his idea continued, tracking, as Edwards would have it, the attention of his mind in thinking, with unmatched exacting precision, as he structured materials and steps and recorded results, variously and repeatedly describing how "Light is immitted [sent] into a dark Room."[37] Newton's meticulous care in recording all aspects of his experiments belonged to his stated intention to set down his methods so that the procedures could be repeated in such a way that whether or not one had facility in the mathematics underlying the process, the results could be produced, in Edwards's terms, as "actual ideas." It is impossible to know whether Edwards attempted any of Newton's experiments in one of his own actual rooms, but it is clear that what he came to see through repeated readings of Newton's text about the different properties of refraction, reflection, inflection, diffusion, diffraction, attraction, repulsion, and the infinite variability of the spectrum contributed to what would become his lifelong preoccupation with the interrelated natures of matter and spirit, mind, consciousness, being. In addition, while tracking his own mind thinking, Edwards isolated significant words which he used as prisms to focus his attention.

In "Things to be Considered an[d] Written fully about," a section of *"Natural Philosophy" and Related Papers* containing numbered items, the following two entries, made sometime during his eight-month (August

1722 – nearly May 1723) ministerial service in New York after his graduation from Yale, beautifully exemplify how deeply he had been affected by both Newton's speculations and his speculative manner of perception:

13. To observe that, all the rays of one sort being obstructed by any medium and others still proceeding, as by the air in smoky weather, etc. – to inquire how it can be; and to observe that its so doing makes it probable that there are some other properties in light and mediums yet wholly unknown; and to observe that the unaccountable phenomena of reflections prove the same: and to inquire what it is. And also to seek out other strange phenomena, and compare them all together and see what qualities can be made out of 'em; *and if we can discover them, it's probable we may be let into a new world of philosophy.* (Emphasis mine)

and

21[b]. Relating to the thirteenth [above]: to observe that it is certain that the stopping of one sort of rays, and the proceeding of others, is not because that sort of rays alone are stopped by striking against the particles of the medium, from this experiment, viz.: as I was under the trees I observed that the light of the sun upon the leaves of the book I was reading in, which crept through the crevices of the leaves of the tree, to be of a reddish-purplish color; which I supposed to be because many of the green rays were taken up by the leaves of the tree and left all the rest tainted with the most opposite color; which could be no otherwise than by the stopping those green rays which passed near to the edges of the leaves.
    N. B. That this light of the sun would not appear colored except the crevices through which the rays came was very small.
    Corol. 1. Hence it is certain that bodies do attract the same sort of rays most strongly that they reflect most strongly.
    Corol. 2. Hence bodies do attract one sort of rays more than another.
    Corol. 3. Hence it is probable that bodies do reflect and attract by the same force, because that they both attract and reflect the same sort of rays.[38]

Striking here is the manner in which the Newtonian information wove itself into one of Edwards's most constant habits: being in an isolated natural setting, engaged in observing, in an attitude of reception, a version of piety, taking in and reading through the signs around and inside him to establish a relation, meaning, his typological training extending itself through Newton's text. Striking as well, to those familiar with Newton's presentation in the *Opticks*, as well as in the *Principia* (which Edwards also knew), is the precision with which Edwards records his observations and following "corollaries." The benefits to perception of practicing the scientific method are as evident in Edwards's thinking as they are in the work of any productive scientist. These benefits equally informed his ministerial function and contributed directly to Edwards's fashioning a new language, charged with, *excited* by, "actual ideas" he projected in the room of his mind concerning the properties of light. We recall from his ordination sermon his direction that the minister's "instructions [be] clear and plain, accommodated to the capacity of his hearers," and it is to be noted in this context that "in the vast majority of sermons," what he called his "Opening of the Text," consisted of "several brief numbered heads, frequently designated 'Observation' or 'Inference,'"[39] the exact terms Newton used in the *Opticks* following the "Propositions" of his experiments. The power of Edwards's projection, hinted at by the comment italicized at the end of the thirteenth entry above, he presciently recognized, would mean a "new world of philosophy." He had come to realize "that the universe is created out of nothing every moment; and if it were not for our imaginations, which hinder us, we might see that wonderful work performed continually, which was seen by the morning stars when they sang together."[40] The line that would be drawn through nineteenth-century work on light and magnetism into Einstein's new world of spacetime was being inscribed, the work of translating the Book of God into the Book of Nature begun. In this context, Edwards's suggestion that the work of imagination had to be reconceived is especially important in its forecasting of the function Alfred North Whitehead would later term "prehension," the contribution made by activating imagination to be able to understand the underlying process accounting for facts observed that permitted, for example, Charles Lyell in the nineteenth century to contravene Bishop Ussher's dating of earth's existence according to Scripture with his intellectually calculated findings.[41]

In Edwards's place and time the work at hand, the work inflected by his faith, was to *affect* his congregations with the realizations by which he had been affected, his majestic perception into the ways of God's creation. Indeed, in his *Personal Narrative*, written sometime after January 1739, he "explains how his experience of conversion . . . brought a new sense of the presence of God in nature: 'God's excellency, his wisdom, his purity and love, seemed to appear in everything; in the sun, moon, and stars; in the clouds and blue sky; in the grass, flowers, trees; in the water and all nature; which used greatly to fix my mind.'"[42] The task of directing the steps toward possible conversion for others demanded that, like the prophets of the Old Testament and the apostles of the New, Edwards communicate his vision in words capable of transforming his audience from doubters into believers, overcome their resistance in phrasings that would themselves repeatedly illustrate, perform as signs, as formulae or the steps of an experiment, the act of converting matter into spirit, pure being, since, as he had understood, the relation of matter to spirit was in the constant activity of God as pure being:

Since, as has been shewn, body is nothing but an infinite resistance in some part of space caused by the immediate exercise of divine power, it follows that as great and as wonderful a power is every moment exerted to the upholding of the world, as at first was to the creation of it; the first creation being only the first exertion of this power to cause such resistance, the preservation only the continuation or the repetition of this power every moment to cause this resistance.

So that the substance of bodies at last becomes either nothing, or nothing but the Deity acting in that particular manner in those parts of space where he thinks fit. So that, speaking most strictly, there is no proper substance but God himself (we speak at present with respect to bodies only). How truly, then, is he said to be *ens entium* [entity of entities].[43]

As Newton had detailed and as Edwards repeated in elaborating what he derived from Newton in his "Things to be Considered," "Of Atoms," and elsewhere, both light itself and all bodies were constituted by differences in intensity, speed, and density that issue in consequent forms of attraction or repulsion and in the existence of "spaces or pores" of greater or lesser size and number; in the case of bodies, the differences being the products of varying combinations and mixtures of elements. The larger and more numerous the "spaces or pores," the greater the bodies' capacity to receive light, and, indeed, the bodies with greater space between matter become "lighter," less resistant, increasingly transparent on the way to becoming once again the "nothing" that is God – "Nothing that is not there and the nothing that is."[44] Colors, hues, tones, shades moving into darkness, as described by Newton and understood by Edwards, were products of the constantly changing relations of excitement between the infinitude of light rays, each with its specific wave intensity, and the compositional properties of bodies. The work of the minister, as Edwards applied this understanding, was to convert into available terms for different auditors, more or less disposed to being graced by their varying material/spiritual composition, what he had understood about the apposite relation between what was recorded in the Book of God and what he increasingly learned in the Book of Nature. As Knight observes:

For the reader of Edwards's text or the auditor of his sermon, . . . natural types communicated in concentrated form (almost like a pictograph) the thesis unfolding in the treatise itself. The historical narrative [from the biblical text] and the natural image were merely alternative ways to understand the work of redemption and to retain it in the mind; the preacher, like God himself, used both to instruct and edify.[45]

Edwards's directions for conversion would be actualized, in his sense of presenting the "actual idea," in the mutations of utterance that represented the experiential discrepancy between fact and feeling, fact including, following Locke, the description of the world imparted in the grand narrative provided by Christianity's sacred text. The "alternative ways to understand the work of redemption," the natural types added to the historical narrative, following the Newtonian paradigm, were different kinds of wave intensities, different frequencies, along which the words from God's great book of creation could be communicated to potential receivers of His grace. As Emerson would later phrase it, the process Edwards attempted to stimulate in his audience was based on the premise that "Spirit is matter reduced to an extreme thinness."[46] This process could only be effected by the success of his style, his manner of using words as actions to prompt consequent mimicking actions in the members of his congregation to open greater spaces in the matter of their being.

The success of the mutation of Edwards's style was, of course, enabled by his ministerial function. The repetitions with variations in his sermons of his understanding of the relations between the work of God and the manifestations of nature would foster in his audiences an increasing disposition to being graced, depending on how often they attended to his words and on how effectively these words touched their sense of being threatened. As Kimnach has observed, the more the members of his "rustic congregation" listened to his sermons, the more "their minds moved in grooves dictated by the form" Edwards had devised.[47] During the 1738–9 period, for example, attempting to spark another revival by communicating this sense of threat to his congregation, Edwards developed his distinctive preaching style. Commenting on his mastery of this mature style, Ava Chamberlain notes his technique of repetition with variation:

The sermon series was a traditional Puritan vehicle for the exposition of doctrine, and in 1738–39 Edwards mastered and transformed this homiletical style by delivering three extended series . . . [I]n November 1737, Edwards began to preach a nineteen-preaching-unit series on Matthew 25:1–12, the parable of the wise and foolish virgins. The series extended at least until February and must have been completed by the end of March, because between April and October 1738 Edwards delivered the twenty-one-unit series on I Corinthians 13, known as *Charity and Its Fruits*. In March 1739, only five months after finishing the *Charity* series, he began the thirty-unit series on Isaiah 51:8, known as *A History of the Work of Redemption*.[48]

Edwards, of course, could not have known that repetition with variation is the prime motive of evolutionary change, but he sensed its effectiveness nonetheless from his performance of it, both in attending closely to his own thinking and in executing his ministerial function. By the time he composed *A History of the Work of Redemption*, this sense of the effectiveness of amplification by repetition with progressive variation of focus on the same biblical text had spiralled to increase the number of sermons on a particular text from the nineteen preaching-units on Matthew 25: 1–12, to the twenty-one on I Corinthians 13, to the thirty on Isaiah 51:8, *A History of the Work of Redemption*. That this last series was to have one of the greatest impacts in nineteenth-century religious consciousness in America only serves to underline the rhetorical power of the motive he had so successfully elaborated.[49]

The actual information about the essentially recursive–progressive model Edwards had recognized and deliberately practiced would only begin to become available after the implications of Darwin's monumental contribution were illuminated by the delayed addition of Gregor Mendel's investigations into what we now know as genetics. It was only quite recently, in the 1940s, with Ernst Mayr's description and delineation of "imperfect replication" that the elements of Darwin's laying out of the workings of natural selection were combined with Mendelian genetics to permit the establishment of the "modern evolutionary synthesis," which has been of singular importance in evolutionary thought ever since.[50] "Imperfect replication," termed more recently "errors of descent" by Steve Jones, one of Darwin's latest explicators, is a shorthand for genetic variation caused by mutation, the engine of evolution. Variation in the ability to copy earlier genetic information at the same time preserves certain core features of the preceding generation, necessary for continuing survival, while producing a number of variants that account for what Darwin called the "profligacy" of nature. The variants optimize the chances of matching random changes in the environment; some of the variants will survive if they happen to fit a particular niche or need.

Extending this notion to the ability of a text to survive (one of Darwin's central concerns for *Origin*, as noted earlier, p. 6), to maximize its chances for success a text must at the same time preserve elements that have worked in the past to sustain a necessary balance of "belief" and introduce "the more than rational distortion[s]" embodying what is coming to be, what is experienced as *feeling*, not yet codified into *fact*, during a more or less extended historical moment.[51] Such a text expresses the temporal reality of being, its "historical drift," to borrow a term from the language of contemporary biology of cognition.[52] "Style," in a particular time and place, represents the homeostatic adjustment which enables an individual, and, if the style is successful, a population, to adjust what Emerson called "the axis of vision" to things as they are understood to be in that moment.[53] Style, in other words, is a membrane, a structure whose particular components form a boundary differentiating it from the larger system in which it participates, exchanging nourishment from a specific environment for the propagation and preservation of the transformations that constitute its form.[54] Edwards's success in his time, in *affecting* his congregations toward conversion, and in continuing into our time to demand the attention of readers, is directly linked to his having translated into his writing a fully grounded imaginative grasp, an "ideal apprehension," in his terms, of the actual behavior of our most constant element, light, and of the constant and pervasive property holding all in the universe, gravity. His achievement in this respect came from his disciplined attention to bringing these apprehensions into the "room of the idea" he had constructed and repeating his experiments for himself and for his congregations: "The way that the Work of Redemption . . . respecting the souls of the redeemed is carried on from the fall <of man to the end of the world> is by repeating after continually working the same work over again, though in different persons from age to age . . . repeating and renewing the same effect on the different subjects of it."[55] Edwards interpolated his understanding of Newton into the grand Christian narrative to produce texts "saluted by the emotions as well as the intellect," texts that were "signals to positive action." An example of how actually realized this conceptual practice was for Edwards is offered in the passage just quoted where the angle brackets enclose one of the phrases he repeated and stressed in this sermon, which, in the handwritten booklet made, as was his practice, to fit the palm of his hand, is simply an open space, to be filled by what he knew by heart. As John F. Wilson notes, "Edwards . . . used this method to indicate his intention to repeat words or phrases as he built the rhetorical structure of his preaching."[56]

In this connection it is interesting to consider, as well, another aspect of Edwards's immersion in biblical texts which together make up the grand narrative of Christianity. Stephen Prickett, in recalling the work of Robert Lowth, originator of the English Higher Criticism of the Bible, notes as one of his central observations that the Hebrew poetry of the Old Testament "worked not by the common European devices of rhyme, assonance, rhythm etc., but by what he called 'parallelism', [*sic* punctuation] where one phrase or sentence is amplified or contrasted with another, immediately juxtaposed with it. The origins of this parallelism . . . lay in the previous oral tradition – in this case in the antiphonal chants and choruses we find mentioned at various points in the Old Testament."[57] In reading a passage from I Samuel 18:7, Lowth distinguishes, as Prickett observes, "no less than eight different kinds of parallelism, ranging from simple repetition, to echo, variation, contrast and comparison."[58] Elsewhere, in discussing the appropriateness or inappropriateness of certain languages for translations of the Hebrew Bible, Prickett, following William Tyndale, notes the affinity between Hebrew and English in their both having a flexible word order which permits a rhetoric dependent on particular choices and arrangements of words.[59] In addition, as we have been reminded recently by Judith Shulevitz: "Biblical Hebrew has an unusually small vocabulary clustered around an even smaller number of three-letter roots, most of them denoting concrete actions or things, and the Bible achieves its mimetic effects partly through the skillful repetition of these few vivid words. The translators who gave us the King James version appear . . . to have understood this."[60] Edwards's long and repeated study of scriptural texts, combined, most importantly, with having to write and deliver, in the face of communal dissolution, sermons that were "signals for positive action," inscribed a template, as it were, a perceptual habit, that would enable him to recover what Emerson would call in *Nature* (1836) "an original relation to the universe," that "original relation" being a new language. Edwards used "key words" as the prophets had, as "connective tissue"[61] around which grew descriptions nourished by his personal experience of grace. Emerson, it should be noted, offered his interrogative injunction having been prepared in biblical texts and in the necessity of composing effective sermons in the same way as Edwards. The situation of America, its spiritual life at different moments threatened, endangered, alerted both Edwards and Emerson to "the realization that a talent for speaking differently, rather than for arguing well, is the chief instrument for cultural change."[62] The features common to Edwards's and Emerson's styles connect both of them to the manners of utterance belonging to the Hebrew prophets. All were attempting to make the invisible visible, though the idea of the invisible necessarily changed over time.[63] Edwards's and Emerson's utterances would be, as it were, amplified by what they replaced as the content of what Lowth termed "parallelisms," and in the different forms and arrangement of words they deployed. The identifying paradigm of what would come to be known as Pragmatism, "Truth *happens* to an idea,"[64] was beginning to be set down: "a natural habit, or foundation for action," in Edwards's phrase (see p. 34 above), the seed of belief.

Of practical interest in connection with Edwards's redaction of sacred texts is his habit of setting down his amplifications in his "Blank Bible," a small printed version with blank pages interleaved for notes. Marsden notes that "from 1730 to 1758 Edwards made perhaps ten thousand entries, or an average of more than one entry for every weekday, in this collection alone"; there were, in addition, four large notebooks called "Notes on Scripture," which he kept throughout his career.[65] This exercise of returning again and again to texts, so much from them learned by heart, each time taking account of his own earlier notations as well, a performance of recursiveness, would be replayed in its secular variety by Emerson in his manner of going back again and again to his own earlier lectures and essays and indexing and re-indexing them for salient words, phrases, and concepts which he kept in separate notebooks to use in amplifying later work. His earlier ministerial training and practice in the method of typology – like Edwards, returning repeatedly to the Testaments – he translated into his purpose of fashioning a "Natural History of the Intellect." And Wallace Stevens, though he did not, like Edwards, keep a "Blank Bible," nor like Emerson index his journals, did return to certain central texts, notably to Psalms, to Proverbs, and to Emerson, exemplifying in the development of his corpus the same kind of performance of recursiveness and amplification. While not trained in the ministry, Stevens was steeped in cyclic returns to Bible stories and sermons from childhood through late adolescence, both at home and in church, through his mother's deep religious commitment. Without formal education in typology, he nonetheless learned as well, as we shall see, to "look [not] at facts, but through them," the instruction inscribed to himself in his journal the summer before he returned for his last year at Harvard.[66] Each of these men, their spirits textually trained like vines on the trellis of the sacred, cultivated the strong stock of familiar salvific phrases and grafted into them new strains.

Further discussion of Emerson or of Stevens will be left at this point for following chapters; they have been invoked here because of the continuity their examples offer in mapping the development of Pragmatism out of a particular set of circumstances and practices. Emerson's experience in the biblical texts, as a minister, in the work of studying words and shaping language, is remarkably close to that of Edwards, and yet, of course, different. Imperfect replication, the mechanism of evolutionary change, can be applied figuratively in this instance, as it can be later to William James in relation to Emerson and Edwards, to Wallace Stevens in relation to James, Emerson, and Edwards. Information is both replicated and passed along imperfectly through texts from one generation to another in different experiential environments, as, for example, Locke and Newton read by Edwards, who adapted them through his particular inflection to America's environment of fact.

Edwards's contribution to the idea of the invisible, what he learned from Newton was, for his practical purposes, detailing additional aspects of the mind of God. The perceptual lacunae of prophetic speech, where either an antiphonal rephrasing or a gnomic response, for example, blocked, in an Old Testament text, further imagining of the invisible mind of God, Edwards would begin to fill with more of what had been disclosed to him, through Newton, about that mind. Indeed, he shared this faith with Newton who believed "that the fundamental truths about nature had been known to the wise men of antiquity and the Biblical prophets, who (he thought) had chosen to conceal their knowledge from the 'vulgar' by using symbols and allegory."[67] For Edwards, it was consistent with faith that God's love could be understood as gravity and His grace as actual light. The content of the "parallelisms" of the biblical texts represented, for Edwards, an earlier stage in the "ascent of being to Being." As Knight observes:

God's communications accelerate as the work of redemption progresses; the unfolding of each successive period in sacred history brings greater knowledge of the divine, especially at the thresholds when one providential era gives way to the next. Describing the shift from the Old Testament world to that of the New, Edwards remarked "what a great increase is here of the light of the gospel . . . [H]ow plentiful are the revelations and prophecies of Christ now to what they were in the first Old Testament period." [*HWR*, p. 240] Prophecies become more exact; types become more frequent and more perfect in their prefiguring of the Messiah. This is, of course, a highly traditional interpretation of biblical types.

Less conventional was Edwards's claim that divine communications will continue to expand, in frequency and in kind, with the approach of the millennium. Just as the gospel light intensified with the first coming of Christ, so with the coming of the kingdom knowledge of heavenly things will increase, extending beyond the Bible to include revelation through nature and human history. In his most jubilant moods Edwards expressed faith that this process was already underway. He observed, for example, that "the late invention of telescopes, whereby heavenly objects are brought so much nearer and made so much plainer to sight . . . is a type and forerunner of the great increase in the knowledge of heavenly things that shall be in the approaching glorious times."[68]

GOD IS A COMMUNICATING BEING[69]

Before going on to consider passages from Edwards illustrating his deployment of the various behaviors of light he had apprehended as "actual ideas," it is useful to keep in mind the general features of what he imagined and understood from his reading. Newton's experiments led him to theorize that while light was omnipresent, its manifestations ranged through the

colors of the humanly perceived spectrum and into darkness. To recapitulate somewhat the description offered earlier, these manifestations were
to be imagined as the products of relations between the invisible, pure
light of the sun and the myriad elements with which it interacts, each
of these elements affecting the wave function of the sun's light to register particular colors. Moreover, light itself is composed of an infinity of
"diverse kinds of light." As Newton concluded in Experiment 6 of Book I,
Part II of the *Opticks*: "From all which it is manifest, that if the Sun's
Light consisted of but one sort of Rays, there would be but one Colour in
the whole world, nor would it be possible to produce any new Colour by
Reflexions and Refractions, and by consequence that the variety of Colours
depends upon the Composition of Light."[70] The varying elements, because
of their differing compositions, attract the "diverse kinds of light," rays, in
a gravitational way according to the densities and wave intensities both
of the diverse rays within light and of the elements interacting with it to
effect reflection, refraction, diffusion, absorption, etc. Understood as the
most immensely complex relation of degrees of interactivity on a spectrum
extending to the infinite, scintillant degree of God, light, as described by
Newton, actualized each and every element of God's creation as indeed, in
Emerson's later phrasing, "part or particle of God,"[71] of that light.

Additionally, light, by increasing exposure of itself, exciting more heat,
gradually transforms elements, receptive according to their composition,
from opaque to transparent, to nothing if consumed in the light of fire. The
possibilities of such transformations depend on the various dispositions of
the elements being affected by light, these dispositions, again, being conditioned both by their composition and by their varying motions, speeds:

For the Rays to speak properly are not coloured. In them there is nothing else than
a certain Power and Disposition to stir up a Sensation of this or that Colour. For
as Sound in a Bell or musical String, or other sounding Body, is nothing but a
trembling motion, and in the Air nothing but that Motion propagated from the
Object, and in the Sensorium [the place of sensation] 'tis A Sense of that Motion
under the Form of Sound; so Colours in the Object are nothing but a Disposition
to reflect this or that sort of Rays more copiously than the rest; in the Rays they are
nothing but their dispositions to propagate this or that Motion into the Sensorium,
and in the Sensorium they are Sensations of those Motions under the forms of
Colours.[72]

In Edwards's vocabulary this idea of propagation became "excellency," the
disposition of individuals to ascend toward God's eternal "excellence" by
excelling, increasing speed in receiving more and more light. For Edwards,
"disposition" was literal, a dis-positioning, a shift in spiritual valence and

receptivity occasioned by the relation of the subject as object of light. The work of the minister was to ignite auditors' attention to the truth of the gospels:

When light and heat are thus united in a minister of the gospel, it shows that each is genuine, and of a right kind, and that both are divine. Divine light is attended with heat; and so, on the other hand, a truly divine and holy heat and ardor is ever accompanied with light.[73]

The greater the reception of light, the more excited the mind by "holy heat," the quicker the transformation of matter into spirit, the speedier the combustion of fallen human impediments to delight in pure being.[74] As the young minister had offered early on in "Beauty of the World" (1725), parenthetically acknowledging – "(as Sir Isaac Newton has shown)" – his debt:

'Tis very probable that that wonderful suitableness of green for the grass and plants, the blue of the sky, the white of the clouds, the colors of the flowers, consists in a complicated proportion that these colors make with one another, either in the magnitude of the rays, the number of vibrations that are caused in the optic nerve, or some other way. So there is a great suitableness between the objects of different senses, as between sounds, colors, and smells – as between the colors of the woods and flowers, and the smell, and the singing of birds – which 'tis probable consist in a certain proportion of the vibrations that are made in the different organs. So there are innumerable other agreeablenesses of motions, figures, etc.: the gentle motions of trees, of lily, etc., as it is agreeable to other things that represent calmness, gentleness and benevolence, etc. The fields and woods seem to rejoice, and how joyful do the birds seem to be in it. How much a resemblance is there of every grace in the fields covered with plants and flowers, when the sun shines serenely and undisturbedly upon them. How a resemblance, I say, of every grace and beautiful disposition of mind; of an inferior towards a superior cause, preserver, benevolent benefactor, and a fountain of happiness.[75]

For Edwards, Newton's catalogue of the behaviors of light, precisely detailed following his experiments, translated into a spiritual catalogue of the states of mind of individuals seeking salvation, "of every grace and beautiful disposition of mind; of an inferior towards a superior cause." Diffraction, refraction, reflection, absorption, diffusion would assume in Edwards's ministerial lexicon meanings which would direct the inflection of his words to assist the activity of his auditors' imaginations in the work of understanding God's creation. He would, moreover, examine himself first and continually, following the attention of his mind in thinking to set down the words serving as the prisms through which he might scrutinize the state of his own soul.

In the "room of the idea" once constructed – like Newton's chamber darkened to permit directed, sharp focus – Jonathan Edwards discovered the "sense of the heart," derived from the "Sense of that Motion" Newton described as the contents of the different "Sensoria" agitated by their disposition to receive sensations as forms. Here was the experience of the aesthetic in its purest sense, in its "actual idea" as feeling, sensation, making forms. Edwards's important addition to sensationalist conceptual equipment is best conceived, in its most primitive and apparent form, as a pulsing, a motive not thought, not, that is, predicated, but *felt*, a motive which allowed idiosyncratic emotive perception to be an organizing principle, the actual increased heart beat and increased "heat" of brain-activity as described by William James, who, recuperating and advancing Edwards's contribution, stated as one of the primary objectives of his *Principles*, the establishment of the emotions as a valid basis for judgment.[76] Whitehead would further particularize this process: "The direct perception whereby the datum in the immediate subject is inherited from the past can thus, under an abstraction, be conceived as the transference of throbs of emotional energy, clothed in the specific forms provided by the sensa."[77] This sense of the heart, identical for Edwards with mind, was an analogue for what he had come to understand about the behavior of light. As detailed earlier, this response was, indeed, a physical experience, a "sensuous apprehension," in Miller's words, of the effect of what Edwards believed to be being excited by grace, by the spirit of God. In place of the logic of predication that his Puritan forebears had inherited by way of the Augustinian replays of the Aristotelian system, Edwards fashioned a new kind of typological reasoning informed by his immersion in the sensationalism of Locke, specified and concretized by his reading of Newton, as well as by his actual situation in the New World natural setting where he found himself, literally, without the categories of thought, without the grammar and syntax, with which to account for what he saw and heard and felt. The logic he devised seems, in some ways, oddly backward-looking, as has been noted by Stephen Daniel, drawing as it does on typology and the Renaissance system of signs,[78] where "the whole universe, heaven and earth, air and seas, and the divine constitution and history of the holy Scriptures, [are read to] be full of images of divine things, as full as language is of words."[79]

And yet, as also observed by Daniel, what Edwards accomplished using this retrieval was a major change in habit of mind. Edwards embodied, as a sixth sense, what Locke had merely hinted at in the closing chapter of his *Essay*, where he suggests the extension of "'the doctrine of signs' beyond a simple analysis of words or the relation of ideas to the study of the order by which thought itself is possible." In pointing toward this extension, Locke invokes *semiotike*, which, as a term, most interestingly, derives from the art of musical notation as used by Locke's friend John Wallis in his 1682 edition of Ptolemy's *Harmonics*: "In this expanded sense, Locke notes, semiotics is 'aptly termed also *Logike*, logic: the business whereof is to consider the nature of signs the mind makes use of for the understanding of things, or conveying its knowledge to others.' To understand ideas and words in the context of just such a doctrine 'would afford us another sort of logic and critic, than what we have been hitherto acquainted with.'" At the end of the *Essay*, as Daniel observes, Locke points to a project which would explain why words, "in their primary or immediate signification, stand for nothing but the *ideas* in the mind of him that uses them."[80]

Edwards's faith as a divine permitted him to trust that the "sense of the heart" is that which "consider[s] the nature of signs the mind makes use of for the understanding of things, or conveying its knowledge to others." This sense was for him as much a gift of God as any of the other five senses; thus he pursued Locke's project, informed with what he had learned from Newton as its semiotic. While in theological terms being graced meant the restoration of this sense, lost with original sin, in Lockean terms, Edwards's "heart" was the container/organ of the resonances and residues of lived and living speech and experience, the place of Lockean *Reflection*, a conceptual space being explored by Edwards as he began to free himself from the Puritan constraint of keeping consciousness confined to conscience. In doing so, he realized language to matter, or, rather, *as* matter, capable of creating sensations as actually as seeing, hearing, touching, tasting, and smelling. While Locke had pointed the direction, he had not *practiced* language, *performed* it, as it were, in the manner his realizations were suggesting. These indications would only be pursued in England later, most notably by John Keats, by Samuel Taylor Coleridge (endeavoring to "elevat[e] . . . words into things, & living Things too"), and experimentally by Charles Bell, whose work, pursuing a "neurologically-based 'natural language,'" which would be of central significance not only to Keats but to Darwin and to Emerson, gave proof to Edwards's "sense of the heart": Bell found "in the interplay of nervous system, heart, blood, and skin a telling example of the embodied mind in action . . . The 'filaments' of the nervous system are 'extended to the heart, and wind about the vessels in their course through the body.'"[81] Locke, however, remained, to the greatest extent, within the logic of predication that was the soil of his intellectual experience.

In contrast, Edwards, finding himself and his congregations lost amidst "the wild, the ruinous waste"[82] of the New World experience, his congregations, the community, dissolving, yet with his own faith in place, abandoned himself to God's grace, as it were, and so yielded his consciousness to mimic the open spaces of the landscape where, without script or map, he was forced to read everything as sign. Realizing the condition of being lost as the natural and unavoidable condition of life in this savage setting, Edwards allowed "the convergence of scientific curiosity and typological vision," that Lawrence Buell has noted in characterizing his thought,[83] to figure, or, perhaps better, to *dis*-figure, like emergent properties, reason's conceptual categories. But, again, because of his faith, Edwards was able to do so with conviction, with his confirmed sense of the heart, that it was a matter of life and death for words to come to mean in whatever manner he could divine. As he described in *Thoughts on the Revival of Religion in New England*, "Our people don't so much need to have their heads stored, as to have their hearts touched; and they stand in the greatest need of that sort of preaching that has the greatest tendency to do this."[84] Elsewhere, in *The Distinguishing Marks of a Work of the Spirit of God*, he particularizes how this sort of preaching is effected:

I think it is a reasonable thing to endeavor to fright persons away from hell . . .'tis a reasonable thing to fright a person out of an house on fire . . . When ministers preach of hell, and warn sinners to avoid it, in a cold manner, though they may say in words that it is infinitely terrible; yet (if we look on language as a communication of our minds to others) they contradict themselves; for actions . . . have a language to convey our minds, as well as words.

In addition, as Kimnach points out, Edwards understood that it was the "gesture of language," specifically the images and metaphors employed analogically in making an argument concrete,[85] that would make words actions, matter. While Edwards believed his insights to have come from God, from our later point of view it is easy to see that his response was animal, that is, the response of a creature struggling to survive in an environment where "the squirming facts exceed[ed] the squamous mind."[86] We recall Feyerabend's observations cited in the introductory chapter here (p. 5); Edwards admitted panic, and the space panic unavoidably opens in the mind – "but yet it never seemed to be proper to express my concern that I had, by the name of terror"[87] – to inform, by silently withholding its name, the direction and shape of his thought, as his sermons abundantly exemplify, and as his notes on "The Mind," where he introduces and explores "the sense of the heart," justify.

Moreover, his ministerial charge in the face of threat to community enabled Edwards to preserve and extend the implications of Locke's empiricism without imperiling the existence of the divine. Rather, with his "sense of the heart" understood as the correspondent of God's grace, he embedded the divine within the empirical. Lockean epistemology had, of course, posed a serious political problem, how not to become Hobbesian in a world of fact, how to maintain connection to community if each individual was nothing more than the container of a different set of facts. Faced with this problem, though not with immediate political threat, the Scottish philosophers Lord Kames, Thomas Reid, and his student Dugald Stewart devised a common moral sense, based in intuitionism. While Edwards's intention was consistent with what was emerging in Edinburgh at roughly the same time, his solution, by preserving the divine in the "sense of the heart" and linking this sense directly to words and their "nature as signs," provided the experiential bridge linking belief and investigation.

Edwards's self-imposed charge was to discover for both himself and his congregations how words come to mean, the manner in which they might perform the work of salvation and so convert the fallen into saints. To understand ideas and words in the context of "the doctrine of signs," as *semiotike*, as Locke suggested, Edwards introduced the Newtonian information, which he was, in effect, "learning by heart" from the Book of Nature, into the thought experiment he would conduct throughout his career. In this experiment, feeling his heart quicken and "burn within" and questioning the source of the excitement, he allowed the words which would serve him as prisms to break up the light of an idea into its various rays, its various components and aspects. (It is interesting to note in the context of "thought experiment," that David Brainerd, Edwards's son-in-law, described Edwards's project as "experimental religion.") In deliberately pursuing the use of certain words as instruments enabling analysis, Edwards was, of course, reenacting and continuing the instigating motive of the Reformation, "a quarrel over words," as Michel de Montaigne described it, in a "culture of grammatical transformation."[88] We recall Martin Luther's recounting his preoccupation with the word and idea of "grace," and that it was his determination in turning, troping, the idea this way and that, over and over again, in attempting to align the concept of God's grace with the actualities of suffering and evil, that eventually provided the occasion for his *feeling* grace, hearing the call to his election. It was this sensible understanding of grace, attendant on his own interpretation rather than on doctrine, which provided him access to the divine. For Edwards, the reason for his repetition of certain words and repeated observations of natural facts was grounded in typology, as Knight has observed in quoting from him, "to signify the great importance of the antitype," Christ; "the sun is a type of Christ," "so the seasons of the sun," as she paraphrases from *Images or Shadows of Divine Things*, "continually re-present a 'lively' image of the divine."[89]

Among the words Edwards used as prisms to focus this "divine and supernatural light," whose valence and intensity he would assiduously measure and chart in his own being – "Sometimes only mentioning a single word, causes my heart to burn within me"[90] – "light," "delight," "excellence" and "excellency," "affect" and "affection," "disposition," "gravity," "depends," "fit," and "suitable" are among those especially inflected. Edwards allowed these words to direct light into the spaces opened in his perceptual syntax by emotions stirred in response to the various threats he faced both individually, in tracking the movements of his spirit, and communally, as minister to those for whom he was responsible. These threats took different forms, from those posed by the inability to understand a scriptural passage or something noted by Newton, for example, through those attendant on his scrupulous self-examination which prompted self-doubt verging on despair, to those consequent on contemplating powerlessness, and ultimately death, to those attendant on the fear of losing faith, through to those he would in fact experience when effectively ostracized by his Northampton community in 1750 because of his adamant stance concerning tests for church membership. A prime instance of the way in which such a threat informed the manner in which he constructed a series of sentences which he could spiritually inhabit for a while is a passage appropriately borrowed, for the argument being presented here, from the opening of Perry Miller's biography of Edwards. This passage, from a Public Lecture Edwards gave in Northampton on Thursday, July 8, 1731, exemplifies the kind of word usage he deployed following what he had learned about light; I have italicized the variants of the word "affect," his prisms here:

When the mind is *affected* with a thing much, it is led into such schemes of thought about it, as, if they were written down, would seem very impertinent to one that was not *affected*. It is so in all matters. The scripture falls in with the natural stream of one's thought [a possible source for William James] when the mind is *affected* with the things of which they speak; but are very wide of their series of thought, who are not *affected*. For instance, the text that says "one generation passeth away and another cometh, but the earth abideth forever," seems to me in a common frame of mind insipid; the latter part of the verse seems impertinently to be brought in, as what may better tend to illustrate the former: the thought of the earth being the same, does not seem very naturally and *affectingly* to fall in after the thought of one generation passing, and another coming. What is it to the purpose whether the earth remains the same or no? This makes not the changes of the inhabitants either more or less *affecting*.

But yet when, upon an occasion, I was more than ordinarily *affected* with the passing of one generation after another; how all those, who made such a noise and bluster now, and were so much concerned about their life, would be clean gone off from the face of the earth in sixty or seventy years time, and that the world would be left desolate with respect to them, and that another generation would come on, that would be very little concerned about them, and so one after another: it was particularly *affecting* to me to think that the earth still remained the same through all these changes upon the surface: the same spots of ground, the same mountains and valleys where those things were done, remaining just as they were, though the actors ceased, and the actors just gone. And then this text came into my mind.[91]

The most distinctive feature of Edwards's style, both in the writings he kept as his own and in his sermons, as indicated earlier, is this manner of progressive repetition of certain words in their variants. This practice, internalized from the method of typology, also grounded his understanding of ideas as set down in "The Mind": "IDEAS. All sorts of ideas of things are but the repetitions of those very things over again, as well as the ideas of colors, figures, solidity, tastes and smells, as the ideas of thought and mental acts,"[92] his realization of repetition as the active principle in producing ideas prefiguring later psychologists', most notably William James's, descriptions of how information is inscribed in neuronal pathways. In the passage above, the different grammatical uses and syntactic positions of "affect" break up, analyze, the idea to be examined. In the room of the idea of human transience, the feelings brought into focus through the prism of *affected* four times repeated in variant syntactic relations, followed by *affectingly*, then *affecting*, before the reappearance of *affected* and *affecting* once more, function, indeed, like the *semiotike* of musical notation to elicit a performance through a movement scaling the ascent from "speculative" to "sensible" knowledge, "the order by which thought itself is possible," in Locke's terms. From the "speculative" consideration of a proposition, in the first sentence presented by the polarization of the extremes possible – "is affected" against "not affected" – Edwards conducts his audience to the next modulation of feeling by introducing, first, recognition – represented by the repetition of the opening phrase, "when the mind is affected," where now "affected" locates for attention an experiential cognate, each listener's sympathetic consideration of his/her manner of regarding the passing of particular ideas/memories/projections in consciousness when considering "the natural stream of one's thought" when stirred, "affected with the things of which they [the voices of the prophets and apostles in scripture] speak."

The construction of this third sentence elicits an amplification in feeling "when the mind is affected" by calling on auditors to shift from speculative reflection by responding with their individual content to mimic the activity of the general mind in elaborating a proposition; the positioning of "when the mind is affected" in the center of this first clause diffracts the initial meaning of "affected" to produce, as different shades, the necessarily different contents in auditors under the commonality of sympathetic identification. This sympathetic identification is induced, as well, by the personification of "scripture" to evoke the prophets and disciples who "speak" through the biblical books. "Not affected" in the terminal position of this sentence reflects "not affected" closing the first sentence, thus reinvoking the negative pole of the speculative moment, light bounced back, meaning not penetrated by feeling. Diffraction and reflection combine in this sentence to produce a feeling of uneasiness in auditors invited to engage their sympathy while reminded of the threat of being "not affected." The room of the idea prepared, light is directed through its aperture and prisms.

In the fourth sentence the feeling of uncertainty is drawn into Edwards's own being by example, illustrating and mimicking for his auditors the process which they have been prepared by the previous sentence to experience in searching for individual illustrations of being "affected with the things of which they [the scriptures] speak." Coming near the end of this fourth sentence, "affectingly" refracts the rays of meaning, of light, through Edwards's personal experience following the mode of refraction differentiated from reflection as described by Newton in Proposition XII of Book II, Part III; the "Proposition," presented in a different type face in *Opticks* (here in italics) is followed by observations and explanation in regular type:

PROP. XII. *Every Ray of Light in its passage through any refracting Surface is put into a certain transient Constitution or State, which in the progress of the Ray returns at equal intervals, and disposes the Ray at every return to be easily transmitted through the next refracting Surface, and between the returns to be easily reflected by it.*

so the Rays of Light, by impinging on any refracting or reflecting Surface, excite vibrations in the refracting or reflecting Medium or Substance, and by exciting them agitate the solid parts of the refracting or reflecting Body, and by agitating them cause the Body to grow warm or hot; that the vibrations thus excited are propagated in the refracting or reflecting Medium or Substance, much after the manner that vibrations are propagated in the Air for causing Sound, and move faster than the Rays so as to overtake them; and that when any Ray is in that part of the vibration which conspires with its Motion, it easily breaks through a refracting Surface, but when it is in the contrary part which impedes its Motion, it is easily reflected.[93]

Edwards uses his "instance" as an indication of a step he has taken on the "ascent to actual being," his position on this scale effecting in him greater, faster agitation by the "Rays of Light," meaning, "propagated" by the "vibrations" of the text it is his intention to elucidate for his audience, the greater number of whom may be assumed to be still "reflecting," even literally "reflecting on" the meaning of the text, having not yet been "affected" in the way Edwards will show himself to be by the end of the passage. The stretched adverbial usage, "affectingly," perfectly mimics the preacher's desire to break through the reflecting surfaces of his auditors, which "impede the Motions" of the rays of meaning he is at pains to communicate. While they, too, have grown "warm or hot," they are still in need of being put into "a certain transient Constitution or State" in which they, too, might begin to refract the "affection" attendant on feeling what it means to be transient in this world. Truth, for his auditors, and for us, his readers, is what is happening to the idea of their transience as a result of the way he is casting light on his words. We begin to see, to feel, why we still read him.

The fifth sentence in the passage is a question: "What is it to the purpose whether the earth remains the same or no?" From the speculative point of view, this is a rhetorical question, but from the sensible point of view, conditioned by what has come before, a pained utterance, a recording of one of the spaces of panic opened by Edwards's inability at a certain moment to respond to a passage of Scripture, an inability to converse with the author of the utterance which is the subject of this lesson. Edwards's auditors, no less than we, would recognize similar responses to those things that prompt the wish to dismiss them, to send, reflect, them back to their source, but which still gnaw at the mind. "What do I care if . . ." is the colloquial container of such responses, thrown up like dust in the eyes of an enemy as we turn to flee. The refusal to enter the conversation the temporarily opaque surface of the text offers deflects the threat posed to the state of one's being at that moment, a state of resistance in which understanding is "impeded." Attention to the mind in thinking is the only possibility of salvation at such points, attending to what is being felt, to what is being experienced as threat in such moments. Edwards's response (the sixth sentence) to the question posed, "This makes not the changes of the inhabitants either more or less affecting," focuses precisely for scrutiny the deflective impulse to dismiss the threat, but by introducing the present participle "affecting" as the prism, announces the unfinished business to which attention must be given. "Affecting" is the transparency function, alerting Edwards's audience to the auguring "of good or evil" dependent, like the light of the sun finding in its objects the spaces/"pores" which would permit the "conspir[ing] with its own Motion," on their feeling the sensation of his words fill the spaces of their being, effect the refraction of meaning into "truth," happening to them.

The seventh sentence then performs the activity of Edwards's becoming increasingly transparent, admitting greater and greater light into the spaces/pores opened by the "sense of the heart" making *sensible* to him the *feeling* of transience by his recollection of the "occasion" when in the "room of the idea" of transience he admitted his pain in facing this fact. Most notably, the sentence begins by imitating the effect of this opening to feeling by actually opening the spaces between the adverbial deictic "When" which begins the first sentence of the passage and "affected": in place of "When the mind is affected," here is "But yet when, upon an occasion, I was more than ordinarily affected," with the personal pronoun "I" centrally positioned, the aperture admitting light, the homonymic "eye" observing the projection into the "room of the idea" of what will follow, an extended description of how the idea of transience came to mean for him when illuminated, sensed, through his experience. Revealingly, in translating the abstraction of "the passing of one generation after another," Edwards uses colloquial terms to express his feeling: "those, who made such a noise and bluster now," who would be "clean gone off from the face of the earth," which would be left "desolate," pathetically personified in his description, before "another generation would come on, that would be very little concerned about them." Edwards's "prehension," in Whitehead's terms, signals the contribution to sensationalist philosophy indicated earlier (p. 47). That is, in bringing to bear in reading, in receiving, any text or experiential moment that holds attention for an initially indeterminate reason, one's individual fund of associations held in trust, in faith, by the "heart," as understood by Edwards, one could access the "sensible knowledge" necessary to "convert" what was before merely "speculative knowledge" by the "sense of the heart" into *feeling* it as "actual idea." This sense, then, fully awakened, feels its "appetite" for the divine, for "the consent of being to being," and draws up the text that will satisfy, that will "please," "placing of it right by our imagination," to reestablish the "relation" of "complicated harmony" with God:[94]

the greater a being is, and the more it has of entity, the more will consent to being in general please it. But God is proper entity itself, and these two therefore in him become the same; for so far as a thing consents to being in general, so far it consents to him. And the more perfect created spirits are, the nearer do they come to their creator in this regard.[95]

Edwards's conception of the "APPETITE of the mind,"[96] intrinsic to accessing the "sensible knowledge" that converts "speculative knowledge" into "actual ideas," is, insofar as I have been able to determine, the original instance of thinking the mind an active organ, seeking nutriment for survival, in his terms variously "panting," "thirsting," "hungering" for the words that will satisfy, catalyze the raw materials of experience into necessary intellectual, spiritual nourishment. Edwards thus converted, before Hume's skepticism and Kant's a priori clouded the idea of the mind as *tabula rasa*, Locke's notion to his own use, an instigating example of the method that would later define Pragmatism. This understanding of the mind as an organ would, of course, come to inform the thinking of later theorists, Darwin, Emerson, and William James primary among them, with Whitehead then elaborating his philosophy of "organism" around what he called the "appetition of thought"; these aspects will be taken up in the chapters following.

To return to the present discussion, in connection with making the speculative sensible, specifically in relation to Edwards's incantatory repetition of certain words and their variants, it is illuminating to consider recent findings by neuroscientists on the electrochemical effects of chanting, meditation, and prayer. Brain scans have shown that these practices produce strikingly low activity in the posterior superior parietal lobe, a region dubbed by researchers "the orientation association area" (OAA), which provides bearings for the body in physical space. Prayer, meditation, and chanting induce the same feelings of "lightness," a "blurring of the lines between feeling in body and out of body," a feeling of oneness with the universe or God, or of floating above one's body, similarly reported in patients resuscitated from clinical death, who also often report seeing a light at the end of a tunnel. (Edwards's several repetitions of being "swallowed up in Christ" attendant on his intense experiences of prayer, "to be emptied and annihilated" as described in his *Personal Narrative*, should be recalled here.) This same region of the temporal lobes when subjected to patterns of magnetic fields in laboratory conditions produces the same effect in volunteers. When this region is undisturbed, when, that is, the OAA activity is not lowered as in deep meditation or prayer, or in the laboratory, "there is a sharp distinction between self and nonself."[97] Edwards's experience of "a divine and supernatural light" was, indeed, a fact of feeling. As the author of the article describing this research observes,

In reality, all experience is mediated by the brain . . . Of course, we are not aware of the workings of our own electrochemical systems. What we experience is what philosophers call qualia, or subjective states of thought and feelings that arise from a concatenation of neural events . . . It is the fate of the paranormal and the supernatural to be subsumed into the normal and the natural. In fact, there is no paranormal or supernatural; there are only the normal and the natural – and mysteries yet to be explained.[98]

Nearly 300 years earlier, Edwards observed: "So the soul may be said to be in the brain, because ideas that come by the body immediately ensue only on alterations that are made there, and the soul most immediately produces effects nowhere else."[99]

In Edwards's *Personal Narrative*, a text bridging the private and public, the words "delight" and "sweet," with their variants, strike readers with a litanic, if not obsessive, rhythm. Most notably, the narrative begins with his remarking "those new dispositions" which he experienced as a first moment of conversion "diffused" as "a new sense" by the words of I Timothy 1:17: "Now unto the King eternal, immortal, invisible, the only wise God, be honor and glory forever and ever, Amen," which he "kept saying, and as it were singing over," in the manner which, as described above, would have induced what he describes here of being "as it were swallowed up in him [God]."[100] Further along, Edwards particularizes this repetitive, meditative practice as identical with experiencing the "gently vivifying beams of the sun . . . diffusing," and himself "receiving" as a flower "the pleasant beams of the sun's glory," in like manner himself "opening . . . to drink in the light of the sun."[101] In such settings, he records,

I had then, and at other times, the greatest delight in the holy Scripture, of any book whatsoever. Oftentimes in reading it, every word seemed to touch my heart. I felt an harmony between something in my heart, and those sweet and powerful words. I seemed often to see so much light, exhibited by every sentence, and such a refreshing ravishing food communicated, that I could not get along in reading. Used oftentimes to dwell long on one sentence, to see the wonders contained in it; and yet almost every sentence seemed to be full of wonders.[102]

In these remarkable passages, we see Edwards naturalizing the supernatural, without in any way diminishing that divine supernatural, his soul/mind informed by what he had learned from Newton, that information transfiguring the expected temporal sequence of narrative with pools of light *diffused* throughout his account, in the varying appearances in the text of "delight" and "sweet" and their combinations, the interpolations of his spiritual calculus, evidences of his having been "affected" by divining the "actual ideas" "vivifying" the words of Scripture. These incidences mimic the actual "dispositions" of the matter of his being opened to feel its "appetite" for increasing light. (We should here also recall "dispositions" as a salient term in Newton's delineations of light's effects; see p. 45 above.) As Edwards describes on several occasions in the *Narrative*, this "affect" was felt as a "panting" or "thirst" for more light, "the knowledge that surpasseth understanding." In terms of the aesthetic he was fashioning, "the more than rational distortion[s]" provided in their interruptions of linear thinking a model for the distinctive style that would enable later "doers of the Word" in the New World to continue to perform their ministerial function for following generations. As Ann Taves has observed in describing Edwards's effectiveness as a minister in activating a "new spiritual sense," and advising other ministers to observe reactions to certain words and their repetitions in their parishioners, his "insight into mimetic action awaited the development of more sophisticated theories of magnetic and then unconscious interaction,"[103] the physiological grounding provided, for example, by the research described above, linking the effects of incantation and what for Edwards and his congregations would have been perceived as spiritual vision.

In this context, and before returning to the central features of the *Personal Narrative*, it is apt to note the comments of some of Edwards's nineteenth-century reader–critics concerning the success of *A History of the Work of Redemption*. The impact of this discourse on nineteenth-century American spiritual life has earlier and generally been remarked (note 49). Noteworthy as indicative of this response is that *A History* was prominently reviewed by the British cultural elite, as well as by central figures in America's cultural conversation. An anonymous essay in the *Monthly Review* negatively criticized Edwards's discourse as displaying "a method *entirely new*," a "confused rhapsody," the reviewer commenting, "He has enriched his history with every thing that could be suggested by the most unbridled imagination," seeing Edwards as an "intoxicated visionary presuming to see the will of God."[104] Another explicit discussion of *A History*, by Edward W. Grinfield in *The Nature and Extent of the Christian Dispensation with Reference to the Salvability of the Heathen* (London, 1827), while also critical, nonetheless observed: "I would hope, that hereafter it will be no more doubted, that the general system of doctrine which they [the apostolic writings] exhibit has a universal reference to the human race; than it is now doubted, that the principles of the Newtonian philosophy hold good to the world at large, whether believed in or not by the majority of mankind."[105] In America, at the same time, George Bancroft, as observed by Wilson, reflecting upon

the "deeper import and meaning of historiography". . . argued that "exact observation" is necessary for the "historic enquirer," but that the true meaning of the activity lies "behind" the observations: "Facts faithfully ascertained, and placed in proper contiguity, become of themselves the firm links of a brightly burnished chain, connecting events with their causes, and marking the line along which the electric power of truth is conveyed from generation to generation." His point is that "historic truth" should "establish itself as a science." When it does, it will "become the highest demonstration of the superintending providence of God."

This striking position leads Bancroft to affirm a belief in "progress in human affairs." Indeed, he sees universal history as an attempt "to relate 'the sum of all God's works of providence,'" and in so quoting Edwards credits him with this decisive formulation.

> In America, the first conception of its office, in the mind of Jonathan Edwards, though still cramped and perverted by theological forms not derived from obser-
> vation, was nobler than the theory of Vico: more grand and general than the
> method of Bossuet, it embraced in its outline the whole "work of redemption,"
> – the history of the influence of all moral truth in the gradual regeneration of
> morality.[106]

The "gradual regeneration of morality," would, of course, become the pre-occupation of those who followed Edwards: Emerson, Peirce, William and Henry James, Stevens, and Stein. The manners and methods they devised from their pondering what would suffice to evidence "the activity of the most august imagination"[107] in its ongoing "relation to the universe" constitute the subjects of the chapters following.

But, to return, in closing, to Edwards's *Personal Narrative*, it is important to comment on the idea of "dependence," noted in opening this chapter, as a controlling motive of his understanding. Nearing the end of his record of illumination, Edwards observes, "I have vastly a greater sense, of my universal, exceeding dependence on God's grace and strength, and mere good pleasure, of late, than I used formerly to have."[108] By the time he comes to offer this summation, his text has exuberantly performed feeling the fact of "exceeding dependence" through the crescendoing appearances of "delight" and "sweet" alternating with their variants to focus attention sensibly on the progressive thinning of his matter into spirit as he comes to "pure delight in being." His delight, following Newton, is the sensible embodiment of his dependence on light: his existence is of and from, *de-*, light, just as all in God's creation is an effect, *de*-pending on that same light. That dependence is not metaphorical, but actual, the varying manners of its being felt a product of the interactivity of individual beings with Being, "consent to being" a description of so aligning – "inclining" in Edwards's words – the receptive pores so that increasing rays of grace continue to transform matter into spirit, gradually clearing the material obstructions that produce opacity and so reflection, which, as Edwards would have known from his study of Newton's delineation of light's transmission in

Query 24 of Book III of the *Opticks*, "disturb and interrupt the Motions of this Medium."[109] For Edwards, "sweetness," "pleasure," is concomitant with greater and greater transparency and attendant heat, making himself more and more able to receive and transmit "the Motions of this Medium."

Moreover, it was by reconceiving dependence, not as submission and passivity, as child to parent, but as the activity of consent, of deploying the will to rediscover its connection with divinity wherein the actuality of physical reality is understood more accurately, this understanding, in turn, optimizing the choices for successful survival of the spirit, that Edwards effected his transformation of the Lockean scheme. The imagination of Locke belonged as fully to the orders of British society and nature tamed as Edwards's did to the spiritual stress of his society and to the elemental sensations of what was still a threatening frontier. As noted earlier, while occasionally falling into analogy, Locke's conceptual habit was trained in predication, while Edwards, for all practical purposes, like so many of the Puritan divines before him, was thrown back into the situation in which, as Barbara Maria Stafford in her splendid study of analogy has observed, the pre-Socratics had found themselves before nature, their "innovation" using analogy as the primary mode of establishing a "mediation with the divine world through a tangible link." She continues, in a sentence which could just as easily describe the rhetorical practices of John Cotton, Cotton Mather, Edward Taylor, or Edwards: "Wind, smoke, shadow, dream, fire, and image were the phenomenological terms of comparison they borrowed to marry the suprasensible to the sensible realm," adding, "it was Heraclitus (536–470 B.C.), the greatest of the Ionians, who turned analogy away from simple, vertical anthropomorphism and honed it into a general tool for scientific explanation."[110] Recovering this kind of instrumentality was a necessity for Edwards, feeling himself as truly as the Psalmist and the ministers preceding him in his task, "a stranger in the earth." The ground and development of analogy Stafford describes apply neatly to Edwards in his moment, moving back and forth from the secure anchorage offered by the sacred texts into his imperfect imaginings of the unfathomable Being of God, Light:

Analogy, born of the human desire to achieve union with that which one does not possess, is also a passionate process marked by fluid oscillations. Perceiving the lack of something – whether physical, emotional, spiritual, or intellectual – inspires us to search for an approximating resemblance to fill its place. That theological, philosophical, rhetorical, and aesthetic quest gave birth to the middle term: the delayed not-yet or the allusive not-quite. This fleeting entity – participating both

in what one has and what one has not, like and unlike the yearned for experience –
temporarily allows the beholder to feel near, even interpenetrated by, what is distant,
unfamiliar, different . . . retreat and advance, absence and presence . . . mark the
capriccio dynamics of analogy's jumps from antithesis to synthesis and back again.[111]

Thus dependence becomes activity and the seed of imagination, conceived
as constituent of what is known, planted:

We should imagine analogy, then, as a participatory performance, a ballet of cen-
tripetal and centrifugal forces . . . . Analogy correlates originality with continuity,
what comes after with what went before, ensuing parts with evolving whole.

[A]nalogy is a demonstrative or evidentiary practice – putting the visible into
relationship with the invisible and manifesting the effect of that momentary uni-
son . . . the earthly or natural thing establishes a temporary resemblance with a
hidden mystery that one cannot otherwise see. All of analogy's simile-generating
figures are thus incarnational. They materialize, display, and disseminate an enigma
that escapes words.[112]

The effects of analogy, as Stevens would later describe, exist in the spaces
between, above, and around words, illuminating them, like light, but it is
nonetheless the words, their histories hidden in the turns of their letters,
their sounds spoken and unspoken, sparking the actual firings in synaptic
gaps that create the illuminations. The title of Edwards's Miscellany no. 782,
"Ideas. Sense of the Heart. Spiritual Knowledge. Faith," serves well as template for this process, a shorthand description of the work of the aesthetic
understood to be a secularized soteriological impulse, as William James
would carefully lay out and exemplify, providing the "complex ecstasies"[113]
necessary for belief and action.

CHAPTER THREE

Emerson's moving pictures

Indeed, what reason may not go to school to the wisdom of bees, ants, and spiders?

Thomas Browne, *Religio Medici*

IN THE BEGINNING WAS THE WORD

"We too must write Bibles, to unite again the heavens and the earthly world. The secret of genius is to suffer no fiction to exist for us; to realize all that we know; in the high refinement of modern life, in arts, in sciences, in books, in men, to exact good faith, reality, and a purpose; and first, last, midst, and without end, to honor every truth by use."[1] Thus, retrospectively, in 1850, having in 1845 delivered the lectures which would be collected under the title of "Representative Men," Emerson closed "Goethe; or, The Writer." His coda clearly restates the continuing necessity of a sacred office, a ministerial function, but now "in the high refinement of modern life," the performance of this office is no longer to read through received testaments but to "write Bibles," records of a new, "original relation to the universe." The questions opening *Nature* (1836) are to be explicitly answered by this ongoing activity: "But when a faithful thinker, resolute to detach every object from personal relations, and see it in the light of thought, shall, at the same time, kindle science with the fire of holiest affections, then will God go forth anew into the creation."[2] Informed by "speculation," the inner vision variously illustrated in the portraits of "Representative Men," this activity evidences the mutation of Divine Providence into self-conscious intentionality, "purpose . . . to honor every truth by use." The line from Edwards to Peirce and James is drawn. Where Edwards read and offered "Images, or Shadows of Divine Things," Emerson reads and offers "Representative Men": "Our age is secular," he broadly announced. Unnamed, of course, is Emerson himself, receiver and transmitter of the spirits whose translations of the invisible, by degrees, *realize* nature as mind's precipitate:

Nature is the incarnation of a thought, and turns to a thought again, as ice becomes water and gas. The world is mind precipitated, and the volatile essence is forever escaping into the state of free thought . . . Man imprisoned, man crystallized, man vegetative, speaks to man impersonated . . . Every moment instructs, and every object: for wisdom is infused into every form. It has been poured into us as blood; it convulsed us as pain; it slid into us as pleasure.[3]

Emerson's idea that it is possible to recognize, through what he calls the "rotation" of time, the residues of human experience and thinking, "scoriae,"[4] which in recombination contribute to the survival of the species, constituting what he and, later, Charles Sanders Peirce and William James call "common sense," belongs to his having himself imagined the process Darwin was to name "evolution": "We are tendencies, or rather, symptoms, and none of us is complete. We touch and go, and sip the foam of many lives. Rotation is the law of nature."[5] How Emerson came to have this understanding and how, through his work, it inflected the emergence of Pragmatism is the subject of this chapter. He announced it variously and with subtle boldness: ". . . it slid into us as pleasure."

At forty-seven, when he published *Representative Men*, Emerson was well poised to be retrospective concerning the evolution of his own mind. The instances of its process are, in his terms, "useful" for what is "reported" in their details, the "precipitates" remaining in the "alembic"[6] of his spirit of the thought experiments he had been conducting throughout his life. These experiments yielded results in the form of his "relations" with what he called in *Nature* the "NOT ME," extended here to include "other men": "Other men are the lenses through which we read our own minds. Each man seeks those of different quality from his own, and such as are good of their kind; that is, he seeks other men, and the *otherest*. The stronger the nature, the more it is reactive"; and, further, "The world has a sure chemistry, by which it extracts what is excellent in its children, and lets fall the infirmities and limitations of the grandest mind."[7] Notably, in *Nature*, there are certain key words, elements, as it were, shared in their emphasis and repetition with Jonathan Edwards: delight, scale and degree, relations, affection, excellent/excellence, love. Concentrated in the "Introduction" and Chapter I ("Nature"), they reappear throughout the volume, as well as in later essays, especially in *Representative Men*, where they are also most concentrated in its opening, "The Uses of Great Men," but also run throughout that collection. So much is this the case that it would be difficult for a reader familiar with both Edwards's and Emerson's bodies of work but not immediately fresh from immersion in either to identify one or the other as author of the following examples:

All things in the universe arrange themselves to each person anew, according to his ruling love. Man is such as his affection and thought are. Man is man by virtue of willing, not by virtue of knowing and understanding. As he is, so he sees . . . Whatever the angels looked upon was to them celestial.

What we call gravitation, and fancy ultimate, is one fork of a mightier stream, for which we have yet no name.

The soul of man must be the type of our scheme, just as the body of man is the type after which a dwelling-house is built.

There is no office or function of man but is rightly discharged by this divine method, and nothing that is not noxious to him if detached from its universal relations.

I think no man can go with his thoughts about him, into one of our churches, without feeling, that what hold the public worship had on men is gone, or going. It has lost its grasp on the affection of the good, and the fear of the bad.

And so lovely, and with yet more entire consent of my human being, sounds in my ear the severe music . . . of the true God.

The problem of restoring to the world original and eternal beauty, is solved by the redemption of the soul.

Learn that none of these things is superficial, but that each phenomenon has its roots in the faculties and affections of the mind.

The world thus exists to the soul to satisfy the desire of beauty.

The greatest delight which the fields and woods minister, is the suggestion of an occult relation between man and the vegetable.

The commonality of vocabulary and concept is not surprising once the commonality of experience, reading, and purpose of these two self-described natural historians of the soul is taken into account. As Lawrence Buell observes in his welcome portrait of Emerson as himself a "representative man," the "moral sentiment" informing his work

was a secularized descendant of Jonathan Edwards's "divine and supernatural light," the Holy Spirit pried away from the wrathful father-judge. It draws on scriptural sources as the prologue to the gospel of John that Edwards also loved, which renders divine logos abstractly as light contending against darkness. It goes back still further to the "prophetic voice" that would unexpectedly keep Socrates from error, even "in the middle of a sentence."[8]

Indeed, both Edwards's and Emerson's imperfect replication of the work of original ministration performed by the prophets of the Old Testament and the apostles of the New, adapting their purposes for and in their own time and place, illustrates Emerson's observation concerning the preservation of vital species of utterance and thought, the spiritual version of nature's process as he had come to apprehend it: "Jesus and Shakespeare are fragments of the soul."[9] As he noted in making a point about the continuing success of Shakespeare's work and of the English Bible, their languages evolved "by wide social labor, when a thousand wrought like one"; borrowing from Hugo Grotius, he observed as well that "in respect to the Lord's Prayer, that the single clauses of which it is composed were already in use, in the time of Christ, in the rabbinical forms. He [Jesus] picked out the grains of gold,"[10] a selective breeder of words. Emerson no less than Edwards was trained in the method of typological interpretation, read the sacred texts, was affected by Henry More's Platonism, transformed by Newton's explanations of light and the movement of the planets, and conceived his mission to be conversion, but now fully naturalized to adjust "the axis of vision . . . with the axis of things":[11]

A life in harmony with nature, the love of truth and of virtue, will purge the eyes to understand her text. By degrees we may come to know the primitive sense of the permanent objects of nature, so that the world shall be to us an open book, and every form significant of its hidden life and final cause.[12]

Developing the theme of ascending spiritual being articulated by Edwards, Emerson's signature figure of transparency is informed equally by Newton's description of the behavior of light as translated by Edwards to describe the progress of the soul, through "fits of easy transmission and reflection," giving "consent to being." Moreover, having himself ascended a few steps on the stair of experience through reading in the science of his time, Emerson broadened his vision of things as they are, adding to his understanding of Newton what he learned, for example, from Michael Faraday's work in electromagnetism with its focus on "Polarity" and wave action:

That great principle of Undulation in nature, that shows itself in the inspiring and expiring of the breath; in desire and satiety; in the ebb and flow of the sea; in day and night; in heat and cold; and as yet more deeply ingrained in every atom and every fluid, is known under the name of Polarity, – these "fits of easy transmission and reflection," as Newton called them, are the law of nature because they are the law of spirit.[13]

When "the axis of vision is . . . coincident with the axis of things, . . . they appear . . . transparent [not] opake."[14] His stated purpose, to "kindle science with the fire of holiest affections," makes explicit what was implicit in Edwards by drawing attention to the individuals whose adjustments of the axis of vision placed them with the prophets and apostles, voices of continuing revelation. It was a bold step. What would have been heresy for Edwards, impossible for a minister to utter in the tenor of his time, was, Emerson realized, necessary in his own, as he had announced in "The Divinity School Address" (1838): "But now the priest's Sabbath has lost the splendor of nature . . . And what greater calamity can fall upon a nation, than the loss of worship?"[15] In the five years since his epiphanic visit to the Jardin des Plantes when, as he recorded in his journal, he sensed "an occult relation between the very scorpions and man" – "I feel the centipede in me, – cayman, carp, eagle, and fox. I am moved by strange sympathies; I say continually 'I will be a naturalist.'"[16] – he immersed himself in natural philosophy and the various natural histories of his moment and reread and reconsidered the work of those he had come to know earlier, before his illumination.

Among the contemporary figures were Charles Lyell, Alexander von Humboldt, Augustin and Alphonse de Candolle, Georges Louis Leclerc (comte de) Buffon, Baron Cuvier, John Herschel, Michael Faraday, Charles Bell, Charles Darwin in his account of the voyage of *The Beagle*, Hans Oersted (who in 1820 performed a key experiment that led to the discovery of electromagmetism and who held that all material objects are embodiments of ideas),[17] Humphry Davy; among those recuperated from earlier generations, Plato, Lucretius, Francis Bacon, Galileo, Newton, Swedenborg, John Flamsteed, Roger Boscovich, Kant, Goethe, and, importantly, as he indicated in his essay on Plato in *Representative Men*, the sages of the East, from whose work, Plato, who had gone "into Egypt, and perhaps still farther east, to import the other element, which Europe wanted, into the European mind,"[18] had expanded his own vision. With these abundant streams feeding his thought, already long breeding spiritual nourishment, Emerson composed *Nature*, "The American Scholar," "The Divinity School Address," "Literary Ethics," and began lecturing regularly on "The Uses of Natural History." Offering a secular sacrament of praise for creation, his eucharist translated into the body of his work elements learned from his studious ghosts that would make his language a new perceptual form.[19] As he described in *Representative Men*, reporting what he shared in understanding with Swedenborg, phrased earlier in different variations in *Nature* and "Circles":

The mind is a finer body, and resumes its functions of feeding, digesting, absorbing, excluding, and generating, in a new and ethereal element. Here, in the brain, is all the process of alimentation repeated, in the acquiring, comparing, digesting, and assimilating of experience. Here again is the mystery of generation repeated. In the brain are male and female faculties: here is marriage, here is fruit. And there is no limit to this ascending scale, but series on series. Every thing, at the end of one use, is taken up into the next, each series punctually repeating every organ and process of the last. We are adapted to infinity . . . in nature is no end . . . Creative force, like a musical composer, goes on unweariedly repeating a simple air or theme, now high, now low, in solo, in chorus, ten thousand times reverberated, till it fills earth and heaven with the chant.[20]

It is to be especially remarked that Emerson's notion of the individual mind seeking nourishment according to its particular need is grounded in the conception of mind as "an organic agent," existing on a scale linking matter and spirit – "Spirit is matter reduced to an extreme thinness: O *so* thin!"[21] – thus making explicit what was implicit in Edwards, and further contributing to what Alfred North Whitehead, also taking into account William and Henry James's elaborations of "interest," would describe as the "appetition of thought," the central feature of the non-vitalist organicism – his "organism" – most comprehensively presented in *Process and Reality*. This understanding takes difference fully into account: "temperament," in Emerson's terms, embodying Edwards's similar perception of the varying "composition" of souls. In giving attention to his own mind thinking, in the manner of Edwards, and in recording the process he witnessed as he performed his lectures, observing the effects of his words on his auditors, Emerson's method represents what might be called ideational natural selection, a physics of personality where "Temperament puts all divinity to rout":[22]

His [the writer's] office is a reception of the facts into the mind, and then a selection of the eminent and characteristic experiences.

Nature will be reported. All things are engaged in writing their history. The planet, the pebble, goes attended by its shadow. The rolling rock leaves its scratches on the mountain; the river, its channel in the soil; the animal, its bones in the stratum; the fern and leaf, their modest epitaph in the coal. The falling drop makes its sculpture in the sand or the stone. Not a foot steps into the snow, or along the ground, but prints, in characters more or less lasting, a map of its march. Every act of the man inscribes itself in the memories of his fellows, and in his own manners and face. The air is full of sounds; the sky of tokens; the ground is all memoranda and signatures; and every object covered over with hints, which speak to the intelligent.

. . .The record is alive, as that which it recorded is alive. In man, the memory is a kind of looking-glass, which, having received the images of surrounding objects, is touched with life, and disposes them in a new order. The facts which transpired do not lie in it inert; but some subside, and others shine; so that soon we have a new picture, composed of the eminent experiences.[23]

His language echoing Edwards – ". . . men's minds . . . by the laws of nature . . . a sensation will spontaneously arise . . ."[24] – and heralding Thoreau, Emerson describes how the elements constituting intellectual being combine and recombine in a manner identified in *Nature* as religious reception, responses converting the invisible into the visible:

A man conversing in earnest, if he watch his intellectual processes, will find that a material image, more or less luminous, arises in his mind, cotemporaneous with every thought, which furnishes the vestment of the thought . . . This imagery is spontaneous. It is the blending of experience with the present action of the mind. It is proper creation. It is the working of the Original Cause through the instruments he has already made.[25]

Certainly, Emerson's familiarity with the eighteenth-century notion of sympathy, with the concepts of *Naturphilosophie* and emerging embryology, with Goethe's earlier elaboration of *Organismus*, and Coleridge's speculations, particularly his *Aids to Reflection* with James Marsh's glosses, had prepared the ground for his imaginative enlargement, but it is this imaginative enlargement and his translation of it into a form of language that are significant, "the present action of the mind" engaged "to the end of mastering in all . . . facts a language by which to illustrate and embody our perceptions."[26] Indeed, as the passage above illustrates, Emerson had by 1836 fully realized the seminal role played by image, specifically as it is described here, as metaphor, in the development and success of an idea, a realization that became in the second half of the twentieth century the salient feature in the discussions surrounding Thomas Kuhn's notion of paradigms in scientific "revolutions." Donna Haraway, in *Crystals, Fabrics, and Fields* (1976), borrowing from theorists engaged in the conversations sparked by Kuhn, offers observations pertinent here concerning the place and operation of metaphor:

Metaphoric systems are the core of structural coherence . . . A metaphor is the vital spirit of a paradigm (or perhaps its basic organizing relation) . . . an intrinsic part of science because metaphor is predictive . . . A metaphor is important to the nature of explanation because it leads to the testing of the neutral parts of the analogy. It leads to a searching for the *limits* of the metaphoric system and thus generates the anomalies important in paradigm change . . . (A metaphor is an image that gives concrete coherence to even highly abstract thought.) . . . Metaphor is a property of language that gives boundaries to worlds and helps scientists using real languages to push against these bounds.[27]

More particularly, in connection with a metaphor intrinsic to biology's emergence as a distinct field, Haraway rehearses the projections of the crystal analogy, beginning with Nehemiah Grew (a seventeenth-century plant anatomist who "regarded regularities in natural forms as evidence that the processes of growth consisted in the repetition of simple steps"), and continuing through Goethe to Ernst Haeckel (whose permutations of the crystal analogy produced drawings of animals conforming "to his belief in the geometrical character of organic form"), to D'Arcy Wentworth Thompson (1860–1948) ("the first to analyze different body proportions by referring them to a Cartesian coordinate system and applying rules of transformation"), and to Otto Butschli (1848–1920) (who "analyzed protoplasm in terms of a geometrical space-lattice").[28] Pursuing the analogy further into the twentieth century, Haraway focuses on the contributions made by Ross G. Harrison, Joseph Needham, and Paul Weiss in their studies of symmetry, polarity, resonance, and pattern as they derive from the examination of crystals and contribute to clarifications concerning field–particle duality. Looking back to Newton's theories concerning the properties of light, with his prescient hypothesizing of a wave–particle duality, and ahead to the concrete, as it were, *crystallization* of that duality in the structure of the DNA molecule uncovered by Watson and Crick in 1953, makes clear the central importance of the crystal metaphor fully visualized and projected in its activity as a model for organic growth. As Haraway points out, "If one sees the world in terms of hierarchically organized levels (the organism becomes the primary metaphor), the crystal becomes an intermediate state of organization."[29] Long before the possibilities offered by crystal spectrography, Emerson gained access to this particular plane of vision through the close attention he gave to his mind in thinking and imagining as he read Davy, Herschel, Lyell, Swedenborg, and Faraday, turning what he found in their descriptions around what he already knew of ideal and real forms from Plato, Galileo, Newton, Kant, Goethe, and the other strong natures with which his own had reacted.

In speaking of the relation between the ideal and the real during Emerson's extended historical moment, the place of Kant in making the invisible visible must, of course, not be forgotten. For the purpose of this discussion, it is especially important to remark his contribution to the installation of the aesthetic into what Locke called "the furniture of the mind." Tracing the effectiveness of the crystal metaphor in leading to the modification of cell theory and later to the description of the DNA molecule, Haraway notes "the significance of aesthetic commitments in the development of biology" made by Matthias Jacob Schleiden, which led to the later "provocative thesis . . . that biology can be seen as a concretization of an initial aesthetic notion."[30] Schleiden synthesized information about crystalline units with the prevailing nineteenth-century notion of the sphere as the perfect cell form to see "globular units of organisms as a fundamental structural basis":

The cell theory provided a representation of the whole organism as an assembly of essentially similar structural units which always arose from pre-existing cells. This was a scientific representation because it referred to structure and function but also because it precisely fulfilled the esthetic requirements of the idea of organic form. In the development of cell theory we witness the transformation of esthetic presuppositions into scientific knowledge in a manner that parallels Kant's statement that the sense of beauty is an aid to the discovery of truth.[31]

It is essential to recall at this point that the aesthetic as a distinct category of thought and experience emerged just at the same moment that different "sciences" were themselves emerging from natural philosophy and natural history; indeed, the term "scientist" was first used only in 1824 by William Whewell, one of Darwin's mentors, who first suggested the idea of "consilience" as the *ur*-principle underpinning all patterns and proliferations of form in nature. The rooms of these ideas opened to offer shelter to spirits being unsettled from hopes of heaven and the security of guidance by divine and supernatural light through the news brought with the Higher Criticism: not only was the story of the God of Abraham and Isaac one of many stories, but implicit in this broadened view was the suggestion that it is the imperfect that is our paradise. Emerson, initially rattled by the accumulating evidence for this realization, even fearing blindness when severe eye trouble, coincident with his first questioning of the idea of divinity, forced him to interrupt his theological studies (a questioning reinforced by the loss of divine light when the death of his first wife confirmed for him the absence of a transcendent soul), regained his balance precisely through the defining experience of religion, being lost and then finding, in the meeting and embracing of demons, "the *otherest*," his new variety of religious experience naturalized to a new environment of fact. Stimulated to reception and reaction as "a newborn bard of the Holy Ghost"[32] in the Pentecost of his time to speak in tongues common to it, Emerson allowed his thinking appetite to nourish him as it needed from the squirming facts disturbing sleep and the dream of reason, thus revealing religion to be as it was in the beginning, an expression of spiritual location: a vector indicating the latitude, longitude, and moment of being on a sphere reeling through the universe, the mind of God – "People wish to be settled; only as far as they are unsettled is there any hope for them."[33] Animated by his instinct for what was useful, "invigorated by habits of conversation with nature"[34] confirming through "delight" what he learned reading the sages of the East, the philosophers of the West, the inquisitorial botanists, geologists, astronomers, and naturalists of his time, and permitting these perceptions to pierce the rotten diction of the tribe to "fasten words again to visible things," Emerson's noble accents and inescapable rhythms, "inflamed with passion . . . exalted by thought," restored to the "aesthetic" theorized by Kant the body and blood it had when the Greeks uttered *aisthanomai*, "I feel, sense." Reiterating the necessity for this restoration in his own later theorizing, following Emerson and William James, Whitehead noted:

The philosophy of organism aspires to construct a critique of pure feeling, in the philosophical position in which Kant put his *Critique of Pure Reason*. This should also supersede the remaining *Critiques* required in the Kantian philosophy. Thus in the organic philosophy Kant's "Transcendental Aesthetic" becomes a distorted fragment of what should have been his main topic.[35]

To attend to this "main topic" was Emerson's ministerial purpose, picking up where Edwards had left off, converting images, shadows of divine things, into the world in the form of aesthetic, feeling, responses recorded in the selection and recombination of words in his sentences:

The world, – this shadow of the soul, or *other me*, lies wide around. Its attractions are the keys which unlock my thoughts and make me acquainted with myself. I run eagerly into this resounding tumult. I grasp the hands of those next me, and take my place in the ring to suffer and to work, taught by an instinct, that so shall the dumb abyss be vocal with speech. I pierce its order; I dissipate its fear; I dispose of it within the circuit of my expanding life . . . A strange process too, this, by which experience is converted into thought, as a mulberry leaf is converted into satin.[36]

"Cut these words and they would bleed; they are vascular and alive"; "Words are finite organs of the infinite mind"; "The use of natural history is to give us aid in supernatural history"[37] – Emerson's persistent reflection on the *other me* described, in what Peirce would later term "firstness," the function specified in current neuroscientific research of "mirror neurons," located in a region of the brain discovered several years ago by Giacomo Rizzolatti, which fire in the same way when the subject is performing an activity or observing the activity performed by another. This discovery has led to the argument that we are "conscious of our own thoughts . . . only because we first evolved the capacity to imagine the thoughts of others."[38]

While Emerson's acknowledgments of the "Representative Men" whose habits of mind became his own vestments of thought have been broadly discussed, much more detailed examination has been given to Plato, Shakespeare, Montaigne, Goethe, and even Napoleon, than to Swedenborg.[39] With the exception of scholars like Eugene Taylor devoted to rescuing the significance of his work, the general critical conclusion concerning Swedenborg in this context has focused mainly on Emerson's criticism of his limited conception of symbols, and has been colored by an undertone carrying over from early reactions in nineteenth-century America dismissing "the Mystic" with suggestions of madness and religious fanaticism.[40] This view is shortsighted. It should not be forgotten that Kant, also a deep reader of Swedenborg, even at one point trying to contact him, had "digested much of [his] philosophy a good four years before his own inaugural dissertation was published, as evidenced by Kant's *Dreams of a Spirit-Seer* [1766]."[41] Swedenborg's thinking spanned the period which included the developments in eighteenth-century intellectual history to which Jonathan Edwards was also witness. As Emerson reminded his readers, "Newton, in the year in which Swedenborg was born [1688], published the 'Principia,' and established universal gravity." For each of these figures "enlightenment" was truly a metaphor that gave "boundaries to worlds" and helped them "push against these bounds." In addition, Swedenborg, "the Lutheran bishop's son," was, like Edwards, fluent in the language of Scripture and even more fluent than Edwards in the language of the Book of Nature, being by training a metallurgist prepared, as Emerson notes, in "chemistry and optics, physiology, mathematics, and astronomy," from all of which he drew "images fit for the measure of his versatile and capacious brain."[42]

Emerson realized that the complex angelology Swedenborg devised and imaginatively inhabited was not a lunatic projection, but a metaphorical translation of all he learned from what he had observed and studied most closely in his twenty-two years as examiner of mines and smelting works, how the crystals composing rocks and minerals grow, change, interact, and transform under the varying conditions and pressures of the earth turning in its gravitational field and orbit around the sun: "His varied and solid knowledge makes his style lustrous with points and shooting spicula of thought, and resembling one of those winter mornings when the air sparkles with crystals."[43] In drawing his analogy for an imagined cosmology from crystalline structures, Swedenborg forecast an observation made later, in the nineteenth century, by Richard Owen, whom Emerson also read. Owen recognized that the vegetative repetition and imperfect repetitive copying responsible for diversification in plants was instigated by the same "polarizing force" which causes the growth of crystals and that this polarizing force is one of the two fundamental forces at work in the organic world.[44]

Swedenborg's universe of angels was, indeed, a perfect example of what Emerson described as the "luminous mental image" accompanying think- ing attended to in its extended process, truly for Swedenborg "a masque beyond the planets," in Stevens's later phrasing.[45] Emerson recognized that Swedenborg's decision, what he called his "illumination," to devote himself, after his "vastation," his threatened loss of faith and sanity,[46] to describing a theological system, "a deranged balance"[47] where angels and what they eat and drink, how they dress, what their houses look like and what they sit on, represented an experientially grounded performance of the aesthetic func- tion, a performance that was "part of the res itself and not about it." This angelology served as an elaborate memory palace in which "The Prophet of the North" could project all he knew of crystalline forms and their trans- formations, the prime model for later nineteenth- and twentieth-century elaborations of organicism. William James would note this same aspect, describing his father's incorporation of Swedenborg's angelic vision as "an account of the 'physics' of creation."[48] Kant, in contrast, would write *about* the *res*; consequently, his language remains uninhabitable, accessible only to those few trained in the skills of intellectual map-making, able to explore and plot the contours of his rare, high terrain and provide translations of what they found and find there, like glimpses of the dark side of the moon.

Kant's earliest cartographers include the strongest figures of Roman- ticism: Coleridge, Wordsworth, Caspar David Friedrich, Alexander von Humboldt, and, of course, in its later, American variety, Emerson. While all commonly rendered the most prominent features of the newly described landscape of the mind with lines defining nature as the source of beauty and motive of the sublime, Emerson understood that his map had to provide the kind of guidance Virgil offered Dante, a key, compass rose, an indication of how to deploy "the instruments . . . already made" to turn back and look long through history to reanimate the still speaking shades, at the same time as calibrating these instruments to follow "the crystal sphere of thought . . . as concentrical as the geological structure of the globe. As our soils and rocks lie in strata, concentric strata, so do all men's thinkings run laterally, never vertically."[49] Unlike his European contemporaries who could assume shared cultural, religious, and linguistic inheritances in and from which their rebellions and revolutions arose, Emerson had first to teach his audiences how to read, how to think, and how to speak, "converse in earnest." Selective continuity and evolution, not revolution, informed his ministerial method, to show through "great power of performance," how each "Man Thinking" could, like Swedenborg, shape his *lingua franca* to embody the particular coordinates of his experience, "a new order of distinctions, a new order of ideas":[50]

Life is girt all round with a zodiac of sciences, the contributions of men who have perished to add their point of light to our sky. Engineer, broker, jurist, physician, moralist, theologian, and every man, inasmuch as he has any science, is a definer and map-maker of the latitudes and longitudes of our condition. These road-makers on every hand enrich us. We must extend the area of life, and multiply our relations. We are as much gainers by finding a new property in the old earth, as by acquiring a new planet.[51]

Just as Dante multiplied the relations of the pagan past with his Christian present, and Swedenborg, like Edwards, "used the earth symbolically" to "extricat[e] from the literal, the universal sense" from the "books of the Old and New Testaments" which he believed "were exact allegories . . . written in the angelic and ecstatic mode" of "organic form,"[52] all creating visions, moving pictures, of what they understood to be the "working of the Original Cause," so too Emerson, except that in "the yet untouched continent of hope glittering with all its mountains in the vast West,"[53] "theism" was to be "the purification of the human mind," a continuing work of Reformation, an "ethical reformation,"[54] heaven emptied of the "gods of fable" to be reconceived as the difficult simplicity of what it is to imagine, "the necessary and structural action of the human mind":

The gods of fable are the shining moments of great men. We run all our vessels into one mould. Our colossal theologies of Judaism, Christism, Buddhism, Mahometism, are the necessary and structural action of the human mind. The student of history is like a man going into a warehouse to buy cloths or carpets. He fancies he has a new article. If he go to the factory, he shall find that his new stuff still repeats the scrolls and rosettes which are found on the interior walls of the pyramids of Thebes. Our theism is the purification of the human mind. Man can paint, or make, or think nothing but man. He believes that the great material elements had their origin from his thought. And our philosophy finds one essence collected or distributed.[55]

"Old wine in new bottles," "Pragmatism, A New Name for Some Old Ways of Thinking": William James would precipitate Emerson's perception into a full elaboration of the difficulty of holding a thought in the mind, developing and refining his spiritual father's insight that "to think is to act"[56] to show that, indeed, "to sustain a representation, to think is, in short, the only moral act,"[57] a recognition shared by his brother. "How well the James boys understand the use of language," Emerson commented early on in their careers, enjoying a premonition of how both would continue his project in their work with words.[58]

In selecting work from the past to "engraft" for future growth,[59] Emerson noted his "veneration" of Swedenborg as one of the "great men" precisely because he "substantiated" the activity of his imagination, showing through the behavior of angels what it is "to perform one more turn through the circle of beings": "He endeavored to engraft a purely philosophical Ethics on the popular Christianity of his time . . . he showed the connection between nature and the affection of the soul. He pierced the emblematic or spiritual character of the visible, audible, tangible world."[60] Even more specifically, and rephrasing Edwards's sense of the heart, Emerson noted, "he must be reckoned a leader in that revolution, which, by giving to science an idea, has given to an aimless accumulation of experiments, guidance and form, and a beating heart."[61] Emerson himself, in turn, took yet another step on the stair stretching upwards, seeing angels in their own original relation to the universe, as words, messengers of the spirit, attracting one another in their identities, being converted from one scale of being to another by degrees, appearing in their radiance, circulating in ranging periods in a purely linguistic cosmology: "We cannot let our angels go. We do not see that they only go out, that archangels may come in."[62] The pattern, however, was the same, imitating nature in a "self-similar" way:[63] the "crystal sphere of thought," crystals in rock, and crystal organization in organisms, "man crystallized," all "grow by accretion . . . addition to each axis . . . proportional to axial relations of the lattice"[64] of time and place. The structure and behavior of crystals in their variety as rocks, minerals, and gems, as well as in other forms of matter, provided Swedenborg with the "luminous mental image" he would use to project his imagined understanding – in Whitehead's later terminology, his "prehension" – of the natural processes elaborating the "Identity-philosophy" he believed to underlie the multiform universe:

This theory dates from the oldest philosophers . . . It is this: that nature iterates her means perpetually on successive planes. In the old aphorism, *nature is always self-similar*. In the plant, the eye or germinative point opens to a leaf, then to another leaf, with a power of transforming the leaf into radicle, stamen, pistil, petal, bract, sepal, or seed. The whole art of the plant is still to repeat leaf on leaf without end, the more or less of heat, light, moisture, and food, determining the form it shall assume. In the animal, nature makes a vertebra, or a spine of vertebrae, and helps herself still by a new spine, with a limited power of modifying its form, – spine on spine, to the end of the world.[65]

At the center of this universe, of course, was the incandescent radiance of the Godhead, pure light. The spiralling ranks of Swedenborg's angels extending out from this center imitated in their ordering and differences the properties of crystals, from the purest transparency of diamonds to the absorbent dark density of obsidian. Self-similar crystalline properties of different gems, minerals, and rocks produce their discrete forms, though growth for all, as he knew, is produced in the same way, by accretion as the result of a particular asymmetry occasioned by movement toward light, which thereby induces a repeated polarity. These lessons would not be lost on "the James boys."

Like Edwards, whose sermons he had read and reread, Emerson had learned early of the affective power of words' patterning both from the close attention to his own mind in thinking, evidenced in his journal-keeping and indexing, and from his practice as minister, observing in his awareness of his constituency's requirement of redemption, their reactions to certain phrasings and images – "we adapt our voice and phrase to the distance and character of the ear we speak to."[66] He shared Edwards's habit of allowing a particular word or phrase to reappear again and again, his later lectures and essays preserving sermonic force, with each of these selected words and phrases circling through his imagination's orbit, the word or phrase accreting some slight newness inflecting its axis, its tilt toward transparency – "The opaque self becomes transparent with the light of the First Cause";[67] "A healthy soul . . . as the magnet arranges itself with the pole . . . stands to all beholders like a transparent object betwixt them and the sun, and whoso journeys towards the sun, journeys towards that person."[68] Here was Newton's description of the behavior of light as translated by Edwards and imagined by Emerson. In Swedenborg he realized the same motive dressed in the habits of angels, displaying how the process of transformation, purification, occurs. Emerson was able to see through the celestial garments Swedenborg wove the accuracy of his perception because of his own studies in "the method of nature." He had, moreover, as will be discussed later in this chapter, read as well in language theory and philology, and so was able to enlarge the scope of this method to include language, thought, mind itself, thus converting Swedenborg's sublime back into its elements and inventing a spatio-temporal grid for mind:

As plants convert the minerals into food for animals, so each man converts some raw material in nature to human use. The inventors of fire, electricity, magnetism, iron, lead, glass, linen, silk, cotton; the makers of tools; the inventor of decimal notation; the geometer; the engineer; the musician, – severally make an easy way for all, through unknown and impossible confusions. Each man is, by secret liking, connected with some district of nature, whose agent and interpreter he is, as Linnaeus, of plants; Huber, of bees; Fries, of lichens; Van Mons, of pears; Dalton, of atomic forms; Euclid, of lines; Newton, of fluxions.

A man is a centre for nature, running out threads of relation through every thing, fluid and solid, material and elemental. The earth rolls; every clod and stone comes to the meridian: so every organ, function, acid, crystal, grain of dust, has its relation to the brain. It waits long, but its turn comes . . .

. . . The possibility of interpretation lies in the identity of the observer with the observed. Each material thing has its celestial side; has its translation, through humanity, into the spiritual and necessary sphere, where it plays a part as indestructible as any other. And to these, their ends, all things continually ascend. The gases gather to the solid firmament; the chemic lump arrives at the plant, and grows; arrives at the quadruped, and walks; arrives at the man, and thinks. But also the constituency determines the vote of the representative. He is not only representative, but participant. Like can only be known by like. The reason why he knows about them is, that he is of them; he has just come out of nature, or from being a part of that thing . . . all that is yet inanimate will one day speak and reason.[69]

Through "the organ of language, – the subtlest, strongest, and longest-lived of man's creations"[70] – this ascendancy continues: religion in its original relation to the universe, naturalized in its ongoing speciation into effective forms of expression, the infinite transformations of matter, of what matters: "Words are finite organs of the infinite mind."

This angelic communication constitutes Emerson's contribution to the vocabulary of experience. Imagination had to be newly conceived, not simply as repository but as "participant," in its successful varieties of linguistic description realized as itself the divine and supernatural light animating all, an instrument continuously tempered by use: "Imagination may be defined to be, the use which the Reason makes of the material world."[71] To teach this use was his end. To accomplish it in the latitude and longitude of his time and place, his location in the great lattice of human being, meant taking fully into account the possibilities of relations among and for the inhabitants of "the nervous, rocky West,"[72] too impatient for the private forms of prayers and poems. The intelligence of this soil, he felt, fed on facts while craving still the taste of the honey of heaven. The Romantic resonance would be scaled here into "anthems of indefinite music" mimicking "the beautiful motion of the snow"[73] instead of into verses musing the obscure interior responses of our "bond to all that dust."[74] The lamp turned inward by the first generation of Romantic poets Emerson turned outward, now to project its light through the multiple prisms offered by the various sciences as they were evolving, like a Fresnel lantern throwing its beacon far out in full sweeps into the night sea around a headland of new fact to those attempting to steer a safe course to harbor. Emerson's was a public voice: "The sentence is the unit of democracy."[75]

Feeling his way through the new environment of classification and description offered by the secular priests of invisible natural processes, following his pastoral inclination to bind his community in a variety of religious experience adapted to "the verve of earth"[76] – "to put science and the soul, long estranged from each other, at one again"[77] – his lectures and essays developed like cities around the needs of the complex organism of nineteenth-century American society. In place of linear progress to the closing "truth" of an argument premised on the rules of classical logic, Emerson allowed his perceptions to deposit themselves according to their specific gravities, as ores in the turning rock of earth accreting through polarity by affinity, by what he called "genial radiation."[78] He included rather than excluded middle terms, letting both/and and more perform their functions, as they did in nature where the profligacy of forms ensures optimal survival of species in constantly changing conditions. In using words in imitation of nature's process, he was uncovering, as he had proposed to himself to do, the "natural history of the intellect," as Darwin had that of species:

the poet turns the world to glass, and shows us things in their right series and procession. For . . . he stands one step nearer to things, and sees the flowing or metamorphosis; perceives that thought is multiform . . . All the facts of the animal economy, sex, nutriment, gestation, birth, growth, are symbols of the passage of the world into the soul of man, to suffer there a change, and reappear a new and higher fact. He uses forms according to the life, not according to the form. This is true science. The poet alone knows astronomy, chemistry, vegetation, and animation, for he does not stop at these facts but employs them as signs. He knows why the plain, or meadow of space, was strown with these flowers we call suns, and moons, and stars; why the great deep is adorned with animals, with men, and gods; for, in every word he speaks he rides on them as the horses of thought.

. . . The poets made all the words, and therefore language is the archives of history, and, if we must say it, a sort of tomb of the muses. For, though the origin of most of our words is forgotten, each word was at first a stroke of genius, and obtained currency, because for the moment it symbolized the world to the first speaker and to the hearer. The etymologist finds the deadest word to have been once a brilliant picture. Language is fossil poetry. As the limestone of the continent consists of infinite masses of the shells of animalcules, so language is made up of images, or tropes, which now in their secondary use, have long ceased to remind us of their poetic origin . . . What we call nature, is a certain self-regulated motion, or change.[79]

Emerson's oscillation between the poles of natural fact and religious feeling similarly characterized the movement of Charles Darwin's mind as he too struggled – within the limits of language and logic developed, until the moment of his inheritance, to communicate belief in a fixed order designed by the First Cause – to describe instead, the "self-regulated motion, or change" of nature he had realized in America's New World environment. And just as Emerson's affinities with Edwards and Swedenborg are products of their commonality of preparation, so, too, are certain remarkable parallels between Emerson and Darwin that account for Emerson's anticipation in the performance of his style, the activity of his language, of the theory which Darwin came to identify. These braidings are central in the evolution of thinking about thinking that issues in Pragmatism.

. . . IN THY BRAIN, THE GEOMETRY OF THE CITY OF GOD[80]

The preceding pages describe Emerson's style as representing a major shift in how the nature and function of imagination were conceived. The pages following will read this shift, in Emerson's terms, as "the necessary and structural action of the human mind" in its response to the increasing evolutionary information available from the late eighteenth through the early nineteenth centuries, accounts which both Emerson and Darwin read.[81] This shift represented what Raymond Williams would term "the structure of feeling" of Emerson's time and place, his age. The age demanded resistance to its most insistent idea of progress. In response to this demand, Emerson reversed the manifest trend of his time, so abundantly noted by recent Marxist and post-Marxist theorists, of transforming nature into culture. His work, in sharp contrast, was to transform, reconvert, culture/language into nature, an endeavor engaged by Darwin as well, though in a style more discursive than poetic, dictated by his necessarily having to account for the unaccountable. This distinction between Emerson's and Darwin's styles will emerge here against a background tracing the common intellectual experiences that contributed to shaping their habits of mind.

Emerson's disrupting the possibility of ordinary reading practice has been duly noted and accounted for in various ways unnecessary to survey here. What does need to be called to attention, however, is that the grammatical and syntactic confusion of his style was created deliberately, an expression of the interest he shared with Jonathan Edwards, to create a template, as it were, of the mind's activity, a template which could then be referred to reflexively and modified. As Emerson observed in "The Method of Nature," "Genius . . . is itself a mutation of the thing described."[82] The repeatedly returned-to words and phrases from his repeatedly indexed journals, from earlier lectures and essays, interpolated into later offerings function like messenger-RNA, preserving elements of his past identity to modify the perceptual code of his present. While Edwards planned in compiling his notes on "The Mind" to compose a later anatomy, Emerson fulfilled his own intention to become a natural historian of the intellect by making the elements of mind itself, words, the human ground and world, the field of his and his audience's exploration and collection. "Where do we find ourselves?"[83] – the question opening "Experience" frames not only the reading of that essay but the attitude to be assumed in order to negotiate the territory of Emerson's language: "We must learn the language of facts."[84] In the same way that Thoreau's *Walden* becomes for its readers what the experience of Walden Pond was for Thoreau, Emerson's texts are mimetic of his discovering himself in a new world of linguistic relation occasioned by the disappearing authority for fixed meaning in a great chain of being. The natural history cabinet with its offering of infinite juxtapositions and suggestions had already broken the chain into its links. As noted in Chapter 1 here, Lee Rust Brown, following certain earlier critics, and, more recently, Laura Dassow Walls have elucidated many of the aspects of this development in connection with Emerson, but more needs to be examined.

Deep readers of Emerson have all had the repeatedly unsettling experience of trying to remember in which essay a particular phrase or sentence, as familiar as a line from "The Star Spangled Banner" to Americans or "God Save the Queen" to Britons, is found. Again and again we are sent tracking through the underlined, annotated pages of our texts, more often than not being led down a path we did not then mean to follow by another one of our marked passages, sometimes a variation on the one being sought. Eventually we recollect ourselves, return to the clearing, and try again. In these excursions, we too find ourselves becoming natural historians of the intellect, going out to survey the territory we have begun to explore and map, finding how the landscape has changed with the seasons of our understanding. This experience is not unlike that provided by Thoreau in his accounts of the changes he observed in the countryside around Concord. Collected under the title *Faith in a Seed*, what emerges from these essays, as noted by Robert Richardson, is Thoreau's first-hand apprehension of the same kind of complex and chance species variations that Darwin also realized.[85] We recall Thoreau's descriptions of the circles of infant pines growing around a mature stand, and then circles around these circles in succeeding years that he remarked in making his zigzag way back and forth from his center, commenting on how a winter storm one year or the prevailing wind on a particular slope altered growth patterns and individual specimens. In this way he was able to map imaginatively the effects of the up and down between the elements from year to year that generated the modifications in those species he had chosen to regard, for the purposes of experiment, as his originals.

In the same way Emerson organized his essays. Beginning with a stand of ideas admired in their full flowering – *experience, self-reliance, history, friendship, intellect,* even *nature* itself – he dropped their seeds in expanding and irregular circles to observe their growth, first through the immediate rough circumference of their references in sentences, then allowed to develop into paragraphs and later lectures and essays, determined by the wind and weather of his informed attention, the figurative sun under which they turned no less than actual plants under the actual sun. The project Emerson set himself was to describe the effects of this phototropism of ideas, through time, into eventual dispersion and diverse forms of maturation. His challenge was to do this in a language whose syntactic and grammatical structures were and are not only linear but two-dimensional, subtended by the notion of continuing progress from simplicity to complex perfection, following a pre-ordained course.[86] Indeed, Darwin faced the same problem, in his revisions of *Origin* attempting to make his language mimic not the teleology implicit in the great-chain-of-being model but the very opposite, the absence of design, chance, which he had uncovered to be the method of nature. The pattern imaginatively deployed by both men, I would offer, was that of the crystal, subtending, as it did, the emergent field of biology: "our act arranges itself by irresistible magnetism in a line with the poles of the world."[87]

Emerson and Darwin equally understood language as a fundamental power, in its function both as the lens determining perception and as the aptest investigative model permitting the account of changes in nature over time. While it is, of course, impossible to know all of the contributing factors in each of their histories that predisposed them to having what has come to be viewed as a modernist and post-modernist (not in the "po-mo" sense, but simply as after the period of modernism) conception of language, it is nonetheless the case that they had been prepared to regard language in this way by astonishingly similar reading experiences at almost simultaneous moments. First and foremost among these is the immersion of both young men in John Milton's *Paradise Lost*.

Darwin's biographers have all commented in one way or another on what the young collector himself detailed in his *Voyage of the Beagle*, in his *Autobiography*, in his correspondence: that he carried a much-thumbed copy of Milton's epic along with him everywhere in his pocket through the years of this all-important apprenticeship. Walking deep into the exuberant, venereal landscapes of South America, he noted again and again, as recorded in *Voyage* and in his diary, and in his later speculative journals, how the only words he could find that came close to describing what he was seeing were lines from *Paradise Lost*. Most particularly, Milton's vivid depictions of Satan's discoveries recurred to Darwin – "O'er bog or steep, through strait, rough, dense, or rare, / With head, hands, wings, or feet, pursues his way, / And swims, or sinks, or wades, or creeps, or flies" – through his fall toward "This pendent World" to find "At length a universal hubbub wild, / Of stunning sounds and voices all confused, / Borne through the hollow dark." As he recorded on October 24, 1832, making way swiftly under full sail for Buenos Aires at night in a luminous sea, the combined sounds of the ocean's rhythmic scudding and rushing wind "assault[ing] his ear with loudest vehemence":

The vessel drove before her bows two billows of liquid phosphorus, & her wake was a milky train. – As far as the eye reached, the crest of every wave was bright; & from the reflected light, the sky just above the horizon was not so utterly dark as the rest of the Heavens. – It is impossible to behold this plain of matter, as it were melted & consuming by heat, without being reminded of Miltons [*sic*] description of Chaos & Anarchy. –[88]

"Thither he plie[d], / Undaunted, to meet there whatever Power / Or Spirit of the nethermost Abyss / Might in that noise reside, of whom to ask / Which way the nearest coast of darkness lies / Bordering on light." And, indeed, Darwin asked and found his answer.

It was not only Darwin who found himself thus overtaken by the genius of Milton in his inquiries into nature's mysteries. John Tyndall, his contemporary, the Irish physicist, also a member of the Royal Society's elite Philosophical Club (both Darwin and Tyndall received the Royal Medal from the Society in 1853), pointedly observed that his work on radiation had been enabled by an unusually developed awareness of relations in space trained by his early reading of Milton's epic of cosmic and syntactic spaces in *Paradise Lost*:

English grammar was the most important discipline of my boyhood. The piercing through the involved and inverted sentences of Paradise Lost, the linking of the verb to its often distant nominative, of the relative to its transitive verb, of the preposition to the noun or pronoun which it governed, the study of the variations in mood or tense, the transpositions often necessary to bring out the true grammatical structure of a sentence, all this was to my young mind a discipline of the highest value, and a source of unflagging delight.[89]

Similarly, Charles Lyell, whose literally groundbreaking *Principles of Geology* (1830–3) was to provide another of the common formative reading experiences for Emerson and Darwin, credited the temporal extension and syntactical inversions of classical poetry such as in Ovid's *Metamorphoses*, cited repeatedly in his own "teaching" volumes, with allowing him to realize that if a text were to accomplish the primary work of changing the way nature was perceived it had to transform the function of imagination. As noted by Martin Rudwick in his introduction to the reissued *Principles*, after commenting on Lyell's realization that the greatest factor regarding the progress of geology had been an inadequate conception of the time scale in earth history:

In placing such emphasis on the sense of geological time scale, Lyell shows a penetrating awareness of the nature of the task of persuasion. For although his scientific colleagues (unlike the Mosaic pseudogeologists) readily accepted a vast time scale on the intellectual level, Lyell recognized that it was their scientific *imagination* that needed transforming. Much of the detailed argument of the *Principles* is therefore designed to draw out the full implications of a belief which they already claimed to know.

Although a vast time scale is now more generally conceded, Lyell maintains, other habits of mind still continue to retard geology. Of these the most important is a failure to recognize the distorting effect of our viewpoint as subaerial terrestrial beings. This causes us to underestimate the magnitude of submarine and subterranean geological processes. An intelligent aquatic being and a "gnome" confined to subterranean regions would form very different but equally distorted views on geology.[90]

Addressing the same aspect of Lyell's work, Gillian Beer comments additionally and perspicaciously that drawing on poetic forms and classical references fosters a sense of what she calls "human spaciousness" in the mind of the writer who can appraise relations across time, and that Lyell held that the power to re-imagine the remote past was the characterizing property of human reason.[91] Indeed, Lyell stated his intention to be no less than the establishment of life through time.[92] This attempt and goodly achievement was fully appreciated by both Emerson and Darwin as evidenced in their diary and journal comments concerning the effects of reading *Principles*, and was the reason, as well, they both valued friendship and conversation with Lyell. In the *Descent of Man* Darwin noted, for example: "A language, like a species, when once extinct, never, as Sir C. Lyell remarks, reappears . . . The survival or preservation of certain favoured words in the struggle for existence is natural selection."[93]

Poetry offered these men the "particular formal resources to think with . . . By cross-setting a considerable number of systems in simultaneity (natural speech word order, metric units, line units, grammatical units, cursive syntax – all play[ing] across each other). By means of metre in particular, and sometimes by rhyme, the poet sets up multiple relations between ideas in a style closer to the form of theorems than of prose."[94] Again in his essay on the use of the scientific imagination, John Tyndall invokes Milton in illustration of his point: "The study of natural science goes hand in hand with the culture of the imagination . . . We have been picturing atoms and molecules and vibrations and waves which eye has never seen nor ear heard, and which can only be discerned by the exercise of the imagination."[95] Rephrasing this perception for the twentieth century, Whitehead also used the example of Milton, particularly the description of Satan's journey across Chaos which had served as Darwin's guide – "Milton is here performing for Plato the same poetic service that Lucretius performed for Democritus"– to underline the necessity of breaking the mould of a language shaped by a deterministic world view:

The appeal . . . in this section has been an appeal to the facts against the modes of expression prevalent in the last few centuries. These recent modes of expression are partly the outcome of a mixture of theology and philosophy, and are partly due to the Newtonian physics, no longer accepted as a fundamental statement. But language and thought have been framed according to that mould; and it is necessary to remind ourselves that this is not the way in which the world has been described by some of the greatest intellects. [His appeal is to recall the language of process of Democritus, of Plato in the *Timaeus*.][96]

Darwin and Emerson used Milton's telescoping, tumbling forms as theoretical frames in which to view emergent aspects of evolution. I have digressed a bit from citing the evidence of Emerson's regard for Milton and *Paradise Lost* in order to sketch this background of the early nineteenth century's cultural climate, a background which has been considered in connection with the development of Darwin's thinking, but which has not been put to work imaginatively in considering the structure of feeling in which and out of which the other major work of the century grew. It is a simple point in a complex field: that is, that it was language theory and comparative philology which provided models for thinking, particularly for discoveries in geology and in evolutionary theory, complementary to those offered by crystallography and morphology for biology. We have grown so used, in our time, to disdaining if not dismissing the products of sciences that cannot be quantified in deference to those of the "hard sciences," that it is difficult for us to conceive of the intellectual temper at a time when both different "sciences" and "aesthetics" were themselves precipitated as distinct categories of thought. This was the period when men and women of letters in America and Britain, whether literary historians, poets, journalists, or natural historians, would have read an article by Faraday, followed by another on the Higher Criticism, followed by another on Milton's prosody, collected in the same issue of the *Edinburgh Review*, the *Fortnightly Review*, the *Westminster Review*, the *North American Review*, the *Quarterly Review*, or any one of a number of other journals and magazines which shaped Victorian sensibility. As Beer observes:

The wonderful inclusiveness of generalist journals at that time, from the *Literary Gazette and Journal of Belles Lettres, Science, and Art*, to the *Contemporary Review* and the *Nineteenth Century*, meant that philosophers, lawyers, evolutionary theorists, politicians, astronomers, physicists, novelists, theologians, poets, and language theorists all appeared alongside each other, more often with the effect of bricolage than synthesis, true enough. But their lying alongside on the page encouraged the reader to infer connections between their activities by the simple scan of the eye and by the simultaneous availability of diverse ideas . . . That desire to cross disciplinary bounds was itself part of the insistence on kinship in evolutionary thought.[97]

It was not, then, a soft-minded or "poetic" thing to do to privilege poetic discourse and language theory as modes of knowing, but, rather, the opposite. Thomas Carlyle was not alone in insisting on the corporeal aspects of language, retrieving from his Puritan forebears, as had Edwards, their understanding of the ability of metaphors and tropes to produce "physical effects: fear, excitement, bodily recognition of past persons."[98] As Beer goes on to note:

(In his work on fantasy, Todorov has characterized its method as prolonging the moment of hesitation between interpretations and has reminded us that the removal or varying of categorical boundaries itself "represents an experience of limits." [It is useful to recall in this connection the comments cited earlier on the importance of metaphor for the development of biology.]) Carlyle was greeted by his contemporaries as a philosopher and a historian, but his method is never analytical. His enterprise was a formative force in the Victorian search for synthesis and (apparently contradictorily) for taxonomic refinement.[99]

It was in this intellectual atmosphere that Emerson, beginning during the same transforming sojourn abroad that included his famous visit to the Jardin des Plantes, not only felt his kinship with Carlyle, as abundantly evidenced in his journals, in their correspondence, and long-lived mutual ideational midwifery, but realized as well the fullness of what Milton had to teach him. From the earliest year of his journal-keeping in 1820 (when he was seventeen) and well through the period of his writing *Nature* (1836), there is not a year in which Milton or *Paradise Lost* is not referred to either as having been read or reread, or in memorial evocation. Emerson grasped the signal value in Milton's refashioning the inherited typological scrim to accommodate the new world view described by Galileo and Newton. What Emerson attended to most specifically in Milton's style was the manner in which it communicated the mind's feeling of losing itself in this revolutionary dispensation and its simultaneous attempt, within the free-fall out of what had seemed certain, to get some bearings again, to find, if possible, a new orienting star: "It is very unhappy, but too late to be helped, the discovery we have made, that we exist. That discovery is called the Fall of Man. Ever afterwards, we suspect our instruments."[100] The syntactic spaces Milton opened for musing, suspending us in the heavenly air with Satan, between words on the way to earth, invite, even demand, interpretation. It is as though Milton forces us to perform the defining act of the Reformation. Through the extended moments of grammatical hesitation, for a while outside the margins of sense, we finally justify our way, calling on meaning from our envisioning, thus making the text our own. The scope of Milton's periods spirals through an imaginative mindscape conceived not as two-dimensional but three-, the third corresponding appropriately to the pictorial addition of perspective in painting coincident with the incorporation of navigational, astronomical measurement and observation into the basic vocabulary of thinking. It was not simply that the telescope allowed Galileo and others to confirm Copernicus's disturbing news by following the shadows of the mountains of the moon, but that in order to have this information *mean* it had to be experienced, tried on again and again as a new habit of mind, and this could only happen by forcing attention through linguistic mimesis ("linguistic" here including the languages of art, music, etc.) of the processes necessary to understand in order to be able to *see* this new world, a world of invisible but nonetheless real relations. The discipline so well described by Tyndall as effected by his reading of *Paradise Lost* addresses the issue being emphasized here.

Emerson, no less than Milton, found himself on the shores of a new world, gradually being transformed through the years of his life by speculations and discoveries as unsettling as those consequent on Copernicus's finding. The most significant feature of the accumulating evolutionary information against which all theorists tested their mettle was that organisms seemed to be self-determining, and that the direction of their actions, always over-determined by myriad accidental relations/causes, was ultimately the product of chance, which Darwin himself equated with what philosophers called and call, in human terms, free will: "free will is to mind what chance is to matter."[101] The force figured by Darwin as motivating one choice over another, and stated simply as such by him, was pleasure, the satisfaction at some level at a given moment of appetite, whether for nutriment, water, sleep, or sex.[102] "Whenever a true theory appears," wrote Emerson in the Introduction to *Nature* (1836), "it will be its own evidence. Its test is, that it will explain all phenomena. Now many are thought not only unexplained but unexplicable; as language, sleep, madness, dreams, beasts, sex."[103] Emerson's catalogue, which he goes on to explore in the unorthodox arrangement of the chapters following, does not, in light of Darwin's observations, seem as incommodious as it first appears. Where and how did they come to this common understanding? While Milton provided the imaginative form, the content came from variations on themes played out in the work of natural historians important in their time, as well as in the work of certain key figures of earlier generations, all read carefully by both Emerson and Darwin.

Before noting those who nourished the thinking of Emerson and Darwin and whose work would later be converted into lines of relations radiating the energy of the light they refocused – Peirce, William and Henry James, and through them, Stevens, Stein, and Whitehead – it is illuminating as well to observe, in connection with the "self-regulated motion" of nature perceived by both Emerson and Darwin, a more recent parallel. Oliver Selfridge, Norbert Weiner's star dissertation student and "one of the few living people mentioned," as Selfridge notes, in the acknowledgments of *Cybernetics* (1949), also attributes to his reading and rereading of *Paradise Lost*, particularly to the image of Pandemonium – "the shrieking of the demons awoke something in me" – his break-through recognition of the pattern he would adapt as a way of teaching a computer itself to recognize patterns. It is this "self-regulated motion" that characterizes what are known today as "emergent systems," the systems on which so much current technology depends:

"We are proposing here a model of a process which we claim can adaptively improve itself to handle certain pattern-recognition problems which cannot be adequately specified in advance." These were the first words Selfridge delivered at a symposium in late 1958, held at the very same National Physical Laboratory from which [Alan] Turing had escaped a decade before. Selfridge's presentation had the memorable title "Pandemonium: A Paradigm for Learning," and while it had little impact outside the nascent computer-science community, the ideas Selfridge outlined that day would eventually become part of our everyday life – each time we enter a name in our PalmPilots or use voice-recognition software to ask for information over the phone. Pandemonium, as Selfridge outlined it in his talk, was not so much a specific piece of software as it was a way of approaching a problem. The problem was an ambitious one, given the limited computational resources of the day: how to teach a computer to recognize patterns that were ill-defined or erratic, like the sound waves that comprise spoken language.[104]

The brilliance of Selfridge's paradigm lies in his having *prehended*, to vary Whitehead's term, from his reading of *Paradise Lost*, the same pattern of natural selection Darwin and Emerson similarly saw moving. There will be more to say concerning Emerson's use of this pattern in his evolving style which, in turn, is a method of teaching thinking about thinking.

A comprehensive survey of Darwin's and Emerson's common library of literature, philosophy, natural philosophy, and natural history demands a volume in itself. Here there is only space to list the items which, in the intellectual world they inhabited, any educated reader might have borrowed from the same library, so to speak. In the journals, reading records, and letters of Darwin and Emerson there are, in addition to Milton and *Paradise Lost*, Lyell, and Tyndall, as outlined above, the following frequently "borrowed" volumes and authors over roughly the same period of years: Sir Thomas Browne's *Religio Medici*, Locke's *Essay concerning Human Understanding*, Dugald Stewart's *Philosophy of Mind* (and particularly on the sublime), David Hume, William Paley's *Natural Theology, or Evidences of the Existence and Attributes of the Deity*, Coleridge's and Wordsworth's poetry (Darwin noted in one of his diaries that he had gone through the *Excursion* twice carefully), Carlyle, Charles Bell's *The Hand its Mechanism and Vital Endowments as Evincing Design* (No. 4 of the Bridgewater Treatises on the Power Wisdom and Goodness of God as Manifested in the Creation [3rd edn., 1834]; this and No. 5, Peter Mark Roget's *Animal and Vegetable Physiology Considered with Reference to Natural Theology* were the only "good ones" in the series according to Emerson),[105] Richard Owen, Baron Cuvier's *Anatomie des mollusques*, Alexander von Humboldt, John Herschel's *Preliminary Discourse on the Study of Natural Philosophy*, Augustin de Candolle's *Théorie élémentaire de la botanique* and *Organographie*, Robert Chambers's *Vestiges of the Natural History of Creation*, L. A. J. Quetelet's *A Treatise on Man*, and, of course, Robert Malthus's *Essay on the Principle of Population*. Primary among these for Emerson were Herschel's *Preliminary Discourse*, Lyell's *Principles of Geology*, Bell's *The Hand* and, for both Emerson and Darwin, Humboldt's volumes as they appeared. The prehension of the celestial pantomime offered by each of these earlier figures permitted both Emerson and Darwin to attempt "to annul that adulterous divorce which the superstition of many ages has effected between the intellect and holiness" through the "discovery and performance"[106] of what Francis Bacon had called the "general law . . . of continuity." The shape of this law was emerging as a wave: "Society is a wave. The wave moves onward, but the water of which it is composed does not. The same particle does not rise from the valley to the ridge. Its unity is only phenomenal. The persons who make up a society to-day, next year die, and their experience with them."[107] Emerson's figure embodied the statistical research into social phenomena done by Quetelet, whose work would later importantly inform James Clerk Maxwell's model for the random distribution of molecular motion, which, in turn, would prompt C. S. Peirce "to postulate a 'universe of chance' which would include the laws of physics themselves."[108] Maxwell's and Peirce's contributions to articulating the law of continuity more precisely will be taken up again in the following chapter.

The reflections to follow will throw light back on the passages cited in opening this chapter illustrating the continuity between Edwards and Emerson to illuminate that continuity itself as being a developing revelation appearing, as though miraculously, yet, ordinarily, on the first photographic plates, of the properties of light gradually transforming the idea of God into Nature. "*De*-light," "gravity" described as "affection" and "love," "relations," "degrees" and "scale," "excellence," continued to excite energy in the crystal of thought because they were terms of the metaphor for the mind of God, precipitating out to show themselves as actual parts or particles of nature in its "self-regulated motion." Naturalized by selection into the conceptual vocabulary of the nineteenth century under the pressure of accumulating fact describing polarity, the place of pleasure, wave motion, resonance, chance, and change, varieties of these words survived to become strong stock of the twentieth. "Affection," for example, became the "interest" of William and Henry James; the "relations [that] stop nowhere" of Henry; the basis of Stevens's "It Must Give Pleasure." Informed by the facts being brought to light in the nineteenth century, the brief catalogue of excerpts opening this chapter – all from Emerson[109] – could be used as a secular catechism, "a missal found in the mud,"[110] to prepare the "faithful thinker" to extract and convert from the exacting contingency of environment the elements that in fitting recombinatory formulations will work to express the law of continuity in nature "that we might celebrate its immense beauty in many ways and places."[111] Emerson himself accomplished this work in sentences fashioned to excite the heat of their words into motion, light, translating religious experience into aesthetic performance through "the summersaults, spells, and resurrections, wrought by the imagination"[112] into moving pictures. His understanding of the processes underlying the transformations of matter and of words as matter derives from the sources he shared with Darwin.

In addition to the sources listed above, Darwin and Emerson were equally prepared in different ways by Humphry Davy's work in chemistry, Adam Sedgwick's in geology, and Hensleigh Wedgwood's in philology. The chemistry laboratory that Darwin as a boy shared with his brother Erasmus was set up following the principles of Davy, many of whose experiments they reproduced; Emerson read Davy diligently and studied, as well, the work of, and attended lectures given by, Faraday, himself indebted to Davy's thinking, as was Samuel Taylor Coleridge.[113] Sedgwick, with whom Darwin worked while he was at Cambridge, was "the first of the Cambridge men known as the 'Northern Lights,'" as noted by Janet Browne, "a bluff Yorkshireman and liberal Anglican priest whose . . . rapprochement between geology and religion helped create much of the nineteenth-century view of the natural world."[114] During his 1848 visit to London, Emerson made a point to seek out Sedgwick with whom he dined on April 5 together with other members of the "Geologic Club" ("a limited number of fellows of the Geologic Society who usually dined together on Society evenings and adjourned from their dinner at Clunn's Hotel, Covent Garden, to the meeting of the Society at Somerset House . . . The program of the 5th was formally reported in *The Athenaeum*, April 22, 1848"[115]); in a letter to his wife, Lidian, the following day, Emerson commented that Sedgwick was the "best man" of the Society.[116] A few days later, on April 13, Emerson dined with another man he had been anxious to meet and talk with, Hensleigh Wedgwood, the cousin of Charles Darwin, preoccupied since his youth with the development and history of language, its relationship to thought, and the doctrine of chance and free will, a subject on which he published a volume, which his cousin carefully read.[117] Deeply read in philosophy, and following the cues provided by John Horne Tooke and Lord Monboddo as to what could be learned by studying etymology,[118] Wedgwood realized the problem with Locke's notion of a "train of ideas"; he communicated his insights excitedly from early on in his career to his cousin Charles, who shared his enthusiastic interest.[119] Indeed, in a letter to his wife in July 1844, worrying about his health and taking precautions against possible early death, Darwin instructed her in that event to entrust to Hensleigh all his work as well as "all [his] books on Natural History, which are either scored or have references at end to the pages, begging him carefully to look over & consider such passages, as actually bearing or by possibility bearing on this subject –." He continues in the same letter, "I wish you to make a list of all such books, as some temptation to an Editor. I also request that you hand over [to] him [Hensleigh] all those scraps roughly divided in eight or ten brown paper portfolios: the scraps with copied quotations from various works are those which may aid my Editor."[120]

The richness of Darwin's relationship with Wedgwood cannot be overly emphasized.[121] Wedgwood's major preoccupation with language theory is abundantly evidenced in the years he spent working on his etymological dictionary from 1833 onwards (published in three volumes from 1859 to 1867). From the time of his return from his voyage on the *Beagle*, Darwin was in almost daily contact with his cousin, who was at the time actively involved in his researches for the dictionary, itself greatly modeled on and indebted to Jacob Grimm's *Deutsches Wörterbuch*, published over several decades, which together were among Emerson's most prized volumes.[122] Edward Manier, in *The Young Darwin and his Cultural Circle*, comments on Darwin's relation to some of Wedgwood's dictionary's definitions, such as the several meanings of the term "struggle."[123] In 1833 Wedgwood published an extensive technical exposition of Grimm's achievement for workers in language theory in the *Quarterly Review*; the same issue of the journal opened with a review of four of the Bridgewater Treatises (those of Whewell, Kidd, Bell, and Chalmers).[124] Emerson, a regular reader of the *Quarterly Review*, certainly would have read Wedgwood's review article, while Darwin, still away on the *Beagle*, would either have received it as part of the regular shipments of books and periodicals sent to him during his years at sea and traveling in South America or have read it on his return. In any event, as Beer observes, "given his current interest in the subject [of language theory] and close ties between [him and his cousin] . . . [h]e could not . . . have failed to become aware of the importance of Grimm's work for Wedgwood's enterprise."[125] She goes on to emphasize that Wedgwood makes his point about Grimm's contribution "using unselfconsciously the genetic discourse ('descendant', 'stock') which Darwin raises to the level of argument" in a key passage from *Origin* where he turns "to comparative grammar, and to the different rates at which languages change, to make clear what is novel in his ideas: evolutionary genealogy would explain the relations of diverse languages. And, as important, not all forms (linguistic or organic) need change in an evolutionary system."[126] Here, then, is the passage from *Origin* to which she refers:

It may be worthwhile to illustrate this view of classification, by taking the case of languages. If we possessed a perfect pedigree of mankind, a genealogical arrangement of the races of man would afford the best classification of the various languages now spoken throughout the world; and if all extinct languages, and all intermediate and slowly changing dialects, had to be included, such an arrangement would, I think, be the only possible one. Yet it might be that some very ancient language had altered very little, and had given rise to few new languages, whilst others (owing to the spreading and subsequent isolation and states of civilisation of the several races, descended from a common race) had altered much, and had given rise to many new languages and dialects. The various degrees of difference in the languages from the same stock, would have to be expressed by groups subordinate to groups; but the proper or even only possible arrangement would still be genealogical; and this would be strictly natural, as it would connect together all languages, extinct and modern, by the closest affinities, and would give the filiation and origin of each tongue. In confirmation of this view, let us glance at the classification of varieties, which are believed or known to have descended from one species.[127]

The closeness of Darwin's mapping of what Beer nicely calls his "thought model" of language theory to evolutionary theory cannot be gainsaid, and what he adapted he recognized by way of Wedgwood's incisive analysis of Grimm's method. After praising Grimm's thoroughness in accounting for every German dialect and inflection, Wedgwood goes on to comment on Grimm's achievement as being all the more remarkable, as Beer notes, "because its thoroughness does not draw on an even spread of material *evidence*. It relies instead upon the discovery of fundamental *laws*" (her emphasis; as did the work of Charles Lyell in *Principles of Geology*, as both Darwin and Emerson similarly recognized). "Herein," continues Beer, "lies the crucial attraction and challenge of language theory as a thought model for Darwin during the period in which he was organizing his theory. The gaps in the fossil record were a notorious problem in assaying evidence and in arguing for a consecutive history of law bound change."[128] What Darwin practiced was an imaginative calculus, prehension, inserting probable forms in an invisible yet actual mindscape.

Beer goes on to observe that "Wedgwood makes the comparison with the fossil record (which he represents as relatively complete) and suggests that the linguistic record is harder to recuperate and to interpret" and continues, quoting Wedgwood:

like the organic remains of the external world, these particles were formed of the most striking portions of the sentences which they represent, whilst the more perishable portions have mouldered away. [We recall here the passage quoted earlier around Emerson's observation that "Language is fossil poetry."] In some respects the fossil remains have met with a more fortunate destiny than the relics of the immaterial world, for, whilst the former have for the most part been preserved by the protecting soil in which they were embedded, so that a skillful anatomist has little difficulty in deciding to what portion of the skeleton of living animals they correspond, the latter, from their everyday and universal use, have been worn, until, like the pebbles on the beach, they have lost every corner and distinctive mark, and hardly a vestige remains to indicate their original form. Yet even here we are not left entirely without traces which may enable us to form some conjecture of the origin of one or two of these pronouns.[129]

She then goes on to observe:

Wedgwood emphasizes the morphological similarity between past and present life-forms which, he argues, allows "a skillful anatomist" to interpret the fossil record. Darwin, in the course of the next twenty years' work, became ever more conscious of the gaps and of the problem of discriminating between "true affinity" and mere similarity. He needed to construct a historical register, and to formulate laws governing change, as it seemed [Franz] Bopp [the famous Sanskrit scholar] and Grimm had already done in their own field.[130]

With this background in place, we can return to the observation made above, that both Darwin and Emerson addressed themselves to solving the same problem concerning the possibilities of adequate description in language but projected different thought experiments to demonstrate their results. Though both learned key lessons about the organization and presentation of ideas and envisioning from the same core of texts, their purposes were different. Most significantly, Darwin had to integrate the actual facts evidenced by his explorations in the fossil record into his account. Emerson, poised just earlier enough in time and without the first-hand experience in the field of bones and rocks, could present his evidence figuratively. As remarked by Beer, Darwin "needed to construct a historical register, and to formulate laws governing change" following his findings;[131] this he eventually did over the course of the several revisions of *Origin*, where the accumulations of his details, presented as fruit burdening his branching speculations, fall of their own weight, finally, into the ground of his readers' imaginations, there to seed the understanding of the process of life itself, "that first, foremost law."[132]

Complementarily, Emerson's work provides a record of his exploration in the field of words, experienced by him, following the conceptions of Grimm, Bopp, Wedgwood, and other language theorists, and as imaginatively projected by Swedenborg, as life forms themselves. It is as though with Emerson we walk through the territory of language disordered by the catastrophe of evolutionary information, yet preserving its history in its parts; we witness an intellectual landscape broken, disrupted into rifts, chasms, and new accidental juxtapositions. A student with whom I met regularly to discuss Emerson in preparation for her final oral examination and eventually a dissertation dealing with Emerson's aesthetics remarked on one occasion that she felt as though the Sage of Concord were trying to drive her insane. I burst out laughing in recognition and then said that was precisely the point. The experience of reading Emerson is somewhat like what it must have been inside the mind of Darwin, walking in the mountains of South America, seeing the geological evidences of both gradual and catastrophic changes, but suspending the idea of design and fixed plan, not yet able to make sense of what he saw. It is not surprising that he was to suffer psychological strain throughout the rest of his life as he struggled, like Jacob with his necessary angel, to express what his inherited language still fights powerfully to deny, that God has fallen from his heaven and all is not right with the world.

Of course, what has been presented here about the work of both Darwin and Emerson will not have meaning unless their texts have been engaged fully by an imagination become itself the process of turning through light, projecting the invisible, through its reeling making sense of what otherwise remain still, discretely framed ideas. The difference between reading either Darwin or Emerson without and with this kind of imaginative engagement is like the difference between "ideas about the thing" and "the thing itself."[133] We recall the passage from William James's "Stream of Thought" quoted in the opening chapter above (p. 7), calling attention to the inadequacy of English's grammatical and syntactic categories for expressing the "real relations" of nature's accidental transitivity and of the human implication in its process, "We ought to say a feeling of *and*, a feeling of *if*, a feeling of *but*."

As noted earlier, Whitehead called William James "that adorable genius" because he had, following Darwin's lead, exploded the " 'idea' idea," theorizing the place of pleasure, the aesthetic, as the function satisfying the appetite of thought for a place of rest.[134] Truth happens to an idea in a reciprocal relation with an environment, as Jonathan Edwards had recognized within a still sacred frame. New meanings and new varieties: if they fit and work in an extended moment, they become species that last for a while in the forms they have found. Edwards, Emerson, Darwin, William and Henry James, Stein, and Stevens realized that words must break out of their stillness, their fossil forms, and be reconceived, reimagined moving, moving pictures of what might happen *if* this or *if* that, of what might have happened in the past, animated by the animal feeling of what might work in this instance, what in that: "for wisdom is infused into every form. It has been poured into us as blood; it convulsed as pain; it slid into us as pleasure; it enveloped us in dull, melancholy days, or in days of cheerful labor; we did not guess its essence, until after a long time."[135] The dissociation of imagination from the "'idea' idea," of words as and in fixed categories, is the distinctive feature of nineteenth-century thinking about thinking, an adaptation to the accumulated facts of experience bursting their containing syllables as we recognized ourselves to be descended as Darwin described, from "a hairy quadruped furnished with a tail and pointed ears, probably arboreal in his habits."[136]

The common characteristic informing the natural historical texts of those so valued by Darwin and Emerson – Lyell, Herschel, Bell, Humboldt – is that what is imagined through them, what they mimic, is the process of coming to see the invisible, not embodied in mythological figures, but as the *real relations* themselves, "suffer[ing] no fiction to exist for us." In noting details and finding ways of recording their descriptions, these natural historians made images into moving pictures by accounting for the unaccountable, the feeling of time passing that makes every fact. Darwin and Emerson recognized that to represent the effects of time required so framing the objects of consideration that they would reveal themselves simultaneously as products of transient conditions and of constant, though evolving, laws or principles; this complex relation was both the nature of objects, and nature itself. Humboldt's texts are exemplary in this respect, offering, intentionally, accounts of both the external and internal scenes of his explorations. In *Aspects of Nature*, for 19 pages of description in his chapter on "The Physiognomy of Plants" there are 125 pages of "Annotations and Additions" offering what he knew about his examples from what he had read. Following his Kantian faith in the identity of mind and matter, and, even more specifically, following Kant's wish for a future philosopher who would compose a geography of the world that all could equally inhabit imaginatively, Humboldt recorded his experience taking account always of frame and lens, manifesting, like the best of ethnographers, what James Clifford calls "the rhetoric of accounts."[137] In this way he contributed, together with Georg Hamann and Johann Gottfried von Herder, as Ian Hacking observes, to the major shift in the "conception of language not as a mental but as a public object with a history."[138]

Humboldt's accomplishment in this area was emphatically remarked in their journals and letters by both Emerson and Darwin, who each adapted it to their respective intellectual environments. As Emerson reminded his audiences on numerous occasions, America needed to express its original relation to the universe: the message was part of the dispersion of the evolutionary news that everything and everyone were now conceived to be in such an original relation. Just as Lyell had realized that he had to get his audiences to think about the place of the planet in the universe in a different way in order to reveal the processes of geological change once thought to be "original" to be ongoing in the globe's circling through time, both Emerson and Darwin, tracing a more invisible process, realized that they had to get their audiences not only to think differently, but to think about thinking differently. Once the model of comparative philology combined in its affinity with the crystal analogy had worked to reveal the modifications in and over time and situation of all aspects of nature, including language, then, by extension, the process of producing language, thinking itself, had to be understood as subject to change under varying conditions. While thinking for Edwards, for example, even if informed by Newton's descriptions, was still imagined as a type of divine light, the synthesizing of the information drawn off, abstracted, from the descriptions of different nineteenth-century scientists produced in Emerson a kind of phase transition, an idea of thinking as the activity of light naturalized as it effects, in fact, the growth and transformation of crystals, the various atoms/ions accreting through polarities produced by asymmetries and realignments turning, "continually falling forward"[139] in gravity through electric fields toward light: "Without electricity the air would rot."[140] Light, the eighteenth century's dominant metaphor, projected and reinflected through nineteenth-century work in electricity, optics, astronomy, wave theory, and crystallography, created what Whitehead called a "new mentality," one which "altered the metaphysical presuppositions and the imaginative contents of our minds; so that . . . the old stimuli provoke a new response."[141] Out of this excitement psychology would emerge, the beam it cast then directed by William James to "the thing itself," *pragma*, in his Pragmatism spelling out the elements constituting the thing we call mind: "Thought is all light."[142]

Thinking, while understood by Emerson and by Darwin in its actual poetic potential, was regarded, at the same time, as simply another cultural practice or even tribal artifact, with the human considered as a tribe or species of animal. They understood, moreover, that thinking evolves its particular types of structure by the laws of natural selection, this realization forecasting the work that would emerge as the study of "intelligent systems" in the last half of the twentieth century.[143] Emerson recognized as well that the relation of language to thinking is reciprocal, a relation in which the subject moves both inside and outside the process in a constant rhapsody. As part of thinking "America . . . a poem in our eyes"[144] where English adapted to the "intelligence of [t]his soil,"[145] Emerson knew that language when set down in writing and made record functions as a kind of cabinet or museum case in which thinking itself can be regarded, as it was and continues to be – an exotic object. The function of the poet is to make metaphors, to make strange, to break museum cabinets, as Cuvier did, whether apocryphally or not, and let the specimens move from one case into the next: in this sense, Milton, with his slithering, sliding syntax, was not speaking English. Accomplishing this end, the poet recreates again and again for each generation the experience of language and thinking that Emerson had of nature and species in the Jardin des Plantes. Becoming aware of this relation alerts us to how exotic indeed the accidental feature of our constant falling forward on this globe is: "betwixt the snows and the tropics, somewhat of the gravity of nature will infuse itself into the code."[146] The task of describing the nature and operation of this code would be taken up by William James.

This chapter has offered a case history, a theory of a kind. After Darwin, nothing can be taken for granted or fixed. Everything becomes, naturally, a matter of display, holding up for consideration, a theory an invisible case in the invisible museum of mind.

CHAPTER FOUR

William James's feeling of if

I fear we are not getting rid of God because we still believe in grammar.
Nietzsche, *Twilight of the Idols*

If aesthetics wants to rise above empty chatter, it must expose itself, stepping out into the open where there is no place to hide. This means aesthetics must give up that sense of security which it had borrowed from the sciences.
Adorno, *Aesthetic*

BUT CAN A HERMENEUTICS OF THE RELIGIOUS DO WITHOUT UNBALANCED THOUGHTS?[1]

In New York City on a lecture tour in 1842, months after the death of his five-year-old son, Waldo, from scarlet fever, Emerson, between engagements, visiting Henry James Sr., then resident with his wife and infant son at Astor House, asked to be "taken upstairs" to see the babe, on whom he bestowed a blessing. The beneficence was realized. William James took on most seriously his role as his godfather's spiritual heir.[2] The legacy was a true one in passing on the most valuable items from a past lived in a particular place to a future imagined, of *if.* The value of the conversations overheard and participated in by both William and Henry James as boys and young men on the continuing occasions of Emerson's visits to the James household – where, in one of the more permanent residences there was, even, "Mr. Emerson's room"[3] – and of the many visits made later, during the 1860s and '70s, by William to the Emerson family in Concord, was to show itself in the use to which William put his legacy, in what he was "to lecture or teach or preach," as Henry, early on, described his brother's vocation,[4] the necessity of taking into full account feeling in the ongoing activity of describing an "original relation to the universe": "Individuality is founded in feeling; and the recesses of feeling, the darker, blinder strata of character, are the only places in the world in which we catch real fact in the making, and directly perceive how events happen, and how work is actually done."[5] It was such "real fact" that, following Emerson's realizations attendant on the death of his son, constituted "experience" for James:

A conscious field *plus* its object as felt or thought of *plus* an attitude towards the object *plus* the sense of self to whom the attitude belongs . . . such a concrete bit of personal experience may be a small bit, [but] it is a solid bit as long as it lasts; not hollow, not a mere abstract element of experience, such as the "object" is when taken all alone. It is a *full* fact, even though it be an insignificant fact; it is of the *kind* to which all realities whatsoever must belong; the motor currents of the world run through the like of it; it is on the line connecting real events with real events. (Emphases James's)[6]

Following Emerson's insight into the scaling continuity of matter and spirit, William James pursued its actualization through his own "darker, blinder strata" of experience, to develop, over a twelve-year period from 1878 to 1890, a wholly articulate set of principles of psychology, which continue today to provide areas of productive research. This pursuit was realized in the face of both "the irreducible and stubborn facts" of the matter being uncovered in related fields by fellow scientists and the facts of what he referred to, in a letter to a friend during the period of his most severe psychic symptoms during 1869, as "a family peculiarity."[7] In suffering through this and later periods of crisis, which recurred into the mid-1870s, James came to know the terror of religious experience untethered by the myth of heaven, the reality of Emerson's observation that "Temperament puts all divinity to rout."[8] The "NOT ME" invaded him with all its power. He found himself – oddly, since neither he nor his siblings had been reared in any religious tradition, but rather in what Henry James Jr. called a "pewless state"[9] – as Jonathan Edwards would have: "if I had not clung to scripture-texts like 'The eternal God is my refuge, etc. . .' I think I should have grown really insane."[10] This clinging represented what he would eventually come to recognize, purely, as an aesthetic solution – in his case, at this point, an atavistic reflex reaction offering him redemption, temporary balance, made possible by the language of his culture. Indeed, though the James children had not been brought up religiously, Henry James Sr. had read to them from both the Old and New Testaments, preparing their imaginative ground with the linguistically descriptive richness offered by the King James translation. Out of William James's later recognition of the intrinsic connection between perception and language would develop his variety of the philosophy that came to be known as Pragmatism, where in place of any lingering idea of God the Creator or any lesser *deus ex machina*, he substituted the machinery of the mind, "that invented world," as *pragma*, "the thing itself."[11] Exchanging the light of Divine Providence for that of the microscope focused on and, self-reflexively, with, the mind's primary evidence, language, William James anatomized perception to ground its fact in feeling.

The centrality of the aesthetic in shaping all aspects of James's thinking has been remarked by Ralph Barton Perry, Gerald Myers, and Jacques Barzun, and, most recently, richly discussed by Jonathan Levin.[12] Myers, in linking this motive for William and Henry to their father's repeatedly insistent instruction that they "design" all manners of reporting their experience as "aesthetic reactions," observes:

The aesthetic interest shared with Henry is especially relevant; and what is a sizable piece of unfinished scholarship is a comprehensive interpretation of the aesthetic in William's philosophy and psychology . . . The claim, for instance, that philosophical preferences are aesthetically motivated recurs in James's work, including the first chapter of *The Principles of Psychology*, appearing years earlier in an 1878 essay that scolded Thomas Henry Huxley and W. K. Clifford for not recognizing in their praise of *disinterested* information, that "the love of consistency of thought . . . and the ideal fealty to Truth . . . are so many particular forms of aesthetic interest." Even physical science, James claimed, ultimately rests on decisions that are partly aesthetic and therefore partly subjective.[13]

Myers goes on to comment, astutely, that "Religion . . . William's main concern all his life . . . was a further aspect of the aesthetic and impressionistic . . . [a] way of giving meaning to impressions recorded in letters, diaries, memories." More recently, Paul Jerome Croce has elaborated the connection between religious and scientific experience for James.

It is important to clarify William James's understanding of religion in order to avoid a fall into the habit of what Alfred North Whitehead called "misplaced concreteness" so easy when dealing with terms like "religion" or, as James himself points out, "aesthetic":

It is a monstrous abridgement of life, which like all abridgements is got by the absolute loss and casting out of real matter. This is why so few human beings truly care for philosophy. The particular determinations which she ignores are the real matter exciting needs, quite as potent and authoritative as hers. What does the moral enthusiast care for philosophical ethics? Why does the *Aesthetik* of every German philosopher appear to the artist an abomination of desolation? . . . The entire man, who feels all needs by turns, will take nothing as an equivalent for life but the fullness of living itself. Since the essences of things are as a matter of fact disseminated through the whole of time and space, it is in their spread-outness and alteration that he will enjoy them.[14]

To avoid his approach and method being so narrowly conceived, James provided a corrective description of religion and religious experience not only in the lectures constituting *Varieties*, but even in its titling, *The Varieties of Religious Experience: A Study in Human Nature*. Religion is presented as a kind, a species, of experience of which there are many varieties, and these varieties are to be studied as constituting not the soul or spirit, but human nature.[15] It should be noted that the conceptualization indicated by the title belongs to natural history and that the distribution of the concept through the examples illustrating the many forms the experience takes is Darwinian. The adaptation of this frame to consider the numinous, a central aspect of the "vague," the "reinstatement" of which "to its proper place in intellectual life" James had earlier announced as the aim of his *Principles*, is not surprising given his expressed desire in *Principles* and elsewhere "to embrace the darwinian facts" and unfold their implications in considering the evolution of the mind.[16] Opening *Varieties*, he reiterates this intent and method: "To understand a thing rightly we need to see it both out of its environment and in it, and to have acquaintance with the whole range of its variations."[17] Further on, he is explicit: "But in that 'theory of evolution' which, gathering momentum for a century, has within the past twenty-five years swept so rapidly over Europe and America, we see the ground laid for a new sort of religion of Nature."[18] In the second lecture of *Varieties*, "Circumscription of the Topic," James offers his description of religion; the emphasis is his:

Religion, therefore, as I now ask you arbitrarily to take it, shall mean for us *the feelings, acts, and experiences of individual men in their solitude, so far as they apprehend themselves to stand in relation to whatever they may consider the divine*. Since the relation may be either moral, physical, or ritual, it is evident that out of religion in the sense in which we take it, theologies, philosophies, and ecclesiastical organizations may secondarily grow.[19]

Before presenting this working definition, James "proclaims" that his "wish" in the lectures is "to interest" his audience "particularly" in "personal religion pure and simple . . . the inner dispositions of man himself which form the centre [*sic*] of interest, his conscience, his deserts, his helplessness, his incompleteness . . . the relation [which] goes direct from heart to heart, from soul to soul, between man and his maker."[20] The reader who hears in his definition and proclamation inflections of Edwards and of Emerson has been prepaˌed not only by what I have been suggesting in the argument of these chapters. Nearing the close of his first lecture, "Religion and Neurology," James announces his continuation of Edwards's project, further naturalizing it in the context of the contemporary inquiry into empiricist investigations of belief; again, the emphases are James's:

In other words, not its origin, but *the way in which it works on the whole*, is Dr. Maudsley's [author of *Natural Causes and Supernatural Seemings* (1886)] final test of belief. This is our own empiricist criterion . . . By their fruits ye shall know them, not by their roots. Jonathan Edwards's Treatise on Religious Affections is an elaborate working out of this thesis. The *roots* of a man's virtue are inaccessible to us. No appearances whatever are infallible proofs of grace. Our practice is the only sure evidence, even to ourselves, that we are genuinely Christian.[21]

James goes on to quote a passage from Edwards's *Treatise* to sharpen his focus on "practice" as evidencing morality, "God's grace" in Edwards's terms. In later lectures/chapters, James draws on other of Edwards's texts, reminding his audience of their significance for him.[22]

And just following the description of his circumscribed topic, James expends three long paragraphs to voice his affiliation with Emerson in pursuing the idea of religion as an experience of "Not a deity *in concreto*, not a superhuman person, but [of] the immanent divinity in things, the essentially spiritual structure of the universe," citing "The Divinity School Address" with its illustration of "These laws . . . [which] execute themselves."[23] He continues, reflecting on Emerson in a kind of paean of praise, to observe:

The universe has a divine soul of order, which soul is moral, being also the soul within the soul of man. But whether this soul of the universe be a mere quality like the eye's brilliancy or the skin's softness, or whether it be a self-conscious life like the eye's seeing or the skin's feeling, is a decision that never unmistakably appears in Emerson's pages. It quivers on the boundary of these things, sometimes leaning one way, sometimes the other, to suit the literary rather than the philosophic need. Whatever it is, though, it is active. As much as if it were a God, we can trust it to protect all ideal interests and keep the world's balance straight. The sentences in which Emerson, to the very end, gave utterance to this faith are as fine as anything in literature.[24]

In acknowledging Edwards and Emerson as honored guests in the room of his idea of religion, James ordained himself next in the line of priests of the invisible while suggestively particularizing his scope and method. He would continue the seemingly oxymoronic work of plotting the "natural history of the soul,"[25] deploying both terms in their informed senses, examining natural history as a history of feeling belonging to "the apperceiving mass" constituting complex organisms, and the soul as fact, *the* fact of the matter:

"So all of our raptures and our drynesses, our longings and pantings, our questions and beliefs. They are equally organically founded, be they of religious or of non-religious content."[26]

To this end, the lessons learned from Emerson pointed out by James are especially significant. As he indicates after quoting sentences from Emerson, "the inner experiences that underlie such expression of faith as this and impel the writer to their utterance are . . . religious experiences."[27] Such sentences transcend the limitation of philosophical abstraction precisely because they "quiver on the boundary of . . . things, sometimes leaning one way, sometimes the other, to suit the literary rather than the philosophic need," thereby enabling in their potential the activity of consciousness at its most acute in its function of preserving the "balance," the perceptual homeostasis, of the individuals who engage them: "Every bit of us at every moment . . . quivers along various radii."[28] For James, words used in this way stimulate "the normal evolution of character [which] chiefly consist[s] in the straightening out and unifying of the inner self."[29] James's defense of Emersonian faith made explicit its basic tenets: refusal of reification; and identification of the religious with the aesthetic, what he calls here the "literary," the aesthetic non-pejoratively understood, reinvested and reinvigorated with the unsettling experiences in confronting the "NOT ME," where "I" is found to be nothing more than "this thought which is called I, – . . . the mould into which the world is poured like melted wax."[30] As Emerson illustrates and James anatomizes, this recognition attends the conversion of experiences that would once have been denoted as "religious," traditionally understood, into available secular expressions of the uncertain yet luminous relation *between* the human and whatever can be even imperfectly glimpsed of the great order in which it finds itself. James clearly never forgot his father's "constantly repeated" injunction to his children: "Convert, convert, convert . . . to convert and convert . . . everything that should happen to us, every contact, every impression and every experience."[31] In this conceptualization of conversion, subjectivity is reconstituted: the Romantic individual, the Genius in Nature, breaks down into its genesis, the feelings of being in nature: "personality implies the incessant presence of two elements, an objective person, known by a passing subjective Thought and recognized as continuing in time. *Hereafter let us use the words* ME *and* I *for the empirical person and the judging Thought.*"[32] James realized this deconstruction to be required by what Darwin had uncovered. Moreover, the terms of James's description of "decision," or intention, "quivering" around Emerson's sentences are informed by James's understanding of the most essential feature of organic life, the electrical polarity "sometimes leaning one way, sometimes the other" on which change, growth, depends: "*'perishing' pulses of thought . . . recollect and know.*"[33]

For James, these feelings of being, the distinguishing features of religious experience, no matter the variety, spring from facing death and/or non-being, the ultimate "NOT ME." These manifestations include: melancholy; "fear and trembling"; exaltation; ecstasy; vision; willing to some order; participation, whether actual or imagined, in a community; and, very importantly, utterance or verbal performance of some kind. Each of these aspects describes, in one way or another, standing back or away from the occasion of the self, even if momentarily. The space of that removal can be experienced, depending on its valence, as terror or joy, loss or gain – it has a "cash-value," as it were: "You must bring out of each word its practical cash-value, set it at work within the stream of your experience."[34] James recognized that the work of the aesthetic is, through "interest" – through attention to and expression within that space of "in between being," *inter-esse* – to offer the possibility of gain, redemption, or, at least, recuperation of loss: "As much as if it were a God . . . to protect all ideal interests and keep the world's balance straight." Abundantly in the examples offered in *Varieties*, James illustrates how "sick souls," including himself, considered "biologically and psychologically,"[35] recuperate their loss of being by performing a variety of religious practice that, in requiring attention to the space opened when the idea of the self is, in James's words, "sacrificed," extends the idea of reception Emerson had in *Nature* (1836) described as inspired linguistic activity.[36] The key for Emerson is, most significantly, an *if*, an offering to choice, to will, an *if* that follows Edwards into his "room of the idea" to focus the "close attention to the mind in thinking":

A man conversing in earnest, *if he watch his intellectual processes*, will find that a material image, more or less luminous, arises in his mind, cotemporaneous with *every* thought . . . This imagery is spontaneous. It is the blending of experience with the present action of the mind. It is proper creation. It is the working of the Original Cause through the instruments he has already made. (Emphases mine)[37]

In this invitation to spiritual voyeurism, Emerson, James realized, opened the conceptual space once occupied by grace understood in theological terms to the possibilities of subjective imaginings brought with the Darwinian information. The key unlocking the possibilities of individual expression James would articulate in secular terms as an act of free will to believe – taking account of "experience" blending with the demands of "the present action of the mind" to produce "interest" – in an imagined "structure of the universe,"[38] the description of which enables acting, living: "the

belief that there is an unseen order, and that our supreme good lies in harmoniously adjusting ourselves thereto."[39] Depending on the individual's
"experience," this description will be more or less informed, more or less an
expression of an accurate understanding of relation with the universe. The
prerequisite in all cases, however, preserves the essential element of "religious" experience, recognized by James "from the merely biological point
of view," as "an essential organ of our life, performing a function which no
other portion of our nature can so successfully fulfill," the conversion of
the idea of the subject. Through choosing to take on "that personal attitude
which the individual finds himself impelled to take up towards what he
apprehends to be the divine . . . a helpless and sacrificial attitude," the
subject is converted from specially created being outside or above nature,
"I," to "part and particle" of "it," "absolutely dependent on the universe":[40]
"I – this thought which is called I, – is the mould into which the world
is poured like melted wax." The point of view of the converted subject
is *in relation*, a moving vector expressing changing conditions within the
matrix: "New truth is always a go-between."[41] This is the aesthetic subject,
aware of its "interesting" place in the universe, the description of which
gives pleasure, restores the balance of being.

The translation of religious feelings into forms of communal expression
issues in chant, prayer, ritual; translated into forms of personal expression,
it issues in art, and, equally, as James indicates, in philosophical speculation
and science; the "cash-value" of these conversions, as emphasized by James
in his text: "*Immediate luminousness . . . philosophical reasonableness* and
moral helpfulness."[42] His signal contribution was to articulate the identity
of aesthetic with religious experience within the Darwinian framework,
in his examples and explanations naturalizing and legitimizing this experience as an "organ" with the functions of any other organ and having a
species-specific survival value: "It is a biological as well as a psychological
condition."[43] Darwin in *The Descent of Man* provided the explicit basis
for James's refinement, developing in that volume the notion of mind as
a thought-secreting organ, a notion around which he had begun to speculate already in 1839: "Why is thought being a secretion of brain, more
wonderful than gravity a property of matter? It is our arrogance, our admi-
ration of ourselves."[44] In this frame, for Darwin, "intelligence" is simply
the "central feature of adaptive change."[45] James developed this suggestion,
drawing also on what he had learned from Locke, Edwards, and Emerson
in considering thinking and its products as matter, extending the consideration, through his training as a physiologist and continued reading in the
science of his moment, to regard this matter as subject to the same laws of

stimulus and response, action and reaction, as all life forms. While his idea of consciousness and the operation of thought in nature developed from an understanding of evolution – his view of the universe as "unfinished, growing in all sorts of places where thinking beings are at work"[46] – his notion was informed and particularized by his studies in neurology. In opening the third lecture of *Varieties*, "The Reality of the Unseen," widening the scope of religion to describe the field of aesthetic potential, James makes these elements clear:

Were one asked to characterize the life of religion in the broadest and most general terms possible, one might say that it consists of the belief that there is an unseen order, and that our supreme good lies in harmoniously adjusting ourselves thereto. This belief and this adjustment are the religious attitude in the soul. I wish during this hour to call your attention to some of the psychological peculiarities of such an attitude as this, of belief in an object which we cannot see. All our attitudes, moral, practical, or emotional, as well as religious, are due to the "objects" of our consciousness, the things we believe to exist, whether really or ideally, along with ourselves. Such objects may be present to our senses, or they may be present only to our thought. In either case they elicit from us a *reaction*; and the reaction due to things of thought is notoriously in many cases as strong as that due to sensible presences. It may be even stronger . . . in general our whole higher prudential and moral life is based on the fact that our material sensations actually present may have a weaker influence on our action than ideas of remoter facts. (Emphasis James's)[47]

The first three sentences, reflecting Edwards and Emerson and projecting Stevens, importantly remind his audience of the actuality both of his performance and of the capacity of his listeners/readers to give close attention to his and to their own minds in thinking. As though delivering a lay sermon, James "call[s our] attention" – significantly preserving in the printed text the manner of direct address – "during this hour" to the aspects of mind to be examined. Both the notion of voiced delivery, a feature maintained throughout the lectures published as chapters, and the reminder of how long he will claim the spiritual breath of attention, are aspects of the stylistic reality principle James practiced in *Varieties*. In its "acts," its lectures/chapters, he staged the dramatic idea of "the variety of religious experience" as epitomizing the place of emotions in mind – "If religion is to mean anything definite for us . . . we ought to take it as meaning this added dimension of emotion."[48] In this way he would satisfy, as had Emerson in his work, "the literary rather than the philosophic need." He had, after all, already explicitly addressed himself to satisfying the philosophic need in *Principles*. The acting out in *Varieties* of the effects of words as matter, as vitally effective in stimulating a "*reaction*" – fear, panic, dread – as a lion leaping out of the jungle, an example James cites when presenting the scene of his own disguised terror during his most severe nervous collapse, successfully illustrated what he had laid out in *Principles*. This performance at the same time became the experience informing what he would phrase a short time later, notably after having reread all of "the divine Emerson"[49] in preparation for the lecture celebrating his centenary, in and as *Pragmatism*, one function of which he described as being "a happy harmonizer of empiricist ways of thinking with the more religious demands of human beings."[50]

In retrospectively analyzing his own "vastation," James had come to experience the truth of what happens to an idea, specifically the Lockean idea of the power of words to create primary impressions, "with the force of a revelation": "An idea, to be suggestive, must come to an individual with the force of a revelation."[51] He realized that the success, the survival, of the Christian myth belonged to its having provided the script for assuming the attitudes most necessary to achieving the "supreme good" of harmonious adjustment to "an unseen order." These attitudes he named helplessness and sacrifice, humility and reception: "The whole force of the Christian religion . . . so far as belief in the divine personages of the believer, is in general exerted by the instrumentality of pure ideas, of which nothing in the individual's past experience directly serves as a model."[52] He realized, moreover, that the force exerted by having given close attention to these material representations of feelings could itself stimulate the opening of a neurological circuit, a need, requiring the closure of response to reestablish homeostasis: the "nervous system [is] a mass of matter whose parts, constantly kept in states of different tension, are as constantly tending to equalize their states":[53]

Through this hovering of the attention . . . the accumulation of associates becomes so great that the combined tensions of their neural processes break through . . . and the nervous wave pours into the tract which has . . . been awaiting its advent. And as the expectant, sub-conscious itching there, bursts into the fulness of vivid feeling, the mind finds an inexpressible relief.[54]

His enactment of this process is the description of the occasion informing *Varieties*, the account in Lecture VI, "The Sick Soul," of a "sufferer . . . evidently in a bad nervous condition at the time of which he writes."[55] James's costuming himself in the person, or, perhaps more tellingly, in the *language* of a French correspondent, is most suggestive both in the deflection it attempts and in its potential energy, or, more precisely, using the terminology of contemporary neuroscience, its *action potential*, carrying as it does, one of the strong currents of his thinking in and about words as what current researchers call *wave packets*.[56]

The fact of James's fluency in French and German, acquired from extended stays abroad during childhood and adulthood, from tutoring, as well as from his ongoing reading in both languages, has not yet been considered in the light of what has here earlier been remarked, following the indications in *Principles* in connection with Jonathan Edwards's having read Newton's *Opticks* in its Latin version, concerning language learning. James's particular ease in French was evidenced even by frequent punning and word-play in conversation and letters. When his central and extensively repeated use of *vague* – "wave" in French – is thus considered, the room of its idea is brightly illuminated with the close attention he gave to all that was being explored through the second half of the nineteenth century and into the early twentieth, following Faraday's work and, of course, reflecting Newton's major contribution, concerning the behavior of waves in the propagation of light, sound, electricity, and magnetism.[57] Following James into the dressing-room where he prepares himself as the most necessary actor in the drama to unfold will provide the evidence grounding words as things, *pragmata*, material objects.

The account of James's French melancholic persona, which he "translates freely," is centrally significant; readers with an edition of *Varieties* at hand will get a fuller sense of James's own "quivering" style by reading through the entire "excellent example" with its complete frame in place.[58] The first paragraph of the fictionalized account, the actor emerged from the "dressing-room" of the prologue into the "dressing-room" of the scene, is quoted in its entirety; I have emphasized passages having specific resonances that will be taken up in the paragraphs following. (Worth comment, in addition, is that James's manner of setting the scene of the narrative, deflecting and mediating its source, is the manner employed so effectively by Henry James in *The Turn of the Screw*, where "the reality of the unseen" is the subject as well.) Here, then, is the description of the "case":

Whilst in this state of philosophic pessimism and general depression of spirits about my prospects, I went one evening *into a dressing-room in the twilight* to procure some article that was there; *when suddenly there fell upon me without any warning, just as if it came out of the darkness, a horrible fear of my own existence. Simultaneously there arose in my mind the image of* an epileptic patient whom I had seen in the asylum, a black-haired youth with greenish skin, entirely idiotic, who used to sit all day on one of the benches, or rather shelves against the wall, with his knees drawn up against his chin, and the coarse gray undershirt, which was his only garment, drawn over them inclosing his entire figure. He sat there like a sort of sculptured Egyptian cat or Peruvian mummy, *moving nothing but his black eyes and looking absolutely non-human. This image and my fear entered into a species of combination with each other.* THAT SHAPE AM I, *I felt, potentially.* Nothing that I possess can defend me against that fate, if the hour for it should strike for me as it struck for him. There was such a horror of him, and such perception of *my own merely momentary discrepancy from him, that it was as if something hitherto solid within my breast gave way entirely, and I became a mass of quivering fear. After this the universe was changed for me altogether.* I awoke morning after morning with a horrible dread at the pit of my stomach, and with a sense of the insecurity of life that I never knew before, and that I have never felt since.* It was like a revelation; and although the immediate feelings passed away, the experience has made me sympathetic with the morbid feelings of others ever since. It gradually faded, but for months I was unable to go out into the dark alone.[59]

The asterisk above replaces James's footnote indication to the following; again, the emphases are mine:

Compare Bunyan: "There was I struck into a very great trembling, insomuch that at some times I could, for days together, feel my very body, as well as my mind, to shake and totter under the sense of the dreadful judgment of God, that should fall on those that have sinned that most fearful and unpardonable sin. I felt also such clogging and heat at my stomach, by reason of this my terror, that I was, especially at some times, as if my breast-bone would have split asunder . . . Thus did I *wind, and twine, and shrink,* under the burden that was upon me; which burden also did so oppress me *that I could neither stand, nor go, nor lie,* either at rest or quiet.

The cadence and setting of the first passage italicized above, *into a dressing-room in the twilight* eerily echo Emerson's famous prelude, *Crossing a bare common . . . at twilight.*[60] (I have italicized passages from Emerson and James in this paragraph for ease of reading; using quotation marks with roman type face would, I felt, have made difficult seeing the parallels I am drawing.) The shading deepens: *when suddenly there fell upon me without any warning* covering *without having in my thoughts any occurrence of special good fortune;* and Emerson's *under a clouded sky* becoming *just as if it came out of the darkness,* to shrink from *I am glad to the brink of fear* into *a horrible fear of my own existence.* Replacing the "spontaneous" image of the transparent eyeball – *This imagery is spontaneous. It is the blending of experience with the present action of the mind* – illuminating Emerson, his *head bathed by the blithe air, and uplifted into infinite space,* in James's mind *Simultaneously there arose . . . the image* of the epileptic patient *moving nothing but his black eyes and looking absolutely non-human.* Where, *all mean egotism* vanished, Emerson *becomes* identical with *uncontained and immortal beauty,* to announce *I am part or particle of God,* James's actor, wrapped still in the horror attending loss of self, cannot yet separate the *non-human* from a human representation: THAT SHAPE AM I, *I felt, potentially* – a reduced version of clinging to the idea of an anthropomorphic god, precisely the conceptual atavism being experienced most virulently by the culture in the face of the Darwinian information at the moment of James's first nervous collapse. (A version of this reaction had been experienced by Henry James Sr., as well, though his crisis in 1844 obviously pre-dated the specific prompt occasioned by the publication of *Origin*; significantly, as we shall see further on, his recovery involved a Swedenborgian adaptation of the Christian myth.) Emerson bursts *in perfect exhilaration* the syllable of the self – *I am nothing; I see all; the currents of the Universal Being circulate through me . . .* – while for James in the guise of his letter-writer it *was as if something hitherto solid within my breast gave way entirely, and I became a mass of quivering fear.* Yet for both, after these experiences, the *universe was changed . . . altogether*; for both it was *a revelation.*

While a strict Bloomian might, at this point, read James's cloaked account in relation to Emerson's famous description of his conversion as a prime instance of the anxiety of influence, I would like to suggest a more specifically inflected, naturalized reading of this introversion and inversion, following both James's investigation of the mechanism of religious conversion and the abiding physiological point of view underlying his teaching and practice of psychology. This reading will not gainsay the parts played in James's personal drama by the ghosts of his father, Emerson, or God, but will shift the scenery to foreground the *relation between* these and other factors, this activity itself cast as the protagonist, so to speak, the relation, the *it*, the subject reconceived in its plasticity and transitivity, "part or particle" of the "wave" that is its "society." This kind of "bottom-up" reading of personality emerges, of course, from applying the Darwinian information to what Emerson called "temperament" and underlies Karl Marx's perception of the relation between society and the individual no less than it does Emerson's, as well as it does current work in cognitive psychology.[61] What is central for Emerson and, following him, for James, as it would be for Nietzsche (as Stanley Cavell and Richard Poirier have importantly reminded us, recent cultural criticism tends to forget or ignore Nietzsche's debt to Emerson[62]), is the location of this relation in the practice or performance of language. Whitehead would continue investigating and theorizing this relation, as would, of course, Freud and Wittgenstein, each in a different manner.

Freud, though also trained as a physiologist, retained, as James realized, an idea of the subject, his *ego* distinct from the *id*,[63] that preserved a hierarchical structure, itself a Romantic residue, where the ego emerges as a hero if successful in waging its battle of interpreting the id's wants in the language of the super-ego. This structure is reflected in Harold Bloom's critical framework and preserves the idea of the dominant individual, from Gilgamesh and Theseus and through the Hebraio-Christian myth, of the virile youth who in one way or another kills, conquers, transforms, or damns the forces of the unknown. Freud figured the unknown as drives residing in the dark unconscious; sex and death were the monsters to be slain, or, at least, confined to a labyrinth. James criticized Freud and distinguished his own understanding of psychology from his European colleague precisely around the idea of what constitutes this unknown, the unconscious, and how it operates. James thought Freud had limited the understanding of the psyche by restricting motivation primarily to sexuality and describing the unconscious mythologically as a sort of hell where these forces, condemned like demons, might be released if converted by a strong redeemer/interpreter/reader.[64] James, in contrast, considered the unconscious simply as the chaos of feelings that had not yet found words – "a feeling of *and*, a feeling of *if*, a feeling of *but*, and a feeling of *by*" – and the labyrinth, the inherited grammatical structure in which these feelings paced and bellowed as half-human expressions at its center. His experience, as presented in his veiled account with his demon, to which we shall now return to consider James's footnote to Bunyan, reflects how he came to have this knowledge of men made out of words.

It is interesting to remark in this context, of James's noting of Bunyan, that foot- or endnotes, when they contain more than brief references to sources, function, literally, as *hyper*text, casting light from above onto and into the discursive progress permitted by the conventions of linear structure of argument, offering the necessary overview, the map of the mind in and from which the argument, the thread leading out of the labyrinth, is constructed.[65] This function was paradigmatically illustrated and described as designed to such an end by Alexander von Humboldt in *Aspects of Nature* as well as in *Cosmos*, where, following his Kantian aim, he observed, as remarked here in the last chapter, the significance of recording not only what he saw around him as he explored the new world of American nature but also what he knew as cognate phenomena from his store of reading and thinking. This feature was not lost on Emerson who incorporated and refined it to shape his essays into palimpsests where the texts he overwrote swim and glitter beneath the surface of his sentences, enticing readers to catch the real fact quivering in the making of his sentences: "The drop is a small ocean"; "The world globes itself in a drop of dew"; "Without electricity the air would rot"; "the earth lies in the soft arms of the atmosphere"; "All things are in contact; every atom has a sphere of repulsion; – Things are and are not at the same time"; "The whole world is the flux of matter over the wires of thought to the poles or points where it would build."[66] Newton, Davy, Faraday, Lyell live in the imaginings these sentences imitate for the writer and stimulate for the reader or listener. The imitation is in the performance of reception, the imperfect replication in the words of the writer of "the working of the Original Cause through the instruments he has already made"; it is religious experience, and it gives pleasure. The stimulation for the reader or listener opens a circuit of reception. In James's footnote to Bunyan, the mechanism of this activity can be observed.

The space of mind, James understood, is filled with what has been caught from texts that embody such possibility. In offering his pointed comparison to the passage from Bunyan, James provided the key unlocking the material image of his dread. While within his own familial context, he would have been exposed to the stories of "divine personages" as described in biblical texts through Henry James Sr.'s reading to his children from Scripture, the language of the culture was itself a translation of these stories. Milton's *Paradise Lost*, Swedenborg's *Heaven and Hell*, Bunyan's *Pilgrim's Progress* (after the Bible, the second most-published volume in the nineteenth century) served as well as any gospel to be the book in which to read himself: *This image and my fear entered into a species of combination with each other.* THAT SHAPE AM I, *I felt, potentially.* These texts, their "scoriae" preserved in cultural referents and/or recorded in past experiences of reading, contained the images, the available terms, with which to clothe the present action of his mind, its feeling the *horrible fear of . . . existence.* Emerson's project was to replace these terms with those of a naturalized scripture. The continuing work of the Reformation required ongoing iconoclasm, getting rid of the verbal icons still remaining after the destruction of idols and graven images. At the time of his most serious crisis William James did not yet have sufficient practice in the language of transparency Emerson was teaching. He was twenty-five, trying to find a way to set down his multiple impressions – "the enormous difficulty I experience in turning out my clotted thought in a logical & grammatical procession. I find more freedom however in each successive attempt."[67] He had begun to experience episodes of deep depression, verging repeatedly on thoughts of suicide, during the period of resuming his studies at Harvard Medical School after his return in February 1866 from a Brazilian expedition with Louis Agassiz, following which, in the summer, he completed his undergraduate internship at Massachusetts General Hospital. Through this same time, Henry James Sr. was steeped in Swedenborg, reading and rereading from his worn, faded red morocco-bound volumes, as he worked on the interpretation of the Swedish mystic's theology he would publish as *The Secret of Swedenborg* in 1869, which, an early reviewer commented, in negatively criticizing the volume, the author had kept well, a sting of shame felt by William.[68]

It might not be accidental that it was, in fact, after this exposure and his own reading of *The Secret*, prompting a qualified appreciation of his father's "great & original ideas" in dealing with "pure theology" if not "philosophy,"[69] that he experienced the critical episode expressed in the image of the still, shrunken, and silent figure, which first appeared as a notebook drawing of himself, "seated on a chair, hands on knees, bending forward toward the floor, his face obscured with the words 'Here I and Sorrow Sit' [written] above him."[70] Between the earlier incidents of depression and this moment, James had again interrupted his progress toward a degree at Harvard Medical School with an eighteen-month stay of recuperation and study in Germany, taking the thermal baths at Teplitz and Dresden before going on to Berlin to learn what was newest there in the fields of psychology and physiology. James's pursuit of his scientific interests was, from the moment he chose to begin a course of study in chemistry at the Lawrence Scientific School of Harvard University in 1861, in the midst of the excited debates following the publication of Darwin's *Origin*, itself the field in which he would both align and separate himself from his father. Henry James Sr. had initially encouraged his eldest son's scientific interests, which had shown themselves early on in his boyhood; his younger brother Henry, recalling William's preoccupations in 1857, at age fifteen, during one of the James family's extended residences in Europe – having moved that summer from Paris to Boulogne, where William received his first formal scientific training – provided a catalogue of how William investigated his "interest in the 'queer' or the incalculable effects of things": "The consumption of chemicals, the transformation of mysterious liquids from glass to glass under exposure to lambent flame, the cultivation of stained fingers, the establishment and the transport, in our wanderings, of galvanic batteries, the administration to all he could persuade of electric shocks, the maintenance of marine animals in splashy aquaria, the practice of photography."[71] For Christmas that year William received from his parents a microscope, armed with which he would, like a latter-day Jonathan Edwards, "go out into the country, into the dear old woods and fields and ponds. There I would try to make as many discoveries as possible," and, echoing the young Emerson as well, announce, "I'll . . . do as much good in the natural history line as I can."[72] Henry James Sr., hoping, with so many in his generation, that future evidences in natural history would confirm divine purpose and design, could not have anticipated, in sending William to the Lawrence School, where the pious Louis Agassiz was prominently installed and delivering the gospel of natural theology, the effects of the Darwinian information, not only on his son but on the nature of perception and expression both within the Harvard community and in the culture at large: "With Darwinism, the long-standing break in the harmony between science and religion became dramatically manifest, and the fissure between religious belief and professional science, which Agassiz's flamboyant personality had held together so well, became an open chasm."[73]

At the point of his stay in Teplitz in March 1868, William was deepening his understanding of Darwin, reading for review his latest, *The Variation of Animals and Plants under Domestication*,[74] which reinforced his understanding of the evolutionary view premised on accident against the idea of nature designed by God as Agassiz maintained; William wrote to his brother Henry, expressing the insecurity of his burgeoning judgment: "The more I think of Darwin's ideas the more weighty do they appear to me – tho' of course my opinion is worth very little – still I *believe* [emphasis James's] that that scoundrel Agassiz is unworthy either intellectually or morally for him to wipe his shoes on, & find a certain pleasure in yielding to the feeling."[75] He was also reading Claude Bernard (who first conceptualized the notion of cellular homeostasis) on the progress of the study of physiology in France, and the *Odyssey*, concretizing his experience of the last with visits to the museum in Dresden to see the collection of Egyptian and Greek casts – "like a bath from Heaven," at the same time as having "[his] S. Am indians . . . rising before [him] as [he] read the O."[76] He simultaneously reflected on the possibilities of "intellectual and moral" companionship in America – "My organ of perception-of-national-differences happened to be in a super-excited state."[77] And, significantly, he thought again of Emerson, further differentiating himself from his father, prompted by Henry Sr.'s recently announced "mingled enchantment and irritation with Emerson." William James wondered about who the "honest men" might be who would show themselves his true "intellectual offspring."[78] Without his yet having conceptualized the structure of the feeling mind that became the work of *Principles*, not yet having devised his own way out of the labyrinth of "grammatical & logical procession," the manner of argument expected by his culture which he would have to escape, James's circuits were, in fact, overloaded. How to determine what to believe was, indeed, the problem of his age, its *dis*-ease.[79] The nerve-tracts established by the habit of mind shaped over 2,000 years of Christianized Western belief were deep; even when emptied of their content, the stories of divine personages and progress to a perfected end, the need to believe remained. Some, like Agassiz, Herbert Spencer (though a declared atheist, still believing in "progressive advance" and "postulating the existence of an 'Unknowable power' behind all knowable phenomena"[80]), and Henry James Sr., with his idiosyncratic Fourierist sense of socially perfectible spirituality, attempted to patch the thinning fabric, preserve the protective garment; William James, experiencing it as mummifying winding cloth, feeling its restriction, recognized the need for cutting up and refashioning.

What happens to an idea when it comes to be experienced as "a revelation" is what James set out to investigate and, even more importantly, to communicate. As he would come to realize and later theorize in *The Varieties of Religious Experience*, it is "mental states that have . . . substantive value as revelations of the living truth."[81] One of the lessons learned from his father that neither he nor Henry would ever forget was "that the 'feeling' mind is measured . . . by the verbal style that it invents for itself," a lesson grounded in the belief expressed by Socrates in the *Phaedo* that "to express oneself badly . . . does some harm to the soul."[82] William James found in the midst of his crisis of identity the terms for his own horror of existence in Bunyan's description of feeling fear and trembling before the experience of redemptive "grace abounding to the chief of sinners"; this was precisely at the point in his life when he would have to begin to select from what he had learned from the experiences of others the elements to combine with what he had learned from his own. The psychological process underlying his imitation of some strains and his differentiation from others – his own "pilgrim's progress"– is disclosed in a verbal mechanism which itself illustrates the continuity of the laws concerning matter and spirit, in this instance, the law of self-identity/imitation, which, we know today, also underpins the information transfer between DNA and messenger-RNA strands. Emerson, extrapolating from Goethe, from Swedenborg, and from his own thinking, had repeatedly emphasized and illustrated this law of organism in connection with perception and knowing: what we notice, question, pursue, strikes the chord of forgotten majesty within us, the recognition an actualizing experience of Platonic idealism. The opening of this feeling circuit of reception is what permits real learning, understanding, belief.

Whatever the particular trigger that made Bunyan and his text the portion of the strip of the cultural code along which the young William James, as presented in his disguised account, would align himself, the pattern he would imperfectly replicate in his own description – whether it was the idea of the "pilgrim's progress," whether the vivid imagery perhaps remembered from childhood reading of the "Slough of Despond," whether his noting that Bunyan had, like Henry James Sr. and Swedenborg, found the temporary resting-place offering the possibility of salvation in passages recalled from the Bible, whether because feeling his own incipient pride in beginning to make judgments about his "fathers"– he clearly found there the fact of feeling expressed in a way with which he identified, found himself revealed "more truly and more strange":[83] "Thus did I *wind, and twine, and shrink*" became, through the process Freud would later term "condensation," his own *mummified* image, "*This image and my fear entered into a species of combination with each other.*" Interpreting the nightmarish vision, rebus-like – the mechanism Freud identified as key in *The Interpretation of Dreams* – in the words of his fictionalized account, James unwound, surrendered and sacrificed himself, "*and I became a mass of quivering fear.*" Pulling away from the template, the spaces between the letters of Bunyan's description were filled with his actual experience coded in his memory of the asylum and seeing the epileptic, the Peruvian mummy residue from his South American trip, and the Egyptian cat from his visit to the museum in Dresden. The recombinant form of his being would, most significantly, emerge, loosened from still images to recover and describe itself as an active abstraction, or an abstract activity, the choice to believe in free will, a de-mythologized, secular variety of "the reality of the unseen." Out of this "vastation" came his full understanding of the power of words themselves, of what it was Emerson, shaping Kant's ideas into moving syllables, embodied, that indeed Nature could, if adequately described, take the place of God, that such words create new "mental states that have . . . substantive value as revelations of the living truth":

Immanuel Kant held a curious doctrine about such objects of belief as God, the design of creation, the soul, its freedom, and the life hereafter. These things, he said, are properly not objects of knowledge at all. Our conceptions always require a sense-content to work with, and as the words "soul," "God," "immortality," cover no distinctive sense-content whatever, it follows that theoretically speaking they are words devoid of any significance. Yet strangely enough they have a definite meaning *for our practice.* We can act *as if* there were a God; feel *as if* we were free; consider Nature *as if* she were full of special designs; lay plans *as if* we were to be immortal; and we find that these words do make a genuine difference in our moral life . . .
   . . . The sentiment of reality can indeed attach itself so strongly to our object of belief that our whole life is polarized through and through, so to speak, by its sense of the existence of the thing believed in, and yet that thing, for purpose of definite description, can hardly be said to be present to our mind at all. It is as if a bar of iron, without any touch or sight, with no representative faculty whatever, might

nevertheless be strongly endowed with an inner capacity for magnetic feeling; and as if, through the various arousals of its magnetism by magnets coming and going in its neighborhood, it might be consciously determined to different attitudes and tendencies. Such a bar of iron could never give you an outward description of the agencies that had the power of stirring it so strongly; yet of their presence, and of their significance for its life, it would be intensely aware through every fibre of its being.

It is not only the Ideas of Pure Reason, as Kant styled them, that have this power of making us vitally feel presences that we are impotent articulately to describe. All sorts of higher abstractions bring with them the same kind of impalpable appeal. Remember those passages from Emerson which I read at my last lecture. The whole universe of concrete objects, as we know them, swims, not only for such a transcendentalist writer, but for all of us, in a wider and higher universe of abstract ideas, that lend it its significance. (Emphases James's)[84]

A proclamation of intense devotion to the lessons learned from his fathers informs this passage, itself a description of spiritual activity as natural process following the laws of electromagnetic activity as illustrated by Faraday and continuing to be explored in the work of Helmholtz and Clerk Maxwell in their studies of polarization, of sound and optical wave activity; by 1865 Maxwell described the mathematical relation between electricity and magnetism, proving that there is only one force, electromagnetism and that light itself is an electromagnetic wave.[85] James's description also provides an implicit explanation of his striking inversion of Emerson's account of his *crossing* illumination in *Nature*. Emerson's description of his naturally transcendental religious conversion was imperfectly replicated by James in a negatively polarized version because the letter-writing character had not yet converted Emerson to his own use. At the moment of James's actual "vastation" the terms for this experience were generated by nerve tracts activated by the habit of mind shaped by the common language, the currency or, more precisely, the current, of his culture: in his case, Bunyan's terms of spiritual devastation and recuperative pilgrimage. This habit was to show itself to be not a good fit, though it would, through its negative capability, prompt the turn to its opposing pole, James's initiating act of free will, following, again, in a seeming charge of the power of words, the appropriately named "Renouvier," to believe in free will.

Important to note in reflecting on the passage above in the context of the discussion here is that the terms chosen by James to elucidate the reality of *as if,* his description being his "variety," that is, his adaptation of Kantian idealism to the nascent twentieth-century environment of fact, belong to the language of electromagnetism, a language he had begun to learn even before beginning his studies at the Lawrence School. In another ironic turn on his father's spiritual aspirations and guidance, William James's early introduction to the work of Faraday was to provide additional energy moving him toward what Henry Sr. regarded as "the opposing law."[86]

Henry James Sr., when still a young man, twenty-six, having left the Princeton Theological Seminary where he had enrolled in what proved to be an unsuccessful attempt to satisfy his religious appetite within the Presbyterian tradition in which he had been reared, embarked on one of the many European journeys he would make during his lifetime, searching, much like Emerson at roughly the same moment, and like Henry Adams, later, to find something that would "take the place/Of . . . heaven and its hymns."[87] During this 1837–8 visit, in England, first attracted by the thought of Robert Sandeman with his pristine version of Reformation practice and belief, Henry James met Faraday, to whom he was particularly drawn because he thought he might find in him, as a scientist and noted Sandemanian, someone who had successfully combined a pure form of Christian belief with the facts of matter. James continued to follow Faraday's work throughout his career, years later recommending reading him to his scientifically curious son. William was equally as impressed by what he learned about polarization and patterns of magnetic fields as about the alignments between matter and mind suggested by the diligent and bold scientist, whose contributions to wave theory Einstein (who kept a photograph of Faraday in his office in Bern) noted as seminal to his formulation of the concept of spacetime.

An 1859 notebook evidences the seventeen-year-old William James's recorded responses to his varied reading and thinking about what he had been learning; among these traces we find: Emersonian admonitions to himself, "Nothing can be done without work"; Darwinian perceptions concerning what individuals "are naturally adapted to produce"; and a paraphrased passage from Faraday's essay, "Observations on Mental Education": "Moderate ability on a mere mechanical instrument, ought not to be discouraged by the irksomeness inevitable in the learning to use that far more delicate & personal instrument the mind."[88] Faraday's concentration on the importance of practicing, as one would a musical instrument, the uses of mind, combined with the Emersonian stress to "Do your work," which Henry James Sr. also strongly encouraged, produced in the young William James a rephrasing of the most significant feature of Jonathan Edwards's moral and intellectual economy, the importance of the "habit of *cultivating the attention*" (emphasis James's).[89] It is not surprising that James would later recognize in Edwards his own best thought, incorporating and developing what he found, using as catalyst what, in the form of the contributions of Faraday, Helmholtz, and Maxwell, had evolved from what had focused Edwards's attention, Newton's work on optics. James, experiencing his spiritual wavering and finding salvation, balance, through his conversion, his exchange, of religious for secular terms informed by his growing understanding of natural and scientific processes, began to practice a premonition, as it were, a hunch, hypothesizing that currents operate no differently in mind than they do in matter, and that these currents are charged by words. His first experiment was to act *as if*: his first act of free will, to act as if there were free will: "We can act *as if* there were a God; feel *as if* we were free; consider Nature *as if* she were full of special designs; lay plans *as if* we were to be immortal; and we find that these words do make a genuine difference in our moral life." The first proof was, of course, the success of this deliberate verbal act. Subsequent tests and proofs became the content of his life's work and the work of others following, as experiments today continue to be designed from the theory set down by James in *Principles*.[90]

It may seem ironic that James's initial act is a teasing tautology, an act to believe in itself. And yet, if free will, apparently the defining human characteristic, is identified, as hypothesized by Darwin, as the operation of chance as experienced by the creatures we happen to be (see page 87, and note 101, preceding chapter), then to locate precisely this aspect of life in a probabilistic, *as if*, rather than divinely determined, cosmos, was to announce the only apt morality, "an original relation to the universe," indeed, one which became the basis for the pluralism in religious belief James suggested in closing *Varieties* as the only possible solution for the democracy, or any democracy. It was and was not accidental that this formulation, significantly a prime instance of conceptual/epistemological/syntactic cognitive feedback (an aspect to be discussed further on), the only paradigm shift offered to morality since that to monotheism, emerged in a society premised on freedom of belief. The words framing this concept had had their effect on the "mental states" of the James family, freedom of thought and possibility being the constant theme played, especially for his two older sons, by Henry James Sr. It was and was not accidental, as well, that Darwin realized the identity of chance and free will when and where he was, voyaging in and around this New World of probable possibles: "I might add I have drawn all my illustrations from America, purposely to show what facts can be supported from that part of the globe."[91] By degrees measuring and calculating the advance of his thinking, no less than Captain FitzRoy the progress of *The Beagle*, Darwin, at the points observation could not provide, imagined a sighting, in the shape of a bit of fossil evidence or an intermediate shape of a finch's beak, the probability of evolutionary direction, by a kind of mental dead reckoning, a calculus of spacetime's precipitates on the planet, completing the line plotting his course. Approximation, long familiar to navigators, became, after Leibniz's and Newton's formulations of the calculus, by the nineteenth century the single most important contribution to methods of thinking, and extended into practical as well as speculative fields: "We live in a system of approximations."[92] A central feature of Darwin's theory as presented in *Origin*, immediately recognized as such by C. S. Peirce, is its basis in probability and its expression in persuasive rhetorical phrasing and organization, relying "more on the plausibility of explanation than on the certainty of proof": "Probabilities allow the more moderate alternative of measuring 'the proportion of cases in which . . . a mode of argument . . . carries truth with it.'"[93] Recalling the motive of the search initiated by Francis Bacon, Peirce in his own "Doctrine of Chances" (1878) described Darwin's method as embodying a new kind of logic, "the idea of continuity," which used imagined probabilities, fictions, to fill in retrospectively the gaps in the record of the past – notes toward a supreme fiction, indeed.[94] Darwin's reading of Lyell, of Quetelet, of Malthus, had, as has been observed in the preceding chapter, offered him, no less than Emerson, intellectual exercises which he diligently practiced to shape a new habit of mind; Peirce, one of whose first memories was of being taken to hear Emerson lecture, reflexively grasped what was at issue.[95] Ironically, Agassiz, while in constant "earnest protest against the transmutation theory," and in 1874 specifically criticizing Darwin's use of imagination as a "faulty" addition to scientific method, nonetheless pinpointed his signal contribution to advancing the mode of reasoning, of thinking itself:

Darwin . . . has brought to the discussion a vast amount of well-arranged information, a convincing cogency of argument, and a captivating charm of presentation. His doctrine appealed the more powerfully to the scientific world because he maintained it at first not upon metaphysical ground but upon observation. Indeed it might be said that he treated his subject according to the best scientific methods, had he not frequently overstepped the boundaries of actual knowledge and allowed his imagination to supply the links which science does not furnish.[96]

Precisely in this addition lay Darwin's genius, as James, as well as Peirce, would realize: imagination is the organ through which chance operates on the human scale; its function, to effect variability. The uncertain space of imaginative projections, what James came to call *the vague*, is, in fact, what today's physicists describe, as noted earlier, as a *wave packet*, a probability amplitude composing a range, a scale of *possibles*, of *action potentials*: "The important fact which this 'field' formula commemorates is the indetermination of the margin . . . It lies around us like a 'magnetic field,' inside of which our centre of energy turns."[97] Describing this "field" demanded, as James, but not Peirce, recognized, the other aspects Agassiz noted: "well-arranged information, a convincing cogency of argument, and a captivating charm of presentation" – in another word, *style*, "the more than rational distortion," the spaces of possibility/probability filled with analogies, speculations, guesses at the riddle, dressed in persuasive phrasing, "captivating charm." James was well prepared to practice his rhetorical gift, both by his father's persistent training of his sons in argument around the dinner table and by what he had internalized from his reading, listening, and learning. Moreover, his spiritual father's lesson was never forgotten: while Peirce, in defining what he meant by "abduction," reiterated Emerson's grounding observation aligning "Inspiration" with "the alliance of man with the divinity," and named this a crucial "new mental Element . . . shrewdness . . . the essence of genius,"[98] he failed to follow Emerson's example, to dress his "intellectual processes," the new logic he was devising, in the "material image[s], more or less luminous, aris[ing] in his mind, cotemporaneous with every thought." It is precisely this "spontaneous imagery," as Emerson indicated and William James recognized, that reveals, in making available for one's own and others' reflection and meditation, "the working of the Original Cause," religious/aesthetic experience, as described early in *Varieties*.

Peirce himself acknowledged that in "dwelling so much upon merely logical forms," he was unlikely to reach any but the most astute who had been equally motivated by the impact and implications of the Darwinian information and method to pursue "research into the manner of reality itself," investigating "how and what we think." In comparing his own writing style with that of James, whose words work as the wave packets he imagined, Peirce observed: "I am a mere table of contents, so abstract, a very snarl of twine."[99] Fortunately, William James, one of those few on whom nothing was lost, had been equally unsettled and stimulated by Darwin's work, as were the other members of the Cambridge circle organized in the 1860s and named by Peirce the "Metaphysical Club." Their primary purpose was "how to proceed through the tangle of ideas about evolution"; they "sought to find metaphysical and moral truths not *despite* their interest in Darwinism and other sciences but rather *through* scientific inquiry. Darwin's plausible but unprovable theory of natural selection, with its probabilistic method of explanation, became a focal point for reconstruction of the place of certainty in science and religion."[100] Louis Menand has provided a splendid and comprehensive account of the historical context and concerns of this group and of its central characters, focusing particularly on the Civil War and the challenges posed to belief by the issues involved, with their consequent impact on the development of pragmatism.[101] Earlier, Croce, as noted above, importantly directed close attention to the complex interplay between science and religion in the nineteenth century as it affected the thinking of the major figures of the Metaphysical Club, among whom, as both Croce and Menand discuss, in addition to Peirce and James, Chauncey Wright – like Peirce, another mathematical prodigy – figured centrally. Wright's untimely death in 1875 precluded the possibility of his formally working out and publishing, in the manner of Peirce and James, the ideas germinal to the conversations, which he seems most often to have instigated during the early meetings of the circle, about the "new intellectual style" necessary to the changed environment of uncertainty, the "cosmic weather" as he put it; indeed, in true Emersonian spirit, invoking the "original relation" offered to inquiry by the Socratic model, Wright believed in practicing "philosophy as a conversation,"[102] another habit James would methodically cultivate. (James incorporated "cosmic weather," without attribution or quotation marks, into one of his descriptions in *Pragmatism*.)[103] Wright did publish, however, in 1873, an article in the *North American Review*, the core of which was also of signal concern to James: the will. Notably, it was Darwin, who, equally "impressed by Wright's analytic powers, asked him [in correspondence, as Wright was one of the first, after his teacher Asa Gray, to defend the theory of natural selection] to make clear when a thing may 'be properly said to be effected by the will of man.'" Wright's response was his article, "The Evolution of Self-Consciousness," which Philip Weiner remarked as "his major contribution to scientific psychology – or, as [Wright] called it, psycho-zoology."[104] James attended carefully.

It is unnecessary to rehearse the details covered by Croce, Menand, and Weiner before them, as well as the many others whose work informs these pages; readers not yet familiar with their contributions will, no doubt, following the indications in notes here, go to them. My interest, complementing previous research, is in further elaborating William James's crucial contribution to the development of Pragmatism in his identifying the scientific with religious and aesthetic experience specifically around what he realized as the actual power, energy, of language, in its performative function of translating imagination's products understood as expressions of the fact of feeling. James realized that the mind is tuned by experience in a particular extended moment of spacetime to certain resonant frequencies along which it can receive information. He put Emerson's "temperament" under the microscope, translating its behavior in physiological terms. James understood that in order to adjust temperament, wave bands, nerve pathways, must be re-tracked. In the same way that time was needed for musical performers and audiences during the Baroque period to adjust to hearing as sonorous and pleasing the change from just intonation to equal temperament, the shift in adjusting the instrument of mind would take time and practice.

WILD FACTS[105]

A few months after returning from Brazil, James attended at least one of the lectures on "The Logic of Science" given by Peirce at Harvard and at the Lowell Institute in the mid-1860s; others had been delivered while James was abroad. He reported to his sister late on the night of November 14, 1866: "Where have I been? 'To C. S. Peirce's lecture, which I could not understand a word of, but rather enjoyed the sensation of listening to for an hour.'"[106] Drawn by this "sensation," as by one of the magnets activating his own potential, the "spontaneous imagery" he would later use to describe the effect of abstract ideas in their presentation by Kant and Emerson, James continued to attend assiduously both to learning from Peirce and, significantly, to selecting from his thinking, like a careful breeder, strains he would engraft into his own and cultivate to produce his vigorous hybrid variety. During the winter of 1869–70, in another series of lectures at Harvard, organized by the new president, Charles Eliot Norton, Peirce repeated and elaborated material from the lectures James had missed while in Brazil; these later versions James found more accessible, if still philosophically demanding.[107] Manuscript copies of the lectures, which Peirce continued to work on well into the 1870s, were circulated to members of the Metaphysical Club and excitedly discussed individually and collectively with their author, who drew from his colleagues' comments in shaping the six essays he considered as the basis for a planned book on a logic of probability to supersede the logic of sequence which had been in place, with modifications, since Aristotle. While this book was never completed, out of the conversations generated by the essays crystallized the sought-for new form of thinking: "Much like Ralph Waldo Emerson's reading of 'Nature' at the Transcendentalist Club in the middle 1830s, Peirce's logic papers were a thunderbolt that generalized and highlighted the implications of the perspectives on philosophy and scientific method the group had been grappling with for years . . . Peirce remembered that 'it was there that the name and doctrine of pragmatism saw the light.'"[108] "I used to preach this principle as a sort of logical gospel," Peirce recalled in a later article published in 1908.[109] Revised versions of these papers were eventually published in 1877–8 issues of *Popular Science Monthly* under the title of "Illustrations of the Logic of Science," and have served since as readers' introduction to Peirce's work. (Indeed, Wallace Stevens's father, a subscriber to *Popular Science Monthly*, was among the earliest readers, a fact not lost on his son, as will be considered later.)

James immediately recognized the "cash-value" of Peirce's brilliant adaptation of Darwinian method "to provide the legitimation of beliefs that go beyond the limits of 'one's own ratiocination.'" Peirce demonstrated how – by attending to the elements contributing to statistical patterns in thinking, leading to "common sense"; by sharpening the focus Alexander Bain (like Emerson, another visitor to the James household) had earlier cast on "habit of mind" in its relation to belief and action, and his definition of belief as "that upon which a man is prepared to act";[110] and by "taking advantage of the laws of perception – we can ascertain by reasoning how things really are," as there are "real things" that "affect our senses according to regular laws."[111] While James would never fail to acknowledge Peirce's seminal role in drawing up pragmatism's master-plan and would mindfully practice its aspects as outlined by Peirce (a lesson he had learned from reading Faraday which he later incorporated into *Principles*), he recognized as well that Peirce's Luther needed a Melancthon. As Croce has observed, Peirce, "true to his unteacherly style," himself repeatedly realized "his limits as a popular communicator," commenting again in closing the published essays, that his "reasoning [was] somewhat severe and complicated." In order for the continuing Reformation project to succeed, in order for each individual to be prepared to divine "an original relation to the universe," to justify the ground for "personal religion," the points Peirce outlined would have to be "clarified . . . with metaphor and vivid application."[112] James, "that adorable genius," took on this charge, becoming in his time one of what the Puritan divines called "doers of the word," performing the task of "making the invisible visible."

"[T]aking advantage of the laws of perception" was precisely what James by nature and training was best equipped to do, and in pursuing this end all of the accidents as well as deliberate directions he followed came together to inform his imagination. Predisposed by his father's idiosyncratic educational ideas to entertain and synthesize the varieties of experience to which he had been exposed, William James continued throughout his life to learn from as many sources as were available to him; his brother Henry recalled in 1913, "William, charged with learning – I thought of him inveterately from our younger time as charged with learning."[113] Equally interested in the subjective and objective elements of perception, as he began formulating what it would be necessary to take into account in what would become the chapters of his *Principles*, and as is evident in the encyclopedic nature of his references there, James learned all that was then current not only in neurology, physiology, and psychology, but in optics, electromagnetism, and wave theory. In these last areas, it was the work of Helmholtz he found most useful in providing descriptions that would inform his key notion of *the vague* as both the experience of optimal consciousness and the feature permitting our only access to knowledge of time and space, "[s]ince the essences of things are as a matter of fact disseminated through the whole of time and space." Indeed, it was after studying Helmholtz, using his work on optics as the template for his own larger projected description of the operation of consciousness, that James was able to begin to imagine how this notion would make philosophy useful. Helmholtz's pursuit, aimed at naturalizing and thus simplifying Kant's several kinds of judgment, was to uncover a unified cognitive process, to find a solution answering to "man's lifelong attempt to construct a meaningful world picture not only from his sensations but also from his emotions, fantasies, deductions, unconscious inferences, and memories. In defining cognition as a symbolic construction of reality, Helmholtz launched the modern search for general theories of signs and symbols to account for human understanding."[114] Consequently, as Ross Posnock observes, "by 1879 [James] was able to teach philosophy because he had found a way to conceive of philosophy as a source of stability, like the natural sciences."[115] It should be further observed that James's understanding and delineation of the operation of consciousness, as he would lay out in *Principles*, already provide a comprehensive description of what has been most recently offered as Gerald Edelman's current "break-through" theory of neuronal group selection (TNGS), with the notion of "reentrant signaling" he has advanced as the mechanism for such selection.[116] Just this sentence from *Principles*, for example, contains the essential concept derived from Darwin and Helmholtz, which Edelman's work elaborates: "The definitively closed nature of our personal consciousness is probably an average statistical result of many conditions, but not an elementary force or fact."[117] I shall expand on what I mean here shortly.

Gillian Beer has observed that, "The prevalence of Helmholtzian physiological optics and acoustics as a reference-point in English Victorian intellectual life has received singularly little attention from scholars or theorists."[118] (His "sublime discovery of the conservation of energy . . . in 1847," as remarked by Peirce, has, of course, been widely discussed.)[119] While this is similarly the case for American intellectual life of the same period, William James's familiarity with Helmholtz's contributions, available to him in their original German, as well as through John Tyndall's popular representations of his work beginning in 1867 and later translators' English editions, is especially to be remarked; James had, as well, attended lectures given by Helmholtz. The fact of James's readers not having followed his abundant indications of the significance of this work is surprising, particularly since, as Beer also observes, "By the end of the 1870s Helmholtz is, with Darwin, the recurrent point of reference for writers in *Nature* and *Mind* . . . In the fourth volume of *Mind* (1879), for example, almost all the essays allude to or discuss his work." Moreover, as she also notes, "William James in 'Are we Automata?' refers to 'Helmholtz's immortal work on *Physiological Optics*,'" and "G. Stanley Hall discusses Helmholtz's influence on the philosopher C. S. Peirce."[120]

James's reliance on Helmholtz's lucid descriptions of optical and acoustic wave activity is richly evidenced in *Principles* and central to grounding his chapter on "Attention," the aspect of mind crucial to the understanding of morality which James was at pains to explain in the probabilistic universe he found himself contemplating, urgently so after the crises he had experienced which culminated in his first act of free will. Sharing Darwin's insight into considering free will as the operation of chance on the human scale, James was intent on discovering what the physiology of this experience might be and on making the understanding of it, previously confined to descriptions of theological intervention, available in naturalized terms, in the "exquisite environment of fact . . . of fact not realized before."[121] Through Helmholtz's detailed trackings, James, who never lost the interest in experimenting with batteries and electricity recalled by his brother above,[122] realized that in this environment the human being, "this thought which is called I," is, literally, a "transformer," a receiving instrument, a "vector quantity" in the language of Helmholtz appropriated by Whitehead, who would later be specific: "the human body is to be conceived as a complex 'amplifier' – to use the language of the technology of electromagnetism";[123] "Feelings are 'vectors'; for they feel what is *there* and transform it into what is *here*."[124] By careful tuning, turning through the surrounding hiss and hum, this "I," attending to the pitch and strength of signals "disseminated through the whole of time and space," can find, by a chance turn, free will, the resonant frequency along which a message can be felt "with the force of a revelation": "*The sense-organ must . . . adapt itself to clearest reception of the object, by the adjustment of its muscular apparatus*" (emphasis James's).[125] This conceptualization is a translation into the work of the mind in its play with ideas through words and images of what Helmholtz discovered concerning optical attention, specifically "retinal rivalry."

In the chapter on "Attention," James quotes lengthily a passage from Helmholtz describing how the continual shifting of the eye's focus is prevented by associating "with our looking some distinct purpose which keeps the activity of the attention perpetually renewed . . . *If we wish to keep it upon one and the same object, we must seek constantly to find out something new about the latter*" (emphasis Helmholtz's). James sums up Helmholtz's finding by extending the process to mental activity generally:

> These words of Helmholtz are of fundamental importance. And if true of sensorial attention, how much more true are they of the intellectual variety! The *conditio sine qua non* of sustained attention to a given topic of thought is that we should roll it over and over incessantly and consider different aspects and relations of it in turn.[126]

In the working of the optical system, James realized, lies the explanatory mechanism for imagination, for subjective experience, and the key, as well, to Pragmatism's method where the "truth" that "happens to an idea" depends on hypothesizing an end for the activity of thinking about it, this understanding itself being an adaptation of the method Darwin practiced and illustrated in *Origin*. As Helmholtz further observed: "*we must form as clear a notion as possible of what we expect to see. Then it will actually appear.*"[127] In James's psychologized synthesis, in order for any object of mental vision to be attended to fully, in the "room of the idea," it is first necessary to admit and entertain the motley panoply of characters dressed in flickering, scintillant words and moving images. These are the currents in the stream of one's thought, the residue of experience dressed in the costumes from the wardrobe of the languages available to each individual; the richer and more various the performances of these actors, the greater the possible span of attention as it is turned through the offered spectrum, actually riding the waves firing neural connections, to find a resonant frequency which will, temporarily, close the circuit opened by the initiating interest or stimulus. Finding this frequency is the second stage, directing the actors in a performance convincing enough to produce a belief capable of sustaining action. This space of mental activity James called *the vague* because he properly understood it to be in fact constituted by electro-chemical waves, a particular probability amplitude of stored past experience being stimulated by each new object of attention. From this amplitude the selection made to close the circuit, the response, is an expression of the relation the sensate individual experiences between itself and the universe it inhabits at a moment in spacetime, its morality, following Emerson's definition as being the expressed "relation" between man and nature.[128]

In this realization, of course, James was not alone, "wave action" and "azure" being, as Beer has reminded us, "the stirring topics of then current scientific enquiry," with not only scientists and psychologists immersed in their conceptualization, but writers, poets, and general audiences eager to hear another lecture demonstration about "the real presence of unforeseen phenomena 'out there': singing flames, invisible rays made visible, artificial blue skies."[129] The public was also made aware of the pervasiveness of waves by the press which, after the invention of the telephone in 1876, widely printed patterns made by sound waves.[130] Tyndall, who, like James, found his life's inspiration to investigate and describe nature as miracle in the thought of Emerson (and used a passage from him as epigraph for his most famous essay, "Scientific Use of the Imagination"), was first among those who, in popularizing the astonishing work of Helmholtz, Maxwell, William Thomson, as well as his own on radiation – the polarization of sunlight accounting for the sky's azure – and ice crystallization, consistently attended to the physical properties of words and the activity of imagination as equally participant in the other processes he described. Indeed, he practiced exemplifying the power of language to produce sensible effects. As Beer observes:

Much of the power of his writing came from making visible to the imagination forces beyond the reach of sense . . . his work posed questions about cosmic order and extent. His work on radiation emphasized "the incessant dissolution of limits" (*Fragments*: i. 2). His picturing of the outmost reaches of space was figured as sensation: "It is the transported shiver of bodies countless millions of miles distant, which translates itself in human consciousness into the splendour of the firmament at night" (i. 4). Heat and light are both modes of motion and in the spaces of the universe both classes of undulations incessantly commingle. Here the waves issuing from uncounted centres cross, coincide, oppose, and pass through each other, without confusion or ultimate extinction. Every star is seen across the entanglement of wave-motions produced by all other stars. It is the ceaseless thrill caused by those distant orbs collectively in the ether, that constitutes what we call the "temperature of space." (i, 34)

Beer goes on to note that "Tyndall prefers words that are at once precise, sensational, and evaluative: here, 'thrill' technically signifies penetration and oscillation, and also communicates excitement," and that his "talent for rousing sensation . . . was firmly grounded in materialism," and in the "tendency of [his] rhetoric" for "making visible . . . [t]he idea of the universe as waves, of the parallels between light, heat, and sound, and the single process expressed through them," all "elements of a repertoire shifting across fields" which significantly included language. The multivalent nature of language was now coming to be realized as a prime instance of wave behavior and effect, something that Maxwell also emphasized in his work, being "highly conscious of the changing functions of metaphor as they extend across scientific fields, shifting from technical description toward generalization that allows productive switching to take place between two fields."[131] Tyndall traced this awareness in Maxwell as he shared the concern with shaping new grammar and syntax more adequate to describe "things as they are." It was Tyndall, too, who, in opening his widely read *Sound*, "first published in 1867 and going through numerous editions," pointed out the "aesthetic developments" importantly considered by Helmholtz.[132]

William James was, as is evident in his references, familiar with Tyndall's work as he participated in the spirit of the age to speculate on "the universalizing of wave theory . . . to account for all phenomena" since "Waves were not only the visible waves of the sea, now, but any kind of periodic disturbance in a medium or in space," affecting the intellect[133] and brain matter equally: "It was not easy to know where the application of the principle stopped. It could be made into a description of mind; it could become grounds for spiritualism." Beer cites Walter Pater in *Plato and Platonism* echoing what was in the air: "These opinions too, coming and going, these conjectures as to what under-lay the sensible world, were themselves but fluid elements on the changing surface of existence. Surface, we say; but was there really anything beneath it . . . Was not the very essence of thought itself also such perpetual motion?"[134] James, however, objected in *Principles* to the vitalistic assumption in what he referred to as the "minddust" theory of panpsychism presented by the mathematician W. K. Clifford, an aspect in which he differed from Henri Bergson as well, their premise being that evolution's application to the mind requires that some element of consciousness be present in all matter: "The only thing that we can come to, if we accept the doctrine of evolution at all, is that even in the very lowest organism, even in the Amoeba which swims about in our own blood, there is something or other, inconceivably simple to us, which is of the same nature with our own consciousness."[135] James, again following Helmholtz's important indication that "the impressions of sense are the *signs* of external things,"[136] and combining this observation with what he had learned from Peirce, was coming to understand that the nature of consciousness belongs to the sign system itself, recursively "eddying," as he described in his "Stream of Thought" chapter, each new signal triggering reinforcing flashbacks to associative encoded similarities in neural wave activity, which he paralleled to the overtones and undertones around a musical note and elsewhere to the magnetic field movement of the aurora borealis:

whilst we think, our brain changes, and that, like the aurora borealis, its whole internal equilibrium shifts with every pulse of change. The precise nature of the shifting at a given moment is a product of many factors . . . But just as one of them certainly is the influence of outward objects on the sense-organs during the moment, so is another certainly the very special susceptibility in which the organ has been left at that moment by all it has gone through in the past. Every brain-state is partly determined by the nature of this entire past succession. Alter the latter in any part, and the brain-state must be somewhat different. Each present brain-state is a record in which the eye of Omniscience might read all the foregone history of its owner.[137]

Here James provided descriptions of dimensionalized and moving nonlinear feedforward and feedback loops that drive cognition, recently specified in their mechanism by Edelman's "theory of neuronal group selection" with its "reentrant signaling," used as well by deterministic chaos theorists in relation to information systems:

the brain backdates both action and awareness, that is it draws from memory to predict future circumstances so that it may respond appropriately and in a timely manner in the present moment which it realizes. There is mounting evidence that sensory information and motor plans are indistinguishable in the cortex, suggesting a fusion of present awareness and responsive action, that is action that is future to it. Past, present, and prediction interpenetrate, and become impossible to disentangle in the simplest instances of unself-conscious awareness and instinctual action . . . As events transpire along the arrow of time, the past is altered unpredictably by the present as the strange attractors that access memory are continually modified by new input.[138]

Compare the above, from the most recent literature, to James in 1890:

The natural way of conceiving all this is under the symbolic form of a brain-cell played upon from two directions. Whilst the object excites it from without, other brain-cells . . . arouse it from within. The latter influence is the "adaptation of the attention." *The plenary energy of the brain-cell demands the cooperation of both factors*: not when merely present, but when both present and inwardly imagined, is the object fully attended to and perceived. (Emphasis James's)[139]

In relation to the "aesthetic developments" indicated by Helmholtz as attendant on conceptualizing the activity of optical and acoustic waves, he comments on observing the waves of the sea, large and small, moving forward, back and across, that this "spectacle . . . laid open before the bodily eye what, in the case of the waves of the invisible atmospheric ocean, can be rendered intelligible only to the eye of the understanding, and by the help of a long series of complicated propositions."[140] That "long series of complicated propositions," could be expressed, as James, following Helmholtz, realized, only in some kind of language constituting another invisible atmosphere which nonetheless behaved in the same way. Different patterns of thought were as different waves, superpositions, the determining of which would crest and break, uncertain yet dependent on a critical convergence, where, in terms of meaning and belief, "consciousness and information connect at the level of semantic significance."[141] As James observed:

The simplest thing, therefore, if we are to assume the existence of a stream of consciousness at all, would be to suppose that things that are known together are known in single pulses of that stream. The things may be many, and may occasion many currents in the brain. But the psychic phenomenon correlative to these many currents is one integral "state," transitive or substantive . . . to which the many things appear.[142]

And, further, in two perfectly concise Jamesian phrasings, "the thoughts themselves are the thinkers," and "A word is a conceptual system."[143] In such a system, the imagining of which underpins James's radical empiricism as it does the current radical view of information following developments in quantum mechanics, causal processes and the syntactic and grammatical structures expressing them are seen as only *one species* of information transfer, but it is not expected that all information "connections" will be restricted to such processes.[144] With this apprehension, James would – like Maxwell, who "complained of the want of a 'Grammar of Quaternions' and 'the proper position of . . . Contents, Notation, Syntax, Prosody, Nablady,'"[145] and following "the divine Emerson," with his model "language . . . vehicular and transitive"[146] – call for such a grammar and syntax to begin to take account of "a feeling of *and*, a feeling of *if*, a feeling of *but*, and a feeling of *by*" like the waves of the sea, moving back, forth, and across the mind's object of attention. While within individual sentence boundaries James did not experiment, realizing the processual nature of changing habits of mind and respecting the ingrained habits of his audiences, following from having himself experienced the breakdown resulting from overloading neuronal circuitry with too much new and incompatible information, he did experiment with larger syntactic boundaries with "the eclectic and vivid styles of *Principles of Psychology* and *Varieties of Religious Experience* . . . [in] chaotic and constructive in stimulating ways,"[147] thus illustrating how probability operates in consciousness on a comparatively macrocosmic scale, "revealing the cognitive activity embedded within its structures":[148] "it is in their spread-outness and alteration that he ["[t]he entire man, who feels all needs by turn"] will enjoy them." It would remain for his literary heirs to continue the work at the level of the sentence, while his brother continued to work somewhere in between.

Ross Posnock has observed of Henry James's "enchantment" with *A Pluralistic Universe*, that "Although Henry leaves unsaid what particularly enchanted him, William's plea that we should 'fall back on raw unverbalized life as more of a revealer' of life than concepts would probably have touched a responsive chord in the novelist [*Pluralistic*, p. 121]," and further, that "Henry's application ["rather than simple endorsement" of pragmatism] historicizes William's thought, moving it . . . toward a dialectical fluency alive to creative, experimental action produced by socially committed agents" through the representations of his characters' thinking and behavior, as well as of his own in the prefaces, in his *Autobiography*, and in *The American Scene*.[149] Delineating Henry's application of the philosophy he found himself "unconsciously" practicing all his life, Posnock continues:

> Believing that "only concepts are self-identical," William locates all dynamism in nature: "Nature is but a name for excess; every point in her opens out and runs into the more" . . . [William] insists that if we are really "curious about the inner nature of reality . . . we must turn our backs upon our winged concepts altogether and bury ourselves in the thickness of those passing moments" (*Pluralistic* 112). Henry, however, neither limits himself to imaginative projection nor momentary burial. Instead he chooses a more difficult alternative, one that uses the material medium of language to represent the inner life's thickness . . . He stylistically registers thickness by setting language in motion, creating a ferment of suggestiveness and indeterminacy.

> [Henry] James suspends his will to originate, to order and master, preferring from the start to let impressions fall "into a train of association" . . . His leisurely, meandering sentences embody this train in motion, moving backward and forward, from the "vibrations" of "extreme youth" to the "mere looming mass" of the blank future, yet most intensely receptive, indeed, dependent on the vagaries and improvisations of present flaneries. In other words, the mimetic has begun to act itself out in the style and conduct of James's sentences.[150]

ICH KRYSTALL[151]

In closing this chapter and moving toward Henry James's contribution to fashioning a Pragmatist habit of mind, I shall recall Swedenborg and his angels to offer an imagined lesson in imagining that will illustrate, by way of a forecasting analogue, what Posnock points to above and beautifully phrases elsewhere as the novelist's "mimetic logic."[152] George Santayana observed that William and Henry James "were as tightly swaddled in the genteel tradition as any infant geniuses could be, for they were born in . . . a Swedenborgian household."[153] While Santayana went on to comment that the brothers "burst those bands almost entirely," Henry James was explicit in noting Swedenborg as one of the elements of experience not lost on him. He invoked angels repeatedly in his notebooks, journals, and letters; recorded in *A Small Boy and Others* that the most constant feature of the James family's peripatetic existence was his father's Swedenborg volumes accompanying them everywhere, "forming even for short journeys the base of our father's travelling library";[154] and incorporated a Swedenborgian hero in the character of Lambert Strether as well as Swedenborgian imagery in *The Ambassadors*.[155] And William James realized in Swedenborg's creation of a universe populated and energized by angels with whom he regularly communed one of the most fully articulated and achieved examples of "personal religion." Both brothers knew, as well, of course, of Emerson's recognition of Swedenborg's genius and that Peirce was even more directly affected by him. In addition, as we know, Henry James Sr. read Swedenborg literally and shared his "belief that the physical world possesses a deeper spirituality which is here and now merely clothed in matter," and, like him as well, "envisioned religious truths as empirical facts," and equally "pushed the limits of language's ability to describe the spirit."[156] Further, as Croce has astutely observed, Henry James Sr.

defined the spirit in ways that show a marked similarity to the future pragmatic philosophy of his son William, as the intention or purpose of things as they are used. The son's theory is a secular version of his father's outlook, with psychological rather than spiritual explanation of a larger purpose; yet, in concert with his father's work, William's pragmatism is also a rejection of the strictly factual orientation of traditional empiricism in favor of a focus on practical application and an awareness of the way relations influence perception and meaning.[157]

Extending this perception and connecting it with his own "embrace of the darwinian facts" to include attention to the relation between an individual and its particular environment of space and time in shaping its habit of mind, William James, following Emerson, also recognized in Swedenborg's angelology an accurate metaphorical translation of organic process. Moreover, what Posnock accurately observes concerning the "paradoxical organicism" of Henry James's manner, which Posnock profitably connects with that of Walter Benjamin, seems not at all paradoxical if we imagine the novelist on whom nothing was lost himself imagining, as his brother did, the radiant fiction Swedenborg inhabited. Posnock notes that "James's self-confessed 'habit of finding a little of *all*' his 'impressions reflected in any one of them' . . . has striking affinities with Benjamin's method, which the latter described as the effort at 'discovering the crystal of the total process in the analysis of the small discrete moment.'"[158] Precisely this notion of any form being composed, one would say today "fractally," of increasingly microcosmic iterations of itself is the central trope of Swedenborg's organic cosmology which Emerson was careful to point out in his essay on Swedenborg, quotations from him bracketing his gloss:

"It is a constant law of the organic body, that large, compound, or visible forms exist and subsist from smaller, simpler, and ultimately from invisible forms, which act similarly to the larger ones, but more perfectly and more universally; and the least forms so perfectly and universally, as to involve an idea representative of their entire universe." The unities of each organ are so many little organs, homogeneous with their compound: the unities of the tongue are little tongues; those of the stomach, little stomachs; those of the heart are little hearts. This fruitful idea furnishes a key to every secret. What was too small for the eye to detect was read by the aggregates; what was too large, by the units. There is no end to the application of his thought . . . "Man is a kind of very minute heaven, corresponding to the world of spirits and to heaven. Every particular idea of man, and every affection, yea, every smallest part of his affection, is an image and effigy of him. A spirit may be known from only a single thought."[159]

Emerson was also familiar with the work of Geoffroy Saint-Hilaire, who, extending Baron Cuvier's manner, attempted to understand the whole from an intimate understanding of the smallest fragment, in his theory of analogies illuminating the idea of wholeness through the relation of anatomical parts of diverse organisms.[160] Thus, Henry James's offering that from the observation of the behavior of one of his characters in one scene it would be possible to project a narrative account of the development of the entire personality and William James's central concept of the integral identity of each consciousness are similarly linked to the lessons from Swedenborg informing their father's instruction always "to convert, convert."[161] These insights were linked as well to what they learned from Emerson's translation of the angelic message: to attend to the "luminous material image" appearing in the mind, using it as a key to unlock the door to the "room of the idea" being contemplated, the mystery of one's "interest"– "Interest alone gives accent and emphasis, light and shade, background and foreground – intelligible perspective, in a word"[162] – and thus reveal an aspect of "things as they are" in nature.

There is not space, nor is it necessary here, to detail Swedenborg's universe of angels and its parallels with the developments in crystallography through the nineteenth and into the twentieth centuries. That tracing will be part of a subsequent study, complementary to this one, recursively extending the argument here by increasing the depth of field, returning with narrowed focus to this and other signal moments occasioning the imaginative events which describe the emergence of Pragmatism, realized as itself a self-reflexive, recursive theorizing of the activity of imagination in its essential aesthetic function. The aesthetic functions to restore temporary balance within a system, individually in mind, collectively in a society when the offered imaginative solution, whether in the form of a religious system, poetry, music, or a scientific hypothesis, happens to work in the larger order.

We recall here from the last chapter Haraway's discussion of the crystal metaphor to add:

there are only alternate world views with fertile basic metaphors . . . the fundamental objection raised against a positivist view of science and history has been that inadequate attention is given to the role of metaphor . . . The question ultimately concerns the nature of language . . . Metaphoric systems are the core of structural coherence . . . A metaphor is an image that gives concrete coherence to even highly abstract thought . . . It is important that metaphor be seen as *intelligible*, with real impact and consequences explored by communities sharing the language and image . . . Metaphor is predictive because it is embedded in a rich system not private to any one man . . . Metaphor is a property of language that gives boundaries to worlds and helps scientists using real language to push against these bounds.[163]

Haraway's detailing of the fecundity of the crystal metaphor, which, it will be remembered, even allowed later theorists to recognize in the work of Nehemiah Grew prefigurings of genetic coding, traces the extension of the metaphor to project the continuity between inorganic and organic forms, the essential feature common to all forms – whether mineral, plant, or animal – being tropism, turning toward light: on our planet, the sun. In discussing the work of Jacques Loeb (1859–1924), Haraway notes that he was "tormented by a deep need to resolve the issue of free will and determinism in human action, [and that he] found a solution in his doctrine of animal tropisms, first elaborated about 1880," work with which William James was familiar. For Loeb the idea of "the animal machine" was a "powerful abstraction," of which he observed that its tropisms are "Such determinisms [as] underlie even the most complex phenomena, *including those of that other great abstract entity, the 'will'*"(emphasis mine).[164] The line from Jonathan Edwards's extrapolation of his idea of grace from Newton's work on light, to William James's application of the wave theory, derived from the behavior of light, to the behavior of consciousness, was being drawn, literally, through

crystal: "In the sun's design of its own happiness, As if nothingness contained a metier, A vital assumption, an impermanence, / In its permanent
cold,"[165] Henry James's "frigid vague."[166] Swedenborg's scintillant angels
heralded what was there to be uncovered – in poetic terms, "In the crystal
atmospheres of the mind";[167] in scientific terms, a "demonstrat[ion of] the
role of aesthetic factors in suggesting experimental work and directing its
interpretation."[168]

CHAPTER FIVE

Henry James's more than rational distortion

Then the angel showed me the river of the water of life, bright as crystal, flowing from the throne of God and of the Lamb through the middle of the street of the city.

Revelation, 22:1

Of course, words aren't magic. Neither are sextants, compasses, maps, slide rules and all the other paraphernalia which have accreted around the basic biological brains of *Homo sapiens*. In the case of these other tools and props, however, it is transparently clear that they function so as either to carry out or to facilitate computational operations important to various human projects.

Andy Clark, "Magic Words"

TO THINK IS TO ACT

As much as his brother William, Henry James understood this fundamental of Emerson's "Spiritual Laws," itself an application of what Swedenborg had described as the nature and behavior of his necessary angels. These were not disembodied spirits, but divining insights, communicated "vibrations" embodied in "people" as well as in the other elements of the natural world, which, if attended to, disclose the scaling continuity between the visible and invisible. These insights themselves are angels, revelation unfolding through time, and constitute "heaven." This "angelic wisdom" is experienced as "vision" and communicated in words. As Emerson and William James had realized, Swedenborg's angelology is a cosmology of the linguistic universe, where laws of attraction, polarity, and gravity, in their relation to the "light" contained in both the Book of God and the Book of Nature, operate analogously to those governing the growth and development of all elements in relation to the light of the sun: "The ray of light passes invisible through space, and only when it falls on an object is it seen. When the spiritual energy is directed on something outward, then it is a thought. The relation between it and you first makes you, the value of you, apparent to me."[1]

While the initial interest in Swedenborg might have been prompted by reports circulating throughout Europe during the late eighteenth and early nineteenth centuries concerning his mantic powers – his vision at a distance of the 1759 burning of Stockholm, for instance, which fascinated Immanuel Kant or his prediction of the assassination of Peter III of Russia, as well as of the deaths of other significant political figures, and of his own – more serious consideration was given to him from the middle of the nineteenth century to its end by the increasing availability of translations of his more than sixty volumes of theology and thirty of philosophy and natural history. Kant in Germany, Emerson and Henry James Sr. in America – in spite of the general negative judgment of early-nineteenth-century American readers – and Honoré de Balzac in France recognized, in studying these volumes, that the work the "Prophet of the North" set for himself in the later part of his career was to investigate spirit with the same manner of observation, experimentation, and rigor as would be applied to any other natural phenomenon. Indeed, he denounced and discouraged spiritism, together with ideas of subjective prophecy, as he attempted to uncover an objective basis, following universal laws, for his own "mystical" experience.[2]

A few excerpts from Swedenborg's *Heaven and Hell*, one of the much-thumbed volumes of Henry James Sr.'s traveling library, marked in the imagination of the young Henry with "a sort of black emphasis of dignity,"[3] will serve as backdrop for the scene of attending Henry James in the angelic conversations he enjoyed while developing, executing, and reflecting on what he thought "frankly, quite the best, 'all round' of all [his] productions,"[4] *The Ambassadors*, with its eponymous Swedenborgian hero. Here, then, from *Heaven and Hell*:

The angels all together are called "heaven" because they themselves make heaven.

In the spiritual world each spirit turns himself in the direction of his own love . . . in heaven space is to do with one's inner state, and direction is according to the focus of one's thought . . . a person's love searches deeply into the memory and draws from it everything that is in agreement with the love, gathering and sorting it out for use and rejecting anything that is discordant.

Many people have the mistaken idea that spirits are nothing but disembodied thoughts and feelings but I have never seen anything to suggest this to be so from all my own experience in the spiritual world . . . Angels are people in every sense, and they have faces, ears, bodies, hands and feet, just as people do. They see and hear each other, and they talk among themselves. They lack nothing that a person has, except for one difference; instead of having [only a] material body, angels have a spiritual body that is made up of spiritual substance.

We need to appreciate that people can't see angels by means of their physical senses but only through the eyes of the spirit. This level is in the spiritual world, while everything physical is in the natural world. Like sees like because it is made of similar substance.

[T]he Divine of the Lord is Human in form because it is this that makes heaven . . . The Lord actually appears as an "Angel" in human form to people who acknowledge and believe in a visible Divine but not to people who believe in an invisible Divine.

Since a person is both a heaven in miniature and also a world in miniature, he has a spiritual world and a natural world within him. Everything that occurs on the level of his natural world – his body, its senses and its actions – comes into being from his spiritual world – his mind, its understanding and what it intends – and the two are in correspondence.[5]

Here and throughout *Heaven and Hell*, as well as in his other volumes, Swedenborg variously makes the point that "no one can enter heaven without some concept of the Divine," and that it is the work of angels, in their constant existence and myriad forms, to offer the key permitting entry, the concept. Swedenborg's heaven is immanent, always accessible to those who have received "angelic wisdom." The spiritual world is not an *other* world, but this one perceived in its intensities, seen, as it were, with not only x-ray but all-ray vision. Seeing, understanding, and expressing the correspondences, the relations between all things visible and invisible, constitute the spiritual realm. As Emerson, translating this idea of heaven into that of the transcendental exquisitely observed, "All things swim and glitter."[6] And as Emerson and William and Henry James also understood, as they loosened Swedenborg's cosmology from its theological moorings to restore the idea of "angels" to etymological purity, angels are words, "men made out of words,"[7] words troped, turned in the minds of thinking actors in conversation with them, who *convert* them, both back into the constituent imaginative elements out of which they have been shaped, and forward, projecting their ancient aspects to touch new minds, truth happening to the ideas thus embodied: "It is conversion of all nature into the rhetoric of thought. . . ."[8] Emerson and William and Henry James realized as well that Swedenborg inhabited his heaven and hell, as actually Milton his paradises lost and regained, precisely by transferring into fully imagined fictions both a cosmology and a morality. These fictions offered the possibility of continued spiritual habitation because they were effective mnemonically, literally as *moving* pictures, embodying what Emerson called the "connection between nature and the affections of the soul," "the identity of the law of gravitation with purity of heart."[9] While William James drew on Swedenborg's example to demonstrate the way an individual's local knowledge, when turned on an axis of vision coincident with nature's process, becomes a healthy variety of religious experience, and thereby came to appreciate, at the same time, his father's commitment to communicating what he had learned from the Swedish mystic, in *The Ambassadors* Henry James translated Swedenborg's lesson through what he had learned, turning also to Balzac's *Louis Lambert*, to produce his own fully peopled imagining which could equally serve to represent mnemonically the secular morality he "unconsciously" realized Pragmatism to be. As Ross Posnock has observed,

> A reconsideration of Henry James might begin by recognizing his art as a "process" of "force," for he is above all a believer in "the religion of doing." [James] defines this phrase in an important passage near the end of his final preface:
>> [T]he whole conduct of life consists in things done, which do other things in their turn, just so our behavior and its fruits are essentially one and continuous . . . and so, among our innumerable acts, are no arbitrary, no senseless separation . . . To "put" things is very exactly and responsibly and interminably to do them. Our expression of them . . . belong[s] as nearly to our conduct and our life as every other feature of our freedom.
> This passage better enables us to understand James's famous remark to his brother, after reading *Pragmatism*, that "I was lost in wonder of the extent to which all my life I have . . . unconsciously pragmatised."[10]

The morality of Pragmatism was premised, for both brothers, on an understanding of subjective experience and of language as the life form, the activity, of mindful experience. As John Dewey, later theorizing his variety of pragmatism, which shared central aspects with James's method, would observe, "subjective mind is n[ot] 'an aberration,' as positivism believes, but 'an agency of novel reconstruction' occupying an intermediate position and always situated within a process of inquiry and modification."[11] *The Ambassadors* with its singular point of view offers the paradigmatic instance of this philosophical shift.

Before going on to discuss James's angelic conversations with Swedenborg and Balzac's *Louis Lambert* in relation to *The Ambassadors*, it is useful to consider some of the latest work in cognitive science pointed to by the chapter epigraph borrowed from Andy Clark. The full title of Clark's article is "Magic Words: How Language Augments Human Computation."[12] The research and findings Clark describes complement by experimental extension the signal insights concerning language provided by William James in *The Principles of Psychology*, introduced in the previous chapter and earlier, to be further elaborated in this and following chapters. These insights, as indicated earlier as well, were, for James, part of his spiritual inheritance from Emerson. Indeed, Richard Poirier, responding to a criticism made by Ross Posnock that he had not sufficiently acknowledged Dewey in the pragmatist project of renewing literature, fingered use of language as the feature distinguishing the work of Emerson and William James – and, by extension, Henry James, Robert Frost, Gertrude Stein, and Wallace Stevens – from that of Dewey, and, earlier, Charles Sanders Peirce.[13] It is not that Peirce and Dewey failed to apprehend and foster the view that new ways of managing language were called for in light of the Darwinian information. As noted in the preceding chapter, Peirce was hailed by William James and others as having made the first moves in the language game of pragmatism. What Poirier made clear, however, about Peirce and Dewey is that their writing is not "part of the res," but *about* it.[14] (We recall William James's observation "'about' that, the stolid word *about* engulfing all [the] delicate idiosyncrasies [of "psychic states"] in its monotonous sound.")[15] Language that is "part of the res," like any other part of nature, stimulates wonder, challenges us with questions to which, if we give close attention, we find the answers in ourselves. Reading Emerson, William and Henry James, Stevens, or Stein against Peirce or Dewey makes abundantly clear the difference between language that is pro-*vocative* and language that is not. *The Ambassadors* is a prime and transitional instance of language understood and used this way, pragmatically.

Continuing this chapter's epigraph from Clark to complete his opening paragraph is a listing of analogues for the kind of computational function of language he will detail, the kind of function that both William and Henry James focused on and elaborated in "pragmatising":

The slide rule transforms complex mathematical problems (ones that would baffle or tax the unaided subject) into simple tasks of perceptual recognition. The map provides geographical information in a format well suited to aid complex planning and strategic military operations. The compass gathers and displays a kind of information that (most) unaided human subjects do not seem to command. These various tools and props thus add to generate information, or to store it, or to transform it, or some combination of all three. In so doing, they impact on our individual and collective problem-solving capacities in much the same dramatic ways as various software packages impact the performance of a simple PC.[16]

This listing, pointing to the implications to be explained in Clark's article, fortuitously offers a most apt introduction to Henry James's own "*abracadabrant*"[17] use of language, particularly evident in *The Ambassadors*, which was titled by James sometime after the 1900 titling and rehanging in London's National Gallery of Holbein's *The Ambassadors* (1533), with its extraordinary array of computational instruments displayed on the table extending between the newly named subjects, and with the even more extraordinary blurred image suspended obliquely in the center foreground of the panel, an anamorphic distortion of a skull.[18] The connections between the findings Clark reports and James's use of language will be returned to presently.

Adeline Tintner has already adduced evidence for James's having used Holbein's double portrait as a plane of reference for his novel. She convincingly links the author's unusually delayed titling to the work of Mary Hervey who in 1900 firmly established the identities of the two figures in Holbein's painting, in question until then (it having been thought that the figures represented were Sir Thomas Wyatt and his friend John Leland), as being French ambassadors to the English court of Henry VIII: Jean de Dinteville, Lord of Polisy, and Georges de Selve, Bishop of Lavaur.[19] Tintner comments that, while the panel had been on exhibit at the National Gallery "since 1890 when the Earl of Radnor had, with the help of three wealthy donors, been able to sell the picture to the Nation," it was not until 1900, as a result of Hervey's research, that "it was renamed *The Ambassadors*" and given "a new designation as portraits of the official representatives of French civilization of the Renaissance."[20] Tintner elaborates on James's strong interest in Holbein: he had in 1899 written "The Beldonald Holbein" (published in 1901), based on the painter's portrait of Lady Butts just then acquired by his friend Isabella Gardner; and later, "in 1909 he wrote a play which became a novel, *The Outcry* (1911), to mark the occasion of the rescue of Holbein's *Christina of Denmark* from the clutches of an American millionaire (undoubtedly J. P. Morgan)."[21] From here and from additional points concerning James's penchant for referring to paintings in his titles, Tintner goes on to draw the many parallels between Holbein's pictorial paean to Renaissance France and James's project: "*The Ambassadors* is James's novel of praise of French civilization."[22] Pointing out a series of connections between qualities belonging to the two figures in the painting and qualities belonging variously to Strether and Chad, to Strether and Pocock, to Chad and Little Bilham, and referring to earlier work done by R. W. Stallman on the theme of time in *The Ambassadors*, Tintner argues persuasively for using Holbein's panel as a scrim through which to view James's presentation. In doing this, she focuses on the most striking iconographic feature of Holbein's portrait, the distorted skull, denoting it a *memento mori*, and linking it to James's preoccupation with mortality in the novel:

As death is hidden in the picture, so it is in James's novel. 'Live all you can' for it will be 'too late' if you don't. James says it in the first sentence in the Project for the novel, he writes it in his *Notebooks* [p. 541], and he says it in his letters [*Letters*, vol. IV, p. 194]. It is the main idea in the book and is staged, at the ambassadorial garden party given by Gloriani, in Strether's advice to Little Bilham. Death behind the idea of *carpe diem* stalks the book.[23]

James notes this as the theme once again and finally in his preface added to the 1909 New York edition. What Tintner, and all later interpreters of the novel, including Hazel Hutchison in the most recent analysis of the parallels between James's novel and Holbein's panel, and, importantly, *Louis Lambert*,[24] fail to tease out of their otherwise astute observations, however, are the many implications of anamorphosis, the optical trope employed by Holbein in his depiction, which, like Poe's purloined letter, has remained in full view but unnoticed. This trope, the "more than rational distortion," *par excellence*, was not lost on James who in his preface folded its implications, laid bare in his imagination, back into his own language game, brilliantly played in his fiction. Tintner and other readers have similarly failed to give attention to the controlling navigational metaphor deployed by James throughout the novel and foregrounded in his preface in connection with the instruments displayed in the Holbein panel.[25] In relation to both these aspects, considered generally before scrutiny is given to their elements, the findings provided by Clark are especially instructive.

Clark's work, expanding on that of earlier and contemporary researchers, including Lev Vygotsky, Laura Berk, Peter Carruthers, Paul Churchland, and Daniel Dennett, is to demonstrate the structural features, "external formalisms" of what he calls "public language," language that comprises the "general strategy of 'mentally modelling' the behaviour of selected aspects of our environment [which] is especially important insofar as it allows us to imagine external resources with which we have previously interacted, and to replay the dynamics of such interactions in our heads."[26] This is an "idea of language as a computational transformer which allows pattern-completing brains to tackle otherwise intractable classes of cognitive problems" based on studying the "powerful links between speech, social experience and learning."[27] The role of language understood in this way "is to guide and shape our own behaviour – it is a tool for structuring and controlling action and not merely a medium of information transfer between agents."[28] We recall William James's observation in *Principles*, "to sustain a representation, to think is, in short, the only moral act,"[29] and Henry James's "Thinking is the only morality," and earlier, Emerson's "What is the hardest task in the world? To think."[30] The sustaining of a representation is expressed in its "external formalisms," its syntax and grammar, its "vehicular" function in Emerson's terms, its "transitive aspects" in those of William James. Drawing on the findings of fellow researchers, Clark observes that "such external formalisms are especially hard to invent and slow to develop, and are themselves the kinds of product which (in an innocently bootstrapping kind of way) can evolve only thanks to the linguistically mediated processes of cultural storage and gradual refinement over many lifetimes."[31] As Alfred North Whitehead earlier observed:

Human life is driven forward by its dim apprehension of notions too general for its existing language. Such ideas cannot be grasped singly, one by one in isolation. They require that mankind advances in its apprehension of the general nature of things, so as to conceive systems of ideas elucidating each other. But the growth of generality of apprehension is the slowest of all evolutionary changes.[32]

Clark's observation neatly rephrases one of the central strands of the argument being made in the present study, first articulated in Chapter 2, illustrating the way in which Jonathan Edwards's internalization of Newton's descriptions of the behavior of light fitted and altered the template offered by Scripture in the manner of the "imperfect replication" that is the mechanism of evolution. (See particularly pp. 31–44.) Additional examples of such "cultural storage and gradual refinement" examined here earlier are Emerson's appropriation of Faraday, Lyell, Swedenborg and others, as well as William James's of Bunyan's transmutation of Scripture and his incorporation of the work of Helmholtz. (See pp. 112–16.) Citing the findings of colleagues, Clark notes that all depict "language as a key element in a variety of environmentally extended computational processes," and commenting on an example particularly useful for this discussion in relation to James's navigational metaphor in *The Ambassadors*, offers the following:

This notion of computational processes inhering in larger systems (ones that may incorporate the activities of many individual biological brains) is further developed and defended in Hutchins (1995). Hutchins offers a beautiful and detailed treatment that highlights the ways representation may flow and be transformed within larger, socially and technologically extended systems. Hutchins' main example involves the way maps, instruments, texts, and vocalisations all contribute to the complex process of ship navigation: a process that is best analysed as an extended sequence of computational transitions, many of whose roles is to transform problems into formats better situated to the perceptual and pattern-completing capacities of biological brains. The environmental operations thus *complement* the activities of biological brains.

. . . what is most important . . . is not to try to answer the question, "do we actually think *in* words" (to which the answer is "in a way yes, in a way no"!) but to try to see what computational benefits accrue to biological pattern-completing brains in virtue of their ability to manipulate and sometimes model external representational artefacts.[33]

Henry James's preoccupation with the location of consciousness, especially evident in his late work, has been explored by several readers, most specifically by Sharon Cameron in *Thinking in Henry James*.[34] No reader, however, has discussed James's choice of metaphors for representing, particularly in *The Ambassadors*, his perceptions concerning the nature and operation of consciousness as elaborations of those used by his brother in *Principles*. In the context of the findings noted by Clark in relation to the "notion of computational processes inhering in larger systems . . . that may incorporate the activities of many individual biological brains" as exemplified in the "complex process of ship navigation," it is important to consider: a) in William James, his key figure of the "stream of thought"; his central interest in and use of the idea of the "vague"; his realization, offered in opening the "Stream of Thought" chapter, that a more accurate expression of the activity of thinking in relation to language would be to say "it thinks" (rather than "I think" or "he thinks") coupled with his later interest in psychical research; his comparison, later in the "Stream of Thought" chapter, of the movement of thought to "a bird's life" with its alternating "flights" and "perchings"; and his adaptation, as described in the preceding chapter here, of Helmholtz's work on optical activity for understanding the activity of consciousness; together with: b) in *The Ambassadors*, Henry James's pervasive use of the trope of navigating a vessel of some sort on a stream, river, in a current, at sea (connected with this figure, as well, are figures of mooring, bridges, sinking, shipwreck, the "abyss"); the dominant use of the word "vague" with its variations of "vaguely," "vagueness," "waves" and "wavering," these uses (57 in 329 pages,[35] excluding the plays on "waves," cresting in the Eighth, Ninth, Eleventh and Twelfth Books, with 8, 6, 6, and 9 uses respectively); his use of "itself" to refer to Strether's image of himself in his "real youth";[36] his use, as well, intermittently throughout, of images of flights and perchings;[37] and his equally pervasive use of words and metaphors connected with light, seeing, to disclose a "process of vision," all, most significantly, varieties of "revelation."

This last point, as will be demonstrated in the pages following, provides the beautifully articulated "story of [the] story itself" suspended "in blurred view,"[38] unless seen from a particular point of view – like the skull in Holbein's panel – full center in James's novel, a "story" whispered as though by Swedenborg's angel from one of the "improvised perches" James remembered his father's volumes occupying.[39] Discovering the location of this point of view discloses James's "process of vision," "the story of [the] story," the art transforming the elements of perception and vocabulary he shared with his brother into one of the fictions we know to be a fiction but believe in willingly because it helps us live, adjust to a new environment of fact, acquiring, in learning its language, a computational instrument complementing and amplifying our cognitive capabilities, "a tool for effecting changes in [our] environment."[40]

THINKING ABOUT THINKING

Of special interest in relation to the art of fiction, as paradigmatically conceived by James, is research cited by Clark which finds that "self-directed speech (be it vocal or silent inner rehearsal) [is] a crucial cognitive tool that allows us to highlight the most puzzling features of new situations, and to direct and control our own problem-solving activity." This kind of "linguistic understanding . . .'consists in a grasp of the causal relations into which linguistic signs may enter'" derived from "tak[ing] very seriously the evidence of our own introspection."[41] Here we recall John Locke's pointing, as discussed in Chapter 2 (pp. 47–8), to some future *semiotike* for language abstracted from the manner of musical notation, as well as Jonathan Edwards's self-reflexive treatise on "The Mind," one of the first steps following that pointing. We recall, as well, Emerson's direction for abstraction – "A man conversing in earnest, if he watch his intellectual processes . . ." – and William James's accounts in *Principles* of the neuronal effects of verbal repetition and silent rehearsal. The activities thus described direct attention to the sign system itself, to the "relations into which linguistic signs may enter," above, as it were, or beyond, the communicative, information transfer, function of language. The mental space created by this kind of contemplation is not linear but n-dimensional, connections radiant, multiple, constellated, superpositioned, a "sea of spuming thought,"[42] requiring navigation – bearings, sightings, occulting lights, soundings: "All *felt* times coexist and overlap or compenetrate each other thus vaguely . . . All real units of experience *overlap*."[43] Navigating this mental space, plotting observations, charting the movement of his mind in it, is Henry James's singular writing project.

Significantly, it is on the process of writing that Clark, incorporating the work of other scientists and philosophers, focuses. Citing the work of

Carruthers and Dennett in their elaborations of Vygotsky, Clark notes that "Carruthers suggests 'one does not *first* entertain a private thought and *then* write it down: rather, the thinking *is* the writing,'" and adds that "we can better understand this insight 'by treating writing as an environmental manipulation which transforms the problem space for human brains.'"[44] Elaborating this point, Clark observes:

> It is natural to suppose that words are always rooted in the fertile soil of pre-existing thoughts. But sometimes, at least, the influence seems to run in the other direction. A simple example is poetry. In constructing a poem, we do not simply use words to express thoughts. Rather, it is often the properties of words (their structure and cadence) which determine the thoughts that the poem comes to express. A similar partial reversal can occur during the construction of complex texts and arguments. By writing down our ideas we generate a trace in a format which opens up a new range of possibilities. We can then inspect and re-inspect the same ideas, coming at them from many different angles and in many different frames of mind. We can hold the original ideas steady so that we may judge them, and safely experiment with subtle alterations. We can store them in ways which allow us to compare and combine them with other complexes of ideas in ways which would quickly defeat the un-augmented imagination. In these ways . . . the real properties of physical texts transform the space of possible thoughts.[45]

Contrasting Dennett's theory that the transformation effects "a profound but subtle re-organisation of the brain itself," Clark offers that this kind of language use is "in essence an external resource which complements – but does not profoundly alter – the brain's own basic modes of representation and computation."[46] It functions, in other words, as a prism or lens:

> like a perceptual modality, it renders certain features of our world concrete and salient, and allows us to target our thoughts (and learning algorithms) on a new domain of basic objects. The new domain compresses what were previously complex and unruly sensory patterns into simple objects. These simple objects can then be attended to in ways that quickly reveal further (otherwise hidden) patterns, as in the case of relations-between-relations.[47]

Clark further observes that "for certain very abstract concepts, the *only* route to successful learning may go via the provision of linguistic glosses. Concepts such as charity, extortion and black hole seem pitched too far from perceptual facts to be learnable without exposure to linguistically formulated theories."[48] In addition, as noted above, the repeated rehearsal of linguistic glosses (whether in writing or in vocal or silent inner rehearsal) becomes a "crucial cognitive tool that allows us to highlight the most puzzling features of new situations, and to direct and control our own problem-solving actions."[49] The novelist who observed that "Really . . . relations stop nowhere,"[50] and that "Our expression . . . belongs as nearly to our conduct and to our life as every other feature of our freedom," had clearly realized as he repeatedly rehearsed and revised his sentences to express "a feeling of *if,*" "a feeling of *and,*" "a feeling of *but,*" "a feeling of *by,*" what cognitive science currently confirms, that, "Much of the true power of language lies in its underappreciated capacity to re-shape the computational spaces which confront intelligent agents."[51] As Clark details,

> By "freezing" our own thoughts in the memorable, context-resistant and modality transcending format of a sentence we thus create a special kind of mental object – an object which is apt for scrutiny from multiple cognitive angles, which is not doomed to alter or change every time we are exposed to new inputs or information, and which fixes the ideas at a fairly high level of abstraction from the idiosyncratic details of their proximal origins in sensory input. Such a mental object is . . . ideally suited to figure in the evaluative, critical and tightly focused operations distinction of second-order cognition. It is an object fit for the close and repeated inspections highlighted . . . under the rubric of *attending* to our own thoughts . . . Language stands revealed as a key resource by which we effectively redescribe our own thoughts in a format which makes them available for a variety of new operations and manipulations. [Emphasis Clark's][52]

Henry James, of course, shared such understanding with his brother; we recall from the preceding chapter William James, recuperating what he had learned from Kant and from Emerson, observing, "Our conceptions always require a sense-content to work with, and as the words 'soul,' 'God,' 'immortality,' cover no distinctive sense-content whatever, it follows that theoretically speaking they are words devoid of any signification. Yet strangely enough they have a definite meaning *for our practice*. We can act *as if . . .*" (p. 116 above). William and Henry James, Emerson, Henry James Sr., Jonathan Edwards had all been prepared, through practicing or witnessing varieties of religious experience, to realize the action potential contained in language when repeatedly rehearsed and attended in the "room of the idea."

    Moreover, in hypothetically conceiving of language as the vehicle of the activity of consciousness, enabling its existence as a life form outside of, yet participated in and constituting, individual minds, William and Henry James anticipated current findings in another way, though as discussed in Chapter 3, Emerson had earlier begun to articulate suggestions of this insight, sharing as he did so many crucial sources with Darwin, who extrapolated from the manner of language development and variation the pattern for what would become evolutionary theory (pp. 81–97). Late in his life Henry James in his speculative "Is There a Life after Death?" offered:

What had happened, in short, was that all the while I had been practically, though however dimly, trying to take the measure of my consciousness . . . I had learned, as I may say, to live in it more . . . I had doubtless taken thus to increased living in it by reaction against so grossly finite a world – for it at least *contained* the world, and could handle and criticise it, could play with it and deride it, it had *that* superiority: which meant, all the while, such successful living that the abode itself grew more and more interesting to me, and with this beautiful sign of its character that the more and the more one asked of it the more and the more it appeared to give. [Emphasis James's][53]

William – "The thought is the thinker" – and Henry James were addressing precisely "the question" currently investigated by Clark and others, "of where the mind ends and the rest of the world begins . . . the question [of] how to conceive and locate the boundary between an intelligent system and its world."[54] As Clark observes, evidencing the rightness of perceiving Henry James's work in language as a living "process," a "force," "Our biological brains, after learning, expect the presence of text and speech as much as they expect to encounter weight, force, friction and gravity. Language for us is a constant, and as such can be safely relied upon as the backdrop against which on-line processes of neural computation take shape and develop."[55] We recall James's reflecting in his preface on the manner in which the "story" formed itself around the "hint" at its "centre": "the 'story,' with the omens true . . . puts on from this stage the authenticity of concrete existence. It then *is*, essentially – it begins to be" (emphasis James's).[56]

Underpinning Henry James's realization after reading *Pragmatism* that he had "all his life . . . unconsciously pragmatised" was what he had learned from his own practice in and with language. As Clark states, "profoundly, the practice of putting thoughts into words alters the nature of human experience."[57] The description Clark gives of the manner of this alteration, in technical language the operation of *second-order cognitive dynamics*, provides an explanation of the basis of Pragmatism understood, properly, as a moral activity, and, as I have been suggesting, as continuing the work of the Reformation;[58] it is this kind of activity Henry James recognized as his "unconsciously pragmatis[ing]" in composing his complex linguistic universe. Noting the complementary work of Jean-Pierre Changeux and Derek Bickerton, Clark offers:

By second-order cognitive dynamics I mean a cluster of powerful capacities involving self-evaluation, self-criticism and finely honed remedial responses. Examples would include: recognising a flaw in our own plan or argument, and dedicating further cognitive efforts to fixing it; reflecting on the unreliability of our own initial judgements in certain types of situations and proceeding with special caution as a result; coming to see why we reached a particular conclusion by appreciating the logical transitions in our own thought; thinking about the conditions under which we think best and trying to bring them about. The list could be continued, but the pattern should be clear. In all these cases, we are effectively thinking about our own cognitive profiles or about specific thoughts. This "thinking about thinking," is a good candidate for a distinctively human capacity – one not evidently shared by the other, non-language-using animals who share our planet. As such, it is natural to wonder whether this might be an entire species of thought which is not just reflected in, or extended by, our use of words but is directly dependent upon language for its very existence. Public language and the inner rehearsal of sentences, would, on this model, act like the aerial roots of the Mangrove tree – the words would serve as fixed points capable of attracting and positioning additional intellectual matter, creating the islands of second-order thought so characteristic of the cognitive landscape of *Homo sapiens*.

It is easy to see, in broad outline how this might come about. For as soon as we formulate a thought in words (or on paper), it becomes an object for both ourselves and for others. As an object, it is the kind of thing we can have thoughts about. In creating the object, we need have no thought about thoughts – but once it is there, the opportunity immediately exists to attend to it as an object in its own right. The process of linguistic formulation thus creates the stable structure to which subsequent thinkings attach.[59]

Further elaborating how "linguistic formulations . . . import genuine novelties onto our cognitive horizons," "mak[ing] new thoughts available by effectively freezing other thoughts as types of static object," Clark distinguishes the function of linguistic expression from that of "images" which "are not so easily traded in public exchange": "the value of linguistic formulations (especially in written text) . . . consists . . . in their amenability to a variety of operations and transformations that do not come naturally to the biological brain working in a non-linguistic mode."[60] It is easy to see the connection here with William James's figure of the "cash-value" of ideas expressed as the "currency" of a particular time, location, and situation. A further parallel can be drawn between James's famous description of Pragmatism as "old wine in new bottles" and Clark's observation that the computational operation of public language "involves the use of the same old (essentially pattern-completing) resources to model the special kinds of behaviour observed in the public linguistic world . . . the same old process of pattern completion in high dimensional representational spaces . . . applied to the special domain of a specific kind of *external* representation,"[61] a new relation. And, in connection with the ongoing iconoclasm of the Reformation project, breaking images down into the fluent purity of linguistic analogues, we recall that Emerson's singular criticism of Swedenborg's system of correspondences concerned precisely the fixity of his symbols. Emerson's purpose, in contrast, was to shift the focus to the "vehicular," transitive nature of words, to imagining imagining itself as the ongoing activity of divinity available to each individual who learns to "watch his intellectual processes," to translate what is thus seen, the "luminous material image," into idiomatic linguistic formulations "blending . . . experience with the present action of the mind."

Henry James's "religion of doing" was "to watch his intellectual processes" and transform them into the characters of secular miracle plays where, in place of a Bible story or story of a saint's life, it is "the story of [the] story" of the mind's work in and through words that constitutes the plot and provides the moral lesson. As such, a James novel might be thought of as performing the office of a breviary naturalized to teach us, silently reciting its orders, how to live, what to do, in realizing ourselves to be not specially created but, simply and yet more wonderfully, a language-using species on the planet, as Darwin described. Of course, one of the most difficult aspects to accept in this realization is the accidental nature of the emergence and continuing existence of our species, as well as of all else, in what Peirce described as a "universe of chance." A religion, a philosophy, capable of shifting from belief in a divinely determined order, progressing to an ultimate and just good, to belief in believing itself as the sole mechanism ordering the system inhabited and constituted by the language-using species we happen to be would have to instruct its practitioners repeatedly and in various ways in the fundamental law of this reality, this nature reconceived: that its process is not linear and teleological but stochastic and plural, and that the human mind is both contributing part and particle of this multiform process, itself the agent providing direction by selecting, at each instant, among the myriad possibilities scattered, one course of action. As William James observed in *Principles*, "To be able to banish this 'scattered condition of mind' is to possess a precious faculty": the ability to "voluntarily bring back a wandering attention . . . [This] is the very root of judgment, character, and will";[62] "by attending" to focus on what is of interest from an "indistinguishable swarming continuum, devoid of distinction or emphasis . . . as a sculptor works on his block of stone";[63] and again in *The Will to Believe*, "By 'picking out what to attend to, and ignoring everything else,' the mind reveals its partiality, which is a condition of its efficiency."[64]

Henry James's addition to his brother's work was to script the performance of these abstract, once thought divinely inspired, activities for actors dressed in the clothes they were used to wearing in late-nineteenth-century America's changing scene. In the place of, say, an image of saints climbing a ladder to join the angels in heaven who will reveal, as on a Byzantine icon, the answer to the eternal question "What is this mystery in me?" Henry James illustrates, especially in his later novels, how words behave like the angels described by Swedenborg, like crystals, by attraction, accreting into patterns hovering above the narrative of the text, carrying the possibilities offered to the minds of his characters and his readers, meaning, the truth that happens to ideas in the ever-changing environment of fact. This feature of James's style, abundantly evident in *The Ambassadors*, reveals aesthetic experience as a variety of religious experience, illustrated through James's incorporation of Swedenborg in the person of Lewis Lambert Strether.

The process Clark describes above as *second-order cognitive dynamics* involves the conversion of "complex and unruly sensory patterns into simple objects" that then serve to "reveal further (otherwise hidden) patterns, as in the case of relations-between-relations"; to repeat, "Public language and the inner rehearsal of sentences, would, on this model, act like the aerial roots of the Mangrove tree – the words would serve as fixed points capable of attracting and positioning additional intellectual matter, creating the islands of second-order thought so characteristic of the cognitive landscape of *Homo sapiens* . . . The process of linguistic formulation thus creates the stable structure to which subsequent thinkings attach." It is exactly the operation of this process that James exaggerates in *The Ambassadors*, where, throughout the narrative, certain repeated words form constellations floating above the surface of the text, "fixed points capable of attracting and positioning additional intellectual matter." Following the movements of these constellations enables the reader to navigate the "stream" of "the story of [the] story." "Vague" with its variants, as well as the many words associated with navigation, with flights and perchings, and "seeing" have already been noted; in addition, "conscious" with its different forms, including "conscient"; "present" with its variants; "type"; "matter"; "relation/s"; and the myriad uses of words having to do with time – all combine kaleidoscopically on almost every page of the novel. These "complex and unruly sensory patterns" resolve into "simple objects" that "reveal further . . . patterns" in our minds as the maps of "relations-between-relations," once we, as readers, indeed, become Strether, assume his singular point of view as a voyeur of his mind's life, watching through a keyhole, one eye of his "double consciousness" squeezed shut, so as to be able to resolve, "justif[y] to his own vision,"[65] the "blurred view" of his confused present situation, itself a product of his perception of the past. Other current research in language and memory not mentioned by Clark, but similarly building on the insight of Vygotsky and William James "that all the higher mental abilities of humans are actually socially constructed habits scaffolded by language," "has now made it abundantly clear that our recollections are never literal replays of moments of experience, but rather perceptual reconstructions. Granted, our mental images usually capture the gist of an event; but it is a warped, foreshortened, edited, glossed-over, view of what happened."[66] In the context of the narrative, Strether's "blurred view" becomes an analogue for the identity he has constructed as a result of "the period of conscious detachment occupying the centre of his life, the grey middle desert of the two deaths, that of his wife, and that, ten years later, of his boy"[67] hanging, until his "revelation," in his mind's foreground, yet "(otherwise hidden)" in the same way as the blurred image of the death's head in Holbein's panel.

Further, as critical readers, repeatedly imitating the activity of trying to resolve "the complex and unruly patterns" of James's stylistic distortions in our silent performances of the text, we also, over time, become Henry James, imagining him imagining. Although, at first, reading James is like experiencing a "blurred view" of sense in a language with which we are not yet fully conversant – much like Strether's experience of French would have been – with moments of vagueness hovering between sentences and their comprehension, we gradually learn, by interpolating probable calculations and following cues, in a process of second-order cognition, to extend the structural limitations of translation, which equals the time it takes to see, to understand. Through the "hunt" for meaning over time, matching the segments of James's vision, stretched anamorphically in the structural grid of his syntax and "story," the experience of difference between the consciousness of the reader and the author's consciousness, the "vision" embodied by the text, is collapsed, paradoxically reversing the experience of time, the theme of both the "story" and "the story of [the] story" of *The Ambassadors*. By following James's direction, assuming his point of view, death is resolved into a secularized, pragmatic understanding of the human experience of time, a playing out of the understanding beginning to be explored during the period of his late work.

It should be recalled that James composed the prefaces for the New York edition between 1907 and 1909, when the investigations of non-Euclidean geometries and the fourth dimension explored late in the nineteenth and into the first years of the twentieth centuries were complicated by speculations concerning time by figures such as Henri Poincaré, Henri Bergson, and Charles Howard Hinton – the last two of whom were correspondents of William James. These topics were part of the cultural conversation conducted in the reviews and journals to which Henry James was a regular contributor, the kind of publication, with its pale green cover, of which Lambert Strether is editor ("an expensive Review, devoted to serious questions and inquiries . . . all the colleges, all the cultivated groups scattered about the country take it in and esteem it. It goes to Europe – where they believe it to have attracted attention in high quarters").[68] The news of these significant challenges to inherited notions of space, time, and perception was certainly not lost on James, who, it should also be recalled, entered his late phase just as his friend H. G. Wells published "The Time Machine" (1895) and "The New Accelerator," with "their vividly imagined, almost cinematic descriptions of altered time,"[69] stories seemingly informed by William James's extraordinary "Perception of Time" chapter in *Principles*; Henry James was particularly engaged by "The Time Machine." Holbein's anamorphically blurred image in the foreground of his *Ambassadors* displayed, with an ironic skill James would have recognized, the epitome of pictorial representational possibility offered by the cumulative knowledge of the painter's moment, figured metaphorically in the panel by references to the liberal arts and to the major religious debate surrounding the Reformation, as well as by the various instruments depicted. The navigational instruments enabling the computational advances permitting the Renaissance discovery of the New World and its mappings in Mercator projections also permitted the rendition of the stretched perspective of Holbein's skull. It is not surprising that James would have recognized his *Ambassadors*, with its stretching of perspective, as "the best . . . of all [his] productions." The computational advance to thinking offered by his sentences parallels that offered to navigation by the instruments arrayed in Holbein's painting, while implicit in James's hero's consciousness is the accumulated knowledge of his moment, inflected by proliferating religious uncertainties as the Darwinian information set man, already uneasily displaced by the Copernican revolution, from the center of creation, now at an angle oblique to it. *The Ambassadors* epitomized the possibility of linguistic representation for and of James's time, a "present" most significantly reconceived. James anticipated, in the way he described Strether's perception of self, the "historical drift" of being taking account of time, the reality of the fourth dimension, understood in terms of human phenomenology as a form of anamorphosis, psychological anamorphosis.[70] Quite coincidentally, John Updike, in a recent review of Colm Toibin's fictional account of James's late phase, *The Master*, describes, with his own novelistic insight into his and James's perceptions of time, "the non-writing Henry," his "haunt[ing]" the facts of his lived past and his productions, "with a luminous blur of a face."[71]

THE ABSENCE OF IMAGINATION HAD ITSELF
TO BE IMAGINED[72]

Before continuing with the consideration of the elements of James's style in *The Ambassadors* as linguistic analogues for pictorial anamorphosis, giving attention to the term "anamorphosis" itself yields insight. Deploying it in the manner of a "magic word" "generate[s] a trace . . . open[ing] up a new range of possibilities" for imagining the "pleasure" James describes in his preface as deriving from the retrospective recognition, in his "hunt" for Lambert Strether, of all that was initially "unseen and . . . occult" as the "story"[73] shaped itself around the words eddying into pools in his stream of thought. While, according to the second edition of *Webster's New International Dictionary*, the term properly refers to "an image produced by a distorting optical system or by some other method which renders the image unrecognizable unless viewed by the proper restoring device," its meaning in biology is, "A gradually ascending progression or change in form from one type to another in the evolution of a group of animals or plants," and its meaning in botany is, "A monstrous development or violent change of form in an organ." Its meaning in biology connects it more precisely to its derivation from the Greek *anamorphoun*, "to form anew." In regard to the anamorphic image, in the absence of the "proper restoring device," either a convex mirror or a mirrored cylinder, needed to resolve the distortion, it is necessary that the beholder's point of view be almost parallel to the picture plane and at an approximate angle of 135 degrees from the center of the image. Alternatively, the ideal view is through a keyhole. Only, in other words, by occupying Lambert Strether's point of view, the singular point of view from which the story is related, oblique to but parallel with the actions of the other characters, or by watching the action of his mind through a metaphorical keyhole, can the reader resolve his "double consciousness" into focused understanding. Moreover, only by occupying Henry James's point of view, "the story of [his] story," oblique to but parallel with Strether's "story," can the reader uncover the motive, the "turn of the screw," propelling James's craft in *The Ambassadors* through the stream of thought. To see from Strether's point of view, and then from James's, requires the reader to abandon "normal" reading practices and learn entirely new ways of engagement with the text, voyeuristic in allowing access to knowledge usually hidden. The reader, like the best of ambassadors, must learn a new language, attend most carefully, pick up clues, observe foreign protocols, spy, if necessary, into hidden chambers. James's implicit demand on his reader neatly parallels what Stephen Greenblatt marks as the demand made on the viewer to see the *memento mori* in Holbein's panel: "To see the large death's head requires a still more radical abandonment of what we take to be the 'normal' vision; we must throw the entire painting out of perspective in order to bring into perspective what our usual mode of perception cannot comprehend"[74] – "as quite at an angle of vision as yet untried," as James himself directs in his preface.[75] James forces us to take a position oblique to the meaning of his sentences or to squint at them with one eye shut, and thus lose the binocular perspective of narrative. We are cast out of the garden of meaning, out of Emerson's "field": "The field cannot be well seen from within the field."[76] We must learn, as it were, to fly above it. This point will be returned to later.

The alternative to inhabiting Strether's consciousness is to find or fashion a "proper restoring device," to turn the mind reading into a mirrored cylinder able to reflect James's motive, to participate in what Posnock has termed James's "mimetic logic."[77] The best way to construct such a device is to follow James following his own "interests." Here, recalling William James's noting, in *Principles*, Helmholtz's contribution to the understanding of perception is useful:

Helmholtz says that we notice only those sensations which are signs to us of *things*. But what are things? Nothing, as we shall abundantly see, but special groups of sensible qualities, which happen practically or aesthetically to interest us, to which we therefore give substantive names, and which we exalt to this exclusive status of independence and dignity. But in itself, apart from my interest, a particular dust-wreath on a windy day is just as much of an individual thing, and just as much or as little deserves an individual name, as my own body does.

. . . The ethical energy *par excellence* has to go farther and choose which *interest* out of several, equally coercive, shall become supreme. The issue here is of the utmost pregnancy, for it decides a man's entire career. [Emphases James's][78]

Since we know that one of Henry James's interests during the time of preparing *The Ambassadors* for publication was Holbein's panel, and since we know too that James figured the fiction maker as one "on whom nothing is lost," it is safe to assume that he was attracted by the notion and process of anamorphosis, central as it is to the work from which he borrowed the title of his novel. He would have been most delighted to uncover, in the later "'hunt' for Lambert Strether" that he reflects on in his preface, the parallels of his "process of vision" with that embodied by Holbein's anamorphic projection.

Strether's preoccupation with the idea of how he could have lived had he time – effectively a *memento mori* – distorts the values with which he arrived in the Old World and at the same time marks a "progression or change in form from one type to another in the evolution of [the New World] animal" he represents, as much as it is, from the point of view of Mrs. Newsome and those she stands for, "a monstrous development [, a] violent change" in him as the organ of her sensibility, editor of the pale-green-covered journal she publishes. At bottom, beneath these variants, is the fact that Strether is "formed anew" in and by his experiences as ambassador; there is a change in the "organ" of his consciousness. He is anamorphic. Following the turns of his consciousness as it is presented by James, our consciousness is shaped into the "proper restoring device." As we interpret, we perform the undistorting function, engage in his "mimetic logic," see the art of vagueness. This inverts the process James writes of as his "'hunt' for Lambert Strether," creating his narrative out of "describing the capture of the shadow projected by [his] friend's [Jonathan Sturges's] anecdote" concerning himself and William Dean Howells in a Paris townhouse garden where Howells gave to Sturges the advice Strether gives to Little Bilham. James elaborates on the pleasure of this activity: "No privilege of the teller of tales . . . is more delightful, or has more of the suspense and the thrill of a game of difficulty breathlessly played, than just this business of looking for the unseen and the occult, in a scheme half-grasped, by the light or, so to speak, by the clinging scent, of the gage already in hand."[79] Strether exemplifies I. A. Richards's ideal metaphor, the vehicle transforming the tenor of his author's perception into a reader's understanding. Further, James's later reading of his tale, with *it*, the instrument he had himself devised as "the gage . . . in hand," reflects more of what even to him would have been "unseen and . . . occult" when it was first set down, a practical revelation of mimetic feedback.

The *Oxford English Dictionary* provides additional specific botanical definitions of "anamorphosis" useful in considering James's hero. The entry begins: "Such a degeneration or change in the habit of a plant from different conditions of growth, as gives it the appearance of a different species or genus; abnormal transformation. Chiefly said of cryptogams, as fungi, lichens, and sea-weeds." "Cryptogams," last in the Linnaean sexual system, are plants without stamens and pistils and therefore without proper flowers, plants such as mosses, fungi, algae, as noted above. They are, nonetheless, sexual, though, because of their apparent lack of the usual equipment, covertly so, as their name denotes, "hiddenly married/*gameted*." It is not difficult to see in this designation a bearing on Strether's representation and action in the novel. His sexuality is as ambiguous as the anamorphic skull in Holbein's panel. His son dead, he has no issue, no "flower." It is assumed that his relation with Mrs. Newsome is not physical, although it is as if in his engagement to her he is hiddenly married, at least until the scene of his conversion in Gloriani's garden. From this point on it is as if he secretly plights his troth to Madame de Vionnet. But haunting all his experience is death: "The picture of the stage was now over laid with another image"; "It was at present as if the backward picture had hung there, the long crooked course, grey in the shadow of his solitude."[80]

What does it mean to be preoccupied with death? Intimations of mortality are legion in the literature and painting of the Western tradition, to the point of being read as clichés. They are intimations because death can never be experientially described – a banal but nonetheless useful observation. The realization that death cannot ever be described, in great measure, impelled, as discussed in the preceding chapter, William James's exploration of *The Varieties of Religious Experience*. In his analysis of the function of the anamorphic death's head in Holbein's *Ambassadors*, Greenblatt continues to provide a guide for the present address:

In "The Ambassadors" . . . death is affirmed not in its power to destroy the flesh, or as is familiar from late medieval literature, in its power to horrify and cause unbearable pain, but in its uncanny inaccessibility and absence. What is unseen or perceived as only a blur is far more disquieting than what may be faced baldly and directly, particularly when the limitations of vision are grasped as *structural*, the consequence more of the nature of perception than of the timidity of the perceiver. [Emphasis Greenblatt's][81]

In terms of "structural" "limitations of vision" concerning death, "perceived as only a blur," James's *Ambassadors* can be read as an attempt to deconstruct the cliché notion of what death means back into its elements, to effect the ultimate "re-instatement of the vague to its proper place in our mental life." This kind of analysis demands close attention to precisely what James "discloses" as the "process of vision" framed in his understanding and imagining of this process in the actualities of his moment. In this context, there is a most revealing description of himself offered in *Notes of a Son and Brother*, recalling the experience of sharing a room with William in Boulogne during the period when the older brother's interests shifted from art to science, and all manner of experiments with galvanic batteries, electric shocks, photography, and drugs were constant (see also pp. 113–14): repeatedly, as Henry remembered, there would be "prolonged exposure, exposure mostly of myself, darkened development, also interminable, and *ubiquitous brown blot*" (emphasis mine).[82] Later in *Notes*, he elaborates the suggestion of the photographic effect of light on a plate, a metaphor in the spirit of Henry Fox Talbot's "Pencil of Nature," to describe the process and result of being receptive to experience: "The effect of one's offering such a plate for impressions to play on at their will."[83] And earlier, in *A Small Boy and Others*, he speaks of "reconstituting as I practically am the history of my fostered imagination."[84] Noteworthy, too, is that throughout the volumes comprising the *Autobiography*, variations on the word "vague" are as preponderant as they are in *The Ambassadors*. It is easy to imagine the fascination of both brothers with the process of development, seeing the vague "brown blot" of the photographic negative gradually revealing what had been captured, from a singular point of view, so miraculously, from waves of light. It is, on the other hand, difficult to imagine, without a "proper restoring device," how this process operates, as well, in and as consciousness; the investigation of this process continues to be pursued by current researchers, most notably by Francis Crick and Christof Koch as recapitulated in Koch's *Quest for Consciousness*, and by Oliver Sacks as described in his "In the River of Consciousness" and in "Speed: Aberrations of Time and Movement."[85]

James's language use provides a necessary instrument for this investigation, illustrating the manner in which, over time, from vague impressions develop representations of reality recognized and used as "true" signs of things seen in the light of the mind, "reconstituting" the "I" as "the history of . . . fostered imagination." Early on in his career, James observed that "literary topics would largely gain if writers would wander as far afield in search of a more rigorous method," as had "Professor [John] Tyndall" in giving attention to "the habit of accurate thought." Reviewing an 1871 volume of Tyndall's, James continued to quote from the scientist whose work, as noted in the previous chapter, was equally important to his brother William:

> "The mind," he [Tyndall] excellently says, in his recent "Fragments of Science," "is, as it were, a photographic plate, which is gradually cleansed by the effort to think rightly, and which, when so cleansed, and not before, receives impressions from the light of truth." This sentence may serve at once as a . . . text for remark on the highly clarified condition of . . . intellect. The reader moves in an atmosphere in which the habit of a sort of heroic attention seems to maintain a glare of electric light.[86]

Extending the structural limitations of vision, to provide additional perches on which to rest and observe "this thought which is called I," "the nothing that is" – to borrow the latter phrase from Stevens[87] – in the absence of any metaphysical explanation, was and continues to be the purpose of psychology as conceived by William James and practiced, even before it was named, by Henry: "I had never heard of psychology in art or anywhere else – scarcely anyone then had; but I truly felt the nameless force at play."[88] As both realized, the greatest challenge for "the nameless force" was, and remains, how, in the face of death, without promise of reward or threat of punishment in an afterlife, to shape the "I" – nothing more, in fact, than a habit of mind produced by neuronal currents, a record of thought – into a moral being. Strether, *tether*ed in the *stream* of this thought, *stretch*ed between the fact of his inherited values and his feeling for, his turning toward, the light that Paris symbolizes, is James's "Everyman" in the miracle play first performed not long after God had disappeared from the stage. How to account, without God, for the human "process of vision," for being "face to face"[89] always with the unknown, with death, while still inhabited by the ghostly forms of inherited belief, and desiring to cleanse the mind of their shades, was the problem of the age, experienced and explored by James's hero.

In spite of his initial hesitation, expressed in the "Project of Novel," about choosing Paris, because of its hackneyed use, as the scene for his action, precisely because it is the "City of Light" (originally "Lutetia," capital of the tribe of Parisii), it offered the perfect setting for disclosing Strether's "process of vision," as James later recounted in his preface, the ideal site for a modern allegory of illumination, a secular book of revelation. Strether is guided from the outset by the totally modern but nonetheless angelic Maria Gostrey – "She is inordinately modern, the fruit of actual, international conditions, of the growing polyglot Babel. She calls herself the universal American agent. She calls herself the general amateur-courier," and lives in "her world of reverberations," "full of divination."[90] As the angel necessary for America, she leads him to *go stray*, to stretch his tether until it doubles back on itself like a thinned thread looping into a figure eight, the figure of infinity. Following the "thread" she offers and is, the *ficelle*, Strether will find his way out of the American cultural labyrinth in the center of which the "monstrous haunting image"[91] of Mrs. Newsome waits to devour him. He will come *to see* in Gloriani's garden, at sea in the stream of thought in which he had always been afloat, yet which he had never before been aware of, *it*, the stream. "If we could say in English 'it thinks,' as we say 'it rains' or 'it blows,' we should be stating the fact most simply and with the minimum of assumption. As we cannot, we must simply say that *thought goes on*" – Thus, we recall, did William James introduce "The Stream of Thought" chapter in *Principles*, the core of his brilliant elucidation of the complex emergence of selfhood as the activity of continuous discrimination, steering this way and that in the currents and eddies of the stream: "Consciousness, from our natal day, is of a teeming multiplicity of objects and relations, and what we call simple sensations are results of discriminative attention, pushed often to a very high degree."[92] Henry James dressed this understanding in his modern allegory where Strether is a cipher for the activity his brother theorized, fully elaborating what Emerson had described in "Self-Reliance," the relation of the particle that is "I" to the wave that is society: "Society is a wave. The wave moves onward, but the water of which it is composed does not. The same particle does not rise from the valley to the ridge. Its unity is only phenomenal. The persons who make up a nation to-day, next year die, and their experience dies with them."[93]

Adopting Henry James's navigational troping for negotiating the *stream of thought* offers an interpretative approach to reading pragmatically. Following the indications provided by the variety of computational instrumentation metaphorically implicit in his language, we register the facts impinging on his voyage into his fiction, the invisible world of spirit: " . . . it had been a frank proposition, the whole bunch of data, installed on my premises like a monotony of fine weather."[94] Navigating in this way through James's novel directs attention back again and more fully to Holbein's *Ambassadors* as well as to the other important current running through the fiction maker's stream, Honoré de Balzac's *Louis Lambert*, whose name and spirit Lewis Lambert Strether takes, transforms, and adds to, anamorphically.

In the first two paragraphs of his preface, James provides two unmistakably nautical metaphors; the first, the second sentence: "The situation involved is gathered up betimes, that is in the second chapter of Book Fifth, for the reader's benefit, into as few words as possible – planted or 'sunk,' stiffly and saliently, in the centre of the current, almost perhaps to the obstruction of traffic."[95] The second comes in the middle of the second paragraph and refers to the actual "germ" that was to gestate in the master's imagination to become the novel. This was the conversation referred to earlier, related to him by Jonathan Sturges, a younger man, who had himself been one of the subjects of this interchange with William Dean Howells, described as having taken place in "a charming old garden attached to a house of art, and on a Sunday afternoon in summer" in Paris: "There it stands, accordingly [this "germ" or "note absolute"], full in the tideway; driven in, with hard taps, like some strong stake for the noose of a cable, the swirl of the current roundabout it."[96] In navigating, one is forced constantly to make choices, course corrections, between one direction and another, while always keeping the desired destination in mind. These choices, moreover, depend on triangulation and time, with repeated bearings having to be taken that are oblique to the course, the vessel, the "subject." In this projection, the "subject" is regarded simultaneously as object, from, that is, the still point used as determining pivot for measurement, whether star, sun, light signal, or headland. The navigator plots his course on a chart after recording his observational measurements; on the chart his craft is seen as if from a bird's-eye view, as though from flying above. Navigating is a perfect metaphor for what both Henry and William James understood to be the work of "Man Thinking," Emerson's sharp, thumb-nail description of what the Jameses would understand as "a Pragmatist." The navigational trope works especially well as an interpretive device in considering the central scene in Gloriani's garden. James denoted this scene the "note absolute," the anchorage of thought, because it holds, "imparadised," the impression from the past which is the still point providing necessary bearings, the condition of perception, the past, the invisible spouse joined in hidden marriage to every moment of present seeing. The nature of this experience is greatly illuminated by looking at two passages from *Principles* where William James accounts for the urgency *to place* the objects of our sensations; in extracts in the remainder of this chapter, italics indicate original author's emphases, bold-face mine:

Consciousness . . . cannot properly be said to *inhabit* any place. It has dynamic relations with the brain, and cognitive relations with everything and anything. From the one point of view *we* may say that a sensation is in the same place with the brain (if we like), just as from the other point of view we may say that it is in the same place with whatever quality it may be cognizing. But the supposition that a sensation primitively *feels either itself or its object to be in the same place with the brain* is absolutely groundless, and neither *a priori* probability nor facts from experience can be adduced to show that such a deliverance forms any part of the original cognitive function of our sensibility.

Where, then, do we feel the objects of our original sensation to be?

Certainly a child, newly born in Boston, who gets a sensation from the candle-flame which lights the bedroom, or from his diaper-pin, does not feel either of these objects to be situated in longitude 71 degrees W. and latitude 42 degrees N. He does not feel them to be in the third story of the house. He does not even feel them in any distinct manner to be to the right or the left of any other sensations which he may be getting from other objects in the room at the same time. He does not, in short, know anything *about* their space-relations to anything else in the world. The flame fills its own place, the pain fills its own place; but as yet these places are neither identified with, nor discriminated from, any other places. That comes later. For the places thus first sensibly known are elements of the child's space-world which remain with him all his life; and by memory and later experience he learns a vast number of things *about* those places which at first he did not know. **But to the end of time certain places of the world remain defined for him as the places *where those sensations were;* and his only possible answer** to the question *where anything is* will be to say "*there*," and to name some sensation or other like those first ones, which shall identify the spot.

. . .

The first sensation which an infant gets is for him the Universe. And the Universe which he later comes to know is nothing but an amplification and an implication of that simple germ which, by accretion on the one hand and intussusception on the other, has grown so big and complex and articulate that its first estate is unrememberable. In his dumb awakening to the consciousness of *something there*, a mere *this* as yet (or something for which even the term *this* would perhaps be too discriminative, and the intellectual acknowledgment of which would be better expressed by the bare interjection "lo!"), the infant encounters an object in which (though it be given in pure sensation) all the "categories of understanding" are contained. *It has objectivity, unity, substantiality, causality, in the full sense in which any later object or system of objects has these things.* Here the young knower meets and greets his world; and the miracle of knowledge bursts forth, as Voltaire says, as much in the infant's lowest sensation as in the highest achievement of a Newton's brain. The physiological condition of this first sensible experience is probably nerve-currents coming in from many peripheral organs at once. Later, the one confused Fact which these currents cause to appear is perceived to be many facts, and to contain many qualities. For as the currents vary, and the brain paths are moulded by them, other thoughts with other "objects" come, and the "same thing" which was apprehended as a present *this* soon figures as a past *that*, about which many unsuspected things have come to light.[97]

Henry James navigated the stream of thought with seemingly infinite, almost hypersensible semantic and syntactic adjustments. Obeying what *felt* right, following what he and William called *interests*, as though sensing the wind shift slightly and so tapping the rudder with an adverb or tense variation, Henry used this formless, vague sensation his brother describes above as his still point. Negotiating a successful passage means endless choices, the "discriminative attention" that is "consciousness." "Pushed . . . to a very high degree" consciousness becomes morality: "We select by these constant course corrections the sensations we shall have." This realization is what lies behind Henry James's identification of thinking with morality. "These verily are the refinements and ecstasies of method – amid which, or certainly under the influence of any exhilarated demonstration of which, one must keep one's head and not lose one's way. To cultivate an adequate intelligence for them and to make that sense operative is positively to find a charm in any produced ambiguity of appearance that is not by the same stroke, and all helplessly, an ambiguity of sense."[98] As William James observed, "The ethical energy *par excellence* has to go farther and choose which *interest* out of several, equally coercive, shall become supreme. The issue here is of the utmost pregnancy, for it decides a man's entire career."[99] With this understanding William James established feeling as a legitimate basis for thought and action: "Each of us literally *chooses*, by his ways of attending to things, what sort of universe he shall appear to himself to inhabit."[100] Whitehead made this grounding in feeling explicit, adding a scientifically respectable term to James's perception: "Feelings are 'vectors'; for they feel what is *there* and transform it into what is *here*."[101] Interestingly, the latest work in neuroscience has integrated this understanding into its vocabulary, substituting "valuation" and "affect" for the earlier "feeling."[102] Admitting feeling, sensation, as a determinant of an informed morality was, James realized, the natural consequence of coming to terms with the Darwinian information. As he took pains to elaborate fully in his *Principles*, all of the categories of understanding and judgment on which reasoning depends are nothing more than generalizations of successful instinctual animal behavior made over millennia and all having sensation as their origin:

Conceptual systems which neither began nor left off in sensations would be like bridges without piers. Systems about fact must plunge themselves into sensation as bridges plunge their piers into the rock. Sensations are the stable rock, the *terminus a quo* and the *terminus ad quem* of thought. To find such termini is our aim with all our theories – to conceive first when and where a certain sensation may be had, and then to have it. Finding it stops discussion. Failure to find it kills the false conceit of knowledge.[103]

In *A Small Boy and Others*, Henry James notes the impulse lingering in his autobiographical project to be his "instinct to grope for our earliest aesthetic seeds."[104] Both he and his older brother knew that the Greek root of "aesthetic" is the verb meaning "to perceive, to feel." The difference between the "Project" and the completed novel of *The Ambassadors* is feeling, sensation, "fused into one with it [the "Project" with its "germ"] and . . . become bone of its bone and flesh of its flesh; leaving, it is true, an image of the same *thing* it was before, but making it an image of that thing newly taken and freshly understood."[105] As James synecdochally notes in connection with Strether's relation to Mrs. Newsome in a postscript added to the "Project" and, like it, addressed to his publisher:

Only the difficulty with one's having made so very full a Statement in the present is that one seems to have gone far toward saying *all*: which I needn't add that I haven't in the least pretended to do. Reading these pages over, for instance, I find I haven't at all placed in a light what I make of Strether's **feeling** – his affianced, indebted, and other, consciousness – about Mrs. Newsome. But I need scarcely add, after this, that everything will in fact be in its place and kind.[106]

Elsewhere he particularizes again:

I reiterate these things here on Strether's behalf, in order to intensify the fact that, as he acts now, he does so on full reflection. What this reflection, roughly stated, amounts to then is: "No, I'll be hanged if I purchase the certainty of being coddled for the rest of my days by going straight against the way in which all these impressions and suggestions of the last three months have made me feel, and like to feel, and want to feel."[107]

James describes in the preface that the work of the novel is to explore what is for Strether the virgin continent of feeling that he discovers on his voyage out of what was for him America's ethical and cultural nothingness, a place still puritanically denying the moral valence of sensation, the all-important knowledge the body can provide. It is not for nothing that this information comes to Strether in a garden and that implicated in it is Madame de Vionnet – like Milton's serpent, "subtlest creature."[108] It is also not for nothing that the recognition scene occurs in another garden, that of the Cheval Blanc. It is here where the "story of [his] story," oblique to the plane of the double portrait of Strether and Chad Newsome, is revealed through a beautifully hidden reference to Swedenborg. This scene of revelation thus presented works in the same way as in certain anamorphic Renaissance panels, where simultaneous planes of sacred and profane pictorial representations are depicted, flickering in their alternative visibility.[109]

THE ONE CONFUSED FACT WHICH THESE CURRENTS CAUSE TO APPEAR IS PERCEIVED TO BE MANY FACTS

Recalling Henry James's memory of his father often reading to him and his siblings from the Old and New Testaments, we might imagine how stirring an image, especially for the child who early on recognized his pleasure in visualization, this verse from Revelation, 19:11, would have been: "And I saw heaven opened, and behold, a white horse . . ." We might equally imagine the novelist's later pleasure in contemplating Swedenborg's gloss on this verse in *Apocalypse Revealed*, one of the more popular of his volumes:

A "horse" signifies understanding of the Word, and "a white horse" interior understanding of it . . .; and as the spiritual sense is the interior understanding of the Word, therefore that sense is meant here by "the white horse" . . . Everyone who does not think beyond the literal sense believes that when the last judgment comes, the Lord will appear in the clouds of heaven with angels and the sound of trumpets. But what this means is that He will appear in the Word . . . ; and in the spiritual sense, He is very clearly disclosed . . . the interior understanding of the Word is signified by "the white horse."[110]

In the context of Strether's story, the "interior understanding" that comes to him in the garden of the "White Horse" is recognizing that he will not be able himself to pursue an intimate relationship with Madame de Vionnet because of the now unavoidable acknowledgment of the physical nature of the relationship between her and Chad, the information that, as an ambassador inquiring, literally, into foreign affairs, he has been sent to gather. His acceptance of what this information means for him is the culmination of a "process of vision" – *heaven opened* – itself disclosed in the City of Light, a secular version of the New Jerusalem described in Revelation 21:11 as a city of light: "her light was like unto a stone most precious, even like a jasper stone, clear as crystal." In the context of James's "story of [the] story," it is precisely what Swedenborg means by "the interior understanding of the Word" that signals what James will shape into a new vulgate for experience in a post-Darwinian creation. The nature of this kind of understanding was nowhere better illustrated, before James, than in the character from whom he borrows the name for his hero, Balzac's Louis Lambert.

There are obvious threads borrowed from the "story" of *Louis Lambert* embroidered into the "story" of *The Ambassadors* giving both shade and shape, beginning with the autobiographical features shared by each author in relation to his main characters. Expanding on what Quentin Anderson first noted, it is enough simply to list them, as the deeper interest for the present study is the "interior understanding" of James's "story of [the] story" embodied in Balzac's representation in the character of his Louis Lambert of what I have called earlier Swedenborg's "linguistic cosmology." The threads are: a young man from a provincial background, orphaned, finds himself for three years in Paris, pursuing "son éducation morale"[111] amidst "la civilisation parisienne,"[112] supported by an inheritance; his uncle, his guardian, having a weakness for him, has reluctantly allowed him to stay; the young man has learned to eschew "toute entreprise mercantile";[113] deeply aware of his "double existence,"[114] his "double nature,"[115] the youth comes to enlightenment aided by women, early on an older woman, Mme. de Stael, later a younger, who functions for him like an angel, "un ange-femme,"[116] her surname, "Villenoix," a kind of anagrammatic template for "Vionnet." (There are, in addition, curious accidental affinities between aspects of Balzac's character and aspects of Henry James Sr.'s history, such as the disparagement of bourgeois values noted above; the detail presented in the novel's third sentence, that the Old and New Testaments fell into Louis Lambert's hands at the age of five, and that "this book, in which are contained so many books, decided his destiny";[117] the profound involvement with Swedenborg. There is, too, the similarity between Balzac's hero and William James: as a young man with a passion for science, beginning to explore the nature of the spirit, Louis Lambert, sensing a vertiginous pull, realizes he needs the protection of some system and so composes a "Treatise on the Will."). While in Balzac's hand these threads shape a story distinctly different from James's "story" of *The Ambassadors*, the device of the earlier story, emblematized in the name of Lewis Lambert Strether, is suspended, a monitory shadow in the midst of James's frame: Louis Lambert, a man made wholly out of words, to whom revelation comes through a woman, does not consummate a physical relationship with her, but instead attempts to castrate himself, falls into seeming madness and eventually dies; in his madness, he phrases profound moral perceptions concerning will, substance, language, and thought. The lesson as presented by Balzac is ambiguous since the *ange-femme*, Pauline de Villenoix, remains with and cares for Louis Lambert as his spiritual wife, seeing the "angelic wisdom" in his utterances, which she transcribes until she can no longer understand them. The narrator offers these transcriptions as aphorisms at the novel's end.

Balzac leaves ambiguous whether Lambert's seeming madness represents an excess or a deficiency of consciousness, though the suggestion is that his hero is not truly mad but has transcended the terrestrial world and realized a higher plane of vision accessible only to those who, like his *ange-femme*, have similarly attained the "angelic wisdom" that comes from attending to the "interior understanding" of words. The question of whether or not he is mad circles around whether he has, in the manner of his master, Swedenborg – whom he calls the "Buddha of the North" ("Swedenborg sera peut-être le Bouddha du Nord"[118]) – resolved the central problem of the "double movement" of his consciousness, strained between fascination and communion with words. Either he has attended to ascending assiduously by degrees along the scale of similarity to become, as it were, "the best thing by far," as Aristotle observed, "a master of metaphor," discriminating identities among the names of things to see their underlying processual unity. Or he has lost himself along the way, drawn into the abyss of the endless multiplicity of words when cut off from the subjective apprehension of meaning derived from translating them through his own experience. The closing aphorisms mix spiritist paraphrase with keen insight, suggesting that Balzac's hero had not learned the constraint of system elaborated by Swedenborg, who anticipated, in this system, the dialectic underpinning structuralism, with, in addition, the advantage of an organic genetic model.[119] Nonetheless, because of the observations and comments made by Balzac's narrator – originally a classmate of Louis Lambert's, sharing his interests – throughout the narrative, both what is valuable and what is problematic in following Swedenborg's vision are presented.

Early on the narrator recalls a central lesson he and Louis Lambert learned while boys at school together from one of their masters: the lesson concerned "the different effects produced by words with each different hearing or understanding. The verb has nothing of the absolute: we act on the word more than it on us; its power is in proportion to the images which we have acquired and are able to group."[120] Here were Saussure's signified and signifier already at play, Mallarmé in the wings, and Roman Jakobson's metaphoric/metonymic grid a century in the future. The ongoing conversations between the students concerning the nature of thought and language together with the narrator's reflections on them constitute the greater part of the narrative; subjects touched include: the materiality of thought; the translation into words of vision; the consideration of intelligence as a purely physical phenomenon; the relation of time and place to temperament; the nature of will. While all of these conversations and speculations would, of course, have held interest for James, familiar to him in many of their contours from the non-fictional grapplings of Emerson and his brother William, aspects of the significant issues foregrounded within Balzac's fictional frame informed both Lewis Lambert Strether's "process of vision" and his own as a novelist.

How to account for and describe what one sees when it is unseeable, except in the space of mind, and in the absence of a metaphysical explanation, is the aspect most prominently foregrounded by Balzac. The attempt to express what is seen with the complex of feelings attendant on the attempt, is, of course, the informing motive of the central texts belonging to all varieties of religious experience. Within this attempt Balzac offers particular insights concerning the power of words, both through the meditations of Louis Lambert and the narrator, and through the relations of his characters, including the *ange-femme*, performing as allegorical representations of this power. For Louis Lambert, "Will and Thought are *living forces* . . . Thought is visible and tangible, slow or quick, ponderous or agile, clear or obscure," and apparent in all human activity, directed through "les bizarreries de notre langage."[121] The force of an individual's will and thought increases in proportion to the attention given to the ongoing work that Mallarmé would describe as "purifying the language of the tribe," showing words to be the only angelic messengers: heaven, as Swedenborg wrote, the angels themselves, words. For Jonathan Edwards, this was the work to be accomplished in the "room of the idea." The recognition of one angelic nature by another in the context of Balzac's incorporation of

Swedenborg's linguistic cosmology is an analogue for a reader's response to a text as something "true," what Emerson described as recognizing our own best thoughts in another's "genius," the same impulse prompting conversion for members of Edwards's congregations through the hearing of a particular word or phrase in a sermon. As Emerson described, this kind of experience collapses time:

> The human mind wrote history, and this must read it . . . There is a relation between the hours of our life and the centuries of time. As the air I breathe is drawn from the great repositories of nature, as the light on my book is yielded by a star a hundred millions of miles distant, as the poise of my body depends on the equilibrium of centrifugal and centripetal forces, so the hours should be instructed by the ages and the ages explained by the hours. Of the universal mind each individual mind is one more incarnation. All its properties consist in him. Each new fact in his private experience flashes a light on what great bodies of men have done . . . The fact narrated must correspond to something in me to be credible or intelligible. We, as we read, must become Greeks, Romans, Turks, priest and king, martyr and executioner; must fasten these images to some reality in our secret experience, or we shall learn nothing rightly.[122]

Ongoing participation in this activity is an ascent, with flights and perchings on higher domains, intellectual phase transitions marked by quickened mental acuity, increasing clarity of vision, stimulated, as Swedenborg and Edwards figured, by turning ever closer to the Light, figure of the Godhead. From Plato's figuring of the feeling of fledgling wings sprouting in the *Phaedrus*, through Dante's figuring of Beatrice's function, to Balzac's of Louis Lambert, and to James's of Lewis Lambert Strether, the attraction, disequilibrium, identification, and transcendence offered by the metaphor of love provide analogues for this spiritual scintillation:

> In the spiritual world each spirit turns himself in the direction of his own love . . . in heaven space is to do with one's inner state, and direction is according to the focus of one's thought . . . a person's love searches deeply into the memory and draws from it everything that is in agreement with the love, gathering and sorting it out for use and rejecting anything that is discordant.

How to instruct others in a world without divinity, without catechisms and priests, in this purified, secular variety of religious experience, where consciousness itself takes the place of conscience, constituted the projects of both William and Henry James. As Wallace Stevens observed, "The death of Satan was a tragedy / For the imagination."[123] How was this fall to be redeemed? In place of "empty heaven and its hymns,"[124] Henry James showed the way in which imagination itself works, imagining imagining his revelation.

One of Louis Lambert's central illuminations defines Apocalypse as a "written ecstasy" ("L'Apocalypse est une extase écrite").[125] Elsewhere, feeling drawn toward a brilliant inner light, he realizes his purpose in being to develop the texts to be found in himself, as himself.[126] The method he pursues, following from his early delight in reading the dictionary, is to "voyage" through language, "embark on a word into the depths of the past, like an insect on a blade of grass floated by the will of a stream."[127] He speculates what will be revealed in this "written ecstasy":

What a beautiful book could be composed in recounting the life and adventures of a word . . . to consider it, an abstraction made of its functions, of its effects and actions, isn't this to fall into an ocean of reflections? Aren't most words colored by the ideas that they represent outwardly? . . . The assemblage of letters, their forms, the shape they give to a word, design exactly, following the character of each people, unknown beings whose memory is in us. Who will be able to explain philosophically the transition from sensation to thought, from thought to verb/word, from verb/word to its expression as hieroglyph, from hieroglyphs to alphabet, from alphabet to written eloquence, whose beauty resides in a train of images classed by the rhetoricians, which are like hieroglyphs of thought? Wasn't it the ancient/archaic painting of human ideas configured as zoological forms that served as the first signs used in the Orient to write its languages? Hasn't this [ancient/archaic painting] over time ["traditionellement"], then, left some vestiges in our modern languages, which divided among themselves the fragments ["débris" = Emerson's "scoriae"] of the primitive verb/word of nations, majestic and solemn verb/word, of which the majesty, the solemnity, diminish as societies grow older; with the sounds so sonorous in the Hebrew Bible, so beautiful as well in Greece, weakening, growing faint, through the progress of our successive civilizations? Isn't it to this archaic/ancient Spirit that we owe the mysteries hidden in each human utterance ["parole"]? . . . Isn't it thus with every word? All are impressed/imprinted with a living power which they hold of the soul, and which they restore through the mysteries of the marvelous action and reaction between word and thought. Doesn't one say of a lover that he draws from the lips of his mistress as much love as he communicates to her? By their unique physiognomies, words bring to life again in our brain the creatures for whom they serve as vestments. [Emerson, "vestment of that thought"] As with all beings, there is a particular place where their properties are able to act fully and develop. But this subject suggests a science of its own![128]

In spite of his insight, Louis Lambert fails to achieve the "written ecstasy" of "Apocalypse." Unconstrained by the self-reflexive anchorage of thought that the act of writing would have provided, he floats off on the stream into madness, unable "to sustain a representation" of the order he sees. Curiously, neither did Balzac attempt to implement his vision into the structure of his novel. Henry James, however, provided in the layered structure of his prose in *The Ambassadors* a prime representation of language itself becoming the "subject" which would demand "a science of its own," foregrounding in his stylistic devices the way in which sensation becomes thinking and a basis for belief, how "truth is what happens to an idea." Here, returning to consider the constellations of words that move above the surface of his text will serve as illustration.

There is not space to list all instances of the major themes, the figures, as it were, pictured by these constellations of words. Nor is it possible to reproduce my copy of the text with these words circled on every page. Readers will no doubt have underlined or noted some of these repetitions themselves. I shall, then, offer only a sampling of salient instances demonstrating how Henry James managed, with his "refinements and ecstasies of method," to add dimensions to written language, stretch its capacity to represent the invisible reality of the mind's work in its function of locating itself in the actual spacetime of its existence and deriving, from that multi-dimensional plotting of constantly changing present location, a continuous amplifying of what William James denoted as "*there*," an informed indication for future direction, a morality, a secular apocalypse.

Earlier in the discussion the concept of time as the fourth dimension was presented as part of "the whole bunch of data" Henry James would have "installed on [the] premises" of his imagination. Taking account of time as the fourth dimension in human experience required a fundamental shift in perception and consequent change in the manner of representation. As Sir Arthur Eddington in *The Nature of the Physical World* (1938) lucidly explains:

Our knowledge of space-relations is indirect, like nearly all our knowledge of the external world – a matter of inference and interpretation of the impressions which reach us through our sense-organs. We have similar indirect knowledge of the time-relations existing between the events in the world outside us; but in addition we have direct experience of the time-relations that we ourselves are traversing – a knowledge of time not coming through external sense-organs, but taking a short cut into our consciousness. When I close my eyes and retreat into my inner mind, I feel myself *enduring*, I do not feel myself *extensive*. It is this **feeling of time** as affecting ourselves and not merely as existing in the relations of external events which is so peculiarly characteristic of it. . . .

. . . by long custom we have divided the world of events into three-dimensional sections or instants and regarded the piling of the instants as something distinct from a dimension. That gives us the usual conception of a three-dimensional world floating in the stream of time . . .

We are accustomed to think of a man apart from his duration . . . But to think of a man without his duration is just as abstract as to think of a man without his inside.[129]

It is precisely Lewis Lambert Strether's becoming aware of himself as/in/with his duration, as the "feeling of time," that is the "story" of *The Ambassadors*. James's illustration of this as the condition of being, through his language use in shaping this "story," is "the story of [the] story": "– the chance of being seen in time . . . – had become a fact."[130] Our attention to this "feeling of time," Strether's "inside," is relentlessly attracted throughout the narrative by the specific gravity of words expressing some aspect of temporality, variations on: "clocks," "watches," "hours," "quarters of hours," "moments," "pauses," "seconds," "minutes," "instants," "duration," "delay," "watches of the night," "past," "midnight" (marking two crucial meetings between Strether and Chad), "recent," "tick," and, preponderantly, "time" itself, and, even more, the incantatory repetitions of the syntactic and grammatical varieties of "present," "presence," "presented," "presently," "presentiment." In addition, as though recovering, through Strether's illumination of all that Paris symbolizes, one of the gifts brought with the Norman Conquest, James ranges through verb tenses and modes familiar still to French speakers, discriminations among which speakers of the American vernacular, exemplified by the nonetheless well-educated Waymarsh, would have been hard put to make: uses of the imperfect, perfect, pluperfect, anterior past, past conditional, perfect subjunctive, past subjunctive, imperfect subjunctive in their nuanced relations with different conjunctions and other deictics; he knew, too, of tenses like the imperfect for which we have no neat yet flexible equivalent and that one of the senses of the French reflexive *passé composé* can only be translated imperfectly in English, as all translators of Marcel Proust's famous first sentence of *A la recherche du temps perdu* – "Longtemps, je me suis couché de bonne heure" – would learn. The complex relation to time and kind of action (*Aktionsart*) once enjoyed by the ancient Greeks with their more than sixty verbal forms parsed through four tense systems, through one of which, the aorist, it was possible to conjure a wholly indefinite past, was at least partially preserved in the present of French speakers.

In taking account of the nature of time as the fourth dimension in human experience, its implication of concepts derived from the Second Law of Thermodynamics should not be forgotten. Eddington notes, "The conception associated with entropy must . . . be ranked as the great contribution of the nineteenth century to scientific thought."[131] Indeed, Henry Adams's construing a tragic view of life from this information epitomized the general cultural reaction. But there is nothing tragic about Lambert Strether. Clearly, his future at the end of the "story" is uncertain, but what he comes to see represents, rather, secular redemption. He redeems the notion of a fall from the possibility of perfected end framed by the Christian myth and converts it into acceptance of the fact that the increasing spaces of his being, as "duration," consequent on the increasing disorganization of what had been originally the "*there*" of Woollett, had been filled for more than half his life with the experiences of Puritan America; he was "always . . . occupied, and preoccupied, in one way and another, . . . always, in all relations and connections, . . . ridden by his 'New England conscience.'"[132] He cannot reverse time's arrow, put himself back together again, as in a reverse film of Humpty-Dumpty, jump back on the wall, and begin again: "– he has by this time *seen* too much, felt too much, to retrace his steps to his old standpoint . . . He is conscious of his evolution; he likes it – wouldn't for the world not have had it; albeit that he fully sees how fatal . . . it has been for him."[133] Chad and Little Bilham, however, already fluently filling the spaces of their experience with France's pliant variation of Christian culture, where the idea of the female, *l'ange-femme*, through the language, necessarily defines half the order of being, with genetic polarity activating the current of meaning running through every sentence, both have time to extend their compass of "*there*" to include all the City of Light reveals.

Strether, in contrast, though able to communicate in French, is not "polyglot" like Marie de Vionnet, daughter of a French father and English mother;[134] the structure of his thought and feeling is contained in English, a language in which, as noted earlier, Henry James once observed, trying to express emotions is like trying to dance a quadrille in a sentry box. And in the preface, reaching into French as his hero would, in describing his imagining of "the goal of [Strether's] so conscious a predicament," he goes on, "Where has he come from and why has he come, what is he doing (as we Anglo-Saxons, and we only, say, in our foredoomed clutch of exotic aids to expression) in that *galère*?"[135] There Strether is, his "craft" in French as out-of-date as a galley in which he would have to row strenuously to move through the *vagues* of the stream of thought; he is too old for that. His return to America is a pragmatic choice, a moral decision informed by realizing himself, as the frame of his perspective is stretched to register all the details of what had happened to him in time, *as* time, a "more than rational distortion." "Almost grotesque," as James observes, "becomes the kind of revision [Strether] has to make of the bundle of notions with which he had started from home . . . as he now revises and imaginatively reconstructs, morally reconsiders, so to speak, civilization."[136] This impression, like an undeveloped photograph, a "brown blot," hangs suspended, like Holbein's skull, between the double portrait of himself as he might have become – the possibility represented by Chad, floating out of the wished-for life framed by the remembered Lambinet into its reality – and what, until this present, he had become.

Strether's full sense of the present, his presence, presentiments, his manner of presentation, are appropriately revealed to him in the place from which English speakers received the word: *presence* arriving, too, with William the Conqueror, eventually to color Middle English with its Latinate substantiation of instrumentality – *prae* = "for" + the participle for "being," *ens* < *esse*. Following the lesson whispered by his Swedenborgian angel, James used this "interior understanding of the word" in combination with the others forming his guiding constellations to give as accurate a representation as possible of the actuality of being in time as it had come to be understood in his moment: "Not till . . . he had brought out the words themselves, was he sure . . . that the present would be saved."[137] While Proust, years later in *A la recherche*, translated Bergson's understanding of *la durée* as the center of creative consciousness into the obsession of a neurasthenic, hypersensitive, effeminate dandy, writing from bed in his cork-lined room, and so provided the key to high-toned old Christian soldier–critics ready to lock the aesthetic in the prison of aestheticism – "art for art's sake" having no concern with morality[138] – James illustrated in the form and content of his late work that it is the operation of the aesthetic function that is the foundation of morality. Only by voyaging in the *n*-dimensional spacetime that Emerson described in "Circles" as "the flying Perfect,"[139] coming to see what is *there*, "at-hand," perching on what attracts "interest," what is received in the "Presence-room"[140] of being, can individuals discover the motives of their actions, the bases of their beliefs, and in that process make the course corrections necessary to maintain equilibrium and go on. Each individual must fashion the craft he or she will use for that voyaging, translating what is seen "*there*" from the materials that happen to be at hand. As William James observed:

The connection of the reality of things with their effectiveness as motives is a tale that has never been fully told. The moral tragedy of human life comes wholly from the fact that the link is ruptured which normally should hold between vision of truth and action, and that this pungent sense of effective reality will not attach to certain ideas.[141]

Henry James's search for what would suffice, choosing this situation over that, this image over that, following the particular words on which he would voyage, placing a period, deleting commas, adding a dash, obeyed his vigilant desire not to rupture this moral link, so precisely delineated by his brother:

Everywhere, then, the function of the effort [of the will] is the same: to keep affirming and adopting a thought which, left to itself, would slip away. It may be cold and flat when the spontaneous mental drift is towards excitement, or great and arduous when the spontaneous drift is towards repose. In the one case the effort has to inhibit an explosive, in the other to arouse an obstructed will. The exhausted sailor on a wreck has a will which is obstructed. One of his ideas is that of his sore hands, of the nameless exhaustion of his whole frame which the act of farther pumping involves, and of the deliciousness of sinking into sleep. The other is that of the hungry sea ingulfing him. "Rather the aching toil!" he says; and it becomes a reality then, in spite of the inhibiting influence of the relatively luxurious sensations which he gets from lying still. But exactly similar in form would be his consent to lie and sleep. Often it is the thought of sleep and what leads to it which is the hard one to keep before the mind. If a patient afflicted with insomnia can only control the whirling of this thoughts so far as to think of *nothing at all* (which can be done), or so far as to imagine one letter after another of a verse of scripture or poetry spelt slowly and monotonously out, it is almost certain that here, too, specific bodily effects will follow, and that sleep will come. The trouble is to keep the mind upon a train of objects naturally so insipid. *To sustain a representation, to think*, is, in short, the only moral act.[142]

Henry James provided instruction in attending long and carefully enough to the way words are put together to create an exquisite plane where we learn to exist, to feel more fully in the difficulty of what it is to be: willing, choosing, shaping moving pictures into the words, the fictions, we choose to believe in willingly. His "sacred office"[143] was to offer a secular age an example of religious experience. He is one of our angels. We can imagine him at Lamb House, hunting for Lambert Strether, imagining him imagining the Lambinet, reflecting on *Louis Lambert*, "and of the Lamb through the middle of the street of the city" – voyaging, in the amplitude of the waves of memory, "*there*":

Every definite image in the mind is steeped and dyed in the free water that flows around it. With it goes the sense of its relations. near and remote, the dying echo of whence it came to us, the dawning sense of whither it is to lead. The significance, the value of the image is all in this halo or penumbra that surrounds and escorts it, – or, rather that is fused into one with it and has become bone of its bone and flesh of its flesh; leaving it, it is true, an image of the same *thing* it was before, but making it an image of that thing newly taken and freshly understood.

What is that shadowy scheme of the "form" of an opera, play, or book, which remains in our mind and on which we pass judgment when the actual thing is done? What is our notion of a scientific or philosophical system? Great thinkers have vast premonitory glimpses of relation between terms, which hardly even as verbal images enter the mind, so rapid is the whole process . . . We all of us have this permanent consciousness of whither our thought is going. It is a feeling like any other, a feeling of what thoughts are next to arise, before they have arisen.[144]

Within the "shadowy scheme" of the book he judged "the best 'all round' of all [his] productions," Henry James, a secular "Lamb of God," redeemed, saved in the ongoing present of his words, the spirits who had whispered to him their "angelic wisdom." Between "the garden of the church and the wilderness of the world,"[145] in his garden at Lamb House, reflecting on the scene in the Paris garden that became the "germ" of the novel, remembering, within that reflection, himself as a young man, visiting on Sunday afternoons "an ancient lady," in another but similar Paris garden, "endeared" to him because in an apartment overlooking it had lived Madame Recamier, whom the "ancient lady" knew and had waited on in her last days; this "ancient lady" gave to the novelist "a strange and touching image of her [Madame Recamier] as she lay there dying, blind, and bereft of Chateaubriand, who was already dead."[146] In the "penumbra" surrounding this image and all it contained of the relationship between Chateaubriand and Madame Recamier were: the relationship between Chad and Madame de Vionnet revealed in its fullness on their river; that between Louis Lambert and Madame de Stael (a friend of Madame Recamier) and Mademoiselle de Villenoix; and still another relationship between an *ange-femme* and an impressionable young man who would mature to become the "restless analyst." A river journey of a different kind carried the revelation this relationship contained. In *A Small Boy and Others*, Henry James recalls the memory of a journey down the Hudson made, when he was seven, with his father who received from Washington Irving, while aboard the river-steamer, the news of Margaret Fuller's drowning;[147] elsewhere he recorded, as well, feeling the spirit of Margaret Fuller whispering that he should not forget "the woman question." In the Paris garden, then, "This place and these impressions, as well as many of those, for so many days, of So-and-So's and So-and-So's life, that I've been receiving and that have had their abundant message, make it all come over me. I see it now . . . They immediately put before me, with the communicative force, the real magic of the *right* things."[148]

Magically extending the perspective of linguistic representation in yet another way, the spell of one more garden is cast into "the story of [the] story" of *The Ambassadors*. In Book Second, the scene of Strether's identifying himself with the cover of the Review he edits is presented:

"My name's on the cover," Strether pursued, "and I'm really rather disappointed and hurt that you seem never to have heard of it."

She [Miss Gostrey] neglected for a moment this grievance. "And what kind of a review is it?"

His serenity was now completely restored. "Well, it's green."

"Do you mean in political colour as they say here – in thought?"

"No; I mean the cover's green – of the most lovely shade."[149]

There, at the ends of lines not long enough to spill over into the next in unintentioned enjambments at the typesetter's, "green," "thought," "shade," "planted or 'sunk,' stiffly and saliently, in the centre of the current," sits Andrew Marvell's angel in his "Garden," its theme, from the opening lines, "How vainly men themselves amaze / To win the palm, the oak, or bays. . .," through the lines beginning the fourth stanza, "When we have run our passion's heat / Love hither makes his last retreat," to, blaringly, in its sixth stanza –

> Meanwhile the mind, from pleasures less,
> Withdraws into its happiness:
> The mind, that ocean where each kind
> Does straight its own resemblance find,
> Yet it creates, transcending these,
> Far other worlds, and other seas,
> Annihilating all that's made
> To a green thought in a green shade. –

another of the *ficelles* embroidered into both the "story" and "the story of [the] story" of *The Ambassadors*.

All that we have, finally, are words and pauses:

As we take . . . a general view of the wonderful stream of our consciousness, what strikes us first is this different pace of its parts. Like a bird's life, it seems to be made up of an alternation of flights and perchings. The rhythm of language expresses this, where every thought is expressed in a sentence, and every sentence closed by a period. The resting-places are usually occupied by sensorial imaginings of some sort, whose peculiarity is that they can be held before the mind for an indefinite time, and contemplated without changing; the places of flight are filled with thoughts of relations, static or dynamic, that for the most part obtain between matters contemplated in the periods of comparative rest. *Let us call the resting-places the "substantive parts," and the places of flight the "transitive parts," of the stream of thought*. It then appears that the main end of our thinking is at all times the attainment of some other substantive part than the one from which we have just been dislodged. And we may say that the main use of the transitive parts is to lead us from one substantive conclusion to another.

. . . If there be such things as feelings at all, *then so surely as relations between objects exist in rerum natura, so surely, and more surely, do feelings exist to which these relations are known.* There is not a conjunction or a preposition, and hardly an adverbial phrase, syntactic form, or inflection of voice, in human speech, that does not express some shading or other of relation which we at some moment actually feel to exist between the larger objects of our thought . . . the relations are numberless.[150]

"Then, there we are."[151]

CHAPTER SIX

Wallace Stevens's radiant and productive atmosphere

When we go to expel body out of our thoughts, we must be sure not to leave empty space in the room of it; and when we go to expel emptiness from our thoughts we must not think to squeeze it out by anything close, hard and solid, but we must think of the same that the sleeping rocks dream of; and not till then shall we get a complete idea of nothing.

Jonathan Edwards, "Of Being"

THE POET IS THE PRIEST OF THE INVISIBLE[1]

"I desire my poem to mean as much, and as deeply, as a missal. While I am writing what appear to be trifles, I intend these trifles to be a missal for brooding-sight: for an understanding of the world."[2] Explicit here as elsewhere throughout his work and correspondence about the combined function of his poetry and ministerial office, Wallace Stevens was even more challenged to provide an adequate basis for belief than the earlier priests of the invisible whose heir he was. While Jonathan Edwards had to find words capable of holding together a disintegrating community, he was himself held in the strong embrace of belief in a divine order. While Emerson redefined the concept of the divine, he still believed in an order, the law of continuity he found revealed in the "ecstatic" method of nature. And while William James already experienced the disorder to the order posed by taking into full account the Darwinian information – with chance understood to be nature's method, making the law of continuity a seeming oxymoron – and so framed his probabilistic philosophy to facilitate calculating provisionally functional beliefs, he had not to grapple, as would Stevens, with the yet more unsettling discoveries concerning quantum reality which followed Einstein's magnificently disturbing theory of relativity. Late in his life, Stevens observed in a letter that the greatest problem of his age had been what James phrased as "the will to believe."

He did not elaborate to his correspondent, however, the complexity this problem assumed in the face of the accumulating evidence through the first half of the twentieth century of the impossibility of certainty at the deepest levels of observation and knowledge. This elaboration he recorded, faithfully, in his poems. And sometimes, in speaking to or writing for audiences gathered to honor him or curious to learn how to read his gnomic lines, Stevens would locate the instances prompting the cognitive turbulence attending the attempt to imagine the landscape of reality suggested by the equations of physicists and mathematicians intent on plotting the invisible. Here below, for instance, is his notation gleaned from reading one of the most salient imponderables offered by Max Planck, on whose hypothetical "constant," which obliges us "to attribute an essential element of discontinuity or individuality to any phenomenon we seek to observe,"[3] so much of what continues to be accepted as our universe depends. Reflecting his temperamental shyness in all things, Stevens presented this notation in "A Collect of Philosophy," borrowing from one of those he trusted to express in cool prose what he otherwise voiced in the cries of his poem's occasions:

It is admitted, since Planck, that determinism – the relation of cause to effect – exists, or so it seems, on the human scale, only by means of an aggregate of statistical compensations and as the physicists say, by virtue of macroscopic approximations. (There is much to dream about in the macroscopic approximations.) As to the true nature of corpuscular or quantic phenomena, well, try to imagine them. No one has yet succeeded. But the poets – it is possible.

At this point, Stevens added, before continuing to quote from Jean Paulhan:

And, later, because his mind had been engaged by the subject, he sent a last word. He said,
    It comes to this that philosophers (particularly the philosophers of science) make, not discoveries but hypotheses that may be called poetic. Thus Louis de Broglie admits that progress in physics is, at the moment, in suspense because we do not have the words or the images that are essential to us. But to create illuminations, images, words, that is the very reason for being of poets.[4]

"A Collect of Philosophy" was first delivered as the Moody Lecture at the University of Chicago in November, 1951, when Stevens was seventy-two, commenting on the extra-ordinary developments in perceiving reality he had witnessed, knowing that he had throughout his career taken on the charge "that is the very reason for being of poets," had wrestled long and mightily with what he beautifully named "the necessary angel of reality,"[5] had indeed felt the effects of the disappearance of cause and effect into approximations, and dreamed about words and images essential to create the needed illuminations. He spoke of having read Whitehead's description of the present form of the changing "perceptual field" and quoted from *Science and the Modern World*: "My theory involves the entire abandonment of the notion that simple location is the primary way in which things are involved in space-time. In a certain sense, everything is everywhere at all times, for every location involves an aspect of itself in every other location. Thus every spatio-temporal standpoint mirrors the world." Stevens translated Whitehead's naturalized vision of Augustine's God into its effect: it "produced in the imagination a universal iridescence, a dithering of presences, and, say, a complex of differences."[6] Whitehead had offered his theory first in the Lowell Lectures of 1925, published as a volume later that year. He was providing, as a mathematician and academic philosopher, a historicized account of what, as de Broglie would observe, could not yet be imagined. Describing to the Parisian Academy of Sciences in September 1923 that "waves in motion were – according to the new physics – all the universe consists in," de Broglie emphasized that in so presenting the wave–particle duality "he was not speaking of material waves but of an 'onde fictive.'"[7] At the same moment, Stevens was already embarked on his "voyage, out of goblinry," in a "state of vague receptivity," giving close attention to his mind in thinking, and setting down the "material image[s] more or less luminous" he saw, the first notes toward his own supreme fiction.[8] It should not be surprising that Stevens found himself contemplating the same mysterious "events" as Whitehead – "When was it that the particles became / The whole man?"[9] Both acknowledged their debt to William James. While Whitehead's contribution to mapping the dimensions of the new world of spacetime cannot be gainsaid, Stevens realized, in the same way Darwin had observed of Humboldt's offerings, that, while "the philosopher more or less often experiences the same miraculous shortenings of mental processes that the poet experiences," the language of the philosopher could not begin to represent the actual "vibrations" constituting the reality he was intent to describe. As Stevens specified to his Chicago audience:

The habit of probing for an integration seems to be part of the general will to order . . . The philosopher searches for an integration for its own sake, as, for example, Plato's idea that knowledge is recollection or that the soul is a harmony; the poet searches for an integration that shall be not so much sufficient in itself as sufficient for some quality that it possesses, such as its insight, its evocative power or its appearance in the eye of the imagination. The philosopher intends his integration to be fateful; the poet intends his to be effective.

And yet these integrations, although different from each other, have something in common, such as, say, a characteristic of depth or distance at which they have been found, a facture of the level or position of the mind or, if you like, of a level or position of the feelings, because in the excitement of bringing things about it is not always easy to say whether one is thinking or feeling or doing both at the same time.[10]

Stevens addressed himself persistently to, in his words, the "fact of feeling" ourselves expelled from "the cosmic poem of the ascent into heaven," "creatures, not of a part, which is our every day limitation, but of a whole for which, for the most part, we have as yet no language," where "Yet the absence of imagination had / Itself to be imagined."[11] Within this whole – "our cosmic epoch . . . a society of electromagnetic occasions . . . a society of electrons and protons" – as Whitehead dispassionately described, these "creatures," the primates we happen to be, are nothing more than temporal transformations of patterning electrons and protons, "individuality . . . the transformation of a definite train of recurrent wave-forms":

Accordingly, in the language of physics, the aspects of a primate are merely its contributions to the electro-magnetic field. This is in fact exactly what we know of electrons and protons. An electron for us is merely the pattern of its aspects in its environment, so far as those aspects are relevant to the electromagnetic field.

. . . a pattern need not endure in undifferentiated sameness through time. The pattern may be essentially one of aesthetic contrasts requiring a lapse of time for its unfolding . . . when we translate this notion into the abstractions of physics, it at once becomes the technical notion of "vibration." This vibration is not the vibratory locomotion: it is the vibration of organic deformation. There are certain indications in modern physics that for the role of corpuscular organisms at the base of the physical field, we require vibratory entities. Such corpuscles would be the corpuscles detected as expelled from the nuclei of atoms, which then dissolve into waves of light.[12]

Stevens offers his version:

The material world, for all the assurances of the eye, has become immaterial. It has become an image in the mind. The solid earth disappears and the whole atmosphere is subtilized not by the arrival of some venerable beam of light from an almost hypothetical star but by a breach of reality. What we see is not an external world but an image of it and hence an internal world.

Thus poetry becomes and is a transcendent analogue composed of the particulars of reality, created by the poet's sense of the world, that is to say, his attitude, as he intervenes and interposes the appearances of that sense.[13]

As he commented, "Whether one arrives at the idea of God as a philosopher or as a poet matters greatly."[14] We recall William James: "To think, to sustain a representation, then, is the only moral act." Stevens, the poet of the modern world, extending himself into the "difficulty of what it is to be,"[15] resisted the temptation to fall into categories of substance, instead sustaining in the vibratory breaths of each of his imaginings the exquisite critical opalescence that is our actual condition as our, and all, matter on a planet revolving around its sun slowly dissolves into waves of light.

Especially sensitive from boyhood to light and shadow, to the relation of sun, weather, and seasons, Stevens cultivated his cosmic consciousness throughout his life, even referring to himself in the title of one of his late poems as "The Planet on the Table": "His self and the sun were one / And his poems, although makings of his self, / Were no less makings of the sun."[16] In 107 of the 301 poems comprising *The Collected Poems*, the sun is named, and in another 138 the light of the sun is present in qualities and manifestations of celestial effects and events. This is not to mention the additional number of poems in which seeing, sight, blindness, the eye, and colors play their parts, a dazzling display: "What is there here but weather, what spirit / Have I except it comes from the sun?"[17] While Stevens's fascination with the sun and its effects belonged to what he, following Emerson, called his temperament – "the manner of thinking and feeling . . . of the poet as a whole biological mechanism"[18] – the accidental product of heredity and environment, the conditions of Stevens's environment notably included Einstein's amazing discovery. What idea could more excite the poetic imagination than that of matter speeded by light into pure energy? The letter "C" identified Stevens's "Comedian" with this astonishing glimpse of the invisible making visible all we know: "Nothing that is not there and the nothing that is";[19] "The most provocative of all realities is that reality of which we never lose sight but never see solely as it is."[20] The gradual transformation of Edwards's "Divine and Supernatural Light," beginning with his incorporation of Newton's work, continuing through the developments in optics and wave theory during the nineteenth century, issued in Einstein's brilliant delineation of all as an effect of light, a purely naturalized description that at the same time meant the complete dissolution of the dimensions of what "reality" had been conceived to be, the crumbling of foundations of belief. As Niels Bohr noted in 1929:

The great extension of our experience in recent years has brought to light the insufficiency of our simple mechanical conceptions and, as a consequence, has shaken the foundation on which the customary interpretation of observations was based, thus throwing new light on old philosophical problems. This is true not only of the revision of the foundations of the space-time mode of description brought about by the theory of relativity, but also of the renewed discussion of the principle of causality which has emerged from the quantum theory.[21]

Compounding the already revolutionary impact caused by Darwin's contribution, the reverberations of Einstein's work followed by quantum theorizing set everything "spinning and hissing"[22] – "produced in the imagination a universal iridescence, a dithering of presences . . . a complex of differences." Stevens had chosen his words carefully: the qualities of the rainbow contained in light and captured through the iris of the eye, no longer mythologized or divinely explained, indeed caused a "dithering," quaking, trembling, perplexity, concerning reality and the place and function of the human. Einstein himself noted, "The non-mathematician is seized by a mysterious shuddering . . . a feeling not unlike that awakened by thoughts of the occult" when hearing of the new spacetime universe his equations described.[23] As Arthur Eddington observed in *The Nature of the Physical World* – together with Whitehead's *Science and the Modern World*, one of the most effective texts in making the new physics available to a wide audience –

A rainbow described in the symbolism of physics is a band of aethereal vibration arranged in a systematic order of wave-length from about .000040 cm. to .000072 cm. From one point of view we are paltering with the truth whenever we admire the gorgeous bow of colour, and should strive to reduce our minds to such a state that we receive the same impression from the rainbow as from a table of wave-lengths. But although that is how the rainbow impresses itself on an impersonal spectroscope, we are not giving the whole truth and significance of experience . . . if we suppress the factors wherein we ourselves differ from the spectroscope. We cannot say that the rainbow, as part of the world, was meant to convey the vivid effects of colour; but we can perhaps say that the human mind was meant to perceive it that way.[24]

In "Two or Three Ideas," delivered earlier in 1951, in April, at Mount Holyoke College at a meeting of the College English Association, Stevens offered a moving description of the condition in which the creatures of our culture found themselves in the wake of the wonderful but terrifying discoveries of the modern world:

To see the gods dispelled in mid-air and dissolve like clouds is one of the great human experiences. It is not as if they had gone over the horizon to disappear for a time; nor as if they had been overcome by other gods of greater power and profounder knowledge. It is simply that they came to nothing. Since we have always shared all things with them and have always had a part of their strength and, certainly, all of their knowledge, we shared likewise this experience of annihilation.

It was their annihilation, not ours, and yet it left us feeling that in a measure we, too, had been annihilated. It left us feeling dispossessed and alone in a solitude, like children without parents, in a home that seemed deserted, in which the amical rooms and halls had taken on a look of hardness and emptiness. What was most extraordinary is that they left no mementoes behind, no thrones, no mystic rings, no texts either of the soil or of the soul. It was as if they had never inhabited the earth. There was no crying out for their return. They were not forgotten because they had been a part of the glory of the earth. At the same time, no man ever muttered a petition in his heart for the restoration of those unreal shapes. There was always in every man the increasingly human self, which instead of remaining the observer, the non-participant, the delinquent, became constantly more and more all there was or so it seemed; and whether it was so or merely seemed so still left it for him to resolve life and the world in his own terms.[25]

In opening the talk, he created the atmosphere in which his audience would receive his description:

It is as if we had stepped into a ruin and were startled by a flight of birds that rose as we entered. The familiar experience is made unfamiliar and from that time on, whenever we think of that particular scene, we remember how we held our breath and how the hungry doves of another world rose out of nothingness and whistled away. We stand looking at a remembered habitation. All old dwelling-places are subject to these transmogrifications and the experience of all of us includes a succession of old dwelling-places: abodes of the imagination, ancestral or memories of places that never existed.

He went on to specify the subject of his address: "To speak of the origin and the end of gods is not a light matter. It is to speak of the origin and end of eras of human belief . . . In an age of disbelief . . . it is for the poet to supply the satisfactions of belief, in his manner and in his style." "It is," he clearly announced, "a spiritual role." "But," he was careful to add, "the truth about the poet in a time of disbelief is not that he must turn evangelist. After all, he shares the disbelief of his time."[26] Elaborating Emerson's recognition of nature's ecstatic method for this later moment, "when there is a fluctuation of the whole of appearance," he underlined that "the indifferent experience of life is the unique experience, the item of ecstasy which we have been isolating and reserving for another time and place loftier and more secluded," and clarified,

There is inherent in the words *the revelation of reality* a suggestion that there is a reality of or within or beneath the surface of reality. There are many such realities through which poets constantly pass to and fro, without noticing the imaginary lines that divide one from the other . . . That the revelation of reality has a character or quality peculiar to this time or that or, what is intended to be the same thing, that it is affected by states of mind, is elementary.[27]

Here was a statement fit to the time, incorporating in solemnly reassuring prose the most revolutionary and counter-intuitive facts describing the quantum universe we inhabit – that there are many simultaneous realities, the physicists' "superpositions," and, following Werner Heisenberg's uncertainty principle, that the emergence and description of these possible realities are affected by the states of mind of the observers: "It is as if being was to be observed, / As if . . ."[28] While those of us who pay attention to such things have by now come to accept, if not – as non-specialists in quantum electrodynamics – understand, these facts as elements of the nature we inhabit and constitute, we generally fail to notice how this acceptance has come about and the part it plays in our ongoing participation in the universe. In closing his lecture, Stevens indicated both the ground enabling this acceptance and the part it plays: "It comes to this that we use the same faculties when we write poetry that we use when we create gods or when we fix the bearing of men in reality."[29] Guy Davenport's noting that "a clue to cracking the atom was found in Lucretius by Niels Bohr"[30] illustrates Stevens's point no less than what Darwin found in Milton. The instances of poetic, divine, and scientific creation Stevens recognized as equal, all "sources of perfection. They are of such a nature that they are instances of aesthetic ideas tantamount to moral ideas." Specifically, in the case of poetry, he noted that it "is a unity of language and life that exposes both in a supreme sense."[31] In parallel, "Bohr argued that physics concerns not what nature is, but rather what we can clearly say (and not say) about it."[32] How had Stevens found this faith, this confidence, that "The poet is the priest of the invisible,"[33] at least equal in capability with the scientist to provide descriptions of things as they are?

Even at nineteen, during the spring term of his second year at Harvard, Stevens voiced his perception of the regulating function of art: "Art must fit in with other things; it must be part of the world. And if it finds a place in that system it will likewise find a ministry and relation that are its proper adjuncts." Revealingly, on the way to this announcement in his journal, after opening his entry with a direct attack on "art for art's sake" as "indiscreet and worthless" because it does not take account of the "common run of things" which "are all parts of a system and exist not for themselves but because they are indispensable," the aspiring young writer used as examples the sun and stars:

Take therefore a few specific examples, such as the sun which is certainly beautiful and mighty enough to withstand the trivial adjective artistic. But its beauty is incidental and assists in making agreeable a monotonous machine. To say that the stars were made to guide navigators etc. seems like stretching a point; but the real use of their beauty (which is not their excuse) is that it is a service, a food. Beauty is strength. But art – art all alone, detached, sensuous for the sake of sensuousness, not to perpetuate inspiration or thought, art that is mere art – seems to me to be the most arrant as it is the most inexcusable rubbish.[34]

This early articulation of what he would later term his "rude aesthetic"[35] was sharply defined in opposition to the European variety epitomized by the dandified figure of the poet with whom, ironically, Stevens would come to be identified by his more austere critics after the publication of *Harmonium* in 1923. Unable to recognize the artist of the beautiful outside of the category established by European models, these readers generally agreed with the judgment passed by John Crowe Ransom, that Stevens's poetry "has no moral, political, religious, or sociological values. It is not about 'res publica,' the public thing. The subject matter is trifling."[36] While it was clear from the evidence of his first volume that Stevens was indeed intent on replacing the "honey of heaven" with the "honey of earth,"[37] what the chastising chorus failed to see was that he was as directly involved in expressing and describing religious affections as had been Jonathan Edwards or Cotton Mather, Thomas Shepard, and the other studious ghosts of Puritan forebears who flitted through his lines. The poet's first audiences would not, of course, have been familiar with the complexity of Stevens's religious experience: of his having been, as a boy, haunted by heaven's hymns as he listened to his mother's singing as she accompanied herself on the piano at home every Sunday evening, extending the earlier services at Reading's First Presbyterian Church where he, before attending Sunday school sessions, regularly watched in fascination the counterpointed up and down of the organist's feet on the pedals; of his imaginings as his mother read to him and his siblings from the Bible every night at bedtime; of his pride in participating, as he entered adolescence, in the sacred service as an altar boy, and singing for two years in the choir of Reading's Christ Cathedral, "soprano and, later, alto";[38] of the incipient loosening of the high-toned old Christian woman's orthodoxy as he read and marked passages in the Emerson volumes his mother presented to him during his Christmas 1898 visit home from Harvard. There, as he would later describe, the spirit of William James hung over the yard, the idea of the will to believe permeating the atmosphere.

Indeed, by the time he left Cambridge for New York in 1900 "to try [his] hand at journalism,"[39] it was more and more in nature not in church where he experienced the sacred: "An old argument with me is that the true religious force in the world is not the church but the world itself: the mysterious callings of Nature and our responses," he recorded in his journal on Sunday, August 10, 1902,[40] after having returned from a long walk in the New Jersey countryside and stopped in at St. Patrick's Cathedral to sense, moved by what he had learned from Emerson, the contrast between divinity confined and unconfined. For a while continuing to move up and down between the two elements, he nonetheless preserved the habit of ritual observance, for the next sixteen years on Sundays walking into nature and later back in his room setting down in his journal, as faithfully as any of the "good Puritans" from whom he was descended, his deepening understanding of what he had perceived both of the actuality of the "Invisible" and of the function of what in his 1951 lecture he would call "the satisfactions of belief":

What incessant murmurs fill that ever-laboring, tireless church! But to-day in my walk I thought that after all there is no conflict of forces but rather a contrast. In the cathedral I felt one presence; on the highway I felt another. Two different deities presented themselves; and, though I only have cloudy visions of either, yet I now feel the distinction between them. The priest in me worshipped one God at one shrine; the poet another God at another shrine. The priest worshipped Mercy and Love; the poet Beauty and Might. In the shadows of the church I could hear the prayers of men and women; in the shadows of the trees nothing mingled with Divinity. As I sat dreaming with the Congregation I felt how the glittering altar worked on my senses stimulating and consoling them; and as I went tramping through the fields and woods I beheld every leaf and blade of grass revealing or rather betokening the Invisible.[41]

Stevens's sensibility had been shaped through childhood and adolescence by regular, rigorous religious instruction and practice inscribing the habits of belief and praise, his aesthetic grounded in "glittering altar[s]" and "hankering for hymns."[42] Researchers today, extending Alexander Baumgarten's eighteenth-century investigation into "the science of aesthetics," exploring aesthetics as "sensory cognition" based on recognizing "that sensation itself has a cognitive component," examine how traces of early childhood sensate pleasures become part of the brain's "hard wiring" determining what might appear to the adult as knowledge or knowing.[43] Even as a young man, Stevens was alert to this aspect of his experience. The summer before leaving for Harvard, deliberately steeping himself in the beauty of his native countryside, the area of Pennsylvania's Berk's and Buck's counties, still now a preserve of the pastoral, he recorded in his journal:

The feeling of piety is very dear to me. I would sacrifice a great deal to be a Saint Augustine but modernity is so Chicagoan, so plain, so unmeditative. I thoroughly believe that at this very moment I get none of my chief pleasures except from what is unsullied. The love of beauty excludes evil. A moral life is simply a pure conscience:

a physical, mental and ethical source of pleasure . . . I believe, as unhesitatingly as I believe in anything, in the efficacy and necessity of fact meeting fact – with a background of the ideal.

I'm completely satisfied that behind every physical fact there is a divine force. Don't, therefore, look at facts, but through them.[44]

He went on to describe in delicate detail, as a latter-day Jonathan Edwards might have, the elements of the sunset landscape surrounding him. His yearning for something to "stimulat[e] and consol[e]" his "senses" as effectively as "glittering altar[s]" continued through his years in Cambridge and later moves to various addresses in New York and adjacent neighborhoods, first to work as a journalist, and then, following the failure of this attempt as a result of his incapacity to witness and describe some of the grislier events he had been sent to cover, to heed his father's advice and pursue the study of law. At twenty-two, searching for an order that could take the place of the divine, he found himself "thinking over organic laws etc. the idea of the German 'Organismus,'" and, while commenting, "Wonderfully scientific + clear idea + this *organismus* one," still "lament[ed] that the fairies were things of the past."[45] At twenty-seven, in February, 1906, recording the perceptions of his regular Sunday walk into the countryside stretching from East Orange, New Jersey, where he was then living, to Morristown and back, he observed,

I wish that groves still were sacred – or, at least that something was: that there was still something free from doubt, that day unto day still uttered speech, and night unto night still showed wisdom. I grow tired of the want of faith – the instinct of faith. Self-consciousness convinces me of something, but whether it be something Past, Present or Future I do not know.[46]

By January of 1907, Stevens's letters to Elsie Moll, the beautiful young woman who would become his wife, had almost completely taken the place of his journal entries. He had met her during the summer of 1904, back once again basking idyllically in the fields and woods around Reading. It was significant that he found and, for the next five years of an epistolary relationship punctuated by visits back to Reading and walks with Elsie to favorite glades and nooks, imaginatively kept her in this, as he described, "faery" setting. She was not only local, but, except for her training in music, relatively untutored, not one of those from his cohort in Cambridge to whom he was drawn but by whom, at the same time, he was intimidated. Now confiding his thoughts to her – "My thoughts are my heart" – while guiding what was to him her frailer spirit, the Pygmalion-like suitor communicated his feelings about religion in a way that reflected both the tenor of his more educated cultural moment and his awareness of what William James had located as the neurological effects of the habit of belief:

– I was more interested than you may believe in what you said about religion. A.T.'s [Alice Tragle, a mutual Reading acquaintance] opinions are quite elementary. I have never told you what I believe. There are so many things to think of. I don't <u>care</u> whether churches are all alike or whether they're right or wrong. It is not important. The very fact that they take care of A.T.'s "stupid" people is an exquisite device. It is undoubtedly true that they do not "influence" any but the "stupid." But they are beautiful and full of comfort and moral help. One can get a thousand benefits from churches that one cannot get outside of them. They purify a man, they soften Life. <u>Please</u> don't listen to A.T., or, at least, don't argue with her. Don't <u>care</u> about the Truth. There are other things in Life besides the Truth upon which everybody of any experience agrees, while no two people care about the Truth. I'd rather see you going to church than know that you were as wise as Plato and Haeckel rolled into one; and I'd rather sing some old chestnut out of a hymn-book with you, surrounded by "stupid" people, than listen to all the wise men in the world. It has always been a particular desire of mine to have you join church; and I am very, very glad to know that you are now on the road. – I am not in the least religious. The sun clears my spirit, if I may say that, and an occasional sight of the sea, and thinking of blue valleys, and the odor of the earth, and many things. Such things make a god of a man; but a chapel makes a man of him. Churches are human. – I say my prayers every night – not that I need them now, or that they are anything more than a habit, half-unconscious. But in Spain, in Salamanca, there is a pillar in a church (Santayana told me) worn by the kisses of generations of the devout. One of their kisses are [*sic*] worth all my prayers. Yet the church is a mother for them – and for us.[47]

Setting aside a discussion of the confusion it would have been understandable for Elsie to have experienced on, literally, reading through the lines of her lover, it is important to underline that Stevens's disclosure of the still active force of his religious habit, coupled with his declaring himself not religious yet still saying his prayers every night and feeling the comfort of the church as "human" and as "a mother," reveal precisely the lineaments of the problem he figured as characterizing his age: "the will to believe."[48] Stevens, already embarked on his journey as the "introspective voyager" he would name himself in his mock-heroic autobiography, "The Comedian as The Letter C,"[49] was recounting his first-hand experience of what James had laid out clinically in *The Principles of Psychology* and repeated rhetorically in *The Varieties of Religious Experience*: the channels of reception and perception, determining hunger, need, search and selection, etched into neuronal inheritance by millennia of human behavior recorded in its history, of feasting and fasting, of petition and prayer, of sacrifice and praise, of dreams of paradise and fears of hell, of rejoicing and hoping for redemption, these channels, habits of mind, would continue to hunger for the "satisfactions of belief," the practices, actions, sensory closings of open circuits, beyond anything cool reason might provide – "You know then that it is not the reason / That makes us happy or unhappy."[50] No matter how accurate and verifiable bare reason's product, in describing a universe emptied of what, finally, in all religions represents a power with whom some form of communication is possible, even if only wished-for, this information cannot, in itself, offer the sensory effect necessary to close the neuronal gap and re-establish the homeostatic balance necessary for survival; as the speaker of "Sunday Morning" utters, "But in contentment I still feel / The need of some imperishable bliss."[51] The problem as Stevens realized it was that while the "satisfactions of belief" would have to take the place of "the thought of heaven,"[52] be as "effective" in giving sustenance and solace as a mother humming hymns at bedtime, no immanent protection or promise of future reward could be offered: "My trouble, and the trouble of a great many people, is the loss of belief in the sort of God in Whom we were all brought up to believe."[53] The "satisfactions," in the face of the facts of the modern world, would have to celebrate that "the indifferent experience of life is the unique experience, the item of ecstasy." He would address himself to solving this problem through his experiments with words, translating the "instinct of faith" in God or gods, long cultivated by traditional religions, into an "instinct of faith" in mind alone to offer what would suffice: "It is necessary to propose an enigma to the mind. The mind always proposes a solution."[54]

In another remarkable revelation of his sustained and sustaining religious affections, offered in a letter to his fiancée in the months before their marriage as Stevens approached the closing of his thirtieth year, he describes the aspects attendant on realizing the aesthetic necessity inscribed into human experience by centuries of religious observation and practice. This letter, dated simply "Sunday Evening," as so many others written to Elsie over the years of their courtship, is quoted extensively as it contains strands of perception that were to recombine to shape "Sunday Morning":

My dearest:
  . . . – To-day I have been roaming about town. In the morning I walked down-town – stopping once to watch three flocks of pigeons circling the sky. I dropped into St. John's chapel an hour before the service and sat in the last pew and looked around. It happens that last night at the Library I read a life of Jesus and I was interested to see what symbols of that life appeared in the chapel. I think there were

none at all excepting the gold cross on the altar. When you compare that poverty with the wealth of symbols, of remembrances, that were created and revered in times past, you appreciate the change that has come over the church. The church should be more than a moral institution, if it is to have the influence that it should have. The space, the gloom, the quiet mystify and entrance the spirit. But that is not enough. – And one turns from this chapel to those built by men familiar with Gethsemane, familiar with Jerusalem. – I do not wonder that the church is so largely a relic. Its vitality depended on its association with Palestine, so to speak. – I felt a peculiar emotion in reading about John the Baptist, Bethany, Galilee – and so on, because (the truth is) I had not thought about them much since my days at Sunday-school (when, of course, I didn't think of them at all.) It was like suddenly remembering something long forgotten, or else like suddenly seeing something new and strange in what had always been in my mind. – Reading the life of Jesus, too, makes one distinguish the separate idea of God. Before to-day I do not think I have ever realized that God was distinct from Jesus. It enlarges the matter almost beyond comprehension. People doubt the existence of Jesus – at least, they doubt incidents of his life, such as, say, the Ascension into Heaven after his death. But I do not understand that they deny God. I think everyone admits that in one form or other. – The thought makes the world sweeter – even if God be no more than the mystery of Life. – Well, after a bit, I left the chapel and walked over the Brooklyn Bridge. There was a high wind, so that I put my hat under my arm. I imagined myself pointing things out to you – the Statue of Liberty, green and weather-beaten, Governor's Island, the lower Bay . . . – Then I walked down-town – catching a glimpse, on Madison Avenue, of a yard crowded with tulips. – I dropped into a church for five minutes, merely to see it you understand. I am not pious. But churches are beautiful to see. – And then I came home, observing great masses of white clouds, with an autumnal shape to them, floating through the windy sky . . . – I wish I could spend the whole season out of doors, walking by day, reading and studying in the evenings . . . But after all there are innumerable things besides that kind of life – and I imagine that when I come home from the Library, thinking over some capital idea – a new name for the Milky Way, a new aspect of Life, an amusing story, a gorgeous line – I am as happy as I should be – or could be – anywhere . . . Perhaps, it is best, too, that one should have only glimpses of reality – and get the rest from the fairy-tales, from pictures, and music, and books . . . My chief objection to town-life is the commonness of the life. Such numbers of men degrade Man. The <u>teeming</u> streets make Man a nuisance – a vulgarity, and it is impossible to see his dignity. I feel, nevertheless, the overwhelming necessity of thinking well, speaking well. – "I am a stranger in the earth." [Psalms 119: 19] – You see I have been digging into the Psalms – anything at all, so long as it is full of praise – and rejoicing . . . – Yet if I prattle so much of religious subjects, Psalms and things, my girl will think me a bother, and so, no more, as we used to say when we had stumbled across something unpleasant.[55]

The elements coded into his perception that were to provide the directions for both "Sunday Morning" and his later work are clear. The evocations of Palestine, "the grave of Jesus, where he lay," and "casual flocks of pigeons" were magnificently unwound from this earlier experience and turned through years of reflection and pondering to recombine in a brilliant restatement of paganism redesigned for the American scene. In "Sunday Morning" Stevens presented this restatement through the persona of his imagined "she," as "the effect of conversation with the beauty of the soul,"[56] translating Emerson's description from "The Divinity School Address" into his own inverted conversion narrative, deconstructing the sources of religious worship to complete the work of the Sage of Concord's naturalization of the sacred, restoring "divinity" to purity of response to the actuality of "indecipherable cause[s]":[57]

> Why should she give her bounty to the dead?
> What is divinity if it can come
> Only in silent shadows and in dreams?
> Shall she not find in comforts of the sun,
> In pungent fruit and bright, green wings, or else
> In any balm or beauty of the earth,
> Things to be cherished like the thought of heaven?
> Divinity must live within herself;
> Passions of rain, or moods in falling snow;
> Grievings in loneliness, or unsubdued
> Elations when the forest blooms; gusty
> Emotions on wet roads on autumn nights;
> All pleasures and all pains, remembering
> The bough of summer and the winter branch
> These are the measures destined for her soul.[58]

These strains lingered enduringly in Stevens. Throughout his work elements originally stimulated in the sensory plenum of childhood imaginings, repeatedly excited in the elaborations thinking and reading provided as he moved through life, would reappear, the same but different, traits inherited from the flesh of words, the transformations surviving the braided accidents of time, place, and endless motion: "as if, / In the end, in the whole psychology, the self, / The Town, the weather, in a casual litter, / Together, said words of the world are the life of the world."[59] He presented to Elsie his own direct experience of Platonic recognition, reinforced as it would have been for him through its Emersonian phrasing in "Self-Reliance" – "It was like suddenly remembering something long forgotten, or else like suddenly seeing something new and strange in what had always been in my mind," exemplifying the manner in which a "fitful tracing of a portal" becomes "in the flesh . . . immortal."[60] We recall William James's description of the ongoing amplification through a lifetime of the "*there*" marking the infant's entry through the portal of birth into its particular environment of sensory fact (pp. 162–3). Notably, Stevens's deepening the early tracing of the contours of religious belief returned him, as he recorded to Elsie, both to the beautifully mysterious pleasure of being in a church and to reading the Psalms; in addition, as he observed, his reading the life of Jesus, realizing him as human, distinct from the idea of God, "enlarge[d] the matter almost beyond comprehension."

BUT YOU CANNOT APPROACH NOTHING; FOR THERE IS NOTHING TO APPROACH[61]

In another illustration of the way in which words taken in with what Edwards called "the sense of the heart" become templates for perception, selectors of patterns for growth and change, Stevens's "Sunday Evening" letter, written by a young man at a significant moment of his maturity, as he approached marriage and clarified his beliefs, was a palimpsest. Oddly paralleling the internalization and conversion of Emerson's "Crossing a bare common . . ." passage in William James's description of the scene of first exercising his free will to believe, the erased script beneath the lines Stevens wrote to his future wife is Emerson's "Divinity School Address." That both James and Stevens should have found themselves in spiritual conversation with Emerson in describing crucial, emotionally charged and extended instances of self-consciousness is not as remarkable as it might immediately seem. It was, after all, Emerson's repeatedly and variously expressed purpose "to beget a desire and need to impart to others the same knowledge and love" that is "the effect of conversation with the beauty of the soul." James's acknowledgment of Emerson's guidance has already been discussed. While Stevens did not explicitly announce himself as another of Emerson's heirs, it is abundantly clear from the echoes of phrases, from his imperfect but unmistakable replication of images, from the incorporation and redistribution of Emersonian topics and tropes throughout the corpus of his work, that his being continued to resonate with the words first heard when, while still at Harvard, he began "conversing in earnest" with this benevolent shade, reading, rereading, and marking passages in the twelve-volume edition his mother had given him: "On a few words of what is real in the world / I nourish myself."[62] Emerson's transformations of the patterning of sacred text into his own "book," making it, as he expressly desired, "smell of pines and resound with the hum of insects," instead of echo the language of "Men [who] ha[d] come to speak of the revelation as somewhat long ago given and done, as if God were dead,"[63] performed a sacrament of praise equal in power and effectiveness to the Testaments from which he had learned. Stevens belonged to the third generation of Emerson's descendants, schooled in the lessons and cadences of the New World gospels embodied in the essays and lectures. It was natural for the young American Stevens, preoccupied with the idea of divinity, to recollect Emerson's declaration of independence from the "thoughtless clamor" of "creed outworn."[64]

The parallels between Emerson's address and Stevens's letter are striking, even the ordering of perceptions and ideas of the latter suggested by that of the earlier formal offering. Moreover, in the same way that perceptions recorded in the letter would recombine to shape "Sunday Morning," elements from "The Divinity School Address" written, as it were, beneath those perceptions would recombine in others of Stevens's poems. Emerson opens his oration calling attention to the "air . . . full of birds, and sweet with the breath of the pine, the balm-of-Gilead, and the new hay," introducing his naturalized variety of "religious sentiment" with a figure designed to lift the eyes of the spirit up to the "blithe air" while at the same time grounding his audience in the elements common to American soil and, through his proper naming of the surrounding poplars – "balm-of-Gilead" – to "the devout and contemplative East; not alone . . . Palestine, where it [religious sentiment] reached its purest expression." Emerson then continues to unfold the various aspects of the humanity of Christ before giving the example of stopping into a church one afternoon during a snow storm and hearing the evidence of how "historical Christianity destroys the power of preaching, by withdrawing it from the exploration of the moral nature of man, where the sublime is, where are the resources of astonishment and power":

A snow storm was falling around us. The snow storm was real; the preacher merely spectral; and the eye felt the sad contrast in looking at him, and then out of the window behind him, into the beautiful meteor of the snow. He had lived in vain. He had no one word intimating that he had laughed or wept, was married or in love, had been commended, or cheated, or chagrined. If he had ever lived and acted, we were none the wiser for it. The capital secret of his profession, namely, to convert life into truth, he had not learned. Not one fact in all his experience, had he yet imported into his doctrine.[65]

Similarly, Stevens in his letter focuses attention for himself and his beloved up to "watch three flocks of pigeons circling the sky" before going on to describe how, extending his meditation on the life of Jesus, he dropped into

St. John's chapel, where, echoing Emerson, he too finds that "The church should be more than a moral institution." He concretizes the Emersonian perception, locating the power of the original Christian church in its being "built by men who felt the wonder of the life and death of Jesus . . . Its vitality depend[ent] on its association with Palestine." The "vitality" of "felt" connection with whatever was to replace the supreme fiction offered by early Christianity had to be likewise grounded in a particular environment of fact. This realization would evolve into one of Stevens's poetic principles: "his soil is man's intelligence," he announced in 1922; expanded in the 1936 voicing of "The Man With the Blue Guitar," "Poetry // Exceeding music must take the place / Of empty heaven and its hymns, // Ourselves in poetry must take their place . . . // Ourselves in the tune as if in space, / Yet nothing changed, except the place";[66] and, nearing the end of his career, restated more specifically,

> A mythology reflects its region. Here
> In Connecticut, we never lived in a time
> When mythology was possible – But if we had –
> That raises the question of the image's truth.
> The image must be of the nature of its creator.
> It is the nature of its creator increased,
> Heightened. It is he, anew, in a freshened youth
> And it is he in the substance of his region
> Wood of his forests and stone out of his fields
> Or from under his mountains.[67]

Between his early articulation and this late phrasing, other echoes from Emerson vibrating in him crystallized as he moved through his own seasons – his 1943 description, for example, of "snow . . . like eyesight falling to earth"[68] momentarily catching the sparkle of "the beautiful meteor of the snow" remembered from his earlier imagining of what Emerson saw as he listened to the preacher's lifeless words. Stevens evoked a memory of snow a few years before as well, in his 1936 lecture, "The Irrational Element in Poetry," exploring the idea of writing "poetry to find the good which, in the Platonic sense, is synonymous with God." The lecture opens with a figure chosen to illustrate the mysterious "transaction between reality and the sensibility of the poet from which poetry springs . . . the transposition of an objective reality to a subjective reality":

A day or two before Thanksgiving we had a light fall of snow in Hartford. It melted a little by day and then froze again at night, forming a thin, bright crust over the grass. At the same time, the moon was almost full. I awoke once several hours before daylight and as I lay in bed I heard the steps of a cat running over the snow under my window almost inaudibly. The faintness and strangeness of the sound made on me one of those impressions which one so often seizes as pretexts for poetry.[69]

Elaborating throughout his talk the tension between the "true subject" of poetry, the "irrational element" represented by this magical recollection, and the "poetry of the subject," the development around it – "One is always writing about two things at the same time in poetry . . . the true subject and . . . the poetry of the subject" – Stevens addressed himself to describing "poetic metamorphosis" as a variety of religious experience, as "saintly exercises," but exercises explicitly free of "mystical rhetoric" – "since for my part, I have no patience with that sort of thing." Continuing the necessary work of Emersonian reformation, he called attention, as had Emerson in his time, to "the universal decay and now almost death of faith in society" and the "need . . . never greater of new revelation."[70] The "now" for Stevens in December 1936, with Hitler having reoccupied the Rhineland, Mussolini in Ethiopia, the Spanish Civil War begun, not only reflected loss of faith but portended the end of civilization itself: "The pressure of the contemporaneous from the time of the beginning of the World War [I] to the present time has been constant and extreme . . . It is one thing to talk about the end of civilization and another to feel that the thing is not merely possible but measurably probable." Resistance to this pressure could be accomplished only through a secular form of conversion: "Resistance to the pressure of ominous and destructive circumstance consists of its conversion, so far as possible, into a different, an explicable, an amenable circumstance." And just as for the elect, conversion depended on hearing the word, so was it still for those desiring to save their spirits from the pervasive "sense of upheaval" in this later moment.

In "The Divinity School Address," Emerson invoked "the moaning of the heart . . . bereaved of the consolation, the hope, the grandeur, that come alone out of the culture of the moral nature," asking,

Where now sounds the persuasion, that by its very melody imparadises my heart, and so affirms its own origin in heaven? . . . Where shall I hear these August laws of moral so pronounced, as to fill my ear . . . The test of the true faith, certainly, should be its power to charm and command the soul, as the laws of nature control the activity of the hands, – so commanding that we find pleasure and honor in obeying. The faith should blend with the light of rising and setting suns, and with the flying cloud, the singing bird, and the breath of flowers.[71]

Stevens, before closing his lecture with a clarification of the roles of priest and poet – "The poet cannot profess the irrational as the priest professes the unknown. The poet's role is broader, because he must be possessed, along with everything else, by the earth and by men in their earthy implications" – made his opening, seemingly "trivial trope," the sound of the cat running on the crust of snow, resonate to "reveal a way of truth," the implications folded into his secular sermon, delivered in the midst of the ongoing "war between the mind / And sky"[72] characterizing his century and continuing into ours. ("Americans will go to the polls in a time of threat and ongoing war" – George W. Bush, October 24, 2004.) The topic concerned what he would further specify in "Notes Toward a Supreme Fiction," the necessity of "The fiction of an absolute," of hearing "The luminous melody of proper sound":[73]

The slightest sound matters. The most momentary rhythm matters. You can do as you please, yet everything matters. You are free, but your freedom must be consonant with the freedom of others. To insist for a moment on the point of sound . . . You have somehow to know the sound that is the exact sound; and you do in fact know, without knowing how. Your knowledge is irrational. In that sense life is mysterious; and if it is mysterious at all, I suppose that it is cosmically mysterious . . . What is true of sounds is true of everything: the feeling for words, without regard to their sound, for example. There is, in short, an unwritten rhetoric that is always changing and to which the poet must always be turning.

Turning toward the "unwritten rhetoric," turning toward the dark, open space of "gods dispelled in mid-air," to shape there "an unalterable vibration"[74] as effective as the "beautiful meteor of the snow" in revealing the "cosmically mysterious" atmosphere of being, was what Stevens took on as his "holy office":[75]

The deepening need for words to express our thoughts and feelings which, we are sure, are all the truth that we shall ever experience, having no illusions, makes us listen to words when we hear them, loving them and feeling them, makes us search the sound of them, for a finality, perfection, and unalterable vibration, which it is only within the power of the acutest poet to give them . . . those who understand that words are thoughts and not only our own thoughts but the thoughts of men and women ignorant of what is that they are thinking . . . poetry is words; and . . . words, above everything else, are, in poetry, sounds . . . A poet's words are of things that do not exist without the words . . . It seems, in the last analysis, to have something to do with our self-preservation, and that, no doubt, is why the expression of it, the sound of its words, helps us to live our lives.[76]

"Poetry, then, is the only possible heaven."[77] Stevens answered Emerson's call, itself echoing Edwards's, for a solution to the equation identifying gravity and grace:

I look for the hour when that supreme Beauty, which ravished the souls of those eastern men, and chiefly of those Hebrews, and through their lips spoke oracles to all time, shall speak in the West also. The Hebrew and Greek Scriptures contain immortal sentences, that have been bread of life to millions. But they have no epical integrity; are fragmentary; are not shown in their order to the intellect. I look for that new Teacher, that shall follow so far those shining laws, that he shall see them come full circle; shall see their rounding complete grace; shall see the world to be the mirror of the soul; shall see the identity of the law of gravitation with purity of heart; and shall show that Ought, that Duty, is one thing with Science, with Beauty, and with Joy.[78]

"[E]verything is everywhere at all times, for every location involves an aspect of itself in every other location. Thus every spatio-temporal standpoint mirrors the world." "The solid earth disappears and the whole atmosphere is subtilized not by the arrival of some venerable beam of light from an almost hypothetical star but by a breach of reality. What we see is not an external world but an image of it and hence an internal world."

"Live with the privilege of the immeasurable mind,"[79] Emerson directed. Stevens realized that privilege in realizing mind itself as the "breach of reality," a space scintillant with storms of neurons firing in constant response "its contributions to the electro-magnetic field." To provide within descriptions of this breach the "satisfactions of belief," "that which gives us a momentary existence on an exquisite plane"[80] as did once the Psalms, singing of "that supreme Beauty, which ravished the souls of those eastern men," was Stevens's purpose. The pattern of attention reflected in his 1909 letter to Elsie, moving from noticing pigeons circling in the sky, to probing the sacred power of the original church with its connection to lived experience, to recognizing the humanity of Jesus and naturalizing the idea of divinity, to thinking about "a new name for the Milky Way, a new aspect of Life," to "digging into the Psalms . . . full of praise – and rejoicing," this pattern spiralled out over the course of Stevens's lifetime to include within each of its turns enlargements of the "breach of reality," the space of his mind from its original "*there*," new names, new aspects: "Throw away the lights, the definitions, // And say of what you see in the dark // That it is this or that it is that, / But do not use the rotted names."[81] He followed Emerson's direction to become "a newborn bard of the Holy Ghost," to use words once more "to stimulate the understanding [and] the affection," to "clothe . . . thought in its natural garment": "wise men pierce . . . rotten diction and fasten words again to visible things; so that picturesque language is at once a commanding certificate that he who employs it, is a man in alliance with truth and God."[82] This spiralling was the template of the act, the manner, of his making his poems, the "facture of the level or position of [his] mind . . . of [his] feelings" that he had noted in "A Collect of Philosophy."

The spiralling pattern, the "facture," describing the ecstatic method of nature, from the manner of plant growth and snow crystals which he had learned from studying Goethe and Haeckel, with his notion of the "crystal soul,"[83] to the motion of the stars and planets composing the Milky Way, to the sub-atomic vibrations of protons, electrons, and quarks, springs from cyclic return and advance through an ever-changing electromagnetic field. "Put the Universe under a powerful enough microscope," high-energy physicists currently working at Harvard and at the Fermi Laboratory observe, "and you will find that space itself is a lattice, an array of discrete points,"[84] an infinite crystal: "You will have stopped revolving except in crystal."[85] Stevens returned again and again to Emerson, to the Psalms, and in projecting his "masque / Beyond the planets" described what he saw "in the dark" when he read of the mysterious cosmic uncertainty laid out by the scientists of his moment: "these / The responsive, still sustaining pomps for you / To magnify, if in that drifting waste / You are to be accompanied by more / Than mute bare splendors of the sun and moon."[86] He marked the Psalms as he read and reread, checking, underlining, circling, finding there images he turned into the sound of his words; copied "I am a stranger in the earth" from Psalm 119 not only into his letter to Elsie but again on the inside cover of one of his notebooks; added above Psalm 100, "An exhortation to praise God cheerfully," an indication he would code into his title, "The Comedian as the Letter C," the letter "C" signifying not only the speed of light but the Roman numeral for 100. Psalm 119, its heading underlined twice by Stevens, provided him a lesson in form as well as content.[87] It is worth remarking in connection with Stevens's periodic returns to the Psalms and his celestial imaginings that Einstein similarly paired the voicings of the prophets with cosmic awareness, as he observed in "Religion and Science," an essay for the *New York Times* in 1930: "The beginnings of cosmic religious feeling already appear at the early stage of development, for example, in many of the Psalms of David and in some of the Prophets."[88] It is also worth noting, in terms of Stevens's participation in the ongoing work of the Reformation, that the metrical translations of the Psalms in post-Reformation England became "a crucial part of the Reformers' project to render the Scriptures accessible and appealing," and that "both in medieval and early modern England, the Psalms also had more liturgical importance than any other single book of the Bible."[89] It was this tradition the Reformers brought to the New World and in which

Stevens was reared, listening to and reciting Psalms throughout his boyhood and adolescence: "you can compel by the force of rhythm and sound alone, by getting the right words into the right order at the right speed, and so setting up a kind of movement that the thing being charmed will be forced to imitate."[90]

Of the eight psalms structured as acrostics using the letters of the Hebrew alphabet, Psalm 119, a meditation on the law of God, is the longest and most complex. Each stanza consists of eight lines all beginning with the same Hebrew letter; the twenty-two stanzas use all the letters in turn. In addition almost every line contains the word "law" or a synonym.[91] The artificial structure of the acrostic results in a seeming lack of logical sequence, yet the order imitates the alphabet and its permutations, our most deeply imprinted cultural code, an analog of the law of God, simultaneously as real and abstract as a number system, with the notable difference that it consists of a limited set of variables which, nonetheless, like the elements of the genetic code, combine in unlimited possibilities. The distinctive complementary disorder and order of Stevens's style elaborate this kind of spelling of at first seemingly random natural signs represented by letters into a sequence that only in its wholeness reveals its order: "all language contains its own incommensurable, uniquely constituted infinity."[92] Like Bach's Goldberg Variations or "The Art of Fugue," the repetitions and variations of Stevens's limited set of elements follow the form of a spiral. The iterations of certain words, images, and patterns, over the course of time's spiralling, produce, if imaginatively projected, a lattice, a crystalline form. And in the same way that the regularity of Bach's progressions in "The Art of Fugue" accentuates our suspension in its unresolved ending, Stevens's occasional disruptions of his regular forms properly disturb the peace of expectation, underline the artificiality of the habit of mind built on the relation of cause to effect.

Different kinds of such disruptions, like emergent properties of his system, his style, run through the corpus. A sampling of these mutations includes: the thirteen lines of the third section of "Examination of the Hero in a Time of War,"[93] the other fifteen sections offering in their fourteen lines regular variations on the sonnet; the seeming category error which at first goes unnoticed in *Dry Birds Are Fluttering in Blue Leaves–*, the title of the fourth section of "The Pure Good of Theory";[94] "the adobe of angels" in "Repetitions of a Young Captain"[95] where habitual reading expects "abode"; "rosen" where "risen" is expected in "And for all the white voices / That were rosen once" from "Things of August."[96] Each of these instances of flickering visual/sonic camouflage, like a linguistic Necker cube, imitates how the mind moves – that L. A. Necker, who in 1834 first offered this model for the quivering nature of perception, was a crystallographer is an item of interest – and alerts us simultaneously to how habit shapes perception as well as to how the disruption, once noticed, prompts us to seek an explanation, restore the balance of even just seeming certainty, that seeking itself a consequence of the habit of belief in cause and effect, the design of the universe embodied in our culture's particular ordering of its alphabet's strange signs: "The switching [perception of the cube] is a cortical process, a conflict in consciousness itself, as it vacillates between alternative perceptual interpretations."[97] Introducing Stevens's magical linguistic manipulations as examples of secular transformations of archaic sacred charms, Northrop Frye described how riddle – deriving, as he reminded, from the same root as "read" – "illustrates the association in the human mind between the visual and the conceptual. What is understood must, at least metaphorically, be spread out in space: whatever is taken in through the ear has to form a series of simultaneous patterns (*Gestalten*) in order to be intelligible."[98] Reading through Stevens, finding cognate spots of recognition, matching repetitions, noting variations and disruptions, is code-breaking, a response to his riddling the familiar, making us chase glimpses of what we think we know. This activity, in "mimic motion" of "his mythy mind," a macroscopic version of messenger-RNA transfer, is an imperfect replication of information, an engine for growth, life: *It Must Change*; "Poetry is a health."[99] The code's challenges to meaning produce imbalances, like the asymmetries intrinsic to growth in a crystal, incited by the mind's repeated turnings back through the text to understand, toward light. These experiences of language as matter, constituting one of what William James, borrowing the phrase from Emerson,[100] called "the stubborn facts" against and with which we shape ourselves, were similarly and constantly addressed, as noted earlier, by Whitehead, who pointedly repeated the phrase variously throughout his work, as here, redirecting consideration of the habits of sense belonging to the inherited code and, following James, to the necessity of attending to "the rush of immediate transition":

The macroscopic meaning is concerned with the givenness of the actual world, considered as the stubborn fact which at once limits and provides opportunity for the actual occasion. The canalization of the creative urge, exemplified in its massive reproduction of social nexus, is for common sense the final illustration of the power of stubborn fact. Also in our experience, we essentially arise out of our bodies which are the stubborn facts of the immediate relevant past. We are also carried on by our immediate past of personal experience; we finish a sentence *because* we have begun it. The sentence may embody a new thought, never phrased before, or an old one rephrased with verbal novelty. There need be no well-worn association between the sounds of the earlier and the later words. But it remains remorselessly true, that we finish a sentence *because* we have begun it. We are governed by stubborn fact.

It is in respect to this "stubborn fact" that the theories of modern philosophy are weakest. Philosophers have worried themselves about remote consequences, and the inductive formulations of science. They should confine attention to the rush of immediate transition. Their explanations would then be seen in their native absurdity. (Emphases Whitehead's)[101]

While from early on in his career, still at Harvard, Stevens was aware of James's calling attention to the strangeness of the human arrangement in language, even before, by way of the accident of his father's abiding interest in scientific and philosophical developments, he was indirectly exposed to the contribution Charles Sanders Peirce was making to the theory of signs and to the relations between habit and belief. Garrett Stevens, self-educated after primary school, became first a teacher and later, reading law on his own, passed the bar and practiced as a successful lawyer in Reading. As a subscriber to *Popular Science Monthly* (in the nineteenth century a periodical offering what today's reader might find in a combination of *Scientific American* and *Mind*), Garrett Stevens would have read Peirce's series of six essays, noted here earlier, laying out the method that became pragmatism. (See pp. 123–4.) An indication of Garrett's internalization of Peirce comes from a letter he wrote to his son in November 1897, just after he began his studies at Harvard:

Dear Wallace,
   . . . – I should like to know whether you feel that you are really improving your power to reach proper conclusions, and educating yourself in discerning that after all the positive knowledge the best have is mighty little. You have discerned I suppose, that the sun is not a ball of fire sending light and Heat – like a stove – but that radiation and reflection is [*sic*] the mystery – and that the higher up we get – and nearer to the sun the colder it gets – and a few odd things like that – but you are taught and directed in your studies in a way that you must acknowledge widens your range of vision and upsets your previous notions – teaches you to think – compels you reason – and provides you with positive facts by which you know a conclusion is correct. When this comes to you – you will first begin to absorb and philosophize – . . .[102]

In the example using the sun – most interesting in light of his son's preoccupation with images of the sun and the cold north in his poetry – Garrett illustrated Peirce's Humeian stress on the importance of doubt and of having habitual notions upset. In noting that reason provides the "positive facts" by which a correct conclusion is known, Garrett focused here and elsewhere on using reason as an empirical tool having practical value. As discussed earlier in Chapter 4, this aspect is the keystone of Peirce's thought, where it is the empirical method which gives the answer. For Peirce the rational faculty, rather than a power which is exhausted in the contemplation of things, is a means of transforming them. This lesson Garrett offered as guidance to his son who would practice it throughout his life: "Do not, therefore, look <u>at</u> facts, but <u>through</u> them" – the direction the young Wallace Stevens set down in his journal, he continued to follow deliberately in each of the poems he would compose.

The inscription from Psalm 119, "I am a stranger in the earth," excited a frequency in Stevens's imagination that increased as he learned more of "the indifferent experience of life" described by the scientists of his moment: "in the excitement of bringing things about it is not always easy to say whether one is thinking or feeling or doing both at the same time." Because of the incomplete nature of Stevens's library, it is impossible to know whether it contained publications including articles written in English by Niels Bohr during the 1920s; it is nonetheless worth remarking that Bohr repeatedly referred in these lectures and in earlier work to the "quantum postulate" – the alternating wave–particle duality affected as it is by the scale of observation and the observer himself – as "the irrational element."[103] The complementary, alternating perception of wave and particle describing quantum reality neatly parallels Stevens's description of "thinking" and "feeling," as well as the dithering counterpoint of the "poetry of the subject" and the "true subject" in his own "The Irrational Element of Poetry" illustrated in the actualities of his poems. Apart from the lack of library evidence, we know that Stevens was variously exposed to Bohr's ideas and writings, as he was to those of Planck, Einstein, Heisenberg, and the other scientists who were changing the nature of what reality was thought to be, through both his attention to these developments as they were reported in the *New York Times* and through interviews widely reprinted in journals and magazines such as *Mind, Observer,* the *Nation, Partisan Review,* Leonard Woolf's *New Statesman, Discovery,* and *Philosophy: the Journal of the British Institute of Philosophy* through the 1950s, issues of which Stevens periodically read and quoted from in his notebooks. In addition, the advent of radio enabled the public to listen to lectures on the latest developments in science, spurred especially by the interest in astronomy and the cosmos during the 1920s and '30s.[104] More specifically, during the early part of his career, Stevens was exposed to "frontier instances" of discovery through his participation between 1914 and 1916 in the weekly gatherings organized by his Harvard friend and compeer, Walter Arensberg. The "Arensberg Circle," as it came to be known informally, was modeled by Arensberg, a specialist in the work of Francis Bacon, on the *New Atlantis*, Bacon's imagined utopian community of the best minds in all disciplines speculating about the riddles of the universe: "The meanings are our own – / . . . A text of intelligent men / At the center of the unintelligible, / As in a hermitage, for us to think, / Writing and reading the rigid inscription."[105] In Bacon's view the applications of reason in science grew out of and served an aesthetic intuition of human good. Matter and spirit were not, as for Descartes, separate; rather, for Bacon the work at hand was to investigate the possibility of a transformational continuum, a "law of continuity," what Emerson would later capture in his phrasing, "Spirit is matter reduced to an extreme thinness."[106] At the gatherings in Arensberg's spacious studio apartment on West 67th Street – surrounded by works by Cézanne, Picasso, Braque, Matisse, Derain, Rousseau, Brancusi, Duchamp (who was installed by Arensberg for a time in an adjoining apartment) – Stevens, William Carlos Williams, Mina Loy, Carl Van Vechten, Edgard Varèse (speaking of music as "organized sound" and illustrating his definition with practical exercises on the piano), and others discussed the latest developments in science, philosophy, and psychology, as well as timely readings informally assigned to them by their host. Their collective attempt, as exemplified pictorially in the Cubist style paintings particularly favored by Arensberg, was, following in the line of Bacon, to reconceive the relation of subject and object, figure and ground, shape forms of expression adequate to the paradoxical new world being described through the years of their meetings most prominently by Einstein and Bohr, as well as by Planck, Ernest Rutherford (Bohr's mentor), and Eddington, each of whose discoveries was detailed in the same way as today the latest research into DNA, dark matter, and cosmic strings is reported. In addition, Arensberg, also expert in cryptography, regularly had his guests practice their own code-making and -breaking skills by suggesting they construct works that would serve as challenges to one another to find the "key" unlocking their embedded metaphors.

Bohr's model of the atom was first published in English as a three-part article in *Philosophical Magazine* in 1913; there he presented the first unified description of the "mechanism of radiation," the absorption and emission of energy by electrons in the atom as discontinuous, not only erratic but fragmentary in character. While Bohr mistakenly calculated that the electron exists in determinate positions, acting "like the Cheshire cat, disappearing from one place only to appear in another, without any explanation for its 'quantum leap,'" his model was nonetheless based on sound observations

and prompted further investigation and hypotheses to account for the paradoxical "leap"; thus in the coming years developed the "new" quantum theory elaborating Bohr's model, with Heisenberg's matrix mechanics in 1925,
Erwin Schrödinger's wave mechanics in 1926, and Wolfgang Pauli's work,
all contributing, finally, to a reestablishment of the "visual method" for
descriptions of the invisible sub-atomic field.[107] Indeed, perhaps the most
disturbing aspect of Bohr's discoveries had been the prompting of what
historians of science have called a "crisis of visualization": "The loss of visualization brought about by quantum mechanics represented one of the most
profound transformations undergone by science since the 17th century."[108]
In quantum mechanics "objects figure only as hypothetical phenomena, if
at all," and "bodies are composed of what history and intuitive experience
regard as *nothing*."[109] Schrödinger's "cat paradox," a visual allegory representing the indeterminacy involved in the standing-wave nature of the
electron's relation to the atomic nucleus, both offered a solution to what
had been the problem of the "quantum leap" and proved the value of making the invisible visible, even if his picture offered the impossible "blurred
reality" of "the living and the dead cat . . . mixed or smeared out in equal
parts." As he observed of his thought experiment, "There is a difference
between a shaky or out-of-focus photograph and a snapshot of clouds and
fog banks."[110] Heisenberg, who had with Bohr and others at first unequiv-
ocally maintained the positivist stricture against the use of pictures and
analogies for unobservable sub-atomic processes, came to recognize, as did
Bohr, their necessity and value: "When it comes to atoms, language can be
used only as in poetry. The poet is not nearly so concerned with describing
facts as with creating images and establishing mental connections . . . Quantum theory provides us with a striking illustration of the fact that we can
fully understand a connection though we can speak of it only in images
and parables."[111] It was not necessary, as Schrödinger, Heisenberg, Einstein,
Planck, and other scientists who valued thought experiments and visualization realized, that "the pictures given by scientific theories depict the world
as it exists objectively":[112] "What mattered was that they should bear /
Some lineament or character, // Some affluence, if only half-perceived, /
In the poverty of their words, / Of the planet of which they were part."[113]
As Bohr offered: "What is it that human beings ultimately depend upon?
We depend on our words. We are suspended in language. Our task is to
communicate . . . without losing the objective or unambiguous character
[of what we say]."[114] As C. E. M. Joad, one of those to whom Stevens
was indebted for elucidating the philosophical and ethical implications of
modern science, noted, "the philosophical affinity of modern physics is

distinctly Kantian. The activity of the mind faced with a homogeneous world of spatio-temporal events is, if physicists are to be believed, truly constructive."[115] It was this background radiation, signaling the constructive nature of verbal representation – scientists themselves confirming what Emerson had perceived as the necessary, synthetic function of "a material image, more or less luminous" to furnish "the vestment of thought" – that Stevens used to measure his own "up and down between" imagination and reality: "the relation between the imagination and reality is a question, more or less, of precise equilibrium," "a means by which to achieve balance and measure in our circumstances."[116]

Stevens had been well prepared to accomplish his measures, to "sustain a representation," like the scientists of his moment, of the "blurred reality" of *between*. He had immersed himself in Emerson's varying stylistic repetitions of all he had learned of electricity and waves from Faraday, Leonhard Euler, and even Roger Boscovich, who, in 1763, before Faraday, had anticipated with "a theory of the atom as a point-center surrounded by alternating short-range repulsive and attractive force fields . . . the modern dispersion of the classical atom into fields of radiant energy."[117] William James's lessons extended Stevens's attention to include thinking, consciousness, as itself a wave function, the *vague* resolving itself into a particular image, representation, only when observed, a crystallization, like a snowflake, a precipitate of the mind's weather:

Let anyone try to cut a thought across in the middle and get a look at its section, and he will see how difficult the introspective observation of the transitive tracts is. The rush of the thought is so headlong that it almost always brings us up at the conclusion before we can arrest it. Or, if our purpose is nimble enough and we do arrest it, it ceases forthwith to be itself. As a snowflake caught in the warm hand is no longer a flake but a drop, so, instead of catching the feeling of relation moving on to its term, we find we have caught some substantive thing, usually the last word we were pronouncing, statically taken, and with its function, tendency, and particular meaning in the sentence quite evaporated.[118]

The sentences of Stevens's poetry are such cross-sections of thought realized to be, in fact, like the microscopic events Heisenberg described, "no more than a set of relations, a constellation of discontinuous events . . . observable only when it is *between* stable states, only in the midst of transformation – in essence, when it is no longer identical to itself and has thus ceased to be an object":[119] "The blackbird whistling / Or just after."[120] Just as in "observing [atoms], we have to interact with them through another physical object – radiation," so in observing thoughts we have to interact with the physical object of language, the "physicality of sentences."[121] "What we observe is not the 'object' in its natural state (which is unobservable), but an artifact of the condition of observation,"[122] what Stevens properly named "facture," in the case of his poetry, the words happening to an idea constituting the artifact of the condition of observation, language practiced as *pragma*, "that which has been done . . . res, a thing, fact."[123] And, following what Marie and Pierre Curie had observed already in the mid-1890s of the elements of highest atomic weight, such as uranium and radium, just as they were continually disintegrating through a series of forms, changing their chemical nature and atomic weights, until they reached stable states, as lead,[124] so Stevens pursued what he called "the basic slate,"[125] dis-integrating what he described as the "gawdy"[126] elements of greatest poetic weight constituting *Harmonium*, through the "dithering"series of forms presented in each of his later volumes, until achieving the final stability of "The Rock."

Along the way to fulfilling his early-expressed poetic wish to "be a think-ing stone,"[127] kin to Edwards's exquisite figure of dreaming like "the sleeping rocks," Stevens had additional occasions to consider the perplexing reality of perception described by Niels Bohr and those who continued to elab-orate the theory of quantum electrodynamics. Following his receiving the 1922 Nobel Prize for Physics, Bohr delivered a series of lectures on "The Atom" at Amherst College in 1923. Robert Frost, who had maintained a keen interest in psychology and science, reading *Scientific American* regu-larly, and now teaching English at Amherst, attended two of these lectures, on atomic structure and quantum physics, and enjoyed extended conver-sations about quantum reality with Bohr.[128] While Stevens was not present at these lectures, years later, during the 1930s and '40s, during his regular winter stays in Key West, he established a friendship with Frost, another of the regular members of the vacationing literary community. Frost would also visit Stevens in Hartford. Intent as both were to have their "sentence sound," in Frost's phrase, reverberate with the actuality of things as they had come to be known, Bohr's version of "description without place" is certain to have been one of the subjects about which the two poets shared their thinking and feeling. Again, as Stevens composed "An Ordinary Evening in New Haven," the poem sequence he would read by invitation at the 1949 sesquicentennial meeting of The Connecticut Academy of Arts and Sciences, the change in world view signaled by Bohr would occupy his imagination as he had been informed that one of those representing the sciences at the gathering was to be Max Delbrück, a student of Bohr's (who would himself be awarded the Nobel Prize for Physics in 1969 and refer sig-nificantly in his acceptance speech to Samuel Beckett, the winner that year of the Prize for Literature). Delbrück, strongly influenced particularly by Bohr's *Light and Life* (1932) and by Schrödinger's *What is Life?* (1944), had become a powerful proselytizer for biology. His talk at this jubilee meeting of the Connecticut Academy was entitled "A Physicist Looks at Biology," and echoed in its second sentence, underlining the affinity between poets' and scientists' use of language, Stevens's opening phrase from "Human Arrangement," "Place-bound and time-bound . . . ":[129] "A mature physicist, acquainting himself for the first time with the problems of biology, is puzzled by the circumstance that there are no 'absolute phenomena' in biology. Everything is time bound and space bound."[130] Delbrück elaborated this perception variously with vivid evocations of the unique situation of any living organism against its cosmic background:

the things selected for carry genetic permanence . . . new abstractions . . . bound up with the fact that every biological phenomenon is essentially an historical one, one unique situation in the infinite total complex of life.

. . . The curiosity remains . . . to grasp more clearly how the same matter, which in physics and in chemistry displays orderly and reproducible and relatively simple properties, arranges itself in the most astounding fashions as soon as it is drawn into the orbit of the living organism. The closer one looks at these performances of matter in living organisms the more impressive the show becomes. The meanest living cell becomes a magic puzzle box full of elaborate and changing molecules . . . any one cell represents more an historical than a physical event . . . any living cell carries with it the experiences of a billion years of experimentation by its ancestors . . . a living cell is a system in flux equilibrium . . .

. . . the key problem of biology, from the physicist's point of view, is how living matter manages to record and perpetuate its experiences.[131]

Reflecting on this 1949 occasion in his 1969 Nobel Prize lecture, Delbrück commented on the "irreciprocity" in the Connecticut Academy's having invited the scientists to attend the artists' offerings but not vice versa. (Paul Hindemith was the other artist who had been invited with Stevens to "create" and to "perform"; Hindemith, like Stevens, interested in celestial movements and representing "cosmic drama" in his work,[132] conducted a composition for trumpet and percussion; the other invited scientist was Thomas Hope Johnson.) Though Delbrück's memory was mistaken, both Stevens, Hindemith, and the general public having been invited to the scientists' talks, he observed that this disjunction was "fitting" because, for the scientist, "The medium in which he works does not lend itself to the delight of the listener's ear" – scientists, in general, being asked only rarely to meet with artists and "challenged to match the others' creativeness." "Such an experience may well humble the scientist," he added, having noted as well how greatly the scientists had profited from hearing "An Ordinary Evening in New Haven" and the Hindemith piece. He himself had prepared for that occasion by reading Stevens's poetry. He returned again to the significance of language and form: "The books of the great scientists are gathering dust on the shelves of learned libraries. And rightly so. The scientist addresses an infinitesimal audience of fellow composers. His message is not devoid of universality but its universality is disembodied and anonymous. While the artist's communication is linked forever with its original form."[133] Delbrück's talk at the Connecticut Academy, as well as that of Thomas Hope Johnson – a "Review of Cosmic Rays" – were later available to Stevens in the *Transactions*, and he would have been informed months before the November event of the topics of the talks to be given by Delbrück and Johnson.[134] Given Delbrück's interest in the language of poetry and his preparation in having read Stevens, he is certain to have sought out the poet and talked with him during the dinner, which Stevens described later to Alfred Knopf as "quite an affair,"[135] the exact terms Delbrück used for this "celebration." Given Delbrück's focus in his work on the "time bound and space bound" nature of organic life, its historicity; his investigation, following Bohr's lead, into the possible biological analogs of the complementarity model of wave–particle duality; his particular interest in light, specifically in phototaxic response as a model for sensory perception generally; and his concern with the "key problem of . . . how living matter manages to record and perpetuate its experiences" – given all this, it is useful as a thought experiment illustrating Stevens's premise that poets use the "same faculties" as those who "fix the bearing of men in reality" to consider why the scientist would have remembered twenty years later having so much enjoyed "An Ordinary Evening in New Haven."

Stevens read eleven of the poem's thirty-one sections in that November (I, VI, IX, XI, XII, XVI, XXII, XXVIII, XXX, XXXI, XXIX in this order).[136] Thinking as he did "of the poet as a whole biological mechanism," he would have had in mind as he both composed this long sequence and selected those portions he would read that his first audience would include scientists. The occasion would thus provide the perfect setting in which to present the proofs validating the axioms of Pragmatism, which he, no less than Henry James, would have realized himself to have been practicing throughout his career: (1) "words of the world are the life of the world"; (2) "the theory / Of poetry is the theory of life, // As it is, in the intricate evasions of as, / In things seen and unseen, created from nothingness"; (3) "The poem is . . . / Part of the res itself and not about it"; (4) "It is not in the premise that reality / Is a solid. It may be a shade that traverses / A dust, a force that traverses a shade." Words understood pragmatically, "Part of the res itself," constitute such "a force": "A force capable of bringing about fluctuations in reality in words free from mysticism is a force independent of one's desire to elevate it. It needs no elevations. It has only to be presented, as best one is able to present it."[137] The sections of "An Ordinary Evening in New Haven" describe the superpositions "dithering" in the poet's imagination, "The mobile and the immobile flickering / In the area between is and was" that, in the same way ice crystals ephemerally join to form a snowflake, combine to form the complex "cry of its occasion" that the poem is, a phenomenon illustrating the principle of complementarity no less than an atom observed: the poem is heard as modulated waves of sound, "the beauty of inflection," and seen in a seeming yet simultaneous "just after," in the particles of images made visible in the cloud chamber of mind, "the beauty of innuendo."[138] Giuseppe Ungaretti observed of Petrarch that he was "capable of making us feel in four lines the presence of the material world and of memory, and of how rapid is the transition between the two."[139] Stevens shared this capability.

Each of the sections of the poem is an instance of "flitting" observation of one of the superpositions, "ditherings" – a word Stevens used pointedly and increasingly in his late poetry and prose, together with "fluctuations," "flickerings," "vibrations" – where the interplay of inflection and innu-endo, overlaid and reinforced by equivocating sentences, ambiguous word use (beginning with "evening" in the title where the idea of the sound of a "trumpet ordinary" *evening* in its dissipating reverberations, prompted by the religious suggestion of "vulgate of experience" in the second open-ing line, plays against the *evening* of light during the time when he and Hindemith, with his concerto for trumpet and bassoon, would offer their performances for the Connecticut Academy's "jubilee," a word derived from the Hebrew name for the "ram's horn" used to mark ritual rejoic-ing), combine to produce the verbal equivalent of the "critical opalescence" that Delbrück would have recognized as the perfect figure for both quan-tum reality and the shift marked by Einstein's discovery which permitted it. Freeman Dyson, following Peter Galison's choice to use this exquisite fact as the metaphor for the idea of "coordinated time" and "simultaneity" intrinsic to the evolving perception of the quantum world, offers a lucid and useful description:

Galison uses the phrase "critical opalescence" to sum up the story of what happened in 1905 when relativity was discovered. Critical opalescence is a strikingly beautiful effect that is seen when water is heated to a temperature of 374 degrees Celsius under high pressure. 374 degrees is called the critical temperature of water. It is the temperature at which water turns continuously into steam without boiling. At the critical temperature and pressure, water and steam are indistinguishable. They are a single fluid, unable to make up its mind whether to be a gas or a liquid. In that critical state, the fluid is continually fluctuating between gas and liquid, and the fluctuations are seen visually as a multicolored sparkling. The sparkling is called opalescence because it is also seen in opal jewels which have a similar multicolored radiance.[140]

Stevens's "transparencies of sound // . . . Impalpable habitations that seem to move / In the movement of the colors of the mind," described the common work of scientists, poets, and priests:

> . . . We seek
> Nothing beyond reality. Within it,
>
> Everything, the spirit's alchemicana
> Included, the spirit that goes roundabout
> And through included, not merely the visible,
>
> The solid, but the movable, the moment,
> The coming on of feasts and the habits of saints,
> The pattern of the heavens and high, night air.

Stevens's imaginings in the months during which he put the poem together would also have been stimulated by contemplating what Thomas Johnson would describe in his "Review of Cosmic Rays": "The imaginative transcripts were like clouds, / . . . and the transcripts of feeling, impossible / To distinguish." Fascinated as the poet was by the shimmering displays of the aurora borealis which he had felt privileged to have observed on various occasions in the night sky above his northeastern home, having only recently composed "Auroras of Autumn," and, during the same months in which he composed "An Ordinary Evening in New Haven," thinking of using "Auroras of Autumn" for the title of his forthcoming volume as well – we recall James, ". . . whilst we think, our brain changes, and that, like the aurora borealis, its whole internal equilibrium shifts with every pulse of change"[141] – he would find in what Johnson described further enlargements of his lifelong preoccupation with light and the sun: "To re-create, to use // The cold and earliness and bright origin / Is to search . . . // The sun is half the world, half everything, / The bodiless half." Cosmic rays, he would learn, are actual angels of reality, described by scientists as "messengers from distant regions in our galaxy and beyond," which, when deflected by and combining with the solar cosmic rays of the solar wind meeting the earth's magnetic field, produce the auroral displays, the celestial evidence of our "bond to all that dust."[142] Michael Faraday's prehension of electromagnetic lines of force, so suggestive to Emerson and richly productive for the continuing investigations by Helmholtz and Maxwell which led to Einstein's theory, was by 1949 in fact observable as the "space weather" Johnson described. As Bohr had recognized, reality is, indeed, an activity of the most august imagination shared by scientists and poets intent on providing "the edgings and inchings of final form, / The swarming activities of the formulae / Of statement, directly and indirectly getting at, // Like an evening evoking the spectrum of violet . . ." Understanding the nature and behavior of cosmic rays depends on the same processes as those used for observing electrons on the sub-atomic level; for both kinds of phenomena, light given off in collisions in cloud chambers discloses the ever-changing composition of the invisible, things as they are, the paradox we inhabit, "all of paradise that we shall know":[143]

The acute intelligence of the imagination, the illimitable resources of its memory, its power to possess the moment it perceives – if we were speaking of light itself, and thinking of the relationship between objects and light, no further demonstration would be necessary. Like light, it adds nothing but itself. What light requires a day to do, and by day I mean a kind of Biblical revolution of time, the imagination does in the twinkling of an eye. It colors, increases, brings to a beginning and end, invents languages, crushes men and, for that matter, gods in its hands.[144]

In *QED: The Strange Theory of Light and Matter*, Richard Feynman, offering various visual and verbal metaphors for the paradoxical, counter-intuitive nature of quantum reality, observes:

light is something like raindrops – each little lump of light is called a photon – and if the light is all one color, all the "raindrops" are the same size . . . If we were evolved a little further so we could see ten times more sensitively, we wouldn't have to have this discussion – we would all have seen very dim light of one color as a series of intermittent little flashes of equal intensity.[145]

The work of the poet, as Stevens conceived it, is to shape in language a template of the imagined landscape of those further evolved beings, as Milton provided in *Paradise Lost* the template for the process of evolution.[146] Language used this way, in the case of Stevens used to provide the satisfactions of belief within paradox and perplexity, is like proof theory in mathematics, concerned with the range of possible techniques and methods used in projecting hypothetical answers to still insoluble problems. How is language to describe, for instance, what Erwin Schrödinger remarked as "the most amazing novel aspect in Einstein's 'Restricted' [Special] Theory of Relativity": "that two events may happen in such a way that *either of them* may be regarded as the earlier one" (emphasis Schrödinger's)?[147] As Delbrück noted in closing his Connecticut Academy talk, reiterating the point made by Bohr about the then-current situation in biology, "analysis seems to have stalled around in a semi-descriptive manner without noticeably progressing towards a radical physical explanation" which would demand the stating of "clear paradoxes" such as those which "necessitated [the] revision of our ideals (or prejudices) regarding the description of nature . . . to replace the classical conceptual scheme of particles moving in well defined orbits by the new scheme of quantum states and transition possibilities," the "vibrations" paradoxically accounting for "stability" in the new quantum theory.[148] Delbrück, the physicist looking at biology, speculating "that life . . . evolved from something like crystallization from supersaturated solutions," and searching for "a coherent account of [the] phenomena"[149] of our condition, depended on using "the same faculties" as the poet, "a unity of language and life." He recognized that the poet, "a metaphysician in the dark,"[150] can provide accurate guesses at the riddle, precipitating from the flashes in the cloud chamber of his mind – his "radiant and productive atmosphere"[151] – the sounds of words and shapes of lines that function as what statisticians call "confidence intervals,"[152] and Stevens, "fiction[s] in which we believe willingly," measures that provide the range of possible effects from the available facts. As Gillian Beer has noted, "the power of the creative thinker to outgo the evidence and to generalize convincingly from not-yet-adequate data is a powerful fact of scientific history."[153] For the scientist of the modern world, holding that "every spatio-temporal standpoint mirrors the world," this kind of seeing would of course be possible, "the celestial possible."[154] It is not surprising that Delbrück attended carefully to the sound of words in Stevens's stanzas, the rooms of his ideas, where he described the elements of his naturalized typology, a scientifically informed idealism, a twentieth-century variety of *Images or Shadows of Divine Things*.

Important to remember, in the context of Stevens's ability to fashion a habit of mind fitting to the universe of chance continuing to be described in ever-deepening detail by the scientists of his moment, is his preparation in considering probabilities in his work as a lawyer for the Hartford Accident and Indemnity Company. Not only did statistical projections constitute part of his daily engagement with "reality," but in having to compose the briefs that would make the case for or against the Hartford's issuing a policy or paying on a claim, translating the abstraction of tables into persuasive language, he had to attend to what Ian Hacking in his work on the emergence of probability has called "words in their sites":

Words in their sites. A concept is no more than a word or words in the sites in which it is used. Once we have considered the sentences in which the word is used, and the acts performed by uttering the sentences, and the conditions of felicity or authority for uttering those sentences, and so on, we have exhausted what there is to be said about the concept. A strict version would say we have exhausted the concept when we have considered (*per impossibile*) all the actual specific utterances of the corresponding words.[155]

In a universe considered probabilistically, as Hacking also observes, "the space in which we organize our thoughts has mutated."[156] This new space requires reconceptualizations and so experimental sites. In these experiments, "one conducts the analysis of words in their sites in order to understand how we think and why we seem obliged to think in certain ways."[157] We recall the examples cited earlier of some of Stevens's mutations. He was continuing the work begun by Peirce, James, and the other members of the Metaphysical Club, to shape a method to supersede induction – "a central problem of philosophy" – and redefine "facts":

the problem of induction requires for its formulation a particular conception of the world. It may have had any number of sources, but it seems to be derived principally from commercial transactions, for whose purposes the world, or at any rate its wealth, is so abstracted that it consists only of particulate facts. All data, all rock-bottom givens, are permanent momentary items of fact like those that appear in a ledger book. That is a conception within which the problem of induction seems almost inevitable. Hume thought that all our impressions are of particulate facts. If you want to undo the problem of induction, you have to observe that our impressions are not of particulate facts but of the proverbial balls in motion, and a billiard ball is not something particular, momentary. [We recall here James's use of this example in *Pragmatism*.] In short, one has to undo the starting point. Both modern probabilistic evasions of the problem of induction are quite effective, if not decisive. Here I mean both the Bayesian evasion – the so-called "subjective" approach that analyzes degrees of belief – and the Peircian one – the so-called "objective" approach that analyzes frequencies and confidence intervals.[158]

Stevens, well-practiced in imagining the balls in motion for the Hartford, adapted his skills – his poems, setting up "words in their sites," laboratories for analyzing "degrees of belief," providing "confidence intervals," the range of possible effects comparable with the concepts spun out, as in a centrifuge, during each experiment: "Poetry is nothing if it is not experiment in language."[159] New relations between words were and are required, especially so during periods of major transition in the way we conceive of the universe and our place in it, as we have been experiencing most acutely over roughly the last century and a half. As Hacking indicates, a "therapy model" is called for to analyze and reformulate concepts:

Concepts have memories, or at any rate, we in our very word patterns unconsciously mimic the phylogeny of our concepts. Some of our philosophical problems about concepts are the result of their history. Our perplexities arise not from that deliberate part of our history which we remember, but from that which we forget. A concept becomes possible at a moment. It is made possible by a different arrangement of earlier ideas that have collapsed or exploded. A philosophical problem is created by the incoherencies between the earlier state and the later one. Concepts remember this, but we do not: we gnaw at problems eternally (or for the lifetime of the concept) because we do not understand that the source of the problem is the lack of coherence between the concept and that prior arrangement of ideas that made the concept possible.[160]

Stevens understood: "Poetry is a cure of the mind."[161] His work with words was as deliberate as that of any scientist. Delbrück understood this and so attended as carefully to him as he did to Niels Bohr.

Einstein, commenting on Niels Bohr's achievement, pinpointed the signal feature of his discovery to be like a "miracle" and "the highest form of musicality in the sphere of thought."[162] In this connection, and returning along the way to Stevens's variations throughout his corpus on the figure of "snow like eyesight falling to earth" with its bond to Emerson's snows – the "snow-puddle" at twilight; "the beautiful meteor of the snow"; "the snow-storm was real" – this chapter will close with an exercise illustrating the musicality also evident in Stevens's thinking to show that, indeed, "the theory of poetry is the theory of life."

MUSIC IS A LOGICAL STRUCTURING LIKE A MATHEMATICAL
PROOF OF ITSELF, BUT IT IS NOT MATHEMATICS. IT IS MORE
LIKE A MATHEMATICAL STORY TOLD DRAMATICALLY; NOT
NECESSARILY WITH HIGH DRAMA, BUT WITH PASSION[163]

In "The Irrational Element in Poetry," where, we recall, snow served as his focusing metaphor, Stevens invoked the figure of the poet "of such scope that he can set the abstraction on which so much depends to music." He spoke there too, we remember, of the "unwritten rhetoric that is always changing and to which the poet must also be turning."[164] Throughout his corpus, as many readers have noted, Stevens draws comparisons between this sense and "weather": "What / One believes is what matters. Ecstatic identities / Between one's self and the weather and the things / Of the weather are the belief in one's element."[165] Particularizing this observation, in *Toy Medium: Materialism and the Modern Lyric*, Daniel Tiffany has recently connected Stevens's preoccupation with weather to "the materialist implications of his poetic meteorology," and thereby to the influence of Giambattista Vico and to the Baroque "philosophy of meteors."[166] While concentrating on the modern lyric, Tiffany's project fits well with the argument amplified through the chapters here, as he demonstrates most effectively how "poetry's vision of the corporeal can help to elucidate the sometimes paradoxical bodies conjured by scientific materialism . . . approach[ing] the concept of matter through the category of the aesthetic, but also . . . seek[ing] to articulate the aesthetic through the vocabulary of materialism."[167] Similarly, John Bayley, reflecting on W. H. Auden's speculation that the form of the Petrarchan sonnet embodies the same ratio as other natural objects, as do the trunks of certain trees to their branches, comments that successful poetry is "fathomed through the deepest . . . symmetry of our own mental process."[168] Elaborating the "philosophy of meteors," Tiffany adduces parallels between Johannes Kepler's 1611 treatise on the snowflake – which instances the evanescent crystal as the prime embodiment of the principle of inorganic form, an ever-changing "meteoric" representation of the relation between earth and sky – and Stevens's myriad variations on snow, circling, of course, around the central conceit of "The Snow Man." Pointing out Kepler's delight in playing upon "an interlingual pun between the Latin word for snowflake, *nix*, and the German *nichts* (nothing), calling it 'an omen in the name,'" Tiffany notes the German scientist's hypothesizing that "the meteoric body of the snowflake . . . depicts not only the subliminal atom but also the method by which one visualizes and objectifies the atom," and quotes from the treatise: "Why, my endeavor to give almost Nothing almost comes to nothing! From this almost Nothing I have almost formed the all-embracing Universe itself!"[169] While there is no direct evidence that Stevens was familiar with this work, given "The Snow Man"'s imperfect replication of Kepler's central conceit, "Nothing that is not there and the nothing that is," it is hard to believe that he was not, though it is equally possible that, with his habit of reading dictionaries to search out etymologies and usages and with his own preparation in Latin and German, he could have found himself playing with the same interlingual pun. The fact of influence is incidental to that of the shared perception of realizing snow to be the perfect figure with which to visualize so many simultaneous aspects of the paradoxical reality constituting human nature and habitation: snow making the invisible visible, following the shapes of air in its movements; falling in particles, moving in waves; each crystal a varying of one form depending on the variables of light/heat/cold, pressure; seeming solid yet continuously changing; the perfect figure for making apparent the actuality of "momentary existence on an exquisite plane," protons and electrons shivering into the evanescent drifts we take to be reality – "The snow-storm was real." (We perhaps recall that William Hazlitt's image for Locke's epistemology was snow melting in its fall.) Tiffany cites a historian of science observing of Kepler's treatise, "it defined a new realm of inquiry for exact science: the mathematics of the genesis of form," and established a threshold for "the mathematical physics of small systems."[170] Tiffany does not, however, add that the mathematical form of snow crystal formation, following the logarithmic spiral of the Fibonacci Series characterizing dynamic symmetry and based on the Golden Ratio, the "most irrational" of all irrational numbers, is also that of musical fugue, nor that this formation depends, in the case of both inorganic and organic forms, on the repeated polarity resulting from less-than-momentary asymmetries created by a form's response to light, turning toward the unwritten rhetoric of the universe.[171] It is this repeated "symmetry breaking" that accounts for growth and change from the quantum level to that of cosmological observation.[172] In the middle of this scale, life as described by Darwinism repeats this activity, with the "continual, novelty-generating disequilibrium between [chance and necessity], with aleatory processes (mutation, sexual recombination, migratory mixing) and the elimination of the unfit operating in staggered tandem over time."[173]

Stevens's imagining of himself in "a world in which, like snow, / He became an inhabitant, obedient / To gallant notions on the part of cold,"[174] is a visual embodiment of the musicality of his sphere of thought, his "perceptual field," in Whitehead's terms. The following exercise will demonstrate Stevens's understanding and practice of musicality as an advance in the evolution of language. Those who perform his work learn to see as the more evolved beings Feynman invokes. Stevens's poems are exercises in perceiving the invisible, not only light as photon particles moving in waves and as, in the latest research, thought to be spiralling, "zipping along a corkscrew path," to form (in exhilarating experimental extensions of Swedenborg's imagining of the correspondence between microcosmic and macrocosmic scales) helices and double helices within those amplitudes and frequencies,[175] but equally important in relation to Bohr's and Delbrück's pursuit of the biological analogue of the complementarity principle – which permits the realization of light's nature – as the complementarity of feeling and thinking in consciousness, William James's "perceptual field," a field Stevens also continued to cultivate. I have chosen "Peter Quince at the Clavier"[176] as a sample exercise because of its explicit musical offering, epitomizing, as it were, the project of *Harmonium* as well as of the corpus represented in *The Collected Poems* of 1954, which Stevens had wished to entitle *The Whole of Harmonium* until dissuaded by his publisher.

"Music is feeling, then, not sound" opens the second tercet of the poem's first of four sections. The occasion, by the speaker's account, is "thinking" of a woman in her "blue-shadowed silk," which, it is noted, "Is music." This thinking brings with it, or is identical with, an extended meditation connecting the poem's "I" with the "red-eyed elders" who enter the poem by way of a variation on the Apocrypha story of Susanna. Stevens's elders, well-hidden, watch Susanna bathe and feel "The basses of their beings throb / In witching chords, and their thin blood / Pulse pizzicati of Hosanna." In connection with the multiple "realities through which the poet passes to and fro," the superpositions of consciousness, it is useful to know that in the early years of his marriage Stevens had given his then still beautiful wife a blue silk kimono and a piano, and that he knew Handel's oratorio "Susanna," with which his poem shares certain structural similarities. In Part I, Scene 3, for example, the tenor enters accompanied by the throbbing of basses and intones the pain of his amorous strain. A second elder, a bass, enters next, opening the subsequent scene and adding his voice to the deepening drama of desire. From the first elder's opening strophes, as he begins to describe his yearning, his "thin blood," as it were, and intermittently through the elders' exchange, continuing until the end of Part I, strings pulse pizzicati. These points, condensations of memory's uppourings, function as tonal centers in fugue, around which crystals of thought, here as words, form.

Returning to the poem, we notice that it is not simply "thinking" about this woman, but "that what" the speaker feels, desiring, in an ambiguous relation to "Thinking of [her] blue-shadowed silk," that is the occasion and "Is music." This is an ambiguous relation because it is entirely unclear whether what the speaker feels, desiring, precedes thinking of the figure in the blue-shadowed silk, or whether it is the image that has prompted the feeling, or whether "Thinking of your blue-shadowed silk" is in apposition to, and therefore presented as identical with, "that what I feel . . . desiring you" ("two events may happen in such a way that *either of them* may be regarded as the earlier one"). Moreover, also uncertain is whether the "what [he] feel[s]" is identical with "desiring" the "you." What is abundantly clear, however, is that the poet has confused feeling, thinking, and desiring, or perhaps it would be better to say confused *the relations of* feeling, thinking, and desiring. In doing this, Stevens foregrounded what has become, since Darwin's unsettling news, of central concern – the origin and nature of what we call thinking: "But for that matter, what does 'to think of' mean exactly?"[177] Notably, in Stevens's alignment of thinking, feeling, and desiring with music, he uncovered, as the concealed spring, the same prime motive of all life that Darwin in his *Notebooks* points to: pleasure, most specifically, pleasure as the satisfaction of appetites and the erotic. William James further elaborated this insight, incorporating G. T. Fechner's particularizing the function of the aesthetic, of beauty, to stimulate the mind, "driven," as it is, "by pleasure."[178] Philosophers today studying the cognitive sources of rationality identify four basic grounds, "sensory experience, introspection, memory, and reflection," and note that "basic sources of rational desire include pleasure."[179] Stevens's poem serves well to examine some of the ways in which thinking has been gradually pressed to include feeling, desiring, and pleasure as part of its definition. What Whitehead called the "appetition of thought" craves beauty, pleasure, in order to be satisfied, as Stevens had naively understood even at nineteen: "the real use of . . . beauty . . . is that it is a service, a food."

To describe the work that art does, Raymond Williams uses the notion, deployed here earlier (p. 79), of "structure of feeling," the "particular living result of all the elements in the general organization" of any culture. "Structure," in Williams's view, suggests that any given culture is a distinct entity and unity and manifests a "firm and definite" articulation and shape. But it is necessary, as Williams goes on to say, to take account of "feeling" as well. Any analysis that ignores the fact of feeling remains "reductive and invalid until it incorporates 'the most delicate and least tangible parts of our activity.'"[180] The more than rational distortion that the work of art is allows it to describe more adequately what cannot be so described on what Stevens called the "flat historic scale."[181] Naturally, the more informed and attuned the poet to the myriad aspects of the human environment, the more fully will the "structure of feeling" of the work produced reflect a successful adaptation and so ensure its greater survival value. As Whitehead described in *Process and Reality*, the "physical distortion of the field, leading to instability of the structure" necessitates "the structure accepting repair by food from the environment"; thus distortion is the pre-condition of "appetition," of growth.[182]

Borrowing from the aesthetics of music the basic conceptual grid of pitch as the vertical (harmonic) axis and time as the horizontal (melodic) against and within which a musical work is composed, and connecting this idea of the grid with Williams's "structure of feeling," what is communicated under "pitch" could be understood as the range of what Williams calls "feeling," while time, parsed into tenses and other references to past, present, and future, easily enough slides into the slot of "structure." *Pitch/feeling* represents, then, those "most delicate and least tangible parts of our activity," while *time/structure* provides "firm and definite" articulation and shape. While the nuanced variety of verbal and visual expression cannot be plotted quantitatively in the manner of decibels and measured phrases of a musical composition, imagining the different elements of a poem as coordinates arranged along the vertical and horizontal axes of *pitch/feeling* and *time/structure* provides a schema for the work conceived as the relation between what we could otherwise call the connotative and denotative elements of an extended historical moment: the more "primal" or inarticulate the feeling/pitch, the more immediate, spontaneous, and "simple" the cry, the less time it takes to express; the more complex the feeling/pitch, the more time. The space opened in the plotting of these complicated gestures, "transformation by intervallic expansion" in the language of musicology, is filled by what we call thinking / music / a poem. That is, thinking is what goes on in between the sounds, the images, the words. There is an infinity of possible scales or statements. The images, the words, are not in themselves important except as notes toward the supreme fiction of relationships illustrating the operation of mind in negotiation with its surroundings, its "facture." It is to be noted that "It is the path toward vertical structure intertwined with horizontal structure that western music has taken. This rather than the path of increasing horizontal complexity. In western music the concept of harmony rises up as a dynamic force within music. This is an isolated cultural event that has not happened elsewhere."[183] Thinking is simply another of a culture's instruments, transitional in its time, with its own technology in its time, limited and limiting what can be played.

Looking at the opening of Stevens's poem will help to illustrate what is being described. We read and/or hear the title and first section, "Peter Quince at the Clavier": we imagine a man, a dandy of sorts, somewhat foppish, yet sexual because of his name with its hints of Henry James's ghostly Peter Quint from "The Turn of the Screw" and the quiet play on slang terms for both male and female pudenda; we may also recall Quince the carpenter who fashions an imaginary window – "the fitful tracing of a portal" – in *A Midsummer Night's Dream*. We picture this figure sitting at a clavier, and here our trouble begins. Are we to envision a keyboard instrument capable of holding the bass continuo that will play its part in suggesting "the basses of [the red-eyed elders'] being[s]"? Or are we to see nothing at all, following the abstract indication of "clavier" as the generic name for any keyboard instrument, and thus take Stevens's title to point us to reading the poem as being about the pure good of theory? We go on hoping for clarification through the first stanza and on into the beginning of the second, "Music is feeling, then, not sound"; there are keys, but we still do not know whether they are sounding. And what about "then"? In the parodic syllogism the poet sets up in the second stanza, "then" equivocates any possibility of certainty since we can read it in any of three ways, which will condition how we read "not sound." If we read "then" as part of the logical statement it pretends to inhabit, we have a proposition that separates sound from feeling. Or, we have an observation that the experience of music is feeling not sound, not well, whole, grounded. Or, if we follow the temporal aspect of "then," we have the speaker commenting on the power of music to evoke a past, feeling *then*, not now, and that "that what" is "not sound," not an appropriate response to the present. By thus disrupting our complacency in thinking that we understand what we read, Stevens illustrates William James's central notations in "The Consciousness of Self" chapter of *Principles* concerning the ways in which feelings, desires, divide us up in time, opening spaces in the conventional grammar and syntax of perception:

> Thought is a vehicle of choice as well as of cognition . . . It appropriates *to* itself, it is the actual focus of accretion, the hook from which the chain of past selves dangles, planted firmly in the Present, which alone passes for real, and thus keeping the chain from being a purely ideal thing. Anon the hook itself will drop into the past with all it carries, and then be treated as an object and be appropriated by a new Thought in the new present which will serve as a living hook in turn . . . Its appropriations are . . . less to *itself* than to the most intimately felt *part of its present Object, the body, and the central adjustments*, which accompany the act of thinking . . . *These are the real nucleus of our personal identity* . . . their actual existence, realized as solid present fact . . . these "warm" parts of its present object . . . a firm basis on which the consciousness of personal identity would rest. (Emphases James's)[184]

How these spaces come to be experienced by the body in its central adjustments depends on whether we can find, or ourselves shape, structures of feeling. Without structures of feeling, the spaces opened are experienced as terrifying, the abyss of the existentialists, the "vastations" described by Swedenborg, Henry James Sr., and William James.

In the first section of "Peter Quince," Stevens traces a structure of feeling, a way of thinking, that protects the speaker and the reader from falling into the abyss of uncertainty created by his having forced the realization that ordinary language is inadequate to thinking, that both language and thinking are simply instruments and exist in a reciprocal relation, like the clavier and the possible music it can or cannot produce. His score, the pattern of expression fashioned on the *pitch/time* grid, at the moment the reader's feeling of uncertainty is most intense, moves attention back in time, first to a moment in the speaker's personal past by way of an image of the desired female in her "blue-shadowed silk," and then to an apocryphal historical past redolent with images drawn from a story that simultaneously distracts attention from the reader's discomfort at not knowing how to read and communicates "that what" is the desire that is the motive and content of the thinking evidenced by and in the language of the poem. The images in this section are plotted in time analogously to the musical composer's variations in time on a stated theme, the musical fact from which the audience derives aesthetic pleasure in recognizing the theme through its variations: sameness in difference, a sort of speciation. Stevens manipulates, stretches, feeling by referencing through time by way of images that change from being representations or symbols of any kind to functioning purely as signs. The first image is soothing because derived from a lived past, the following set of images stirring because leading somewhere unexpected while elaborating a thematic connection with the first. This pattern, the feeling of knowing and not knowing at once, is familiar to us from music; we listen and anticipate, not knowing how a progression will develop, yet feel, recognize, its rightness when we hear it.

Raymond Williams's focus on the place of feeling in representation results from the same post-Darwinian reorientation concerning the nature of human experience that prompted Stevens to confuse the relations of feeling, desiring, and thinking in "Peter Quince." Through the Romantic period and well into the nineteenth century in the West the opposition between feeling and thinking was maintained, feeling consistently set aside in the equations of rationality. With the growing acknowledgment of what it means to be an animal, however, and what it is to exist in accidental propitiousness in an equally accidental environment, it has been necessary to rethink thinking. Recent work by neurobiologists Hannah and Antonio Damasio, Gerald Edelman, Jean-Pierre Changeux, and others, as noted here in earlier chapters, all following *The Principles of Psychology* – James's development of Darwin's outline as set out not only in *Origin*, but in *The Descent of Man* and *The Expression of the Emotions in Man and Animals* as well – considers human thinking as a species-specific negotiation with a complex environment based in somatic processes. The experimental evidence adduced by these researchers continues to support what Darwin theorized and grounds the argument amplified in these chapters concerning the nature and function of successful language. Those who come to be recognized as major poets have so attuned themselves to the undertones – what Seamus Heaney calls "under-ear activities" which he properly connects to "the erotics of language"[185] – of what they understand nature to be, an understanding that changes over time, that they are able to anticipate, in the structures of feeling which their works are, what later comes to be common knowledge or, in Stevens's words, "a commonsense beyond the truth . . . a nobility of long descent."[186] As William James and Charles Sanders Peirce observed, what comes to be accepted as common sense is what the species has accumulated over aeons through trial and error of one kind or another that helps it to survive: *It Must Give Pleasure*. The stylistic distortions first greeted as examples of an avant-garde aesthetic – Milton's blank verse in the seventeenth century, Emerson's seeming logical perversity in the nineteenth, Stevens's abstract fictions in the twentieth – presciently represent new forms of thinking that gradually come to be a *lingua franca*, a new "vulgate of experience," once science confirms hints provided by earlier aesthetic speculation.

I am not saying anything new here. Kant made abundantly clear the place of the aesthetic in the ascent to understanding. What has remained unclear, however, is that the aesthetic has a structure, and that this structure is identical to whatever is meant by thinking during a particular historical moment, even if at the time it is initially encountered it is not recognized as thinking, but rather cast as a form of feeling in opposition to or in contrast to what is then commonly accepted as thinking. The work of poetry is to accommodate human beings to their creaturely actuality, stretching the perceptual vocabulary to provide space and form for the animal, for feeling, the aleatory, accidental, irrational element. The more successful the poetry, the more it focuses attention on this aspect to enable its integration and expression within the *pitch/time* grid of a culture. With the increasing information being gathered about human cognition since Darwin, the opposition between feeling and thinking which shaped the syntax and grammar of our inherited ordinary language is dissolving. The fact of feeling need only be feared if there are not forms with and in which it can perform its necessary function in perception. We recall once again James's puissant passage from "The Stream of Thought": "If there be such things as feelings at all, *then so surely as relations between objects exist in rerum natura, so surely, and more surely, do feelings exist to which these relations are known*." It is this unexplored territory to which Stevens directed attention and which is illuminated in considering what music offered him as a way of beginning to understand what it would be to have forms for what James elsewhere described as those "recesses of feeling, the darker, blinder strata of character . . . the only places in the world where we catch real feeling in the making."[187]

Stevens's adherence to the symbolist rubric, derived from the *Naturphilosophen* incorporation of the aesthetic idea as expressed in Kant's

Critique of Judgment, to have all art aspire to the condition of music, has been generally observed but demands closer consideration in connection with the work of both William James and Whitehead as presented here earlier. To recapitulate, following James's exploding the "'idea' idea," Whitehead replaced the notion of "simple location" with a concept precipitated from the imagined atmosphere in which Lyell and Darwin projected their new descriptions of old worlds. What is "seen" under this dispensation of imagination is a movement through spacetime of a principle of organization. The work of thinking within it, then, is to provide a description of what has been "seen" in this way: *It Must Be Abstract* – "the brain automatically infers aspects of the stimulus that are missing and presents these as a fully elaborated percept."[188] The analogues for this kind of description, as Einstein observed in his praise of Bohr's genius, are musical composition and mathematics. Another example is offered in Mozart's description, cited by William James in illustration of the rapidity of mindwork, of seeing and hearing a symphony as whole in one moment before setting it down in time and notation.[189] Stevens's setting down is mimetic of the same kind of apprehension as Mozart's, Darwin's, or Bohr's. All recorded in flawed words and stubborn sounds something perceived only in the mind as a projection through a sequence of some kind that accounts for present fact or feeling. These translations of what is only imperfectly called "insight" represent human adjustment to an ever-changing environment. These adjustments have an animal, animate motive. They give pleasure because they harmonize us, for the extended moment they create, to the reality we inhabit that is and always has been a relation *between*, a relation between what is there outside us, Emerson's "NOT ME," and what/how we interpret that outside to be, "Me." These adjustments feel right because and when they provide the space for us to sense, to give attention, create a "room of the idea." They restore our native, natural senses by forcing us to be silent, like Milton's angels, for as long as it takes to understand. This is the area of experience to which Emerson pointed when he described the difference between "Man Thinking" and "man inhabited by thought." The styles of major poetry represent the historicizing of thinking. Music became the model for all the arts as imagination lost the idea of the static image: "The absence of imagination had itself to be imagined," the effect of time passing making the visible invisible, Cronus devouring his children. Attention had to be drawn to what happens in between facts, to relations in spacetime, to the transitive aspects of language and experience, the "overtones" and "undertones" described by William James, a cinematic sense as of fade-ins, fade-aways, and fade-outs of perception which he derived before cinema from

Helmholtz's 1860 work in physiological optics, an area which continues to be explored by neurobiologists, most specifically by the late Francis Crick in his work with Christof Koch, and by Semir Zeki.[190] Music, embodying – in its fact, its feeling – the wave–particle duality, replaced painting, the *ut pictura poesis* standard in place at least since the Renaissance, as thinking gave up the register of teleology and design and yielded to the increasing evolutionary information of the nineteenth century. Synthetic rather than analytic manners of presentation, adding moving depths of field, taking account of invisible dimensions of time and experience coded in cortical columns, became called for as models for argument.[191]

I want to explain what I mean here a little more closely because the alteration in this habit of mind is something we continue to work on in some way or another, and it is difficult to see a process we are experiencing: again, "The field cannot well be seen from within the field."[192] Moreover, conceiving of the image as discrete and corresponding to what Hacking calls "particulate fact" representing a fixed order of things is a habit worn and practiced for millennia. It is not a habit easily changed. William James and the physiologists and neuroscientists following him have demonstrated that the habits of mind that become common sense and come to seem instinctual do so because neuronal tracks are set down in the brain pan by repeated use. In order to begin to change this hard-wiring, it is not so much that the old system has to be disrupted but, as described earlier, in Chapter 2 (pp. 28–9), side-tracked. New practices must be learned through an effort of will – Peirce's *metaboly*, literally in its etymology, a change, which, in fact, changes the organism's *metabolism* – the first requirement of which is to create the time and open the mental space for attention. If the change is made abruptly, there is system error and breakdown. The hard drive cannot process the information on the new disk. The new information has to be read through the system code in place; a new style, a new aesthetic emerges. It is understandable that from the middle of the nineteenth century and into the period of early modernism those who worked most deliberately at changing the grammar and syntax of perception through their work on language and thinking suffered nervous collapse: Emerson, Peirce, William James, T. S. Eliot.[193]

The model of music offers structural accommodation to an evolutionary view of development. A variation on a particular melodic line will lead to other possible variations from which yet others branch, all having an organic connection with the opening theme but with no one progression predetermined. Possibilities present themselves as the composition grows. The finished piece is one of many potential forms. It can be read backwards to demonstrate how the design grew from its opening, but its shape could have been another. Its rightness, the pleasure derived from hearing it, has to do with what we are capable of hearing, what we are prepared to hear, quite accidentally, from the relations in pitch and time that we have grown used to hearing. A new scale is a sounding of a new spatio-temporal relation, a finding of something *in between* relations that were in place before, a new adaptation, the issue of a marriage of sorts: "We have no questions to ask which are unanswerable."[194] As Plato exquisitely explicated in the *Cratlyus*, the seed of the erotic is the question, the source without which the satisfaction of resolution would be impossible, the concealed spring of all imaginings, asking what is possible between this and that, moving into the spaces opened, feeling at sea, responding with full attention and with the animal need to survive and come to rest for a while: pleasure, renewal. This activity is beyond us, yet ourselves in the most profound sense. When Stevens, coming to the end of his poem, moved the Romantic aesthetic phrased by Keats from the Grecian urn's frozen image to its grounding in the body – "Beauty is momentary in the mind – / The fitful tracing of a portal; / But in the flesh it is immortal" – he addressed precisely the change in structure of thought and feeling occasioned by Darwin's having uncovered our common earthy ancestry:

The enduring personality is the historic route of living occasions which are severally dominant in the body at successive instants. The human body is thus achieving on a scale of concentrated efficiency a type of social organization, which with every gradation of efficiency constitutes the orderliness whereby a cosmic epoch shelters in itself intensity of satisfaction.

The crude aboriginal character of direct perception is inheritance. What is inherited is feeling-tone with evidence of its origin: in other words, vector feeling-tone.[195]

A new aesthetic form forces spaces of attention to open, breaches of reality. We do not first know what to make of what we hear or see. We are in new territory, questioning, alert, interested, literally *inter-esse*, between being one way and another. Coming to understand a new form requires time, *stand*ing *under* it, suffering its discipline, asking questions of it, engaging it again and again until we become fluent in its speech, dressed in a new habit of mind. We map the new space, repeat its contours, its relations. Our responsive accommodation to it shapes a template; we imitate the form while preserving the difference each of us is, theme and variation, adaptation, DNA and messenger-RNA. This response expresses our belief, our interpretation, a fiction in which we believe willingly, and "springs from the belief that we have only our own intelligence on which to rely":[196]

The parts of the bodily event are themselves pervaded by their own enduring patterns, which form elements in the bodily pattern. The parts of the body are really portions of the environment of the total bodily event, but so related that their mutual aspects, each in the other, are peculiarly effective in modifying the pattern of either. This arises from the intimate character of the relation of whole to part. Thus the body is a portion of the environment for the part, and the part is a portion of the environment for the body; only they are peculiarly sensitive, each to modifications of the other. This sensitiveness is so arranged that the part adjusts itself to preserve the stability of the pattern of the body. It is a particular example of the favourable environment shielding the organism.[197]

But what about images? They do form what seems to be the substance of our thoughts, memories, and dreams, and I would not have been able to communicate anything of what I have without them. They are to language what notes are to music; without them no relations could be perceived, like snow making the air visible. Because of sight's primacy in human experience, images hold a species-privileged, accidentally necessary, place. Images will not disappear, as long, at least, as our species continues to have eyes and walk upright, but our understanding of the nature of images and how they ensure our survival, our thinking, is changing and will continue to change: "It seems, in the last analysis, to have something to do with our self-preservation,"[198] product of the sense-making function of consciousness, of thinking. Here it is important to recall the distinction underlined by Andy Clark, and clearly understood by Emerson, Peirce, William and Henry James, and Stevens, between an image and the "linguistic formulation" of an image. As William James observed, "our ideas do not innervate our motor centers directly, but only after first arousing the mental sound of the words."[199] Verbal representations release action potentials, electrical pulses of individual arrangements, associations, stored pictorially, rebus-like. Stevens's repeated stress on the "sound of words" in his prose writings calls attention again to this central mechanism of mind, certainly recognized experientially by Edwards and Emerson as well in their own reflective practice. The sound of a word, each time heard, whether vocalized or in silent rehearsal in reading or thinking, stimulates a different set of neural firings, the process releasing as much of the history of the word hidden in its metaphorical etymology as is known by a particular individual, intertwined with that individual's experiential, metonymical, history of that word, the two strands connected by their changing combinations through and in time, the "occasions" of Whitehead and Stevens. The "material image, more or less luminous" thus produced is not, that is, like a photograph or representation of something out there, but, as scientists like Einstein and Bohr understood, heuristic, more like a cinematic unfolding of spectrometric crystallography, illustrating metaphor and metonymy spiralling around each other connected by particular occasions in time/experience to create a lattice of meaning, a radiant multidimensional web. The meaning produced at any given moment represents the organism's response to an environmental occasion, a "vibration of organic deformation," its "contribution to the electro-magnetic field." Meaning for the organisms we happen to be is one of the essential feedback mechanisms necessary for self-regulation maintained by the brain, "a way of reaching an equilibrium point despite unpredictable – and changing – external conditions."[200] Norbert Weiner termed this self-regulation "homeostasis," borrowing from the vocabulary of cytology, and in *Cybernetics* described its operation: "When we desire a motion to follow a given pattern, the difference between this pattern and the actually performed motion is used as a new input to cause the part regulated to move in such a way as to bring its motion closer to that given by the pattern."[201] If the content of the feedback fits, harmonizes, "in fuller union with the surrounding system,"[202] as Emerson suggested, its vibration survives and contributes to the success of the species, "[e]ach attitude being a syllable in human nature's total message," as William James noted, continuing Emerson's thought: "it takes the whole of us to spell the meaning out completely."[203] We exist in a reciprocal relation to thinking, our feedback complementing "the Darwinian notion of chance production," in fugitive propinquity to things as they are, like music:

Our solar system, with its harmonies, is seen now as but one passing case of a certain sort of moving equilibrium in the heavens, realized by a local accident in an appalling wilderness of worlds where no life can exist. In a span of time which as a cosmic interval will count but as an hour, it will have ceased to be. The Darwinian notion of chance production, and subsequent destruction, speedy or deferred, applies to the largest as well as to the smallest facts.[204]

Stevens's poem illustrates this understanding and the contributory function of the "linguistic formulation" of images – like the reduction of "feeling, then" on the keys of a piano into music, what Mallarmé called the "subdivisions prismatiques de l'Idée"[205] – to the ongoing of thinking. This kind of process, the reduction of natural phenomena to simpler units, is the "hallmark of scientific understanding . . . finding the appropriate abstraction with which to distill an aspect of knowledge."[206] Emerson, in a passage from the "Language" chapter of *Nature*, before describing the manner of addressing attention to one's thinking quoted earlier (see p. 68), had already elaborated this process as it operates linguistically:

Because of the radical correspondence between visible things and human thoughts, savages, who have only what is necessary, converse in figures. As we go back in history, language becomes more picturesque, until its infancy, when it is all poetry; or all spiritual facts are represented by natural symbols. The same symbols are found to make the original elements of all languages. It has moreover been observed, that the idioms of all languages approach each other in passages of the greatest eloquence and power. And as this is the first language, so it is the last. This immediate dependence of language upon nature, this conversion of an outward phenomenon into a type of somewhat in human life, never loses its power to affect us.[207]

Emerson invokes infancy as the muse of language – *infans*, "without words." From this the poem springs and brings us back again in astonishment, to attend in stillness and quiet to who we are and to what is around us, which may be the same thing, as David Hume speculated in describing the self as nothing more than "a bundle of perceptions," a formulation Emerson pointedly modified to "a bundle of relations."[208] The greater the pressure outside us, the more the noise of the world threatens, the greater the necessity for poetry that creates moments in which we can return to our primal condition, animals, infants, and know ourselves and our world more truly and more strange –

For the places thus first sensibly known are elements of the child's space-world which remain with him all his life; and by memory and later experience he learns a vast number of things *about* those places which at first he did not know. But to the end of time certain places of the world remain defined for him as the places *where those sensations were*; and his only possible answer to the question *where anything is* will be to say "*there*," and to name some sensation or other like those first ones, which shall identify the spot.[209]

To these places we attempt to return, in feeling one way or another, throughout life, a naturalized variety of religious experience: "Thus God's purpose in the creative advance is the evocation of intensities."[210] Feelings get temporalized into thinking as we go through experience, gathering additional names for what we encounter along the way, constructing the record of that experience in shimmering images: "Experience is never limited, and it is never complete; it is an immense sensibility, a kind of huge spider-web of the finest silken threads suspended in the chamber of consciousness, and catching every air-borne particle in its tissue. It is the very atmosphere of the mind . . . converts the very pulses of the air into revelations."[211] Yet, throughout life, the nostalgia for the animal condition of our beginning in the world keeps turning us, by its own gravity, back through those images' firing, to infancy, to being without words, reminding us that we feel things before we think them, and that following the thread of the complicated harmony that we make of what we think, back to what we feel, gives pleasure, the strain of being.

CHAPTER SEVEN

Gertrude Stein, James's Melancthon/a

Any literary work, if it accomplishes its purpose, must superinduce in the reader a whole complex of what we are accustomed to call thoughts, emotions and sensations – a state of consciousness, a state of mind; it depends for its effectiveness upon a web of associations as intricate and in the last analysis as mysterious as our minds and bodies themselves.

Edmund Wilson, "Gertrude Stein," in *Axel's Castle*

SLOWLY EVERY ONE IN CONTINUOUS REPEATING, TO THEIR MINUTEST VARIATION, COMES TO BE CLEARER TO SOME ONE[1]

It happened that in February 2001 while I was reading and discussing *The Making of Americans* in one of the graduate seminars where I rehearsed the ideas played out in this volume, news of the mapping of the human genome, seven feet of aperiodic crystal consisting of 3–6 billion nucleotide pairs,[2] was announced and its mapping published on the web. I went immediately to the site and, scrolling through, began to giggle. It seemed as though I were looking at a mapping of the unreeling repetitions and variations of Stein's remarkable verbal experiment. The permutations of the genetic code's ACTG appeared an abstraction of the multifariously inflected phrases running through Stein's amazing text.

I had drafted the sketch of what was to be the chapter on Stein for this volume some time before. I had intended to discuss the "Melanctha" section of *Three Lives* as Stein's version of a teaching text to be used in proselytizing the work of William James, arguing that, in "Melanctha," Stein translates James's major reformation of the way consciousness is conceived into a performative exercise, a kind of catechism demonstrating the necessity of taking the fact of feeling fully into account in understanding rationality, Stein as Melancthon/a to James's Luther, "ready now herself to do teaching."[3] But later in 2001 Steven Meyer's *Irresistible Dictation* appeared, detailing what I would have and more, his analyses extending throughout Stein's corpus to make the solidly constructed case for reading her work as experiments in Jamesian radical empiricism, the fact of feeling indeed taken fully into account, as well as the significance of Stein's scientific and medical background in preparing her for her investigations, aspects central to the discussion I would have presented. Meyer's superb study obviated the need for the extended analysis I had planned. The genome mapping, however, prompted a *Eureka!* moment giving new direction to my task. Subsequently Ulla Dydo and William Rice's *Gertrude Stein: The Language That Rises, 1923–1934* and Joan Retallack's chapter, "The Difficulties of Gertrude Stein, I & II," appeared, adding importantly to the critical conversation about Stein's work. More recently, Janet Malcolm's piece in the *New Yorker* (June 13 & 20, 2005) on *The Making of Americans*, in remarking again some of its salient elements, illustrated "the things everybody is certain of seeing, but which they do not really see,"[4] another "purloined letter" instance – appropriately, Poe having been, as Meyer reminds us, a favorite of Stein's.[5] My contribution in the pages following, then, is offered as coda, both to Meyer and to these other texts, as well as to my own, a closing elaboration on the structure of perception and linguistic transcription in their reciprocal relation as they have been suggested to operate throughout this volume. In the cases of the "frontier instances" who are my subjects, this relation, as demonstrated in the preceding chapters, is such that their linguistic transcriptions are *prehensions*, projected structural analogues of aspects of the nature of being and becoming, *felt* by these writers, all priests of the invisible, to be right, correct guesses at the riddle. "You must have the eyes of science to see in the seed its nodes; you must have the vivacity of the poet to perceive in the thought its futurities," Emerson noted, and Stein followed.[6]

AND I SAID THERE WAS EMERSON[7]

Paralleling the way Emerson's preparation in early-nineteenth-century natural history, geology, botany, physiology, electromagnetism, and more provided nourishment for his thinking and made his style a template of the evolutionary process later described in Darwin's *Origin*, Stein's preparation in the science of her moment, I would suggest, made her style a prehensive template of what we now recognize as the coding mechanism of the genome: "... I cannot repeat this too often any one is of one's period ... And each of us in our own way are bound to express what the world in which we are living is doing."[8] The *Eureka!* attendant on my noticing the close-ness of the genome mapping to Stein's variously recursive phrasings in *The Making of Americans* had to be probed and formulated in the context of what the world in which she was living was doing that might account for her startling anticipation.

"The genomes of many species are dominated by short sequences repeated consecutively called tandem repeats" – the opening sentence of an abstract introducing an article entitled "Methods for Reconstructing the History of Tandem Repeats and Their Application to the Human Genome," appearing October 16, 2001, eight months after the mapping appeared. Following the abstract, the four co-authors of the article present, in illustration:

Assigned to patriarchal poetry too sue sue sue sue shall sue sell and magnificent can as coming let the same shall shall shall shall let it share is share is share shall shall shall shall shell shell shall share is share shell can shell be shell be shell moving in in in inner moving move inner in in inner in meant meant might might may collect collected recollected to refuse what it is is it. ("Patriarchal Poetry," Gertrude Stein)[9]

Revealingly, these scientists studying the patterning of the genome found in Stein something overlooked by her literary readers. While nothing more concerning her example is developed in their article, the simple fact of its having been adduced begs consideration.

Now then, consider the following circumstances:

- Michael Stein attended Johns Hopkins between 1882 and 1886, continuing on for another year's graduate work in biology. For two years beginning in 1883, William Bateson (1861–1926), after studying zoology as an undergraduate at Cambridge with a focus on morphology, pursued post-graduate work at Johns Hopkins, proposing the theory, now generally accepted, that chordates evolved from the primitive echinoderm.

- Gertrude Stein began her studies at Johns Hopkins in 1897, where she would remain for the next four and a half years. As an undergraduate at Radcliffe, in addition to her work with William James and Hugo Munsterberg in psychology, her curriculum included: Zoology 1 and Zoology 2 in 1895–6 (Introductory; B in both); in 1896–7, in addition to Zoology 3 (Comparative Anatomy of Vertebrates; full-year course, B+), Zoology 16 (The Nervous System and its Terminal Organs, Central Nervous Organs and Terminal Organs of Efferent Nerves; half-year, B), Zoology 5 (Embryology of Vertebrates; half-year, A), and Botany 3 (Morphology, Histology, and Physiology of the Flowering Plant; full-year, B). Before beginning at Hopkins, Stein spent the summer of 1897 at the Woods Hole Marine Biological Laboratory taking an advanced course in vertebrate embryology,[10] the area to which William Bateson had, while at Hopkins twelve years earlier, significantly contributed, and with which now Leo Stein – in 1897–8 completing his AB at Hopkins and about to pursue his interest in biology with graduate study there, and in regular conversation with his sister – would have been immediately familiar. At Hopkins she specialized in the anatomy of the brain and the direction of brain tracts, having found that "the practice and theory of medicine did not interest her at all."[11] With Florence Sabin, under the direction of Dr. Lewellys Barker, she "especially studied" a region which presented, according to Barker in his *The Nervous System and Its Constituent Neurones*, "peculiarly puzzling" problems. This was the "nucleus of Darkschewitsch, a bundle of fibers in the medulla oblongata, that pyramid-shaped part of the brain that narrows into the spinal cord."[12]

- William Bateson, after two years of scientific travel in the Russian steppes and in Egypt, returned to Cambridge in 1887, where in 1884 Alfred North Whitehead had begun working on mathematics and logic; Whitehead would remain at Cambridge until 1910. Back in Cambridge, Bateson absorbed himself in the central problems of Darwinian theory, the nature of variation and the mechanism of heredity: "By 1891 Bateson had developed a 'vibratory theory of repetition of parts.' He viewed the organism as a whole and reasoned that when variation occurred it should affect the whole organism. He tried to express this in terms of waves or vibrations";[13] "Variation, Bateson suggested, could be expressed as a rhythmic or 'vibratory' phenomenon analogous to natural phenomena such as ripples, zebra stripes, or morphological segmentation, clearly bounded by natural breaks."[14] In 1894 Bateson published *Materials for the Study of Variation*, explicating his "vibratory" theory and arguing against Darwin that variation within species did not have to be continuous.

- Steven Meyer has observed that "Whitehead's analysis of what he initially called 'rhythm,' and subsequently referred to as 'vibrating pattern' or 'vibratory organism,' provides a scientific framework for understanding Stein's claims to recreate, and not merely represent, individuals in her post-1911 compositions."[15] In Stein's words, she "felt a desire to express the rhythm of the visible world."[16]

- "Following *Materials*, Bateson turned from observing nature to experiments. He bought incubators to store eggs, stocked poultry pens, and focused on poultry and sweet peas as his experimental systems. In 1899 he

suggested that the results of inheritance might not be a simple blending
of parental components."[17]

- "In April 1900, the Dutch biologist Hugo de Vries sent a copy of an
  overlooked article that he had recently rediscovered in the *Proceedings of
  the Natural History of Brunn* for 1866. Written by . . . Gregor Mendel, the
  paper outlined a theory of heredity that Bateson immediately grasped
  could provide a means to account for the discontinuities in organismal
  variation . . . At the annual meeting of the British Association in 1904,
  Bateson's ringing defense of Mendel was an important moment . . . and
  his books *Mendel's Principles of Heredity: A Defense* (1902) and *Mendel's
  Principles of Heredity* (1909) were widely read and enormously influential.
  At Cambridge, he attracted a core of young biologists to his laboratory
  and left his mark on the field as well by coining much of the terminology
  associated with modern Mendelian genetics, from allele and zygote to
  the term genetics itself."[18]

- After reading Mendel's paper, Bateson continued breeding experiments
  using only sweet peas. These experiments resulted in observations that
  purple flowers were inherited almost exclusively along with long pollen,
  and that red flowers almost always had round pollen. These results were
  surprising, as Mendel had stated that characteristics are inherited inde-
  pendently of each other. Later research disclosed that this phenomenon –
  "linkage" – is due to genes sitting close together on the chromosome,[19]
  part of the varied patterning of tandem repeats; "Mendel's laws have since
  become more complex. Linkage, multiple alleles, epistasis, collaboration,
  and modifiers enhance his metaphor."[20]

- Sometime during Gertrude Stein's and Florence Sabin's years at Hopkins,
  on the occasion of a debate on diabetes, the women at Johns Hopkins
  School of Medicine – a distinct minority variously taunted by their male
  counterparts – "were obliged to endure the indignity of receiving a bou-
  quet of sweet peas."[21]

LET ME MAKE BELIEVE THAT I HAVE SEEN IT AND THEN.
I WILL DESCRIBE IT[22]

Let me make believe that Stein had seen diagrams mapping the numerical
ratios of Mendel's Law of Segregation: Short/Short crossed with Tall/Tall
yield four Tall/Shorts; Short/Short crossed with Tall/Short yield two
Tall/Shorts and two Short/Shorts; and on and on. Four elements continuously and variously repeating: "I think I won't / I think I will / I think I
will / I think I won't" (ACTG repeated in a string 3–6 billion units long, its

combinations the markers revealing genetic inheritance). "Out of the two sections printed in sequence" from "On Elucidation," as Ulla Dydo notes, "she makes a checkerboard of texts and voices alternating."[23] Dydo cites another example from the same text: "There are four words in all. / There. / Why. / There. / Why. / There. / Able. / Idle."[24] There are, too, as Mendel and all nineteenth-century breeders knew, random mutations which later researchers learned result from errors in transcription, shifts of one letter in the code, imperfect replications. Of Stein's word-play, Dydo has observed: "she substitutes the homophone 'there' for 'their' or even 'three' for 'there,' or she bends 'and so forth' into a new shape, 'and so fourth'";[25] "It is wonderful the number of mistakes a verb can make."[26] And as in the endless proliferation of life forms, "Always one Stein piece engenders the next, so that each becomes a context for the next."[27] Molecular biology inherited the neo-Mendelian "idea that all of an organism's characteristics were written in a somatic language, generated by a grammar that produced outward sentences distinct but derivable from deep structure."[28] Stein believed no less than Emerson that words are things – "every word I am ever using in writing has for me very existing being"[29] – their present form containing the history of their permutations through time, her writing an example "which has in it all the history of its intellectual recreation . . . language as a real thing."[30] Why not, once the mechanism of generation had been uncovered, experiment in breeding words as well as sweet peas? Since Mendel had observed "that characteristics in intricate organisms were preserved in patterns,"[31] and since language is the unique characteristic of the intricate organisms humans are, why not consider words preserved in patterns equally as elements of the phenotype revealing the otherwise hidden permutations of the genotype unfolding its mechanism over time – in Stein's case, words preserved in patterns of English spoken by "every kind of men and women"[32] in America. She thus "conceived . . . the rhythm of anybody's personality."[33] As she described in "The Gradual Making of the Making of Americans" and elsewhere in *Lectures in America*:

Then at the same time is the question of time. The assembling of a thing to make a whole thing and each one of these whole things is one of a series, but beside this there is the important thing and the very American thing that everybody knows who is an American just how many seconds minutes or hours it is going to take to do a whole thing. It is singularly a sense for combination within a conception of the existence of a given space of time that makes the American thing the American thing, and the sense of this space of time must be within the whole thing as well as in the completed whole thing.

I felt this thing, I am an American and I felt this thing, and I made a continuous effort to create this thing in every paragraph I made in The Making of Americans. . . . a balance a new balance that had to do with a sense of movement of time included in a given space which I have already said is a definitely American thing . . . Within the rhythm of this unfolding pattern . . . each one is themselves inside them and something about them perhaps everything about them will tell some one all about that thing all about what is themselves inside them . . . I had to find out what was inside any one . . . I must find out what is moving inside them that makes them them . . . I began to make charts of all the people I had ever known or seen, or met or remembered . . . I was sure that in a kind of a way the enigma of the universe could in this way be solved.[34]

"READING" SIMPLY IS, IS THERE[35]

At moments in *Irresistible Dictation*, Steven Meyer approaches the suggestion I am making here. He remarks, for instance, "For her [Stein], lasting accomplishment, at once scientific and literary, resided in the singular success she exhibited in rendering the organic mechanisms that operate in all sentence composition and comprehension – that is to say in rendering them *visible*" (emphasis his), and elsewhere that she "was a scientifically trained collector and classifier, a genius at perceiving analogies."[36] Even more closely, in commenting on Stein's late (1934) distinction, "that sentences are not emotional and that paragraphs are,"[37] Meyer draws the comparison between Stein's conception and Whitehead's and to its correspondence with recent work in neurobiology that points to the reciprocal relations of protein molecules and neurons:

In Whitehead's terms, individual sentences are patterns or eternal objects whereas paragraphs are rhythms or vibratory organisms; in Gerald Edelman's more physiological terms, they might even be said to correspond respectively to protein molecules (and the genetic blueprints that determine the configuration of these molecules) and to the neurons that activate, or inhibit, the production of molecules in the outer membranes of cells, regulating cellular adhesion and mobility.[38]

Further, in speaking of Stein's compositional practice as "mapping," Meyer notes "in the broadest sense, as in Edelman's notion of 'reentrant signaling' between neuronal maps, the two activities are genuinely isomorphic."[39] Finally, in concluding his argument, Meyer offers the following:

Whitehead's insistence on "taking time seriously" certainly distinguished him from most of the systematic thinkers who preceded him, if not from James; yet, again, like James, he failed in his philosophy of organism to take writing seriously enough – in particular, to appreciate its capacity, no less than that of speech, to communicate emotion as well as information, to suggest as well as to state. In this respect, Stein's radical empiricism serves to correct, not just complement, theirs; by the same token, the extreme alertness she displayed to the organic mechanisms operating in writing should prove exemplary for the various approaches to the biological sciences that, at the juncture of the twentieth and twenty-first centuries, offer an increasingly nuanced radical empiricist account of the world and how we live in it. The convergence of radical empiricism and the life sciences is hardly due to chance, given that radical empiricists have always tended to frame their intuitions in biological terms. For the radical empiricist, physical concepts such as *energy* exist most immediately within a biological context of *living tissue*, rather than the reverse, and *metaphysics* turns out all along to have been just another way, albeit a fairly abstract one, of talking about biological processes.

Meyer adds, perspicaciously, "To be sure, none of the principal figures I discuss would have been prepared to make so reductive-sounding a claim. Whatever the extent that the biology, and especially the physiology, of their days informed their perspectives, it remained a paltry thing compared to the perspectives thus formed."[40] He notes that Stein shared this point of view, distinguishing, in the case of considering the brain stem as a region, between viewing it "*concretely*" and viewing it "*abstractly* as a clearly articulated set of interlocking structures" (his emphases). Meyer goes on to comment on the other scientists today who, in addition to Edelman, are pursuing, like Stein, "within a Jamesian heritage" that includes Emerson and White-head, "nonreductive approaches to the neurophysiological composition of consciousness."[41] Meyer is careful in closing to remind readers that while his own radical empiricist claim as phrased above may immediately sound reductive in locating metaphysics within biological processes, his approach throughout his study has been and continues to be, in making his final points, precisely to avoid the error responsible for reductionist readings "to which empiricists [as opposed to *radical* empiricists] seem congenitally prone: insufficient attention to context."[42]

Indeed, the last stroke applied to his portrait of Stein as radical empiricist brilliantly highlights his own attention to the abstractly extended context of her literary experiments, reflecting his own prehension of her imaginative activity, stimulated as it was by her early scientific investigations:

Writing and the biological sciences are not *merely* correlated. Viewed from one direction, biological investigation (like all scientific investigation) involves ever more complex extensions of writing practices, ever more broadly distributed tech-nologies of writing; viewed from the other direction, writing is itself an extension or externalization of the human central nervous system. Writing, then, is a func-tion of neurology; the life sciences are a function of writing; and investigations such as Stein's of the organic mechanisms involved in writing ought to prove no less suggestive for biological research than Stein found James's biocentrism to be for achieving her own experimental objective of an ever "fuller" understanding of her "self-understanding" compositions.

Meyer then draws the line completing his portrait, fittingly returning us in the end to Stein's beginning. Describing the pioneering work done by Michael I. Posner and Marcus E. Raichle in using positron emission topography (PET) to explore and picture the neural systems involved in mental operations, Meyer notes their pointing to "an area in the mid-brain called the superior collicus" as responsible for moving attention from one location to another. His paragraph closes: "True to form, the superior collicus directly connects to the neighboring nucleus of Darkschewitsch; it turns out that in her neuroanatomical investigations Stein was examining several of the structures implicated in the innermost mechanisms of close reading or 'reading in slow motion.'"[43]

In a note, Meyer locates the phrase "reading in slow motion" as the method fostered and exemplified by Reuben Brower and Richard Poirier and followed by other teachers of the Harvard General Education course, "The Interpretation of Literature" ("Hum 6"), a method of encouraging students to "enter into, or rather engage in, experiences of imaginative literature" and so "make themselves readers of imagination." The method involves "slowing down the process of reading to observe what is happening, in order to attend very closely to the words, their uses, and their meanings."[44] The method is ideal for reading Stein who observed "so read word by word reading word by word makes the writing that is not anything be something."[45] In offering my acknowledgments I comment that Meyer's thanks to Richard Poirier and to John Hollander in the respective capacities they served for him could, with the substitution of "Stevens" for "Stein," be my own. The similar trajectories Meyer's and my interests and approaches have traced cannot but be owing to the lessons learned from these masters in making ourselves "readers of the imagination," since only by becoming such could we hope to deal adequately with our subjects, both of whom knew indeed that "reality is the activity of the most august imagination." What Steven Meyer and I have seen and described in and through Stein's work, and what I have seen and traced in and through the work of the others who are my subjects here, are performances in slow motion of the prehensive activity of imagination as a life form as it *happened* to be embodied *in time* in the makings of these writers. If the premise of radical empiricism holds, it makes perfect sense that Stein's patterning of words is a prehension of the genome's patterning, no less than Bach's Art of Fugue or Goldberg Variations are prehensions of the structure of the double helix, or Emerson's profligately varied sentences are of the evolutionary process. The emergent properties of these works belong to the system in which we are all unfolding: "The thing in itself folded itself up inside itself like

you might fold a thing up to be another thing which is that thing inside
that thing."[46] Indeed, as Steven Meyer has reminded me, Stein noted that
Marcel Brion, "a certain French critic," had early on compared the "symmetry" of her work "to the symmetry of the musical fugue of Bach."[47]
Any additions offered to the taxonomy are already implicit, "transcription
axiom[s], linguistic" of "the statistics of perhaps"; "The compulsion to find
the pattern of living translation – the way a simple, self-duplicating string
of four letters inscribes an entire living being – is built into every infant who
has ever learned a word, put a phrase together, discovered that phonemes
might *speak*":[48]

... How could a thing if it is a human being if it is anything be entirely contained
within itself. Of course it is, but is it and how is it and how did I know that it is.
    This was the thing that I found then to be completely interesting, this was the
thing I found then to be completely exciting. How was anything contained within
itself.[49]

My addition to the context in which Stein found herself contemplating the above is to suggest that the reappearance of the Mendelian
information and its widespread consideration and elaboration by Bateson and others both provided her a complementary strand of perception to stretch alongside that provided by her earlier preparation in neuropsychology and advanced what she had already learned in studying
nineteenth-century zoology, anatomy, and botany. Reflecting late in her
life on what had stimulated her "habits of attention,"[50] she observed,
"there was nothing more interesting in the nineteenth century than little by little realizing the detail of natural selection in insects flowers and
birds and butterflies and comparing things and animals and noticing the
protective coloring nothing more interesting."[51] "Each detail" she investigated, as Meyer notes, "served to confirm the evolutionary 'principle
which was the basis of all this.'"[52] Beginning, as she described, as a "natural believer in science,"[53] Stein's training prepared her to grasp that there
would be "nothing more interesting" in the twentieth century than genetics. In the same way that, as she commented in relation to the cinema,
she was doing in *The Making of Americans* what the cinema was doing
without at the time ever having "seen a cinema,"[54] whether at the time
she began her literary experiments she was specifically aware of Mendel
or Bateson is incidental. The work surrounding genetics was not only "of
[her] period," but directly affected the concerns of the medical profession
during the time she was at Hopkins, most particularly concerning issues of
eugenics.

YOU SEE MELANCTHA . . . I GOT A NEW FEELING NOW, YOU
BEEN TEACHING TO ME, JUST LIKE I TOLD YOU ONCE,
JUST LIKE A NEW RELIGION TO ME[55]

In a 1997 article, "Gertrude Stein and the Politics of Literary-Medical Experimentation," Daylanne English connects some of the striking stylistic innovations of *Three Lives* with the language of medical histories – the physician's chart, for example, "with its always present-tense verbs" as a source for Stein's deployment of her "continuous present." English's argument develops an observation made by John Malcolm Brinnin in his 1959 study of Stein in her context, *The Third Rose: Gertrude Stein and Her World*, that the author can "seem not to be an artist at all, but a scientist elaborately constructing metaphors in a laboratory of words," and another made by William Carlos Williams who described "Melanctha" as a "thrilling clinical record." English adds:

The "laboratory" that is Stein's *Three Lives* accommodates a specifically medical form of experimental discourse . . . at levels of form and content. The text enacts "elaborately constructed metaphors" of medical documentation through literary experimentation. Stein, as author of *Three Lives*, could even be said to represent a prototype for Pound's modern writer as diagnostician and physician. Indeed, she began writing *Three Lives* shortly after she abandoned her study of medicine at Johns Hopkins in 1902. Set in "Bridgepoint," a thinly veiled Baltimore, Maryland, the book reflects not only Stein's radical use of literary form, but also her ambivalence regarding the poor, largely African American and immigrant population for whom she provided care during her tenure as a medical student.[56]

More particularly, English notes "the book's literary-medical experimentation engages racialist and eugenic . . . thinking" and, in a subsection headed "'Negroes,' Race, and Fitness in 'Melanctha,'" reads Melanctha's "hybrid identity" as her "pathology" and ultimate cause of her death. English sets Stein's portrait against eugenicist Lothrop Stoddard's description of "the genetically-determined fate of mulattoes: 'These unhappy beings, every cell of whose bodies is a battle-ground of jarring heredities, express their souls in acts of hectic violence and aimless instability.'"[57]

One step more and we can see Stein's characterizations of Melanctha Herbert, Rose Johnson, Jane Harden, and Jefferson Campbell as experiments in the genetics of personality, following the protocols of Mendelian crossings of sweet peas, *but*, contra English, critiquing the limited eugenicist view as expressed by Stoddard to examine equally, well in advance of her moment, crossing the effects of nurture/environment/culture with inherited traits in the development of the phenotype.[58] Consider: "Rose Johnson was a real black negress but she had been brought up quite like their own child by white folks"; "Melanctha Herbert was a graceful, pale yellow, intelligent, attractive negress. She had not been raised like Rose by white folks but then she had been half made with real white blood"; "Melanctha Herbert had been raised to be religious, by her mother . . . a sweet-appearing and dignified and pleasant, pale yellow, colored woman"; "Melanctha was pale yellow . . . and a little pleasant like her mother, but the real power in Melanctha's nature came through her robust and unpleasant and very unendurable black father . . . her feeling was really closer to her black coarse father, than her feeling had ever been toward her pale yellow, sweet-appearing mother"; "Jane was a negress, but she was so white that hardly any one could guess it. Jane had had a good deal of education . . . She taught Melanctha many things"; "Jeff Campbell was a robust, dark, healthy, cheery negro"; Jefferson Campbell was "a young mulatto"; "Jefferson's father was . . . a very steady, very intelligent, and very dignified, light brown, grey haired negro"; "Jefferson's mother was a sweet, little, pale brown, gentle woman"; "Jeff Campbell had been raised religious by his people but religion had never interested Jeff very much . . . he really loved best science and experimenting and to learn things."[59]

Stretched alongside the naturally inherited traits unfolded from the genotypes of each one of her characters are those acquired from education and environment. Even before learning from William James to consider words as contributing no less than any other organic factor to the making of a "self," Stein was sensitive to the imprinting of cultural traits through texts. As Meyer reminds us, in *Everybody's Autobiography* Stein "recalled the experience of first reading the Old Testament as a child . . . 'Brought up not a Christian but in Christian thinking,'"[60] so specifically an American situation for the slave populations and their descendants and for the Jewish immigrants arriving increasingly from the middle of the nineteenth and into the twentieth centuries. In a 1923 letter to Edmund Wilson, remarking on the incantatory style of her "Picasso" portrait, which he had praised, Stein commented "the bible lives not by its stories but by its texts."[61] In this vein, Janet Malcolm reports Carl Van Vechten's reaction after reading an early section of *The Making of Americans*: "To me now, it is a little like the Book of Genesis . . . There is something Biblical about you Gertrude. Certainly there is something Biblical about you."[62] In "Poetry and the Imagination" Emerson identified "iterations of phrase," exemplified paradigmatically for our culture in biblical phrasing and in which, he noted, "Milton delights," as the "form of rhyme" characterizing the "genius" who is able to "find" and "say" the "matches made in heaven" for "the rhymes and iterations of Nature" which alone truly express "the piety of the intellect." Only the poet, aware that "the nature of things is flowing, a metamorphosis," can transcribe and write "the adequate genesis" for his moment, sympathizing "not only with the actual form, but with the power of possible forms," realizing that "[f]acts are not foreign, as they seem, but related" metonymically *in time*: "This metonymy, or seeing the same sense in things so diverse, gives a pure pleasure." "American life storms about us daily, and is slow to find a tongue," he observed, and continued, indicating a secularized ministerial purpose for the new American poet:

This contemporary insight is transubstantiation, the conversion of daily bread into the holiest symbols . . . The test of the poet is the power to take the passing day, with its news, its cares, its fears, as he shares them, and hold it up to a divine reason, till he sees it to have a purpose and beauty, and to be related to astronomy and history and the eternal order of the world.[63]

This was the test to which Stein's language would rise, the challenge contained in "translating" into words the "varied forms of the selfsame energy": "Natural objects, if individually described and out of connection, are not yet known, since they are really parts of a symmetrical universe, like words of a sentence; and if their true order is found, the poet can read their divine significance orderly as in a Bible."[64]

To express "connection," "true order," that "relations stop nowhere," is to describe, no less than Jonathan Edwards, "religious affections." Stein was privileged to have as mentor William James, who translated "religious affections" into "radical empiricism" without gainsaying thereby the religious impulse itself, persistently repeating "What is this mystery in me?" as constitutive and informing of identity and perception. Indeed, in transcending the limits of the positivist "who holds that 'we must always wait for sensible evidence for our beliefs' and consequently refuses to admit speculation concerning any 'portion of the total universe' which, 'stretch[ing] beyond this visible world,' takes the form of 'an unseen world of which we now know nothing positive,'"[65] James's radical empiricist furthers the project of the Puritan ministers to "make the invisible visible." James's recognition of Stein's unusual talents bespoke a faith that in her experiments she would, in turn, translate what he had written and lectured *about*, the premises of his philosophy, into the thing itself, *pragma*, language spoken as prayer, as "affection," "with all the unmediated finality of a pain or an intense pleasure."[66] "The poet knows the missing link by the joy it gives"[67] – This was the lesson in "feeling," the "new religion," in which Melanctha would instruct Jefferson Campbell, who, before crossing with

her, was "always thinking,"[68] trained as he was in the Enlightenment principles embodied in his given name and evidenced by his love of science and
experimenting.

One of the great losses to scholarship is William James's copy of *Three
Lives*, dedicated and sent to him by Stein, in which James made marginal
notes as he read. Contained in James's library, given as a gift to Harvard,
it was "appropriated" from the Harvard library, as Stein relates, by "a man
in Boston" who wrote to her sometime around 1930 indicating that as he
thought she would be "very interested in these notes," he would copy them
and send them to her. She replied that indeed she would like to have them
and in return came instead "a manuscript the man himself had written and
of which he wished Gertrude Stein to give him an opinion."[69] Perturbed
by the attempt at literary blackmail, she did nothing. And so we can only
imagine James's comments in the pages of the first-born work of "Dear
Miss Stein," in which he "was enormously interested" no less than in her,
to whom he had written on an earlier occasion, excusing her not writing
a final examination for his course based simply on the fact of feeling she
did not want to: "I understand perfectly how you feel I often feel like that
myself."[70] We have, at least, some indication of his response to *Three Lives*
from the letter he wrote to her after reading: "What a brave new realism
this is!" Her accomplishment in *Three Lives*, of course, was to reproduce
the realism of "thought as it was uttered," with its "delicate idiosyncrasy":
"And if we wish to *feel* that idiosyncrasy we must reproduce th[e] thought
as it was uttered, with every word fringed and the whole sentence bathed
in that original halo of obscure relations, which, like a horizon, then spread
about its meaning."[71]

The place and expression of feeling had, of course, particularly and
periodically disturbed American religious experience, early communities
attempting to prescribe through conversion narratives forms of expression
that would distinguish the genuine gift of grace from mere enthusiasm.
The example Stein offered through Melanctha and pursued through her
attempt to describe the "bottom nature" of "everyone" in *The Making of
Americans* reflected her recognition of the significance of the project of
Jamesian Pragmatism: to braid the Darwinian information about human
nature with a method describing how that information is read/expressed
by human mind under the accidental and varying conditions of environment into individual character/personality. (As we now know, genetic
information is expressed in response/relation to particular cellular and
organismic environments: "Different animal designs reflect the use of the
same old genes, but expressed at different times and in different places

in the organism."[72]) Stein would later, in 1935, further detail her effort in these terms in "The Geographical History of America or The Relation of Human Nature to the Human Mind." America, with its vast and varied environment, was, for Stein, the ideal laboratory in which to observe this relation and continue experimenting, specifically in American language, its control subject, English, already neatly provided. For Stein, "Human mind," as opposed to "human nature," is what "knows," and what it knows, though not identical with language, is expressed in language that, if it is to be effective, must be in relation to geography, particularly in "the sacredness of writing."[73] "Religion" in America's new situation, where, as evidenced in its history, the exigencies of experience all too often forced individuals to revert to the responses of their human nature, had, accordingly, to be newly "invented": "No Europeans and so no European can ever invent a religion, they have too much remembering and forgetting too much to know that human nature is anything."[74] But those Americans, like Jefferson Campbell, steeped in the European "white training" which "had only made for habits, not for nature,"[75] had first to redeem the "human nature" pawned for the European habits that allowed them to pass: "The United States is interesting because in it there are some in it that have no human nature at all . . . what has this to do with the relation of human nature to the human mind."[76] What it had to do with, as Stein had learned from James, was feeling, locating the "*there*": "Individuality is founded in feeling; and the darker, blinder strata of character, are the only places in the world in which we catch real fact in the making, and directly perceive how events happen, and how work is actually done";[77] "Religion has been called natural. Well there is something in that. . . . but religion is timid and so it does not say why or how but it does say where and saying where it must look over there."[78]

As discussed in Chapter 4, William James understood that, following the Darwinian information, religious experience had to be recognized in its varieties, expressive of an organic relation in each individual between human nature and human mind, "*the feelings, acts, and experiences of individual men . . . so far as they apprehend themselves to stand in relation to whatever they may consider the divine.*"[79] Stein attempted to illustrate that such feelings, acts, and experiences find expression for each individual in an idiolect. When Jefferson Campbell, trained in the habits of eighteenth-century thinking that defined the constitution of America, the wished-for ideal republic, begins feeling, being *affected* by Melanctha's teaching, "beginning to feel he could almost trust the goodness in her," he finds that he does not have the language to describe his condition: "He now never thought about all this in real words anymore."[80] His feeling for her gradually affects his language. The experience of affection, of course, is the felt form of some kind of matching, attachment, identification that issues in a transfer of information – a version of "Copy me. Read me." – whether in the form of behavioral imitation, intensification by doubling, as it were, of common traits/interests, or learning, where what is latent in the "darker, blinder strata of character" is drawn up and out to be seen: "I think that if you announce what you see nobody can say no . . . That is what the national hymn says the star spangled banner. Oh say can you see."[81] "Please see my human mind,"[82] draw out, unfold, the implications, the recessive traits of the genotype complicating the behavior of phenotype as much as the traits acquired by cultural imprinting. "To understand a thing means to be in contact with that thing"[83] – in contact with Melanctha Jefferson Campbell's idiolect is expressed, and though he breaks with her, "He never can forget the things she taught him . . . He be like a brother to her always . . . 'I certainly got to go now Melanctha, from you. I go this time, Melanctha really.'"[84] While in their first days of wandering his verb tenses consistently bespoke his "white training" – "wouldn't have been"; "would not have been"; "hadn't . . . to know"; "do think you would have told"[85] – contact with her, in linguistic meiosis, produces as its offspring, in both his voicing and the narrator's, the verbal pattern until then hidden by the "dominant" cultural trait. I certainly do not mean to be reductive here, suggesting that Jefferson Campbell's "bottom nature," as drawn up and out by Melanctha, is an ultimate determinant of his identity – as Stoddard would have argued – or that he will go on to use Black dialect in the future, but rather to illustrate the complexity of Stein's psychological portraiture in attending to the changing landscape of his/her experience as it affects and is part of his language. Indeed, as Meyer has noted, Stein's insight into the complex motivation of behavior revealed in the shadings of her verbal portraiture anticipates the work of current researchers. Antonio Damasio, for example, offers that it is the "concerted activity" of the neocortex "engaged *along with* the older brain core" that produces the "mechanisms of behavior."[86] Similarly, Philip Lieberman observes that "It has become clear that most complex aspects of human behavior, including language, are not regulated in a single localized region of the brain." "The comprehension of a sentence," for instance, "involves circuits that link many cortical and subcortical neural structures."[87]

Joan Retallack describes the plot of what she finely phrases as "Stein's geometry of attention," using the example of *Blood On The Dining Room Floor*, as "a fractal coastline of repetitive/permutative linguistic forms whose semantic shape . . . is constantly shifting in the emotional, social, intellectual weather of interpretive space."[88] She continues to

wonder whether the kind of "positive feedback loop" that generates fractal self-similarities and variations – data reentering the system again and again, each time undergoing slight modifications – might be an illuminating way to think about Stein's writing process. Might in fact give some intuitions about how the mind (that is, the fractal neural networks of the brain) produces complex linguistic forms based on repetition and variation.[89]

What Retallack describes as a "positive feedback loop" in Stein's linguistic activity is more accurately understood, following Meyer, as a prehensive version of the patterning Gerald Edelman details in accounting for the "reentrant signaling" between neuronal maps, which has, as Edelman indicates, analogues on a macrocosmic scale in Darwinian natural selection, and, on a microcosmic scale, in the genetic blueprints that determine the configuration of protein molecules responsible for DNA and RNA-transfer processes: "The double helix is a fractal curve. Ecology's every part – regardless of the magnification, however large the assembled spin-off or small the enzymatic trigger – carries in it some terraced, infinitely dense ecosystem, an inherited hint of the whole."[90] Stein's "habits of attention . . . the reflexes of the complete character of the individual,"[91] stimulated, as Meyer reminds us, by her scientific training, prepared her imagination to project a linguistic model that affects us like a religious text, providing a description of the invisible processes of creation, "an adequate genesis" answering for her moment the question "What is this mystery in me?": "Think of the Bible . . . and think of me."[92] We come "to understand" this process "in contact" with the invisible itself, "wandering" back and forth through her texts, the paradigmatic performance exercise being the recursive, repetitive turnings of the chapters of *The Geographical History of America*, an elaborated brain model mapping what Lyn Hejinian has called in one of her talks on Stein, "the terrain of cognition"[93] – "What has wandering got to do with the human mind or religion. But really wandering has something to do with the human mind."[94] Reading Stein is to experience the mind's associative processes, *feeling thinking*. We identify with the vibratory patterning of her iterations, "enlivened by inversion,"[95] affected by the fact of feeling embodied in her texts, no less than Jefferson Campbell affected by Melanctha, or by the members of Jonathan Edwards's congregations feeling themselves so affected.

BECOME BECAUSE[96]

In establishing the relations between William James, Stein, and Whitehead's "organism," Meyer draws on an observation made by Suzanne Langer, a student of Whitehead's we recall, to locate precisely the address of their common interest in "the mind's associative processes" as the foundation of radical empiricism. Langer distinguishes the "dogmatic empiricism that James rejected as an unexamined inheritance of contemporary science from 'naive empiricism,' with its 'epistemological model' . . . of a 'mosaic of pure sense data linked by a sort of magnetic process, association, into compound entities.'" Meyer continues:

James proposed to treat the intermediate magnetic processes as themselves partaking of the same order of experience as the "purely 'given'" sense-data. (In physiological terms this suggests, as Langer has observed, that for any "intuitive perception" which seems, at least "on the empirical level of knowledge," to be given directly, it nonetheless "take[s] a highly elaborated nervous system to create such an apparently direct presentation." The mind's associative processes are no less embodied than are the sense-data.) "To be radical," James posited in "A World of Pure Experience," an empiricism must neither admit into its constructions any element that is not directly experienced, nor exclude from them any element that is directly experienced. For such a philosophy, *the relations that connect experience must themselves be experienced relations, and any kind of relation experienced must be accounted as "real" as anything else in the system.*[97]

This extension to include as facts relations imagined "in a spiral search back into time"[98] and forward to project, through the mind's magnetic processes, new worlds such as those described by Lyell and Darwin, the realm of experience termed *prehension* by Whitehead, constitutes James's contribution to the continuing project of the Reformation, naturalized as it was by Emerson, and catechized by Stein. In this dispensation, *relations* become _realations_ – "This contemporary insight is transubstantiation," religious experience a repeated, continuously varying expression of "relation to the universe":

Slowly every one in continuous repeating, to their minutest variation, comes to be clearer to some one. Every one who ever was or is or will be living sometimes will be clearly realized by some one. Sometime there will be an ordered history of every one. Slowly every kind of one comes into ordered recognition. More and more then it is wonderful in living the subtle variations coming clear into ordered recognition, coming to make every one a part of some kind of them, some kind of men and women. Repeating then is in every one, every one then comes sometime to be clearer to some one, sometime there will be then an orderly history of every one who ever was or is or will be living.[99]

"The code . . . was not so much a message written *in* a language as all grammar itself"; "Genetic mechanism contains nothing transcendental . . . The grammar does not change from generation to generation – only individual sentences do"; "Inducing mutations, introducing bits of nonsense into the gene's message, can force the code to reveal itself in entirety" –

evolution is not about competition or squeezing out, not a master plan of increasing efficiency. It is a deluge, a cascade of mistaken, tentative, branching, brocaded experiment, secrets seemingly dormant, shouted down from the past . . . programming palimpsests reworked beyond recognition . . . It is about one instruction: "Make another similar something; insert this command; run, repeat." It is about the resultant runaway seed-spreading arabesques, unrelated except in all being variations on that theme . . . That interpretive system seeing the spectrum of natural form as a mirror of God, eager to alert us to His nature through every living, loaded semaphore in creation.[100]

. . . WHAT A GREAT PART IN MAGIC <u>WORDS</u> HAVE ALWAYS PLAYED[101]

"Where do we find ourselves? In a series of which we do not know the extremes, and believe that it has none. We wake and find ourselves on a stair; there are stairs below us, which we seem to have ascended; there are stairs above us, many a one, which go upwards and out of sight":[102]

the double-spiral staircase embodied two identical information queues. The ascending angel order complements and mirrors the descending stream . . . Each angel-file sequence can be entirely recreated from the other . . . All there in Crick and Watson's tantalizing summary: "It has not escaped our notice that the specific pairing we have postulated immediately suggests a possible copying mechanism for the genetic material.". . .
  The heart of the code must lie hidden in its grammar . . . not what a particular string of DNA says, but how it says it . . . a language sufficiently complex and flexible to speak into existence the inconceivable commodity of self-speaking.[103]

"The pragmatic movement . . . seems to have rather suddenly precipitated itself out of the air. A number of tendencies that have always existed in philosophy have all at once become conscious of themselves collectively."[104]
"The world is mind precipitated, and the volatile essence is forever escaping again into the state of free thought."[105]

From Jonathan Edwards, intent on grounding religious affections in the natural world, his "sense of the heart" realizing in his various performances of verbal repetition the fact of feeling himself "part or particle of God," to Stein's experiments tracing "the movement of . . . thoughts and words endlessly the same and endlessly different,"[106] coding the invisible dimensions of time and experience stored in the cortical columns she studied as a young woman, the pursuit of the writers under discussion in these chapters illustrates the method William James described in and as *Pragmatism*, himself pointing its connection, in emphasizing its "look[ing] forward into facts themselves" as "the seat of authority," to the "protestant reformation," even calling the method "philosophic protestantism," a method which "widens the field of search for God."[107] James's calling Pragmatism a "method" was significant. As Martin Heidegger remarked, the Greek word means literally "with(in)-a-path," his recent translator adding that the word means "to-be-on-the-way . . . not thought of as a 'method' man devises but a way that already exists, arising from the very things themselves, as they show themselves through and through."[108] The gradual transformation of religious experience into ongoing revelation of the ordinary as extraordinary is the story of the story told in these pages, looking not at facts but through them, "to find the good, which in the Platonic sense, is synonymous with God."[109] The work of the writers discussed preserves the function of prophetic speech in and as the aesthetic choices they made, feeling for the words and shapes of sentences in the faith that the expressions spun out of their visions, responses to things beyond themselves – forms of prayer, in other words – were necessary apprehensions, their webs of words registering the existence of the invisible as "actual idea," charged, in fact, with radiant currents. Andy Clark's description of "magic words" serving as "fixed points" in a kind of magnetic field, "capable of attracting and positioning additional matter," as presented in relation to reading Henry James, could be applied as productively to reading Edwards, Emerson, William James, Stevens, and Stein: "Human life is driven forward by its dim apprehension of notions too general for its existing language."[110]

A concluding example will serve to recapitulate. Steven Meyer points out that late-twentieth-century speculative biologists, including Clark, Edelman, Damasio, and others, attempting to formulate a "new synthesis" for biology have recuperated key notions "that had been marginalized by the Modern Synthesis of genetics and evolution," the two most prominent of these being *morphogenetic fields* and *homologies of process*.[111] Quoting from a 1996 paper by Scott F. Gilbert, John M. Opitz, and Rudolf A. Raff, Meyer notes:

"*the morphogenetic field*" provided "an alternative to the gene as the unit of ontogeny," or individual development. A "web of interactions" was envisioned, such that any given cell could be defined "by its position within its respective field." Gilbert and his coauthors cite the following definition of such a field, from [Joseph] Needham, as exemplary: "A morphogenetic field is a system of order such that the positions taken by the unstable entities in one part of the system bear a definite relation to the position taken up by the other unstable entities in other parts of the system. The field effect is constituted by their several equilibrium positions. A field is bound to a particular substratum from which the dynamic pattern arises. It is heteroaxial and heteropolar, has recognizably distinct districts, and can, like a magnetic field, maintain its pattern when its mass is either reduced or increased. It can fuse with a similar pattern entering with new material if the axial orientation is favorable."[112]

We recall the discussion beginning in Chapter 3 of the centrality of the crystal analogy and its eventual projection, through the polarizing forces described by Richard Owen, into the fields envisioned by Watson and Crick as the activity of the spiralling double helix (see pp. 68–79). The notion of *homologies of process*, as Gilbert and his co-authors indicate, introduced by Owen, has been recovered by them, as Meyer observes, to investigate "'similarities of dynamic interactions' between organism and ambient," similarities Emerson had prehended in noting the "'perfect correspondence' of man and muskrat."[113] We recall as well the extension of Emerson's prehension into William James's attention to intermediate magnetic processes of cognition, imagined as the movement of the aurora borealis and partaking of the same order of experience as "purely 'given'" sense-data. These were currents charging Stein's thinking, her work, "a field . . . bound to a particular substratum from which [a] dynamic pattern arises," preserving in its recursively proliferating form a template of the "law of continuity" being retrieved by today's researchers: "We are still always aware of her presence . . . eternally and placidly ruminating the gradual developments of the processes of being, registering the vibrations of a psychological country like some august human seismograph whose charts we haven't the training to read."[114] Feeling magic words: "The aesthetic has become the whole of me."[115]

Notes

1 INTRODUCTION: FRONTIER INSTANCES

1 John Locke, *Two Treatises on Government* (rpt. London: Routledge, 1884 [1680–90]), p. 89.

2 While James commented that "there is no logical connexion between pragmatism . . . and 'radical empiricism' . . . [that] [o]ne may entirely reject it and still be a pragmatist," for James himself the connection was intrinsic: *Pragmatism, A New Name for Some Old Ways of Thinking* in William James, *Writings 1902–1910*, ed. Bruce Kuklick (New York: Library of America, 1987), p. 482; references to this title are hereinafter indicated by *P*. I have capitalized "Pragmatism" and "Pragmatist" in this volume to indicate specifically the Jamesian dispensation as there were already in 1908, as described by Arthur O. Lovejoy, at least thirteen varieties; see his "The Thirteen Pragmatisms," *Journal of Philosophy* 5 (1908), 1–42. Ludwig Wittgenstein similarly observed that pragmatism is what he called a "family resemblance" term with no one future running through all its instances, as noted by Russell B. Goodman in *Wittgenstein and William James* (Cambridge: Cambridge University Press, 2002), p. 6.

3 *Charles Darwin's Notebooks, 1836–1844: Geology, Transmutation of Species, Metaphysical Enquiries*, ed. Paul H. Barrett, Peter J. Gautrey, Sandra Herbert, David Kohn, and Sydney Smith (Ithaca: Cornell University Press, 1987), p. 577; hereinafter references to this title are indicated by *CDN*.

4 Alfred North Whitehead most comprehensively elaborates this fact in laying out his philosophy of organism; the articulation of this philosophy is indebted, by his own account in *Process and Reality*, to what he learned from the pragmatists William James and John Dewey.

5 *CDN*, p. 284.

6 Essential reading in this regard are Gillian Beer's groundbreaking *Darwin's Plots: Evolutionary Narrative in Darwin, George Eliot and Nineteenth-Century Fiction* (London; Boston: Ark / Routledge & Kegan Paul, 1983) and Dov Ospovat, *The Development of Darwin's Theory: Natural History, Natural Theology and Natural Selection, 1838–1859* (Cambridge: Cambridge University Press, 1995).

7 Wallace Stevens, *Collected Poetry and Prose*, ed. Frank Kermode and Joan Richardson (New York: Library of America, 1997), p. 29; references to this title are hereinafter indicated by *CPP*.

8 This notion of incommensurability is borrowed from Paul Feyerabend who, in
   Against Method (London: Verso, 1997), describes how, in the face of facts not
   encountered previously, "universal principles" are suspended and that, with
   this suspension, "the rules that are needed for constituting individuals" are
   also suspended. The old logic or system of classification cannot accommodate
   "phenomena outside of its domain" (p. 205). The solution to the problem of
   incommensurability is to "misuse" the inherited language/logic, asking questions that cannot be answered and making demands that cannot be met within
   the current system: "Freed from the fetters of a well-constructed and unambiguous mode of expression and thinking, the elements of A [the inherited
   language/logic] lose their familiar function and start floating around aimlessly –
   the 'chaos of sensations' arises" (p. 204). This understanding implicitly informs
   Richard Poirier's focus on the nature of Emersonian "troping," which, as he
   points out in *Poetry and Pragmatism* (Cambridge, MA: Harvard University
   Press, 1992), pp. 132–3, stretches back to Edwards and forward into the work of
   Stevens, Frost, and Stein. See also his earlier *The Renewal of Literature: Emersonian Reflections* (New York: Random House, 1987). As I shall demonstrate,
   the solutions arrived at by the American writers who are my subjects reflect
   perfectly the situation described here by Feyerabend and centrally addressed
   by Poirier in the critical discussion he initiated and which is continued in these
   pages.

9 The phrase from Emerson is converted for our re-use by Stanley Cavell in
   This New Yet Unapproachable America: Essays after Emerson after Wittgenstein
   (Albuquerque: Living Batch Books, 1989), essential reading, together with
   Cavell's work generally, for all concerned with the evolution of thinking.
   Most pertinent to my argument here – an extended conversation, as it were,
   around thinking of Emerson and so much else stimulated by Cavell's work –
   are: Cavell's "Thinking of Emerson" and "An Emerson Mood" in *The Senses
   of Walden* (San Francisco: North Point, 1981) and *Conditions Handsome and
   Unhandsome: The Constitution of Emersonian Perfectionism* (Chicago: University of Chicago Press, 1990). These essays are recollected in Cavell's *Emerson's
   Transcendental Etudes* (Stanford: Stanford University Press, 2003). In connection with America's ongoing philosophical errand, Cavell points out Emerson's
   preponderant usage of terms beginning with "con-" – *conversation, constitution,
   contradiction, contrariety*, for example – all, by Cavell's account, deriving from
   Emerson's preoccupation with conversion and the forms it would take in a
   secularized environment.

10 *CPP*, p. 22.

11 As Whitehead observes in *The Function of Reason* (Boston: Beacon Press, 1948),
   p. 47: "The men of the early Renaissance never seem quite clear in their minds
   whether they should sacrifice a cock or celebrate the mass. They compromised
   by doing both."

12 The phrase is borrowed from Antonio Damasio's *The Feeling of What Happens:
   Body and Emotion in the Making of Consciousness* (New York: Harcourt, Brace
   and Co., 1999). This volume and his earlier *Descartes' Error: Emotion, Reason,*

and the Human Brain (New York: G. P. Putnam's Sons, 1994) grow out of Damasio's following William James's indications in *The Principles of Psychology*.

13 *CPP*, p. 351.

14 *Process and Reality: An Essay in Cosmology*, corrected edition, ed. David Ray Griffin and Donald W. Sherburne (New York: The Free Press, 1985), pp. 158–9:

> Descartes modified traditional philosophy in two opposite ways. He increased the metaphysical emphasis on the substance–quality forms of thought. The actual things "required nothing but themselves in order to exist," and were to be thought of in terms of their qualities, some of them essential attributes, and others accidental modes. He also laid down the principle, that those substances which are the subjects enjoying conscious experiences provide the primary data for philosophy, namely, themselves as in the enjoyment of such experience. This is the famous subjectivist bias which entered into modern philosophy through Descartes. In this doctrine Descartes undoubtedly made the greatest philosophical discovery since the age of Plato and Aristotle. For his doctrine directly traversed the notion that the proposition, "This stone is grey," expresses a primary form of known fact from which metaphysics can start its generalizations. If we are to go back to the subjective enjoyment of experience, the type of primary starting-point is "my perception of this stone as grey." Primitive men were not metaphysicians, nor were they interested in the expression of concrete experience. Their language merely expressed useful abstractions, such as "greyness of the stone." But like Columbus who never visited America, Descartes missed the full sweep of his own discovery, and he and his successors, Locke and Hume, continued to construe the functionings of the subjective enjoyment of experience according to the substance–quality categories. Yet if the enjoyment of experience be the constitutive subjective fact, these categories have lost all claim to any fundamental character in metaphysics.

Hereinafter references to *Process and Reality* are indicated by *PR*.

15 As observed by Whitehead, *PR*, p. 51.

16 See "The Irrational Element in Poetry," *CPP*, pp. 781–92.

17 Jonathan Edwards, Miscellany no. 782, in *The Works of Jonathan Edwards*, vol. XVIII: *The "Miscellanies" 501–832*, ed. Ava Chamberlain (New Haven and London: Yale University Press, 2000), pp. 452–66. John Locke, *An Essay Concerning Human Understanding*, ed. Peter H. Nidditch (Oxford: Clarendon / Oxford University Press, 1991), vol. II, esp. pp. xix–xxi.

18 This notion is later expressed and explored by William James. In the central "Stream of Thought" chapter of *The Principles of Psychology* (Cambridge, MA and London: Harvard University Press, 1983 [1890]), we find the following remarkably beautiful passage:

> As we take, in fact, a general view of the wonderful stream of our consciousness, what strikes us first is this different pace of its parts. Like a bird's life, it seems to be made of an alternation of flights and perchings. The rhythm of language expresses this, where every thought is expressed in a sentence, and every sentence closed by a period. The resting-places are usually occupied by sensorial imaginations of some sort, whose peculiarity is that they can be held before the mind for an indefinite time, and contemplated without changing; the places of flight are filled with thoughts of relations, static or dynamic, that for the most part obtain between the matters contemplated in the periods of comparative rest.

Let us call the resting-places the "substantive parts," and the places of flight the "transitive parts," of the stream of thought. It then appears that the main end of our thinking is at all times the attainment of some other substantive part from the one from which we have just been dislodged. And we may say that the main use of the transitive parts is to lead us from one substantive conclusion to another. (p. 236)

Hereinafter references to this volume will be indicated by *PP*.

19 Hans Holbein's *The Ambassadors* is perhaps the most famous instance of this kind of pictorial management, though its anamorphic distortion is confined to the skull in the center foreground of the canvas. Henry James was familiar with this painting and titled his *The Ambassadors* within months of Holbein's work being so titled and rehung in London's National Gallery; his deployment of the linguistic/syntactic/grammatical analogue to Holbein's visual anamorphism will be explored here in Chapter 5.

20 See "Seeing Science," special issue, *Representations* 40 (Fall 1992) for a comprehensive and stimulating survey of the changing landscape of perception permitted by the invention of new technologies during this period and later.

21 *Against Method*, p. 16.

22 Ann Kibbey, *The Interpretation of Material Shapes in Puritanism: A Study of Rhetoric, Prejudice, and Violence* (Cambridge: Cambridge University Press, 1986), offers a brilliant extended description of these rhetorical effects. Her analysis of one of John Cotton's sermons is especially illuminating; see pp. 6–41.

23 The literature surrounding the emergence of language and its relation to thought is vast and the subject vexed. Strict evolutionary psychologists, who view themselves as embodying the scientific world view, argue that language is an adaptation evolving from some earlier system of communication, while others working in cognitive science, like Andy Clark (whose speculations will be considered in Chapter 5), and in philosophy, like Jerry Fodor, suggest that the function of language is not limited to communication but permits, especially in its written form, the externalization of thinking, the operations of language complementing and extending the activities of biological brains. Notably, Richard Lewontin, an evolutionary biologist, also takes account of the cultural strand coded in language. I share the views of Clark, Fodor, Lewontin, and others pursuing less restrictive approaches, as later discussions here will illustrate.

24 He observed, for example, that Alexander von Humboldt's *Cosmos* was a monumental contribution to the natural history of the life of the intellect as well as to the natural history of life on the planet, but that because of the failure of its style it did not give pleasure and was not likely, therefore, in his words, "to survive." On Darwin's revisions, see Beer, *Darwin's Plots*, esp. pp. 3–103.

25 The corruption of the idea of the aesthetic that reaches its acme during and after the "art for art's sake" *aestheticism* of the 1890s in Europe is literally foreign to the sense of the term as I have outlined it here and that I hope to make abundantly clear in the chapters following. This sense at the same time restores the aesthetic to its proper source, as indicated by its etymology, in feeling as a

body in its environment, and has all to do with what New World nature offered to those sensitized to perceive a range of experience by certain Renaissance texts, including Locke's *Essay* and Newton's *Opticks*, as indicated above, as well as, centrally, Milton's *Paradise Lost*. The impact of these texts on the figures who are my subjects will be discussed in their particular contexts.

26 *CPP*, p. 14.

27 *PR*, p. 212.

28 *Ibid.*

29 *PP*, pp. 238–9.

30 *Ibid.*, p. 220.

31 Poirier has persuasively made this point in *The Renewal of Literature*.

32 Ralph Waldo Emerson, *Essays and Lectures*, ed. Joel Porte (New York: Library of America, 1983), p. 487; references to this volume will hereinafter be indicated by *EL*.

33 Emily Dickinson, similarly motivated by questioning the idea of design, teleology, also explored the potential of the interstitial transitive aspects of language, but clearly James would not have had the evidence of her poems.

34 Mark Z. Danielewski, *House of Leaves* (New York: Pantheon, 2000), p. 379.

35 The use of "occasion" here is fully informed by Whitehead's definition: "An actual occasion is nothing but the unity to be ascribed to a particular instance of concrescence. This concrescence is nothing else than the 'real internal constitution' of the actual occasion in question. The analysis of the formal constitution of an actual entity has given three stages in the process of feeling: (i) the responsive stage, (ii) the supplemental stage, and (iii) the satisfaction" (*PR*, p. 212).

36 Perry Miller, "Jonathan Edwards on 'The Sense of the Heart,'" *Harvard Theological Review* 41 (1948), 123–45.

37 *PR*, p. 188.

38 *Ibid.*, esp. pp. 25, 184, 186, 224, 259, 263, 273.

39 See Perry Miller, *The New England Mind: The Seventeenth Century* (Cambridge, MA and London: Harvard University Press, 1982 [1939]) for an informing discussion of the "plain style."

40 *EL*, p. 700.

41 *Ibid.*, p. 130.

42 *Ibid.*, p. 7.

43 In describing the contribution of William James, Whitehead, in *Science and the Modern World* (New York: The Free Press, 1985; hereinafter references to this volume will be indicated by *SMW*), nominated James "that adorable genius" for having exploded what W. V. O. Quine called, and Richard Rorty has expansively discussed in *Philosophy and the Mirror of Nature* (Princeton: Princeton University Press) as, the "'idea' idea." Whitehead's comments on James's work belong to his extended discussion of the ways in which the Scientific Revolution begun in the seventeenth century only realized its import during the nineteenth in the recovery of what the pre-Socratics had understood about the centrality of considering periodicity rather than items in descriptions of nature.

Whitehead notes particularly the insight of James's recognition of the necessity of moving away from the Lockean/empiricist notion of "idea" as something that could be impressed on a *tabula rasa* in favor of a "speciated" conception where the "idea" is constantly in process.

44 Richard Poirier, *Robert Frost: The Work of Knowing* (Stanford: Stanford University Press, 1990 [1977]), p. 325.

45 *P*, p. 585.

46 *CPP*, p. 904.

47 John E. Smith, Harry S. Stout, and Kenneth P. Minkema, eds., *A Jonathan Edwards Reader* (New Haven and London: Yale University Press, 1995), p. 282; hereinafter references to this volume will be indicated by *JER*.

48 *Philosophy in a New Key: A Study in the Symbolism of Reason, Rite, and Art* (Cambridge, MA: Harvard University Press, 1996 [1942]), p. 110.

49 The most recent contribution in this area is Laura Dassow Walls, *Emerson's Life in Science: The Culture of Truth* (Ithaca and London: Cornell University Press, 2003). Lee Rust Brown, *The Emerson Museum: Practical Romanticism and The Pursuit of The Whole* (Cambridge, MA: Harvard University Press, 1997) provides keen insights into Emerson's habit of mind and his involvement with natural history. Eric Wilson, *Emerson's Sublime Science* (New York: St. Martin's Press, 1999), which began as a dissertation under my supervision, focuses on Emerson's fascination with electricity through his attention to the work of Davy and Faraday. Earlier, Robert D. Richardson Jr., *Emerson: The Mind on Fire* (Berkeley: University of California Press, 1995) established essential connections between Emerson's reading generally and his developing style. Important as well are Barbara Packer, *Emerson's Fall: A New Interpretation of the Major Essays* (New York: Continuum, 1982) and "Emerson and the Terrible Tabulations of the French," in *Transient and Permanent: The Transcendentalist Movement and Its Contexts*, ed. Charles Capper and Conrad E. Wright (Boston: Northeastern University Press, 1999), pp. 148–67.

50 *EL*, p. 47.

51 *Ibid.*, p. 120.

52 *PR*, p. 212.

53 *PP*, pp. 6–7.

54 *Ibid.*, pp. 5–6.

55 *Ibid.*, p. 246.

56 William James, *The Varieties of Religious Experience* in *Writings 1902–1910*, ed. Bruce Kuklick (New York: The Library of America, 1987), p. 184; hereinafter references to this volume will be indicated by *V*.

57 See Alfred Habegger, *The Father: A Life of Henry James, Sr.* (New York: Farrar, Straus and Giroux, 1994); R. W. B. Lewis, *The Jameses: A Family Narrative* (New York: Farrar, Straus and Giroux, 1991); and F. O. Matthiessen, *The James Family: A Group Biography* (New York: Vintage, 1980 [1947]).

58 Adeline R. Tintner, *Henry James and the Lust of the Eyes: Thirteen Artists in His Work* (Baton Rouge and London: Louisiana State University Press, 1993), pp. 89–90.

59 Charles Darwin, *The Descent of Man, and Selection in Relation to Sex* (rpt. Princeton: Princeton University Press, 1981 [London, 1871]), vol. II, p. 389.

60 The Arensberg Collection now belongs to the Philadelphia Museum of Art. In addition to the works mentioned, canvases by Degas, Cézanne, Picasso, Matisse, and others were subjects for discussion; see Joan Richardson, *Wallace Stevens: The Early Years, 1879–1923* (New York: Beech Tree Books / William Morrow, 1986) for a full discussion.

61 *CPP*, p. 404.

62 *Ibid.*, p. 451.

63 *Ibid.*, p. 135. Jonathan Edwards used the same phrase in pursuing his investigations in "The Mind": "the agreement of our ideas with the things as they are" (*The Works of Jonathan Edwards*, vol. VI: *Scientific and Philosophical Writings*, ed. Wallace E. Andersen [New Haven and London: Yale University Press, 1980] p. 342; hereinafter references to this and other items collected in this volume are indicated as *SP*).

64 *CPP*, pp. 665, 786. The notion of homeostasis was first conceptually articulated in the nineteenth century by Claude Bernard, whom William James carefully read. The term was coined by American physiologist Walter B. Cannon and extended by Norbert Weiner in his investigations into cybernetics, investigations themselves evolved from John Dewey's descriptions in *Art as Experience* (New York: Perigee, 1980) of the aesthetic function understood as a manifestation of the pragmatic impulse. Discussions of homeostasis are offered in the chapters following here.

65 *CPP*, p. 913.

66 *Ibid.*, p. 12.

2 IN JONATHAN EDWARDS'S ROOM OF THE IDEA

1 Jonathan Edwards, *SP*, p. 345.

2 Miller, "Heart," 123–9.

3 The scholarly debate concerning Miller's argument for Locke's impact on Edwards is comprehensively yet concisely traced in Janice Knight, "Learning the Language of God: Jonathan Edwards and the Typology of Nature," *William and Mary Quarterly* 48:4 (1991), 531–51. I follow Knight, and more recently Ann Taves in *Fits, Trances, & Visions: Experiencing Religion and Explaining Experience from Wesley to James* (Princeton: Princeton University Press, 1999), in supporting Miller's view against Norman Fiering, Wilson H. Kimnach, Stephen J. Stein, and Charles J. McCracken. See Knight's notes for full references to opposing voices.

4 The complete title of Newton's text is *Opticks: or, a Treatise of the Reflections, Refractions, Inflections & Colors of Light* based on the fourth edition, London, 1730 (rpt. New York: Dover Publications, 1979). Each of these essential aspects of light, discriminatively and precisely detailed by Newton, would furnish Edwards full imaginative scope. Subsequent references will refer to Newton's text as *Opticks*, except when citing

Wallace E. Anderson who, in his introduction to *SP*, uses the modernized spelling, *Optics*.

Two earlier studies of Edwards's reading of Newton's *Opticks* – James H. Tufts, "Edwards and Newton," *Philosophical Review* 294 (November 1940), 609–22, and Ron Loewinsohn, "Jonathan Edwards' Opticks: Images and Metaphors of Light in Some of his Major Works," *Early American Literature* 8 (1973), 20–32 – open consideration of this relation and offer important observations, but regard Edwards's deployment of what he gleaned from Newton as metaphorical, and neither presents Edwards as himself having, in his terms, an "actual idea" of light's activity as described by Newton. In consequence, neither explores the effect of this "sensible" knowledge on Edwards's style. In addition, Anderson's introduction to *SP* offers a keener appreciation of Edwards's involvement with the *Opticks*, as will be noted further along in this chapter, but also does not connect this involvement with Edwards's style.

　　In contrast, Alan Heimert has observed as perhaps Edwards's "highest achievement" his ability to infuse the inherited language of covenant theology with "radically new meanings derived from his reading of Newton," but, together with most other readers of Edwards, Heimert limits this insight to Edwards's metaphorical appropriation of the concept of gravity. See Heimert's "Afterword," *The Puritans in America: A Narrative Anthology*, ed. Alan Heimert and Andrew Delbanco (Cambridge, MA: Harvard University Press, 1985), pp. 410–11. As will be discussed later in this chapter, Edwards deployed his understanding of Newton in more than a metaphorical sense, attempting, rather, especially in his linguistic adaptation of what he had understood about light, to imitate, as "actual idea," aspects of its behavior in the progress of his sentences. The distinction I am suggesting here between imitation and "as if" constructions will be made clear as my argument proceeds to detail the difference between what Edwards termed "speculative" and "sensible" knowledge, a difference that is the defining feature of his "sense of the heart."

5　Chamberlain's introduction to Edwards, *Miscell. 501–832*, p. 23.

6　Edwards used the 7th edition (London, 1716) of *An Essay concerning Human Understanding*. See *Miscell. 501–832*, p. 454, n. 4. Neither Newton's text nor any other work presenting Newton's discoveries had been used in an American college before 1717/18. Edwards spent almost all of his first three collegiate years in Wethersfield, where some of the Yale faculty had moved, and did not reside in New Haven until 1719, so it is improbable that he would have had an opportunity to study the text before then; see *Miscell. 501–832*, p. 149.

7　*Miscell. 501–832*, pp. 457, 463.

8　Locke, *Essay*, II, iii, p. 121.

9　Jonathan Crary in *Techniques of the Observer: On Vision and Modernity in the Nineteenth Century* (Cambridge, MA: MIT Press, 1991) offers a persuasive description of both Locke's and Newton's familiarity with the *camera obscura* as "a model simultaneously for the observation of empirical phenomena and for reflective introspection and self-observation" (p. 40).

10 This exercise is what Emerson would later describe as the use of life being metonymy, searching backwards for the situating physical moments when connections between things have been "excited." See "Poetry and Imagination," in *Ralph Waldo Emerson*, ed. Richard Poirier (Oxford and New York: Oxford University Press, 1990), pp. 440–73.

11 Taves also notes Edwards's "radical naturalistic understanding of the natural order" (*Fits*, p. 39) while Knight considers Edwards's understanding of conversion to be an individual experience, related to varying states of the soul, an experience that with repeated "awakenings" could gradually move an individual up the "scale of being." See her discussion, "Learning," 541–3.

12 Dennis L. Sepper, *Newton's Optical Writings: A Guided Study* (New Brunswick: Rutgers University Press, 1994), pp. 38–9; hereinafter *NOW*.

13 *Ibid.*, p. 200.

14 Miller was the first to note Edwards's extension of typology to reading nature, which Anderson further elaborates, as does Knight who also discusses Edwards's inclusion of the "rituals of daily life."

15 *CPP*, p. 404.

16 Perry Miller, *Errand Into The Wilderness* (New York: Harper Torchbooks, 1956), p. 195.

17 For additional information about this edition of the *Opticks*, see Anderson's introduction, *SP*, especially pp. 18–19, n. 5.

18 In addition to the *Opticks*, Dummer's gift also brought to the Yale collection Newton's *Principia*; the major scientific works of Robert Boyle; the posthumous papers of Robert Hooke; John Harris's scientific encyclopedia *Lexicon Technicum*; various publications of the Royal Society; Jacques Rohault's *Physica*, a widely used textbook in the Cartesian physics to which Samuel Clarke had added footnotes explaining Newton's corrections of and improvements upon Descartes's theories; Whiston's *Astronomical Lectures* and *New Theory of the Earth*; William Derham's *Astro-theology* and *Physico-theology*; Galileo's *Systema Cosmicum*; Christian Huygens's *Celestial Worlds Discover'd*; David Gregory's *Elements of Astronomy*; and John Ray's *The Wisdom of God Manifested in the Works of Creation*; see *SP*, p. 17, n. 9.

19 *PP*, p. 79.

20 *Ibid.*, p. 105.

21 Knight, "Learning," 532–3; paraphrases and quotations from Edwards as cited by Knight, in order: *Dissertation II. The Nature of True Virtue* in *The Works of Jonathan Edwards*, vol. VIII: *Ethical Writings*, ed. Paul Ramsey (New Haven and London: Yale University Press, 1989), p. 564; *Images or Shadows of Divine Things*, ed. Perry Miller (New Haven and London: Yale University Press, 1948), p. 64; "Types of the Messiah," in *The Works of President Edwards with a Memoir of His Life*, vol. IX (New York, 1830), p. 110.

22 Knight, "Learning," p. 545; quotations from Edwards from *Works*, vol. VIII, pp. 550, 513, 512–13.

23 George M. Marsden in his recent *Jonathan Edwards: A Life* (New Haven and London: Yale University Press, 2003), pp. 79, 129, also notes parallels between

Edwards's sermon style, with its theme and variations, and the "complex harmonies" of eighteenth-century music as exemplified in Bach's fugal structures,
pointing to the divine, but he does not connect this insight to the particularities of Edwards's spiralling style and its embodiment, like Bach's fugues, of
the Fibonacci Series.

24 James H. Bunn in *Wave Forms: A Natural Syntax for Rhythmic Languages* (Stanford: Stanford University Press, 2002) has noted Samuel Taylor
Coleridge's later articulation of this recursive activity from his own attention
to "the pleasurable activity of the mind . . . like the path of sound through air;
at every step he [the reader] pauses and half recedes, and from the retrogressive
movement collects the force which carries him onward" (p. 31).

25 Wilson N. Kimnach remarks on Edwards's "almost feverish search" for new
"books to read" so extensively documented in his "Catalogue" (a manuscript
notebook, quarto of twenty-four leaves, in the Beinecke Rare Book and
Manuscript Library, Yale University). See Wilson N. Kimnach, "General
Introduction," in Jonathan Edwards, *The Works of Jonathan Edwards*, vol. X:
Sermons and Discourses, 1720–1723, ed. Kimnach (New Haven and London:
Yale University Press, 1992), p. 53; hereinafter references to this title will be
indicated by *Sermons 1720–3*.

26 Chamberlain's introduction, *Miscell. 501–832*, p. 39.

27 See *Newton Demands the Muse: Newton's "Opticks" and the Eighteenth-Century
Poets* (Princeton: Princeton University Press, 1966), p. 37.

28 Marsden, *Life*, pp. 54–5.

29 *Sermons 1720–3*, p. 25.

30 *SP*, p. 23.

31 Also noted by Marsden, *Life*, p. 72.

32 These parallels between Darwin's and Emerson's reading are discussed here
in Chapter 3.

33 *NOW*, p. xii. In "Of Being," written when Edwards was fifteen or sixteen,
before, that is, his reading of the *Opticks*, and, as noted above, while persuaded
by More's argument, he boldly wrote, "But I had as good speak plain: I have
already said as much as that space is God." This idea would become refined
through his study of Newton into understanding space itself as a product
of infinite light shading into what to limited human perception appears as
darkness. By 1723 light became identified for him with consciousness, and
consciousness with being. See *SP*, p. 203, n.5.

34 *The Works of Jonathan Edwards*, vol. II: *Religious Affections*, ed. John E. Smith
(New Haven and London: Yale University Press, 1987), p. 206.

35 This quotation from Edwards is also significantly noted by Marsden, *Life*,
p. 44.

36 *NOW*, pp. 24–5, quoting from Newton and elaborating.

37 From Newton's observations following Proposition II of Book II, Part III
of the *Opticks*, quoted in *NOW*, p. 130; the bracketed "[sent]" is Sepper's
addition, the spelling of "immitted," Newton's.

38 *SP*, pp. 221–2, 224.

39 Kimnach's introduction, *Sermons 1720–3*, p. 37. Interestingly, in indicating Edwards's habit of drawing such "Propositions" or "Observations" from a Text for the purpose of "clearing" the Doctrine, Kimnach observes that this manner "brings the entire sermon into a sharp thematic focus, like light rays passing through a lens, if only for a vivid moment" (p. 38), but he nowhere suggests this practice as derived from that of Newton, though he elsewhere compares Edwards's search for "the hieroglyph of the Deity in Nature" with Newton's for "the consistent principle within the event" (p. 45).

40 *SP*, pp. 241–2.

41 Whitehead describes "prehension" as the activity and consequent contribution of active imagination to an apprehension of things as they are. Charles Lyell, for example, had imaginatively to project eons in the evolution of the planet to account for the fossil evidence being made available in his moment, which imagining provided a "fact" about the planet's being in time which could never be experienced as actual by a human observer. See *SMW*, pp. 69–74, 148–9, for a full discussion of "prehension," later denoted "event" by Whitehead.

42 Quoted by Anderson from Samuel Hopkins, *Life and Character of the Late Mr. Jonathan Edwards* (Boston, 1765), p. 27; *SP*, p. 7.

43 *SP*, pp. 241, 215.

44 *CPP*, p. 8.

45 Knight, "Learning," 538. Knight notes her paraphrasing this idea from Edwards's "Types of the Messiah," p. 110 in Mason Lowance and David Watters's typescript version of "Types," which at the time of her writing had not yet appeared in the Yale series.

46 *EL*, p. 475.

47 *Sermons 1720–3*, p. 32.

48 Edwards, *Miscell. 501–832*, p. 6.

49 For a full discussion see John F. Wilson's excellent introduction to *The Works of Jonathan Edwards*, vol. IX: *A History of the Work of Redemption* (New Haven and London: Yale University Press, 1989); hereinafter references to this title will be indicated by *HWR*. Concerning the survival of this text into the cultural life of nineteenth-century America, Wilson notes – following George Bancroft and Harriet Beecher Stowe, who recognized that *A History* "had both set the framework for American collective self-understanding and fostered the remarkable flowering of religious and theological discussion of the nineteenth century" – that,

> With respect to popular culture [as well], *A History of the Work of Redemption* clearly had enormous influence . . . It may not be too much to suggest that Edwards' history was as influential as any other single book in fixing the cultural parameters of nineteenth-century American Protestant culture. It securely anchored American experience in a cosmic setting, locating it by means of reference to sacred Scripture and investing it with preeminent significance for concluding the drama of Christian redemption. It legitimated the social experiment that was the new American culture. (p. 82)

Elsewhere, in appropriately considering *A History* as a "literary document," Wilson brilliantly observes that "Herman Melville's *Moby-Dick* may stand in as close kinship to it as any other American text" (p. 61). A volume contributing a central chapter in American literary and cultural history could be written following the direction he points to here.

50 Tim Flannery, "A Bird's-Eye View of Evolution," a review of Ernst Mayr and Jared Diamond, *The Birds of Northern Melanesia: Speciation, Ecology, and Biogeography* (New York and London: Oxford University Press, 2002) and Ernst Mayr, *What Evolution Is* (New York: Basic Books, 2002), *New York Review of Books* (June 27, 2002), 27. See also Flannery, "In the Primordial Soup," a review of Christopher Wills and Jeffrey Bada, *The Spark of Life: Darwin and the Primeval Soup* (New York: Perseus Books, 2000), and Steve Jones, *Darwin's Ghost: The Origin of Species Updated* (New York: Random House, 2000), *New York Review of Books* (November 2, 2000), 56, for the borrowing of "errors of descent" in the text which follows.

51 Stevens's phrase, "more than rational distortion," is used throughout the chapters here as the figure for the "actual idea" of aesthetic activity embodied in William James's various descriptions of radical empiricism.

52 Humberto R. Maturana and Francisco Varela, *The Tree of Knowledge: The Biological Roots of Human Understanding*, revised edition (Boston and London: Shambala, 1998), p. 61. The application of this concept to the transformation of texts will be elaborated further on here and in following chapters.

53 Taves makes a similar point, though not in particular connection to Edwards:

> a mythic worldview is inscribed on the body of the individual and/or group as people gain mastery of practices in ritual contexts wherein the mythic discourses, images, and/or structures are embedded. As Bourdieu has written, "it is in the dialectical relationship between the body and a space structured according to the mythico-ritual oppositions that one finds the form par excellence of the structural apprenticeship which leads to the em-bodying of the structures of the world." The sacralization of experience thus involves cultivating and maintaining those practices through which a community understands, locates, and experiences the sacred. The relationship between "experience" and "practices" is necessarily dynamic and interdependent . . . Protestants and purveyors of the Enlightenment each attempted in their own way to reinterpret the Christian myth and remap the way in which the bodies of individual Christians and the collective Christian body as a whole were constituted. (*Fits*, p. 47)

54 See Maturana, *Tree*, esp. pp. 43–53 on membranes and forms.

55 *HWR* (Sermon 1), p. 121. It is informing to remark in this context a certain editorial modification of this text. *A History of the Work of Redemption* was first published posthumously, after Jonathan Edwards Jr. had taken possession of his father's manuscripts, by John Erskine in Edinburgh in 1774. It was reissued in 1782 in Edinburgh and reprinted in Boston, before being first issued in New York in 1786. This same version was reprinted three times more in Edinburgh (1788, 1793, 1799) and also in Worcester. Later, "an augmented version, known as the 'Pitcher edition' after its editor, George Pitcher, was brought out in London in 1788." In this version, Pitcher departed from the Erskine version

"in the form of occasionally eliminating a redundant sentence" (Wilson's introduction, *HWR*, p. 26).

56 *HWR*, p. 106.

57 Stephen Prickett, *Narrative, Religion and Science: Fundamentalism versus Irony, 1700–1999* (Cambridge: Cambridge University Press, 2002), p. 36.

58 *Ibid.*, p. 37.

59 *Ibid.*, p. 160.

60 Judith Shulevitz, "From God's Mouth to English," review of Robert Alter, *The Five Books of Moses: A Translation with Commentary* (New York: W. W. Norton, 2004), *New York Times Book Review* (October 17, 2004), 8.

61 *Ibid.*, Shulevitz's terms.

62 Richard Rorty, *Contingency, Irony and Solidarity* (Cambridge: Cambridge University Press, 1989), p. 8; quoted by Prickett, *Narrative*, p. 197.

63 It is exciting, in Edwards's sense, and instructive to consider what the "invisible" includes in today's cosmology:

> The simplest and most popular cosmological model today predicts that you have a twin in a galaxy about 10 to the 10/28th meters from here. This distance is so large that it is beyond astronomical, but that does not make your doppelganger any less real. The estimate is derived from elementary probability and does not even assume speculative modern physics, merely that space is infinite (or at least sufficiently large) in size and almost uniformly filled with matter, as observations indicate. In infinite space, even the most unlikely events must take place somewhere. There are infinitely many other inhabited planets, including not just one but infinitely many that have people with the same appearance, name and memories as you, who play out every possible permutation of your life choices (Max Tegmark, "Parallel Universes," *Scientific American* [May, 2003], 41)

64 *P*, p. 574.

65 Marsden, *Life*, p. 474.

66 Wallace Stevens, *Letters of Wallace Stevens*, ed. Holly Stevens (New York: Alfred A. Knopf, 1970), p. 32; hereinafter references to this title will be indicated by *LWS*.

67 *NOW*, p. 98.

68 Knight, "Learning," 533; quotation from Edwards as cited by Knight in *Images or Shadows*, p. 102.

69 *Ibid.*, p. 543, Knight quoting Edwards from *The Philosophy of Jonathan Edwards from His Private Notebooks*, ed. Harvey G. Townsend (Eugene, OR, 1955), p. 130.

70 Quoted in *NOW*, p. 92.

71 *EL*, p. 10.

72 Newton's "Definition" derived from Experiment 6, Book I, Part II, quoted in *NOW*, pp. 92–3.

73 Quoted from the Worcester edition of Edwards's *Works* by Kimnach, *Sermons 1720–3*, p. 25.

74 Wilson in his introduction to *HWR* underlines Edwards's view in this sermon series that "While Christ, the saints, and the angels ascend toward heaven,

and the church enters eternal blessedness, the world will be set on fire" (p. 40). In Sermon 28 (of thirty), Edwards, alluding to Revelation 20:9, wrote, "The wickedness of the world will remarkably call for Christ's appearing in flaming fire to take vengeance on them" because of their "wickedness" which "will as much call for its being destroyed by a deluge of fire" (pp. 490–1). While in the sermon Edwards incorporates the images from Revelation, in Miscellany no. 803, as noted by Wilson, composed by Edwards as an indication to himself of what he wanted to communicate in his sermon, he indicated that "the theme . . . is the human abuse of divine gifts that provokes the extreme divine vengeance as the world undergoes destruction at the last judgment" (p. 491). "[T]he . . . abuse of divine gifts" for Edwards would have been the sustained resistance to being graced equivalent to the inability to access the "sense of the heart" necessary to create a "room of the idea" in which to entertain, to imagine, the work of God's creation.

75 *JER*, pp. 14–15.
76 "Mental states occasion also changes in the calibre of blood-vessels, or alteration in the heart-beats, or processes more subtle still, in glands and viscera" (*PP*, p. 18). Taking full account of emotions, "feelings," in formulating judgments is the subject of the core chapter of *Principles*, "The Stream of Thought," the greater part of which appeared in *Mind* in January 1884 under the title, "On Some Omissions of Introspective Psychology."
77 *PR*, p. 116.
78 Stephen H. Daniel, *The Philosophy of Jonathan Edwards: A Study in Divine Semiotics* (Bloomington: Indiana University Press, 1994), an excellent study of Edwards's manner and method especially in connection with pointings toward the later work of Charles Sanders Peirce.
79 *The Works of Jonathan Edwards*, vol. XI: *Typological Writings*, ed. Wallace E. Anderson and Mason Lowance, Jr., with David Watters (New Haven and London: Yale University Press, 1993), p. 152.
80 Daniel, *Semiotics*, pp. 15–40, esp. pp. 15, 24; Locke's *Essay*, ed. Nidditch, pp. 720–1, 405, as cited by Daniel, pp. 15–16.
81 Alan Richardson, *British Romanticism and the Science of Mind* (Cambridge: Cambridge University Press, 2001), pp. 4, 137–8, 132, including quotations from Coleridge and Bell. Richardson's superb study, while concentrating on British romanticism, complements mine in uncovering the rich fund of scientific information available to and used especially by Keats, Coleridge, and Wordsworth, some pertinently common to Emerson, as will be discussed in the following chapter here, the crucial difference between the British Romantics and Emerson being his specifically inflected ministerial motive.
82 This phrase is borrowed from Stevens's "The Doctor of Geneva" where the eponymous subject, suggested as a persona or avatar of Calvin, "Lacustrine man," finds himself, like one of the earlier personae of Keats's explorers in "On First Looking into Chapman's Homer," on the newly discovered continent's Pacific shore, in Stevens's rendition brought to tears by the inability of finding words to describe what he sees and feels in the face of "the wild,

the ruinous waste": "Lacustrine man had never been assailed / By such long-rolling opulent cataracts, / . . . the steeples of his city clanked and sprang / In an unburgherly apocalypse. / The doctor used his handkerchief and sighed" (*CPP*, p. 19).

83 Lawrence Buell, "Thoreau and the Natural Environment," in the *Cambridge Companion to Henry David Thoreau*, ed. Joel Myerson (Cambridge: Cambridge University Press, 1996), p. 180.

84 Quoted by Kimnach, *Sermons 1720–3*, p. 26.

85 *Ibid.*

86 *CPP*, p. 195.

87 *Personal Narrative*, in *JER*, p. 283; hereinafter *PN* following the page indications of this edition.

88 Andrew Hadfield, "Erasmus's errata slips," review of Brian Cummings, *The Literary Culture of the Reformation: Grammar and Grace* (Oxford: Oxford University Press, 2002), *The Times Literary Supplement* (March 14, 2003), 31.

89 Knight, "Learning," 542, the quotations and paraphrasing from Edwards, *Images or Shadows*, pp. 95, 59, 95, 119–20.

90 *PN*, p. 292.

91 Perry Miller, *Jonathan Edwards* (New York: Meridian Books, 1959), p. 2. The text which "came into [Edwards's] mind" is I Corinthians 1:29, 30, 31.

92 *SP*, p. 383.

93 Quoted in *NOW*, pp. 140–1.

94 *SP*, pp. 371, 336, 335.

95 *Ibid.*, p. 337.

96 *Ibid.*, p. 371.

97 Michael Shermer, "Demon-Haunted Brain," *Scientific American* (March, 2003), 47. See also Nicole Garbarini, "Heartbeat Poetry: Verse Speaks to Matters of the Heart – Literally," *Scientific American* (October, 2004), 31–2.

98 Shermer, "Demon," 47.

99 *SP*, p. 339.

100 *PN*, p. 284.

101 *Ibid.*, p. 288.

102 *Ibid.*, p. 289.

103 Taves, *Fits*, p. 37

104 Cited by Wilson in his introduction, *HWR*, p. 86.

105 *Ibid.*, p. 88.

106 *Ibid.*, pp. 89–90.

107 *CPP*, p. 471.

108 *PN*, p. 295.

109 Newton, *Opticks*, p. 345.

110 Barbara Maria Stafford, *Visual Analogy: Consciousness as the Art of Connecting* (Cambridge, MA: MIT Press, 1999), p. 105.

111 *Ibid.*, p. 2.

112 *Ibid.*, pp. 9, 23–4.

113 *V*, p. 135.

3 EMERSON'S MOVING PICTURES

1 *EL*, p. 761.
2 *Ibid.*, p. 47.
3 *Ibid.*, p. 555.
4 Emerson borrowed this term from Guillaume Oegger, whom he quotes in the "Language" chapter of *Nature* (1836): "Material objects . . . are necessarily kinds of *scoriae* of the substantial thoughts of the Creator, which must always preserve an exact relation to their first origin; in other words, visible nature must have a spiritual and moral side" (*EL*, p. 25). Emerson extends the term to include the record of thinking in the "material" of language of all those whose work continues to contribute to the successful conduct of life.
5 *Ibid.*, p. 623. Oliver Wendell Holmes was the first to observe Emerson's anticipation of the evolutionary process, even before Robert Chambers's 1844 *Vestiges of Creation.* Joseph Warren Beach extended the discussion in "Emerson and Evolution," *University of Toronto Quarterly* 3 (1934), 474–97. See also William Rossi, "Emerson, Nature, and the Natural Sciences," in *A Historical Guide to Ralph Waldo Emerson*, ed. Joel Myerson (New York: Oxford University Press, 2000), p. 120; Lawrence Buell, *Emerson* (Cambridge, MA and London: Harvard University Press, 2003), p. 176; and Walls, *Culture*, pp. 167–8, 169, 171.
6 *EL*, p. 18.
7 *Ibid.*, pp. 616, 678.
8 Buell, *Emerson*, p. 167.
9 *EL*, p. 301.
10 *Ibid.*, pp. 715–16.
11 *Ibid.*, p. 47.
12 *Ibid.*, p. 25.
13 *Ibid.*, p. 62. See also Walls, *Culture*, pp. 127–65, on the centrality of polarity in the nineteenth century in relation to the development of Emerson's thinking.
14 *EL*, p. 47.
15 *Ibid.*, pp. 84, 87.
16 *Journals of Ralph Waldo Emerson 1820–1872*, vol. III (Boston and New York: Houghton Mifflin, 1910), p. 163.
17 Lynn Gamwell, *Exploring the Invisible: Art, Science and the Spiritual* (Princeton: Princeton University Press, 2002), p. 15.
18 *EL*, p. 635.
19 In a footnote to Emerson's essay "Quotation and Originality" in the Riverside edition of his works, his son Edward Waldo offers: "Dr. Holmes, in several places in his Life of Emerson, has much that is interesting to say about his quotations, which he says 'are like the miraculous draught of fishes'; and he has been at pains to count the named references, chiefly to authors, and found them to be three thousand three hundred and ninety-three, relating to eight hundred and sixty-eight different individuals," quoted by Susan Howe, *The Midnight* (New York: New Directions, 2003), p. 116.

20 *EL*, p. 669.

21 *Ibid.*, pp. 748, 475.

22 *Ibid.*, p. 475.

23 *Ibid.*, p. 746.

24 Edwards, *Miscell. 501–832*, p. 461. It is unlikely that Emerson could have read Edwards's notebooks. He had certainly studied Edwards in Divinity School under Dr. Channing, and his journal notes in 1823–4 evidence particular interest. He knew Edwards's *On the Freedom of the Will* well. See R. D. Richardson, *Mind*, p. 594, nn. 5 and 11; Richardson's view, in sharp contrast to mine, finds Miller's connection between Edwards and Emerson "specious." What is important, whether the connection is direct or not, is the remarkable similarity in their vocabularies and methods in light of the parallels between their spiritual and intellectual preparations.

25 *EL*, p. 23.

26 *Ibid.*, p. 62.

27 Donna Jeanne Haraway, *Crystals, Fabrics, and Fields: Metaphors of Organicism in Twentieth-Century Developmental Biology* (New Haven and London: Yale University Press, 1976), pp. 8–9; hereinafter references to this title will be indicated by *Crystals*. Robert J. Richards in his recent *The Romantic Conception of Life: Science and Philosophy* (Chicago: University of Chicago Press, 2002) has elaborated the central importance of image/metaphor and, of course, the concomitant process of visualization to the development of biology in drawing the parallels between the conceptual fields of the Romantic poets and early "biologists." He does not, however, refer to Haraway's study, which broke ground in this area. Haraway notes, for example, Ross Harrison's citation of Albrecht Dürer's *Treatise on Proportion* as an earlier instance of artists' perception of organic form.

28 *Crystals*, pp. 11, 99.

29 *Ibid.*, p. 11.

30 As elaborated by Philip Ritterbush, *The Art of Organic Forms* (Washington: Smithsonian Institute Press, 1968) and indicated in *Crystals*, pp. 11–13.

31 *Ibid.*, p. 12.

32 *EL*, p. 89.

33 *Ibid.*, p. 413.

34 *Ibid.*, p. 251.

35 *PR*, p. 113.

36 *EL*, p. 60.

37 *Ibid.*, pp. 700, 30, 20.

38 Steven Johnson, *Emergence: The Connected Lives of Ants, Brains, Cities, and Software* (New York: Simon and Schuster, 2002), pp. 198, 200.

39 It has been readers' consensus, following Perry Miller in *The Transcendentalists: An Anthology* (Cambridge, MA: Harvard University Press, 1950), esp. p. 49, that Swedenborgian ideas, introduced through the work of Sampson Reed, were as important in the development of American Transcendentalism as those of Kant percolated through Coleridge, first by way of James Marsh,

sometimes referred to as "the American Coleridge." Emerson certainly read Reed carefully, particularly his *Observations on the Growth of the Mind* (1826), and continued to deepen his knowledge of Swedenborg through the English translations of John Garth Wilkinson and through the writing of and conversations with Henry James Sr. Emerson and the Transcendentalists were to differ sharply from Reed's strict interpretation of Swedenborg which privileged Divine Revelation over what could be revealed through the study of nature.

40 Robert Richardson, for example, while he notes that Emerson was "interested in his work," believes that it was with a "half-fascinated, half-repelled attention" (*Mind*, pp. 197, 436). Richardson does note, in contrast, however, appreciations of Swedenborg and his connections to Emerson's thinking by some of his contemporaries; see p. 612 n. 8. Similarly, Buell, *Emerson*, notes, though in passing, that Swedenborg was significant to Emerson's religious thinking and also that "it is not clear that he ever had the patience to read through a single modern philosophical treatise after he resigned from the pulpit, unless we count the mystical exegeses of Emanuel Swedenborg" (p. 201).

41 Eugene Taylor, "Peirce and Swedenborg," *Studia Swedenborgiana*, 6:1 (June, 1986), 42; see Taylor's note 9 for additional references discussing Swedenborg's influence on Kant.

42 *EL*, pp. 667, 684, 664.

43 *Ibid.*, p. 668.

44 Ospovat, *Development*, p. 133.

45 *CPP*, p. 47.

46 The term "vastation" from Wilkinson's nineteenth-century translation, which made Swedenborg available to English-speaking audiences, would be borrowed by Henry James Sr., and after him William, to describe their own spiritual/nervous crises.

47 *EL*, p. 675.

48 *The Correspondence of William James*, vol. IV: *1856–1877*, ed. Ignas K. Skrupskelis and Elizabeth M. Berkeley (Charlottesville: University Press of Virginia, 1995), p. 220; hereinafter references to this volume will be indicated by *CWJ* 4.

49 *EL*, p. 117.

50 *Ibid.*, pp. 620, 57, 116.

51 *Ibid.*, p. 620.

52 *Ibid.*, p. 675.

53 *Ibid.*, p. 131.

54 *Ibid.*, p. 256.

55 *Ibid.*, p. 616.

56 *Ibid.*, p. 322.

57 *PP*, p. 1170.

58 *The Correspondence of William James*, vol. I: *William and Henry, 1861–1884*, ed. Ignas K. Skrupskelis and Elizabeth M. Berkeley (Charlottesville: University

Press of Virginia, 1992), p. 131, n. 3; hereinafter references to this volume will be indicated by *CWJ* 1.

59 In connection with the notion of "engrafting" in relation to Emerson's appreciation of Swedenborg and his sense of continuity between the inorganic, organic, and spiritual, Arnaldo Momigliano provides a possible link, tracing nineteenth-century scholarship, in that the theory of the correspondence between the parts of the human body and the parts of the whole world is "found in the *Greater Bundahishn*, a Zoroastrian cosmological work of the ninth century A.D., which is supposed to go back to lost sections of the *Avesta*" (*Alien Wisdom: The Limits of Hellenization* [Cambridge: Cambridge University Press, 1991], p. 128). We recall that under Emerson's editorship of the *Dial* some of the first English translations of Indic texts were published together with commentary and consideration of some of the scholarship pointed to by Momigliano. I have not yet investigated the possibility of Emerson's familiarity with this material. William James, in *P*, p. 592, centrally uses this notion as well: "Truth grafts itself on previous truth, modifying it in the process."

60 *EL*, pp. 628, 69.
61 *Ibid.*, p. 670.
62 *Ibid.*, p. 302.
63 *Ibid.*, p. 668.
64 *Crystals*, pp. 98–9.
65 *EL*, pp. 668–9.
66 *EL*, p. 129. See Joan Richardson, "Emerson's Sound Effects," *Raritan* 16:3 (Winter, 1997), 83–101, for a full discussion of this aspect of Emerson's style; see also Buell, *Emerson*, p. 120, commenting on this aspect of Emerson's delivery that he was at the same time expressing "how thinking *felt*."
67 *EL*, p. 631.
68 *Ibid.*, pp. 498–9.
69 *Ibid.*, pp. 618–19.
70 *Ibid.*, p. 106.
71 *Ibid.*, p. 34.
72 *Ibid.*, p. 216.
73 *Ibid.*, pp. 83–4.
74 *CPP*, p. 12.
75 In his lectures Emerson incorporated even forms from newspaper reporting, creating a bricolage. I have not yet been able to relocate the source of this quotation in Emerson, though I know it to come from his work, having borrowed it years ago to entitle one of the first graduate seminars I conducted around his work.
76 *CPP*, p. 12.
77 *EL*, p. 671.
78 *Ibid.*, p. 667.
79 *Ibid.*, pp. 456–7.

80 *EL*, p. 422.
81 For a full discussion of reading available to English-speaking audiences, see Ospovat, *Development*.
82 *EL*, p. 129.
83 *Ibid.*, p. 471.
84 *Ibid.*, p. 422.
85 Henry D. Thoreau, *Faith in a Seed: The Dispersion of Seeds and Other Late Natural History Writings*, ed. Bradley P. Dean (Washington, DC: Island Press, 1993), pp. 3–17.
86 The definitions in Noah Webster's 1828 *American Dictionary*, for example, the standard reference for Emerson and his culture, describe a divinely directed order, and his etymologies, as he indicated in his preface to the dictionary, trace the "American tongue backward through countless transformations to the moment when language began in the Garden of Eden." See Cynthia Griffin Wolff, *Emily Dickinson* (New York: Alfred A. Knopf, 1986), pp. 90–2, for a concise yet comprehensive discussion.
87 *EL*, p. 294.
88 *Charles Darwin's "Beagle" Diary*, ed. R. D. Keynes (Cambridge: Cambridge University Press, 2001), p. 111. Keynes adds the following note:

> CD [Charles Darwin] wrote: "Milton's *Paradise Lost* had been my chief favourite, and in my excursions during the voyage on the *Beagle*, when I could take only a single small volume, I always chose Milton" (see *Autobiography* p. 85). In describing to Henslow (see *Correspondence* 1:280, and also *Journal of Researches* pp. 114–15) a possibly new species of toad coloured black and vermilion, he says "Milton must allude to this very individual when he talks of "squat like a toad"" (*Paradise Lost*, Book 4, line 800). In an entry in Down House Notebook 1.7, written at Coquimbo in May 1835 before setting out for Copiapo, CD reminds himself not to leave the volume of Milton behind.

89 Quoted by Gillian Beer, *Open Fields: Studies in Cultural Encounter* (Oxford: Clarendon Oxford University Press, 1996), p. 211; hereinafter references to this title will be indicated by *OF*.
90 Charles Lyell, *Principles of Geology*, 3 vols., ed. Martin Rudwick (Chicago: University of Chicago Press, 1990), vol. I, pp. xviii–xix.
91 *OF*, p. 210.
92 Lyell, *Principles*, vol. I, p. 234 in the 1881 edition cited by Beer.
93 Cited in *OF*, p. 110.
94 *OF*, p. 210.
95 John Tyndall, "Scientific Use of Imagination," in *Fragments of Science: A Series of Detached Essays, Addresses and Reviews*, 2 vols. (London: Gregg International Publishers Ltd., 1970 [Longman's, Green, 1892]), vol. II, p. 202. Henry James read and admired these volumes, as will be discussed in the chapter on James to follow.
96 *PR*, p. 96.
97 *OF*, pp. 202–3. The titles listed represent only a handful of the selection available to nineteenth-century readers. Exploring the contents of these several

publications in connection with the writers of the period continues to offer a rich field for future investigators.

98 See also Kibbey, *Interpretation*, esp. Chapter 2, "The Rhetorical Imperative," pp. 6–41.

99 *OF*, p. 208.

100 *EL*, p. 487.

101 *CDN*, pp. 526–7: "appetites themselves become changed.– appetites urge the man, but indefinitely, he chooses (but what makes him fix!?<)> – frame of mind, though perhaps he chooses wrongly, – what is frame of mind owing to. – <)> – I verily believe free-will & chance are synonymous. – Shake ten thousand grains of sand together & one will be uppermost: – so in thoughts, one will rise according to law"; further, p 536: "free will is to mind what chance is to matter . . . the free will (if so called) makes change."

102 *Ibid.*, p. 569: "Reason in simplest form probably is single comparison by senses of any two objects – they by VIVID power of conception between one or two absent things. – reason probably mere consequence of vividness & multiplicity of things remembered & associated pleasure &c accompanying such memory. –" In "A Framework for Consciousness," *Nature* "*Neuroscience*" 6: 2 (February, 2003), 119–26, Francis Crick and Christof Koch offer an explanation of neural correlates of consciousness in terms of competing cellular assemblies that incorporates and expands on Darwin's perception. See also Robert J. Richards, *Darwin and the Emergence of Evolutionary Theories of Mind and Behavior* (Chicago: University of Chicago Press, 1987), esp. pp. 85–122, for discussion of the place of pleasure in Darwin's thinking.

103 *EL*, p. 7.

104 Johnson, *Emergence*, pp. 53–4.

105 *The Letters of Ralph Waldo Emerson*, 6 vols., ed. Ralph L. Rusk (New York: Columbia University Press, 1966), vol. II, p. 169.

106 *EL*, p. 130.

107 *Ibid.*, p. 281.

108 Ian Hacking, "Probability and Determinism, 1650–1900," in *Companion to the History of Modern Science*, ed. R. C. Olby, G. N. Cantor, *et al.* (London: Routledge, 1990), pp. 699–700; *OF*, pp. 8, 298; see also Packer, "Emerson and the Terrible Tabulations of the French."

109 *EL*, pp. 678, 669, 692, 125, 87, 82, 47, 48, 19, 11.

110 *CPP*, p. 145.

111 *EL*, p. 620.

112 *Ibid.*, p. 622. It is worth remarking that D. T. Suzuki, as noted by Buell, *Emerson*, p. 197, quotes this same passage to describe the experience of Satori or enlightenment in Zen Buddhism.

113 For an extended discussion of these connections, see Wilson, *Sublime Science*.

114 Janet Browne, *Charles Darwin: Voyaging, A Biography* (Princeton: Princeton University Press, 1995), p. 127.

115 Emerson, *Letters*, vol. IV, p. 51, n. 184.

116 *Ibid.*, p. 51. Among the other scientists Emerson visited during this period were Lyell, Faraday, Richard Owen, and William Hooker.

117 Browne, *Voyaging*, pp. 384, 409.

118 Wedgwood's expertise was such that he corrected even some of Skeat's etymologies; see his *Contested Etymologies in the Dictionary of the Rev. W. W. Skeat* (London: Trubner, 1882).

119 Browne, *Voyaging*, pp. 430, 439, 446.

120 *Ibid.*, pp. 446–7.

121 See especially Beer, "Darwin and the Growth of Language Theory," in *OF*, pp. 95–114.

122 Emerson, *Letters*, vol. VI, p. 188.

123 Edward Manier, *The Young Darwin and his Cultural Circle* (Dordrecht, 1978 [Boston: D. Reidel]), noted in *OF*, p. 102.

124 Wedgwood, "Grimm on the Indo-European Languages," *Quarterly Review* 50 (October 1833), 169–89, as noted in *OF*, p. 102, n. 19.

125 *OF*, pp. 102–3.

126 *Ibid.*, p. 101.

127 Charles Darwin, *On the Origin of Species by Means of Natural Selection*, ed. John Burrow from 1st edn. (Harmondsworth: Penguin, 1968 [London, 1859]), p. 406, as noted in *OF*, pp. 101–2.

128 *OF*, p. 103.

129 Wedgwood quoted by Beer, *ibid.*, p. 103.

130 *Ibid.*, pp. 103–4.

131 *Ibid.*, p. 104.

132 *CPP*, p. 14.

133 *Ibid.*, p. 451.

134 *SMW*, pp. 2, 143–56.

135 *EL*, p. 555.

136 Darwin, *Descent*, vol. II, p. 389.

137 James Clifford, *The Predicament of Culture: Twentieth-Century Ethnography, Literature, and Art* (Cambridge, MA: Harvard University Press, 1988), p. 13.

138 Ian Hacking, *Historical Ontology* (Cambridge, MA: Harvard University Press, 2002), p. 57.

139 *EL*, p. 308.

140 *Ibid.*, p. 549. See also Walls, *Culture*, p. 200, noting Emerson's assimilation of Johann Bernhard Stallo's metaphor of the "solar eye" for his evolutionary narrative where "the metaphor broadened to embrace the creation of life itself: mineral solutions stand 'inert and shapeless, until the magic lines of light' polarize individual molecules into organizing activity."

141 *SMW*, p. 2.

142 *EL*, p. 112.

143 Johnson, *Emergence*, p. 118: "intelligent systems are guided toward particular types of structure by the laws of natural selection."

144 *EL*, p. 465.
145 *CPP*, p. 22.
146 *EL*, p. 217.

4 WILLIAM JAMES'S FEELING OF *IF*

1 Emmanuel Levinas, *On Escape: De l'évasion*, tr. Bettina Bergo (Stanford: Stanford University Press, 2003), p. 113.
2 Henry James, *Autobiography*, ed. Frederick W. Dupee (Princeton: Princeton University Press, 1983), p. 7; hereinafter references to this title will be indicated by *Auto*.
3 *Ibid.*, p. 359.
4 Letter of January 8, 1873, *CWJ* 1, p. 188.
5 *V*, pp. 448–9.
6 *Ibid.*, p. 447.
7 For "peculiarity," see *CWJ* 1, pp. xxvii–xxviii. For "stubborn facts," see letter of March 10, 1887, *The Correspondence of William James*, vol. II: *William and Henry 1885–1896*, ed. Ignas K. Skrupskelis and Elizabeth M. Berkeley (Charlottesville: University Press of Virginia, 1993), p. 59; hereinafter references to this title will be indicated by *CWJ* 2. See also letter of September 1, 1887: "every page of this book of mine is against a resistance . . . the resistance of *facts*, to begin with, each one of which must be bribed to be on one's side, and the resistance of other philosophers to end with, each one of which must be slain" (*CWJ* 2, p. 68). We recall that this notion of "stubborn fact" significantly informs the thinking of Alfred North Whitehead; he repeated the phrase throughout his work and elaborated it fully in *Process and Reality*. The original instance, interestingly for James, is in Emerson, *EL*, p. 180.
8 *EL*, p. 475.
9 *Auto*, p. 133.
10 *CWJ* 1, p. xxxiv. It should be noted, however, that Henry James Sr., especially after his "vastation," did find himself often "absorbed in the study of Scriptures"; see Paul Jerome Croce, *Science and Religion in the Era of William James*, vol. I: *Eclipse of Certainty, 1820–1880* (Chapel Hill: University of North Carolina Press, 1995), p. 52; hereinafter references to this title will be indicated by *SR*.
11 *CPP*, pp. 329, 451. It is important to keep in mind that C. S. Peirce, from whom James took the name of "pragmatism," later changed his own version to "pragmaticism" to distinguish it from James's variety, and that Peirce never freed himself from what James called his "theological inhibition."
12 Perry observed that James probably felt no need to isolate aesthetic as against religious experience for analysis because he "*had* the aesthetic experience, and borrowed the religious," as noted by Jonathan Levin, *The Poetics of Transition: Emerson, Pragmatism & American Literary Modernism* (Durham and London:

Duke University Press, 1999), esp. pp. 67–70, quotation p. 68. For Myers, see introduction to *CWJ* 1, and *William James: His Life and Thought* (New Haven and London: Yale University Press, 1985); Jacques Barzun, *A Stroll with William James* (Chicago: University of Chicago Press, 1983), esp. pp. 71, 100–1. Levin's volume is indispensable to any discussion of pragmatism, both in its extended manifestations and in Jamesian Pragmatism. Indeed, my readings, recuperating the significance of Edwards, the line of ministerial purpose, and incorporating natural historical / scientific information, offer supplemental "transitions" to those he traces in Emerson, William and Henry James, Stein, and Stevens.

13 Myers's introduction to *CWJ* 1, pp. xxx–xxxi. Myers here cites "Remarks on Spencer's Definition of Mind as Correspondence" (1878), in William James, *Essays in Philosophy*, ed. Gerald E. Myers (Cambridge, MA: Harvard University Press, 1978), p. 21. In pointing future scholarship toward a comprehensive account of the aesthetic in James's work, Myers notes his beginning efforts in that direction in his *William James*, pp. 239–40 and 415–22. In the context of the aesthetic aspect of science, see Graham Farmelo, ed., *It Must Be Beautiful: Great Equations of Modern Science* (London and New York: Granta, 2002).

14 "The Sentiment of Rationality," in William James, *Writings 1878–1899*, ed. Gerald E. Myers (New York: The Library of America, 1992), pp. 975–6. James composed "Sentiment" during 1878–9, the period following his most serious nervous/religious crises as well as of his marriage and of his conceiving the idea for *The Principles of Psychology*. It is important to note as well that the conceptualization of "matter of fact disseminated through the whole of time and space" prefigures Whitehead's elaboration of "event," earlier termed "prehension," as indicated here in Chapter 2, n. 41.

15 Taves, *Fits*, p. 271, makes a similar point concerning James's treating "religious experience" as a generic "something," but she does not set his method in a natural historical framework.

16 *PP*, p. 246; second quotation from *P*, p. 535 (see also p. 517). James carefully read and reread all of Darwin; in 1868 he reviewed *The Variation of Plants and Animals Under Domestication*; see *CWJ* 1, p. 36. Also important to remark is James's early reading and later supersession, in titling his ***The** Principles of Psychology*, of Herbert Spencer's *Principles of Psychology*. Where Spencer had generally presented an idea of evolving nature, he had not, like Darwin, presented the accumulating evidence for natural selection; for full discussion, see Janet Browne, *Charles Darwin: The Power of Place, Volume Two of a Biography* (Princeton: Princeton University Press, 2002), esp. pp. 184–6. William James, in contrast, took full account of the Darwinian information. See also Taves, *Fits*, esp. pp. 273–80, for a recapitulation of work on James's use of Darwinian theory. In connection with James's focus on the "vague," it should be remarked, as Ross Posnock has observed, that Henry James was similarly preoccupied, and that Alice "anticipate[d] her brother Henry's discovery of the creative possibilities in the 'saving virtue of vagueness,'" as she recorded

in her *Diary* (Posnock, *The Trial of Curiosity: Henry James, William James, and the Challenge of Modernity* [New York and Oxford: Oxford University Press, 1991], p. 19). It should be noted as well that "vagueness" is the current hot topic in analytic philosophy. For an amusing remark on its currency, see Richard Rorty, "How many grains make a heap?" a review of Scott Soames, *Philosophical Analysis in the 20th Century, London Review of Books* (January 20, 2005), 12.

17 *V*, p. 28.

18 *Ibid.*, pp. 88–9.

19 *Ibid.*, p. 36.

20 *Ibid.*, p. 34.

21 *Ibid.*, p. 26.

22 Perry Miller adduced the continuity between Edwards and James in introducing Edwards's "Miscellany no. 782" ("Heart," p. 128):

> It is fascinating, considering how William James went deliberately back to sources which were also Edwards', and how aware he was of the wrong turning the empirical tradition had taken between Edwards' time and his own, to find how nearly James came to restating Edwards' conclusions. Such reasoning as Edwards here exemplifies seems to have informed many of James' observations:
>> Consent to the idea's undivided presence, this is effort's sole achievement. Its only function is to get this feeling of consent into the mind. And for this there is but one way. The idea to be consented to must be kept from flickering and going out. It must be held steadily before the mind until it fills the mind. Such filling of the mind by an idea, with its congruous associates, *is* consent to the idea and to the fact which the idea represents. (Emphasis James's)

23 *V*, p. 36.

24 *Ibid.*, pp. 37–8.

25 Emerson's phrase, we recall, from "The Method of Nature": "as far as we can trace the natural history of the soul, its health consists in the fulness of its reception, – call it piety, call it veneration" (*EL*, p. 125).

26 *V.*, p. 22.

27 *Ibid.*, p. 38.

28 *A Pluralistic Universe* in *Writings 1902–1910*, p. 762.

29 *Ibid.*, p. 158.

30 *EL*, p. 196. James's identification of the "quivering" quality of Emerson's sentences addresses an issue still live in current theology. Andrew Shanks, incorporating the category of "shakenness," borrowed from the Czech philosopher Jan Patocka, into his argument for a "theological poetics," castigates conventional theology for using the language of philosophy rather than poetry as its model, thereby making actual religious experience unavailable; for him, most religious talk and writing is insufficiently "shaken." As observed by Rowan Williams in "What shakes us?" his review of Shanks's *"What is Truth?": Towards a Theological Poetics* (New York and London: Routledge, 2003), "Truth appears only in the most fundamental apprehension of what thought itself is – in the unappeasable hunger for the sublime or excessive

vision which will break our moral deadlock . . . [T]he 'pathos of shakenness' . . . is visible in the moment when thought understands its own hunger
and so allows itself to be shaken out of habits of power and control" (*The
Times Literary Supplement* [July 4, 2003], 10).

31 *Auto*, p. 123.

32 *PP*, p. 350; James's emphasis.

33 *Ibid.*; James's emphasis.

34 *P*, p. 509.

35 *V*, p. 14.

36 Henry James shared this idea of sacrifice of self, which he termed "surrender."
In *Trial*, Posnock has focused on this aspect of Henry James's personality and
its reflection in his style.

37 *EL*, p. 23.

38 *V*, p. 36.

39 *Ibid.*, p. 55.

40 *Ibid.*, p. 53.

41 *P*, p. 513; John J. McDermott in his introduction to *The Writings of William
James: A Comprehensive Edition*, ed. McDermott (Chicago and London: University of Chicago, 1977), pp. xlvi–xlix, discusses the centrality of James's
"doctrine of relations" to radical empiricism.

42 *V*, p. 25.

43 *Ibid.*, p. 452.

44 *CDN*, p. 291.

45 Darwin, *Descent*, p. viii.

46 Taves, *Fits*, p. 279, quoting David Lambert, *William James and the Metaphysics of Experience* (Cambridge: Cambridge University Press, 1999), chapter
4.

47 *V*, p. 55.

48 *Ibid.*, p. 50.

49 *The Correspondence of William James*, vol. III: *William and Henry, 1897–1910*,
ed. Ignas K. Skrupskelis and Elizabeth M. Berkeley (Charlottesville: University Press of Virginia, 1994), p. 234, from a letter dated May 3, 1903:

> The reading of the divine Emerson, volume after volume, has done me a lot of good,
> and . . . has thrown a strong practical light on my own path. The incorruptible way
> in which he followed his own vocation, of seeing such truths as the Universal Soul
> vouchsafed to him from day to day and month to month, and reporting them in the
> right literary form, and thereafter kept his limits absolutely, refusing to be entangled
> with irrelevancies however urging and tempting, knowing both his strength and its
> limits, and clinging unchangeably to the rural environment which he once for all
> found to be most propitious, seems to me to be a moral lesson to all men who have
> any genius, however small, to foster. I see now with absolute clearness . . . the time
> has come when the remnant of my life must be passed . . . contemplatively . . . and
> with leisure and simplification for the one remaining thing, which is to report in one
> book, at least, such impression as my own intellect has received from the Universe.
> This I mean to stick to . . . – Emerson is exquisite! . . . You too have been leading an

Emersonian life – though the environment differs to suit the needs of the different psychophysical organism which you present.

Hereinafter references to this volume will be indicated by *CWJ* 3.

50 *P*, p. 517.

51 *V*, pp. 107–8.

52 *Ibid.*, p. 55.

53 *PP*, p. 113.

54 *Ibid.*, p. 551.

55 *V*, p. 149.

56 I am indebted to Professor Kathleen Duffy of the Department of Chemistry and Physics, Chestnut Hill College, Philadelphia, PA, for introducing me to the latter term. In response to a paper presenting an outline of the material of this chapter which I gave at the October 2003 meeting of the Society for Literature and Science, she noted that what I describe as James's understanding of the neuronal operation of language is what physicists know as the function of "wave packets." The term belongs to the vocabulary of quantum mechanics and describes the range of frequencies belonging to a particle. The term was first used, as far as I can determine, by Max Born in 1926, and the concept it denotes is carried and expressed by Fourier transforms.

57 James's concept of the "vague" as an analogue for consciousness has, of course, been richly and variously discussed, most particularly by Richard Poirier in *Poetry and Pragmatism* (esp. pp. 129–68) and by William Joseph Gavin in *William James and the Reinstatement of the Vague* (Philadephia: Temple University Press, 1992), but no reader has drawn the connection between the word in French and James's interest in nineteenth-century wave theory. Poirier comes suggestively close, however, in speaking of James's images of streams and the "fluid relations"of words and of the centrality of the sound of words for writers in the line of Emersonian pragmatism.

58 *V*, p. 149.

59 *Ibid.*, pp. 149–50.

60 *EL*, p. 10.

61 See particularly Johnson, *Emergence*. In this connection, note Marx's comment on first reading *Origin*: "It is remarkable how Darwin rediscovers among beasts and plants the society of England, with its division of labour, competition, opening up of new markets, inventions, and the Malthusian struggle for existence" (quoted in Browne, *Power of Place*, pp. 187–8).

62 See especially Poirier, *The Renewal of Literature*, and Cavell's Introduction and "Old and New in Emerson and Nietzsche" in *Transcendental Etudes*, pp. 1–9, 224–33.

63 It is interesting to note that Freud derived his notion of the *id* from his contemporary, Georg Groddeck; see Groddeck, *The Book of the It* (New York: International University Press, 1976).

64 James heard Freud's lecture (given in German, which James, of course, knew very well) at Clark University in September 1909, and recorded his sense of the

limitations of Freud's conception – "a man obsessed with fixed ideas . . . 'symbolism' is a most dangerous method" – in a letter dated September 29, 1909, to Theodore Flournoy.

65 For a full discussion of the various functions of the footnote, see Anthony Grafton, *The Footnote: A Curious History* (Cambridge, MA: Harvard University Press, 1999).

66 In order, these sentences are quoted from *EL*, pp. 69, 289, 549, 385, 585, 965.

67 *CWJ* 1, p. 30.

68 *Ibid.*, Myers's introduction, p. xxxiii. *SR*, p. 55, notes that this reviewer was William Dean Howells. The details of the Swedenborg volumes are variously remembered by Henry James, *Auto*, pp. 331, 340.

69 *CWJ* 1, p. 102.

70 *Ibid.*, p. xxvii.

71 *Auto*, p. 308.

72 *SR*, p. 71, quoting from a letter from William James to Edgar Van Winkle, March 1, 1858, William James Papers, Houghton Library, Harvard University; also quoted in Ralph Barton Perry, *The Thought and Character of William James, Briefer Version* (New York: Braziller, 1954), pp. 52–3, and in Myers, *William James: His Life and Thought*, pp. 3–4.

73 *SR*, p. 99.

74 In two volumes (London: John Murray, 1868).

75 *CWJ* 1, p. 39.

76 *Ibid.*, pp. 39, 42.

77 *Ibid.*, p. 45.

78 *Ibid.*, pp. 45–6.

79 T. J. Jackson Lears, *No Place of Grace: Antimodernism and the Transformation of American Culture, 1880–1920* (New York: Pantheon, 1981), has fully elaborated this idea of *dis*-ease.

80 Browne, *Power of Place*, p. 185.

81 *V*, p. 20.

82 *CWJ* 1, p. xxix.

83 *CPP*, p. 51.

84 *V*, pp. 56–8.

85 Gamwell, *Exploring*, p. 165.

86 *CPP*, p. 47. The phrase, from "A High-Toned Old Christian Woman," offers an apt parallel describing an imagined naturalized, secular response to the law of Christianity.

87 *Ibid.*, p. 137.

88 *SR*, p. 76, quoting from Notebook 1, p. 37 and p. 61, William James Papers, Houghton Library, Harvard University.

89 *Ibid.*

90 Most prominently, in addition to the volumes by Damasio noted earlier: Gerald M. Edelman, *Bright Air, Brilliant Fire: On the Matter of the Mind* (New York: Basic Books, 1992) and *Wider than the Sky: The Phenomenal Gift of Consciousness* (New Haven: Yale University Press, 2004); Joseph Le Doux,

The Emotional Brain (New York: Simon and Schuster, 1996) and *Synaptic Self: How Our Brains Become Who We Are* (New York: Penguin, 2003); John Tooby and Leda Cosmides, eds., *The New Cognitive Neurosciences* (Cambridge, MA: MIT Press, 2000) and Jerome H. Barkow, Leda Cosmides, and John Tooby, eds., *The Adapted Mind: Evolutionary Psychology and the Generation of Culture* (New York and Oxford: Oxford University Press, 1995); Daniel C. Dennett, *Consciousness Explained* (Boston: Little, Brown & Co., 1991) and *Freedom Evolves* (New York: Penguin, 2004); Walter J. Freeman, *Societies of Brains: A Study in the Neuroscience of Love and Hate* (Hillsdale, NJ: Lawrence Erlbaum, 1995) and *How Brains Make Up Their Minds* (New York: Columbia University Press, 1999); Christine Skarda, *The Perceptual Form of Life* (Cambridge, MA: MIT Press, 1999); Semir Zeki, *Inner Vision: An Exploration of Art and the Brain* (Oxford: Oxford University Press, 1999); the several articles published between 1990 and 2003 by Francis Crick and Christof Koch dealing with consciousness and neuroscience and recently recapitulated in Christof Koch, *The Quest for Consciousness: A Neurobiological Approach* (Englewood, CO: Roberts and Co., 2004); V. S. Ramachandran, *A Brief Tour of Human Consciousness* (New York: Pi Press, 2004). I am indebted to all of these studies for deepening, particularizing, and bringing me up-to-date in the continuing research into consciousness; it should be noted that while Ramachandran and Zeki do not directly credit James, it is otherwise clear from their acknowledgments of other sources such as Edelman, Dennett, Helmholtz, etc., that exploration of the field continues in the areas established by *Principles*.

91 *CDN*, p. 25.

92 *EL*, p. 552.

93 *SR*, pp. 198, 86, 216; others, as noted by Croce, have also discussed this aspect of Peirce's understanding of the significance of Darwin's method. Beer, *OF*, pp. 118–19, not mentioned by Croce, properly connects Peirce's concept of *abduction*, or "backward reading," with his understanding of Darwinian evolution.

94 Charles Sanders Peirce, "The Doctrine of Chances" (1878), in *The Essential Peirce: Selected Philosophical Writings*, vol. I: *1867–1893*, ed. Nathan Houser and Christian Kloesel (Bloomington: Indiana University Press, 1992), p. 144.

95 Beautifully recalled by Susan Howe in *The Midnight*, p. 49.

96 Quoted in *SR*, p. 87; earlier quotation from Agassiz quoted on p. 121.

97 *V*, p. 214.

98 Quoted in *SR*, p. 204.

99 *Ibid.*, pp. 182, 204.

100 Croce, first quoting Philip P. Weiner, *Evolution and the Founders of Pragmatism* (New York: Harper & Row, 1965), p. 27, followed by his own observation, *SR*, p. 155.

101 Louis Menand, *The Metaphysical Club: A Story of Ideas in America* (New York: Farrar, Straus and Giroux, 2001).

102 *SR*, pp. 151–2, 157.

103 *P*, p. 532.

104 Weiner, *Evolution*, p. 31.
105 William James, "What Psychical Research Has Accomplished," in *Writings: 1878–1899*, ed. Gerald E. Myers (New York: The Library of America, 1992), p. 682: "if there is anything which human history demonstrates, it is the extreme slowness with which the ordinary academic and critical mind acknowledges facts to exist which present themselves as wild facts, with no stall or pigeon-hole, or as facts which threaten to break up the accepted system."
106 *CWJ* 4, p. 144; also quoted in *SR*, p. 202.
107 *SR*, pp. 202–3.
108 *Ibid.*, p. 205; Posnock describes this as "Peirce's . . . challenge to Cartesianism," which "inaugurated pragmatism" (*Trial*, p. 170).
109 Weiner, *Evolution*, p. 22.
110 *Ibid.*, p. 19, Weiner quoting Bain.
111 *SR*, p. 212; Bain's definition was quoted by Peirce, who continued, "From this definition, pragmatism is scarce more than a corollary; so that I am disposed to think of him as the grandfather of pragmatism" (Weiner, *Evolution*, p. 19).
112 *SR*, p. 222.
113 *Auto*, p. 14.
114 Gamwell, *Exploring*, pp. 136–7.
115 Posnock, *Trial*, p. 63.
116 In *Wider Than The Sky*, a somewhat popularized version of earlier work as described in *Bright Air, Brilliant Fire*.
117 *PP*, p. 331, also cited by Posnock, *Trial*, p. 35.
118 *OF*, p. 245. She goes on in a note and in the text to comment on available translations and on those few figures who were familiar with Helmholtz's work.
119 Quoted by Weiner, *Evolution*, p. 3.
120 *OF*, pp. 247–8.
121 *CPP*, p. 904, from an aphorism which is at the heart of his poetics: "The exquisite environment of fact. The final poem will be the poem of fact in the language of fact. But it will be the poem of fact not realized before."
122 "I am about to recommence with electricity (which has always relieved the fag of College work at home towards spring) using a battery hired here," William wrote to Henry from Rome in late December 1900 (*CWJ* 3, p. 151).
123 *PR*, p. 119.
124 *Ibid.*, p. 87.
125 William James, *Psychology: Briefer Course* in *Writings 1878–1899*, p. 220; hereinafter references to this title will be indicated by *BC*. The edition reprinted in *Writings* is from the 1984 Harvard University Press edition of James's *Works*, and incorporates authorial corrections and revisions made through the fourth (1893) edition of the original 1892 Henry Holt and Company publication. James's stated intention in his "Preface" was to abridge *Principles* so as "to make it more directly available for class-room use" and to clarify the "general point of view . . . as that of 'natural science'": "About two fifths of the volume

is either new or rewritten, the rest is 'scissors and paste'" (p. 3). Notably, the emphasized sentence I have quoted, which does not appear in *Principles*, is labelled "2)" under a bold-faced heading within the chapter on "Attention" which reads "The Physiological Conditions of Attention," and indicated to be "verifiable."

126 *BC*, pp. 218–19.

127 *Ibid.*, p. 225.

128 *EL*, p. 422.

129 *OF*, pp. 296, 305.

130 Gamwell, *Exploring*, p. 152.

131 *OF*, pp. 311–12, 313, 309.

132 *Ibid*, pp. 305, 312, 246.

133 In a passage from his *Hours of Exercise*, quoted by Beer (p. 299), Tyndall comments on "the intellect as a function of temperature," something William James would himself investigate and report on in *Principles*; see here Chapter 2, p. 29, this volume.

134 *OF*, pp. 298, 299, 300–1.

135 W. K. Clifford, "Body and Mind," *Fortnightly Review* (1874), rpt. in *Lectures and Essays*, ed. L. Stephen and F. Pollock (London: Macmillan, 1879), p. 66.

136 Quoted in Tyndall, *Fragments of Science*, vol. I, p. 193, cited in *OF*, p. 305.

137 *PP*, p. 228.

138 Sharon Lattig, Project Statement for "The Orders of Time," unpublished paper, December 2003, p. 3.

139 *PP*, p. 417.

140 Quoted in *OF*, p. 301.

141 William Seager, "Consciousness, Information and Panpsychism," http://members.aol.com/NeoNoetics/CONSC_INFO_PANPSY.html., p. 5.

142 *BC*, p. 195; emphasis James's.

143 *Ibid.*, pp. 209, 212.

144 Seager, "Consciousness," p. 5.

145 Quoted in *OF*, p. 307.

146 *EL*, p. 463.

147 *SR*, p. 240, n. 49, quoting Frederick Ruf, *The Creation of Chaos: William James and the Stylistic Making of a Disorderly World* (Albany: State University of New York Press, 1991), p. 10.

148 Lattig, "Orders of Time," p. 1. To be remarked in this connection are James's directions to readers in the preface to *Principles*, as noted in Chapter 1 here, to take account of their differences; he thus advises various manners of approach including omission of certain chapters, reordering the sequence, etc., depending on their interests and ends: in other words, a Pragmatic approach.

149 Posnock, *Trial*, pp. 90, 93.

150 *Ibid.*, pp. 136–7, 165.

151 *Crystals*, p. 33, quoting Paul Klee.

152 Posnock, *Trial*, p. 155.

153 *Ibid.*, p. 93, Posnock quoting from *Persons and Places*.

154 *Auto*, p. 332.

155 Quentin Anderson, *The American Henry James* (New Brunswick: Rutgers University Press, 1957), reads the major three late novels as embodying an allegory of his father's Swedenborgianism; he does not particularize the details nor comment on James's appropriation of Balzac's hero and novel, as will be presented in the chapter following here.

156 *SR*, pp. 57, 55.

157 *Ibid.*, p. 59; see also, for further discussion of this aspect, Matthiessen, *The James Family*; John Owen King, *The Iron of Melancholy: Structures of Spiritual Conversion in America from the Puritan Conscience to Victorian Neurosis* (Middletown: Wesleyan University Press, 1983); Giles Gunn, "Pragmatic Repossessions," in *Thinking Across the American Grain: Ideology, Intellect, and the New Pragmatism* (Chicago: University of Chicago Press, 1992).

158 Posnock, *Trial*, p. 162.

159 *EL*, pp. 672–3.

160 *Crystals*, pp. 34–6.

161 Eugene Taylor in Taylor, ed., *William James on Exceptional Mental States: The 1896 Lowell Lectures* (Amherst: University of Massachusetts Press, 1984) and "The Appearance of Swedenborg in the History of American Psychology," in *Swedenborg and His Influence*, ed. Erland J. Brock (Bryn Athyn, PA: The Academy of the New Church, 1988), has also drawn the connection between William James's idea of religious transformation and Swedenborg; more recently, Taves, *Fits*, pp. 281–2, has reiterated this view.

162 *PP*, p. 381.

163 *Crystals*, pp. 7–11.

164 *Ibid.*, p. 22.

165 *CPP*, p. 526.

166 Henry James, "Honoré de Balzac," in *Literary Criticism: French Writers, Other European Writers, The Prefaces to the New York Edition*, ed. Leon Edel (New York: The Library of America, 1984), p. 41; quoted by Posnock, *Trial*, p. 94.

167 *CPP*, p. 465.

168 *Crystals*, p. 16.

5 HENRY JAMES'S MORE THAN RATIONAL DISTORTION

1 *EL*, p. 422.

2 Raymond Abellio, Preface to Honoré de Balzac, *Louis Lambert, Les Proscrits, Jésus-Christ en Flandre* (Paris: Gallimard, 1980), p. 10.

3 *Auto*, p. 332.

4 Preface to *The Ambassadors* in Henry James, *Literary Criticism: French Writers, Other European Writers, The Prefaces to the New York Edition*, ed. Leon Edel (New York: Library of America, 1984), p. 1306.

5 Emanuel Swedenborg, *The Shorter Heaven and Hell* (London: Seminar Books, 1993), pp. 14, 16–17, 25, 28–31.

6 *EL*, p. 471.

7 *CPP*, p. 309.

8 *EL*, p. 423.

9 *EL*, pp. 69, 92.

10 Posnock, *Trial*, p. 51. Richard Hocks in *Henry James and Pragmatistic Thought: A Study in the Relationship between the Philosophy of William James and the Literary Art of Henry James* (Chapel Hill: University of North Carolina Press, 1974) also explores the work of the brothers as the "complemental factors of reality" exhibiting "the pragmatist doctrine" William James described (p. 25). Hocks effectively demonstrates "that whereas William is the pragmatist, Henry is . . . the pragmatism; that is, he possesses the very mode of thinking that William characteristically expounds" (p. 4); hereinafter references to this title will be indicated by *HJPT*.

11 John Dewey, *Experience and Nature* (La Salle, IL: Open Court, 1929), pp. 178, 181, quoted by Posnock, *Trial*, p. 94.

12 Andy Clark, "Magic Words: How Language Augments Human Computation," in *Language and Thought: Interdisciplinary Themes*, ed. Peter Carruthers and Jill Boucher (Cambridge: Cambridge University Press, 2003), pp. 162–83.

13 Discussion following Poirier's talk, "Why Do Pragmatists Want to Be Like Poets?" at "The Revival of Pragmatism" Conference, The Graduate Center, CUNY, November 3–4, 1995; rpt. in *The Revival of Pragmatism: New Essays on Social Thought, Law, and Culture*, ed. Morris Dickstein (Durham: Duke University Press, 1998), pp. 347–61.

14 *CPP*, p. 404.

15 *PP*, p. 239.

16 Clark, "Magic Words," p. 162.

17 As Posnock, *Trial*, p. 89, observes, James, in *The American Scene* (Bloomington: Indiana University Press, 1969), describes "the indeterminacy of the nation's future as 'belonging to no known language' and thus expressible only onomatopoetically, as 'something . . . *abracadabrant*'" (pp. 121–2).

18 James entitled his novel between September 1, 1900, when he sent his "Project of Novel" to his publisher, Harper's, and July 10, 1901, when he sent the finished book to his agent, James Pinker, noting in the accompanying letter, "I enclose to you at last, by this post, the too-long retarded Finis of 'The Ambassadors.'" See Adeline R. Tintner, "A Source for James's *The Ambassadors* in Holbein's 'The Ambassadors' (1533)," in *Leon Edel and Literary Art*, ed. Lyall H. Powers assisted by Clare Virginia Eby (Ann Arbor: UMI Research Press, 1988), pp. 135–50; a shorter version is "Holbein's *The Ambassadors*: A Pictorial Source for *The Ambassadors*," in Adeline R. Tintner, *Henry James and the Lust of the Eyes*, pp. 87–104.

19 Mary F. S. Hervey, *Holbein's Ambassadors, the Picture and the Men* (London: G. Bell and Sons, 1900).

20 Tintner, "Source," pp. 135–6.

21 *Ibid.*, p. 136.

22 *Ibid.*

23 *Ibid.*, p. 141. For James's Letters, see *Letters*, vol. IV: *1895–1916* (Cambridge, MA and London: The Belknap Press of Harvard University Press, 1984).

24 Hazel Hutchison, "The Other Lambert Strether: Henry James's *The Ambassadors*, Balzac's *Louis Lambert*, and J. H. Lambert," *Nineteenth-Century Literature* 58 (December, 2003), 230–58. Earlier, Anderson in *American Henry*, pp. 213–16, and James W. Gargano in "*The Ambassadors* and *Louis Lambert*," *Modern Language Notes* 75 (March, 1960), 211–13, noted parallels but did not elaborate their significance in terms of James's "imaginative expansion."

25 David Lodge, "Strether by the River," in *Language of Fiction: Essays in Criticism and Verbal Analysis of the English Novel* (New York: Columbia University Press, 1967), pp. 189–213, comes closest, noting the preponderance of water-imagery and "images . . . explicitly concerned with boats" in *The Ambassadors*. He discusses "the image of the boat" as "a good example of . . . the language of heightened cliché" (pp. 206–7).

26 Clark, "Magic Words," p. 168.

27 *Ibid.*, p. 163.

28 *Ibid.*, p. 164.

29 *PP*, p. 1170.

30 *EL*, p. 420.

31 Clark, "Magic Words," p. 168.

32 Alfred North Whitehead, *Adventures of Ideas* (New York: The Free Press, 1967), p. 24.

33 Clark, "Magic Words," p. 169.

34 Sharon Cameron, *Thinking in Henry James* (Chicago: University of Chicago Press, 1989). Earlier, Dorothea Krook in *The Ordeal of Consciousness in Henry James* (Cambridge: Cambridge University Press, 1962) explored the philosophical implications of James's interest in consciousness and located it in "the ambient air of nineteenth-century speculation, whose main current was the preoccupation with the phenomenon of self-consciousness" (p. 410). She notably excluded both William James's Pragmatism and Henry James Sr.'s Swedenborgianism as possible stimulants to his interest.

35 All references to *The Ambassadors* here will be to the Norton Critical Edition edited by S. P. Rosenbaum (New York: W. W. Norton & Co., 1964); hereinafter references to this title will be indicated by *A*.

36 *Ibid.*, p. 61.

37 *HJPT*, p. 33, notes that Eliseo Vivas in "Henry and William: (Two Notes)," *Kenyon Review* 5 (1943), 580–94, finds William's notion of "flights" and "perchings" to be "an especially helpful analogy to Henry's fictional presentation."

38 *A*, pp. 5, 272.

39 *Auto*, p. 332.

40 Clark, "Magic Words," p. 164.

41 *Ibid.*, pp. 164–5.

42 *CPP*, p. 10.

43 William James, *A Pluralistic Universe* in *Writings 1902–1910*, pp. 734, 742.

44 Clark, "Magic Words," p. 166.

45 *Ibid.*, p. 176.

46 *Ibid.*, p. 167.

47 *Ibid.*, pp. 175–6.

48 *Ibid.*, p. 170.

49 *Ibid.*, p. 164. Clark notes that the idea that advanced cognition involves repeated processes in which achieved knowledge and representation are redescribed in new formats (which support new kinds of cognitive operation and access) is pursued as well by A. Karmiloff-Smith and Dennett; see his note, p. 178. More recently, investigators have found that repetition is key to establishing long-term memory and the "shape" of individual brains/experience:

> The moment-to-moment memories necessary for operating in the present are handled well by transient adjustments in the strength of individual synapses. But when an event is important enough or is repeated enough, synapses fire to make the neuron in turn fire neural impulses repeatedly and strongly, declaring 'this is an event that should be recorded.' The relevant genes turn on, and the synapses that are holding the short-term memory when the synapse-strengthening proteins find them, become, in effect, tattooed. (R. Douglas Fields, "Making Memories Stick," *Scientific American* [February 2005], 75–81)

50 Henry James, preface to *Roderick Hudson* in *Literary Criticism: French Writers*, p. 1041.

51 Clark, "Magic Words," p. 174.

52 *Ibid.*, p. 178.

53 Quoted in Ruth Bernard Yeazell, *Language and Knowledge in the Late Novels of Henry James* (Chicago: University of Chicago Press, 1976), p. 14.

54 Clark, "Magic Words," p. 181.

55 *Ibid.*

56 *A*, p. 4.

57 Clark, "Magic Words," p. 179.

58 Patrick Collinson, "Part of the Fun of Being an English Protestant," a review of Diarmaid MacCulloch, *Reformation: Europe's House Divided 1490–1700* (London: Allen Lane, 2003), *London Review of Books* (July 22, 2004), 22, notes that "English historians . . . have begun to talk about 'the Long Reformation', which was still happening into the 19th century," which MacCulloch plots as "the greatest geological faultline in European civilisation."

59 Clark, "Magic Words," p. 177.

60 *Ibid.*, p. 180.

61 *Ibid.*, p. 168.

62 *PP*, p. 401.

63 *Ibid.*, pp. 274, 277.

64 Posnock, *Trial*, p. 34, quoting from *The Will to Believe*.

65 *A*, p. 83.

66 John McCrone, "Reasons to forget: scientists count the ways we get it wrong," review of Daniel Schacter, *The Seven Sins of Memory: How the Mind Forgets and Remembers* (Boston: Houghton Mifflin, 2001, and London: Souvenir, 2003); James McGaugh, *Memory and Emotion* (London: Weidenfeld and Nicolson; New York: Columbia University Press, 2003); Rusiko Bourtchouladze, *Memories Are Made of This* (New York: Columbia University Press, 2003), *The Times Literary Supplement* (January 30, 2004), 3.

67 *A*, p. 43.

68 "Project of Novel," in *The Complete Notebooks of Henry James*, ed. Leon Edel and Lyall H. Powers (Oxford: Oxford University Press, 1987) p. 550; hereinafter references to this volume will be indicated by *NHJ*. For a complete survey of discussions of the fourth dimension in its spatial and temporal aspects, non-Euclidean geometries, and time and relativity through the middle of the nineteenth and into the early twentieth centuries, see Linda Dalrymple Henderson, *The Fourth Dimension and Non-Euclidean Geometry in Modern Art* (Princeton: Princeton University Press, 1983); on Hinton, see esp. pp. 26–31, and see also Bruce Clarke, "A Scientific Romance: Thermodynamics and the Fourth Dimension in Charles Howard Hinton's 'The Persian King,'" *Science, Technology & the Arts: Weber Studies, An Interdisciplinary Humanities Journal* 14:1 (Winter, 1997).

69 Oliver Sacks, "Speed: Aberrations of Time and Movement," *New Yorker* (August 23, 2004), 60. See also his "In the River of Consciousness," *New York Review of Books* (January 15, 2004), 41–4, with its description derived from Sacks's reading of Crick and Koch's suggestion of "conscious awareness [as] a series of static snapshots, with motion 'painted' on them" to produce a cinematographic effect; see also n. 85 below.

70 "Historical drift," a term belonging to the biology of cognition, describes the progressive transformation of a lineage. See Maturana and Varela, *Tree*, p. 61: "A creative use of this historical phenomenon is what is known in art as anamorphosis. This is an excellent example of historical drift."

71 John Updike, "Silent Master," *New Yorker* (June 28, 2004), 101.

72 *CPP*, p. 428.

73 *A*, p. 4.

74 Stephen Greenblatt, *Renaissance Self-Fashioning: From More to Shakespeare* (Chicago: University of Chicago Press, 1980), p. 19.

75 *A*, p. 15.

76 *EL*, p. 409.

77 Posnock, *Trial*, p. 155.

78 *PP*, pp. 274, 276.

79 *A*, p. 4.

80 *Ibid.*, pp. 48, 61.

81 Greenblatt, *Self-Fashioning*, p. 19.

82 *Auto*, p. 308.

83 *Ibid.*, p. 442.

84 *Ibid.*, p. 65.

85 Koch, *Quest*; for Sacks, see n. 69 above.

86 "John Tyndall," in Henry James, *Literary Criticism: Essays on Literature, American Writers, English Writers*, ed. Leon Edel (New York: The Library of America, 1984), p. 1357.

87 *CPP*, p. 8.

88 *Auto*, p. 194.

89 *A*, pp. 75, 94.

90 *NHJ*, p. 546.

91 *Ibid.*, p. 548.

92 *PP*, p. 219.

93 *EL*, p. 281.

94 *A*, p. 3.

95 *Ibid.*, p. 1.

96 *Ibid.*, p. 2.

97 *PP*, pp. 681–2, 657–8.

98 *A*, p. 13.

99 *PP*, p. 276.

100 *Ibid.*, p. 401.

101 *PR*, p. 87.

102 Crick and Koch, "A Framework for Consciousness," 121.

103 *PP*, pp. 656–7.

104 *Auto*, p. 95.

105 *PP*, p. 246.

106 *NHJ*, p. 576.

107 *Ibid.*, p. 570.

108 *A*, p. 323.

109 For a comprehensive, richly illustrated account of the development and deployment of pictorial anamorphosis, including, of course, a discussion of Holbein's *Ambassadors*, see Jurgis Baltrušaitis, *Anamorphoses ou Thaumaturgus opticus: les perspectives dépravées – II* (Paris: Flammarion, 1996).

110 Emanuel Swedenborg, *Apocalypse Revealed* (New York: The Swedenborg Foundation, 1981), pp. 896–7.

111 Balzac, *Louis Lambert*, p. 107. In the interest of space, in citing from Balzac's novel, I shall not usually offer translations of easily understood phrases; for the same reason I shall provide only the English translation of passages that might not be easily understood; all translations are mine.

112 *Ibid.*, p. 106.

113 *Ibid.*, p. 109.

114 *Ibid.*, p. 65.

115 *Ibid.*, p. 81.

116 *Ibid.*, p. 67.

117 *Ibid.*, p. 25.

118 *Ibid.*, p. 122.

119 Abellio in Preface, Balzac, *Louis Lambert*, p. 16.

120 Balzac, *Louis Lambert*, p. 44.

121 *Ibid.*, p. 86.

122 *EL*, pp. 237–8.

123 *CPP*, p. 281.

124 *Ibid.*, p. 137.

125 Balzac, *Louis Lambert*, p. 99.

126 *Ibid.*, p. 115.

127 *Ibid.*, p. 28.

128 *Ibid.*, pp. 28–30.

129 Sir Arthur Eddington, *The Nature of the Physical World* (London: J. M. Dent & Sons Ltd., 1938), pp. 61–2.

130 *A*, p. 69.

131 Eddington, *Physical World*, p. 107.

132 *NHJ*, pp. 543–4.

133 *Ibid.*, p. 568. In this connection, Crick and Koch in "A Framework for Consciousness," 121–2, describe how oscillations in "winning coalitions" of neurons, those which have been activated more repeatedly over time, sustain and embody "what we are conscious of."

134 *NHJ*, p. 559.

135 *A*, p. 5.

136 *NHJ*, p. 560.

137 *A*, p. 94.

138 John Crowe Ransom, for example, commenting on the poetry of Wallace Stevens, as an example of the "pure" style of "modernity," that it "has no moral, political, religious, or sociological values. It is not about 'res publica,' the public thing," in "Poets Without Laurels," in his *The World's Body* (Baton Rouge: Louisiana State University Press, 1968), p. 59. Ransom's judgment will be discussed further in the following chapter.

139 *EL*, p. 403.

140 We recall Locke's description; see here Chapter 2, p. 25.

141 *PP*, p. 1153.

142 *Ibid.*, p. 1170.

143 James, "The Art of Fiction," p. 46.

144 *PP*, pp. 246–7.

145 Howe, *The Midnight*, p. 130, quoting Roger Williams.

146 *NHJ*, p. 542.

147 *Auto*, p. 37.

148 *NHJ*, pp. 542–3.

149 *A*, p. 50.

150 *PP*, p. 236–8.

151 *A*, p. 345.

6 WALLACE STEVENS'S RADIANT AND PRODUCTIVE ATMOSPHERE

1 *CPP*, p. 908.
2 *LWS*, p. 790.
3 Sandro Petruccioli, *Atoms, Metaphors and Paradoxes: Niels Bohr and the Construction of a New Physics* (Cambridge: Cambridge University Press, 1993), p. 12.
4 *CPP*, p. 861.
5 *Ibid.*, p. 423.
6 *Ibid.*, p. 858.
7 Gillian Beer, "Physics, Sound, and Substance: Later Woolf," in *Virginia Woolf: The Common Ground* (Ann Arbor: University of Michigan Press, 1996), pp. 115–16.
8 *CPP*, pp. 28, 863; *EL*, p. 23.
9 *CPP*, p. 421.
10 *Ibid.*, p. 862.
11 *Ibid.*, pp. 859, 856, 428.
12 *PR*, p. 92; *SMW*, pp. 154, 132–3.
13 *CPP*, pp. 857, 723.
14 *Ibid.*, p. 856.
15 *Ibid.*, p. 330.
16 *Ibid.*, p. 450.
17 *Ibid.*, p. 104.
18 *Ibid.*, p. 716.
19 *Ibid.*, p. 8.
20 *Ibid.*, p. 848.
21 *The Philosophical Writings of Niels Bohr*, vol. I: *Atomic Theory and the Description of Nature* (Woodbridge, CT: Ox Bow Press, 1987), p. 2.
22 *CPP*, p. 19.
23 Quoted by Sergei Eisenstein in "The Filmic Fourth Dimension," in Gamwell, *Exploring*, p. 235.
24 Eddington, *Physical World*, p. 316.
25 *CPP*, pp. 842–3.
26 *Ibid.*, pp. 840–2.
27 *Ibid.*, pp. 847–8.
28 *Ibid.*, p. 449.
29 *Ibid.*, p. 850.
30 Guy Davenport, "Wittgenstein," in *The Geography of the Imagination* (San Francisco: North Point Press, 1981), p. 334.
31 *CPP*, p. 850.
32 Philip Morrison, "Tales Behind the Tags," *Nature* 413 (October, 2001), 461.
33 *CPP*, p. 908.
34 *LWS*, pp. 24–5.
35 *CPP*, p. 29.

36 Ransom, *The World's Body*, p. 59. For a countering argument, see Joan Richardson, "A Reading of 'Sea Surface Full of Clouds,'" *Wallace Stevens Journal* 6:3 and 4 (Fall, 1982), 60–8.

37 *CPP*, p. 12.

38 *LWS*, p. 126.

39 *Ibid.*, p. 34.

40 *Ibid.*, p. 58.

41 *Ibid.*, p. 59.

42 *CPP*, p. 47.

43 Peter de Bolla, "In the Butcher's Shop," a review of Gilles Deleuze, *Francis Bacon: The Logic of Sensation*, tr. Daniel Smith (London: Continuum, 2003), *London Review of Books* (September 23, 2004), 19.

44 *LWS*, p. 32.

45 *Ibid.*, p. 60.

46 *Ibid.*, p. 86.

47 *Ibid.*, p. 96.

48 *Ibid.*, p. 443.

49 *CPP*, p. 23.

50 *Ibid.*, p. 477.

51 *Ibid.*, p. 55.

52 *Ibid.*, p. 53.

53 *LWS*, p. 348.

54 *CPP*, p. 908.

55 *LWS*, pp. 139–41.

56 *EL*, p. 83.

57 *CPP*, p. 75.

58 *Ibid.*, pp. 53–4.

59 *Ibid.*, p. 404.

60 *Ibid.*, p. 74.

61 *PR*, p. 93.

62 *CPP*, p. 273. The volumes of Emerson's *Works* (Boston: Houghton, 1896–8), marked by Stevens, are part of the Wallace Stevens Collection at the Huntington Library, San Marino, California.

63 *EL*, pp. 266, 83.

64 *Ibid.*, pp. 85, 81.

65 *Ibid.*, pp. 75, 10, 78, 86, 84, in order, for the quotations in this paragraph.

66 *CPP*, pp. 136–7.

67 *Ibid.*, p. 476.

68 *Ibid.*, p. 261.

69 Unless otherwise indicated, quotations in the paragraphs following discussing "The Irrational Element in Poetry" are all from that lecture in *CPP*, pp. 781–92.

70 *EL*, p. 83.

71 *Ibid.*, p. 84.

72 *CPP*, p. 351.

73 *Ibid.*, p. 349.

74 *Ibid.*, p. 662.

75 *EL*, p. 85.

76 *CPP* pp. 662–3, 665.

77 *LWS*, p. 360.

78 *EL*, pp. 91–2.

79 *Ibid.*, p. 89.

80 *CPP*, p. 786.

81 *Ibid.*, p. 150.

82 *EL*, pp. 89, 22–3.

83 Martin Kemp, "Spiritual Shapes: Ernst Haeckel's 'art forms in nature,'" *Nature* 413 (October 4, 2001), 460.

84 Joseph D. Lykken, "Disappearing Dimensions," *Nature* 412 (July 12, 2001), 130.

85 *CPP*, p. 351.

86 *Ibid.*, pp. 47, 44–5.

87 What remains of Stevens's library, as well as the greater part of his correspondence, journals, and notebooks, comprise The Wallace Stevens Collection at The Huntington Library, as noted above.

88 Gamwell, *Exploring*, p. 203.

89 Alison Shell, in a review of Hannibal Hamlin, *Psalm Culture in Early Modern England* (Cambridge: Cambridge University Press, 2004), *The Times Literary Supplement* (January 14, 2005), 28.

90 Northrop Frye, "Charms and Riddles," in *Spiritus Mundi: Essays on Literature, Myth, and Society* (Bloomington: Indiana University Press, 1976), p. 125.

91 This description of the structure of Psalm 119 is taken from *The New Oxford Annotated Bible, New Revised Standard Version*, ed. Bruce M. Metzger and Roland E. Murphy (New York: Oxford University Press, 1989), p. 778.

92 Walter Benjamin, "On Language as Such and on the Language of Man," in his *Reflections*, ed. Peter Demetz (New York: Harcourt Brace Jovanovich, 1979), p. 317.

93 *CPP*, pp. 244–50.

94 *Ibid.*, pp. 289–92.

95 *Ibid.*, pp. 271–4.

96 *Ibid.*, pp. 417–22.

97 Sacks, "In the River," 42.

98 Frye, *Spiritus Mundi*, p. 124.

99 *CPP*, pp. 105, 54, 336, 913.

100 From his 1841 lecture, "The Conservative" (*EL*, p. 180).

101 *PR*, p. 129.

102 *LWS*, p. 16.

103 Bohr, "The Quantum Postulate and the Recent Development of Atomic Theory" (1927), in *Philosophical Writings*, vol. I, p. 75, and "Introductory Survey" (1929), collected in same volume, p. 10, offer two such examples.

104 See Holly Henry, *Virginia Woolf and the Discourse of Science: The Aesthetics of Astronomy* (Cambridge: Cambridge University Press, 2003).

105 *CPP*, p. 422.

106 *EL*, p. 475.

107 Daniel Tiffany, *Toy Medium: Materialism and the Modern Lyric* (Berkeley: University of California Press, 2000), pp. 249, 253–4.

108 *Ibid.*, p. 250, Tiffany quoting Petruccioli, *Atoms*, p. 33n.

109 *Ibid.*, pp. 253, 213.

110 *Ibid.*, pp. 270–1.

111 *Ibid.*, p. 211, section epigraph quoted from Heisenberg's *Physics and Beyond*.

112 *Ibid.*, p. 267.

113 *CPP*, p. 450.

114 Quoted by Morrison, "Tales Behind the Tags," 461.

115 C. E. M. Joad, *Philosophical Aspects of Modern Science* (New York: Macmillan, 1932), p. 193. Stevens refers to and quotes Joad in his 1942 lecture "The Noble Rider and the Sound of Words" (*CPP*, pp. 643–65). I have not yet located which of Joad's several texts is the source of Stevens's quotation. In *Philosophical Aspects*, however, Joad prominently explores the idea of the "value" of the new scientific understanding of "reality," as distinct from observable physicality, and speaks repeatedly of "sanctions" afforded by this new view. Stevens's 1948 essay/lecture "Imagination as Value" (*CPP*, pp. 724–39) and his idea of poetry as one of the "sanctions of life" resonate with Joad's discussions.

116 *CPP*, pp. 28, 647, 833.

117 Tiffany, *Toy*, p. 212. Ruggiero [Roger] Boscovich [Boscovitch], a Jesuit mathematician from Croatia, published *A Theory of Natural Philosophy* in 1758. Tiffany does not mention Emerson in connection with Boscovich. Emerson refers to Boscovich, whom Michael Faraday carefully read, as early as 1823 in his journal, as well as later in his 1836 lecture "The Humanity of Science" and in *Nature* (1836), noting that he was one who realized "the central unity, the common law that pervades nature from the deep centre to the unknown circumference" (*The Early Lectures of Ralph Waldo Emerson*, ed. Stephen E. Whicher, Robert E. Spiller, and Wallace E. Williams [Cambridge, MA: Harvard University Press, 1959–72], vol. II, p. 29).

118 *PP*, pp. 236–7.

119 Tiffany, *Toy*, p. 255.

120 *CPP*, p. 75.

121 Bunn, *Wave Forms*, p. 213.

122 Tiffany, *Toy*, p. 255.

123 *Liddell and Scott's Greek–English Lexicon*, new edition (Oxford: Clarendon / Oxford University Press, 1979). It should be noted that Stevens referred to Liddell and Scott as part of his habit of dictionary reading, cultivating the ground of Emerson's, "Every word was once a poem." Also worth noting is that "inference from facture," that is, human making considered in the entirety of its complex negotiations with all aspects of its environment, "the existential relation that is built into the work of art as an 'index,'" is the basis

of some of the latest work in art history; see David Summers, *Real Spaces: World Art History and the Rise of Western Modernism* (London: Phaidon, 2004), reviewed in *The Times Literary Supplement* (July 16, 2004), 19.

124 Stephen Toulmin and Jane Goodfield, *The Architecture of Matter* (Chicago: University of Chicago Press, 1982), p. 273.

125 *CPP*, p. 12.

126 *LWS*, p. 263.

127 *CPP*, p. 10.

128 Gil Abisdris and Adele Casuga, "Niels Bohr and Robert Frost," www.nsta.org/main/news/pdf/tst)109_58.pdf, p. 3. It is of interest, as well, that Frost's choice to attend Harvard had focused around his desire to study psychology with William James; James was on leave the year he became eligible to enroll for this course, however, and Hugo Munsterberg taught James's course using his *Psychology: Briefer Course.*

129 *CPP*, p. 315.

130 *Transactions of The Connecticut Academy of Arts and Sciences* 38 (December, 1949), p. 173, rpt. www.biologie.uni-hamburg.de/b-online/snowbird/prefaces/essay_delbrueck.htm.

131 *Ibid.*, p. 2 of website.

132 Gamwell, *Exploring*, p. 161.

133 Delbrück, "A Physicist's Renewed Look at Biology – Twenty Years Later," Nobel Lecture, December 10, 1969, http://nobelprize.org/medicine/laureates/1969/delbruck-lecture.html, pp. 4–5.

134 Correspondence with Sandra Rux, Connecticut Academy of Arts and Sciences, Yale University, November 30, December 3, 2004.

135 *LWS*, p. 662.

136 *CPP*, pp. 397–417; unless otherwise indicated, quotations in the paragraphs to follow discussing this poem and its occasion are from "An Ordinary Evening in New Haven" as it appears in the pages noted here.

137 *Ibid.*, pp. 639–40. It is interesting to note in passing that in Arthur O. Lovejoy's 1908 article, "The Thirteen Pragmatisms," examining the various points of view expressed by the term's different users in the year following the publication of James's *Pragmatism*, Lovejoy closes his piece by offering it "as a species of *Prolegomena zu einem jeden kunftigen Pragmatismus*," a parodic pastiche of Kant's *Prolegomena to any Future Metaphysics*. The conjunction of his thirteen ways and the appropriation of Kant's title suggest another frame in which to consider Stevens's "Thirteen Ways of Looking at a Blackbird" (1917) and his own "Notes Toward a Supreme Fiction" (1942).

138 *CPP*, p. 75.

139 Quoted by Hugo Estenssoro, "Tell Laura I love her," *The Times Literary Supplement* (July 16, 2004), 13.

140 Freeman Dyson, "Clockwork Science," review of Peter Galison, *Einstein's Clocks, Poincaré's Maps: Empires of Time*, *New York Review of Books* (November 6, 2003), 43–4.

141 *PP*, p. 228.

142 *CPP*, p. 12; Hansjorg Schlaepfer, "Cosmic Rays," *Spatium* 11 (November, 2003), 15.

143 *CPP*, p. 54.

144 *Ibid.*, p. 681.

145 Richard Feynman, *QED: The Strange Theory of Light and Matter* (Princeton: Princeton University Press, 1988), p. 14.

146 A parallel instance of this kind of understanding of evolving vision and reason "beyond reason" (*zaum*) grew out of Russian Suprematism. Kazimir Malevich, made Director of the State Institute of Artistic Culture in Leningrad in 1924, appointed Mikhail Matiushin as head of a laboratory to study hearing and vision.

   Matiushin came to believe that the avant-garde artist's eye itself was evolving and, through proper exercise, could come to have a broader field of vision, to which he gave mystical associations, calling it *zorved* (see-know): "*Zorved* signifies a physiological change from former ways of seeing and entails a completely different way of representing what is seen." Matiushin even predicted that in the artist's eye the cones would grow beyond the fovea (a small depression in the retina constituting the area of most distinct vision), giving the artist detailed peripheral vision in his new expanded visual field. (Gamwell, *Exploring*, p. 108)

   It should be noted that the motive for the new aesthetic in Russia belonged to its becoming a virtual "new world" after the revolutions beginning in 1905 and coincident with the extraordinary developments being made in the sciences.

147 Erwin Schrodinger, *Nature and the Greeks & Science and Humanism* (Cambridge: Cambridge University Press, 1996), p. 152.

148 *Transactions*, pp. 7, 9–10 on website.

149 *Ibid.*, p. 9.

150 *CPP*, p. 218.

151 *Ibid.*, p. 678.

152 Hacking explains "confidence intervals" and their connection with Peircian logic in *An Introduction to Probability and Inductive Logic* (New York: Cambridge University Press, 2001); see also *Historical Ontology*, pp. 13–17.

153 Beer, "Problems of Description," in *OF*, p. 152.

154 *CPP*, p. 433.

155 Hacking, *Historical Ontology*, p. 35.

156 *Ibid.*, p. 14.

157 *Ibid.*, p. 71.

158 *Ibid.*, p. 13.

159 *CPP*, p. 823.

160 Hacking, *Historical Ontology*, p. 37.

161 *CPP*, p. 913.

162 *OF*, p. 153, quoting from Albert Einstein, "Autobiographical Notes," in *Albert Einstein: Philosopher-Scientist*, ed. P. A. Schilpp, vol. I (London, 1970), pp. 45–7.

163 Bill Hammel, "An Essay on Patterns in Musical Composition Transformations, Mathematical Groups, and the Nature of Musical Substance," http://graham.main.nc.us/~bhammel/MUSIC/compose.html, p. 11.

164 *CPP*, pp. 786, 790.

165 *Ibid.*, p. 232.

166 Tiffany, *Toy*, pp. 110–11.

167 *Ibid.*, p. 6.

168 John Bayley, "Silent Music," *New York Review of Books* (November 20, 2003), 46.

169 Tiffany, *Toy*, p. 100.

170 Tiffany, *Toy*, p. 101, citing Lancelot Law Whyte, "Kepler's Unsolved Problem and the *Facultas Formatrix*," in Johannes Kepler, *The Six-Cornered Snowflake: A New Year's Gift* (1611), tr. Colin Hardie (Oxford: Clarendon / Oxford University Press, 1966), p. 62.

171 For an extended discussion of this "most irrational" of numbers, see Mario Livio, *The Golden Ratio: The Story of Phi, The World's Most Astonishing Number* (New York: Broadway Books, 2002).

172 Tegmark, "Parallel Universes."

173 Frederick Crews, "Saving Us from Darwin," *New York Review of Books* (October 4, 2001), 27.

174 *CPP*, p. 443.

175 George Musser, "All Screwed Up: An Obscure Property of Light Puts a Spin on Astronomy," *Scientific American* (November, 2003), 22–5.

176 *CPP*, pp. 72–4.

177 Roland Barthes, "The Brain of Einstein," in *Mythologies* (New York: Vintage, 2000), p. 68.

178 G. T. Fechner, *Vorschule der Aesthetik* "Introduction to Aesthetics" (Leipzig: Breitkopf und Härtel, 1876), cited in translation by Gamwell, *Exploring*, p. 97.

179 Alfred Mele, "We have reasons to believe," a review of Robert Audi, *The Architecture of Reason: The Structure and Substance of Rationality* (Oxford: Oxford University Press, 2001), *The Times Literary Supplement* (August 9, 2002), 24.

180 Raymond Williams, *The Long Revolution* (Peterborough, Ontario: Broadview, 2001 [1961]), pp. 63, 65; see also *Writing in Society* (London and New York: Verso, 1983), esp. pp. 262–6.

181 *CPP*, p. 11.

182 *PR*, p. 106.

183 Hammel, "An Essay on Patterns," p. 4.

184 *PP*, p. 323.

185 Quoted by Anthony Hecht in a review of Heaney's *Finders Keepers: Selected Prose, 1971–2001* (New York: Farrar, Straus, Giroux, 2002) in *New York Review of Books* (December 5, 2002), 54.

186 *CPP*, p. 663.

187 *V*, pp. 448–9.

188 Koch, *Quest*, p. 23n.

189 *PP*, p. 247n.
190 Sacks, "In the River," 41, also notes the connection between James and Helmholtz; see esp. Crick and Koch, "A Framework for Consciousness," 119–25, and Zeki, *Inner Vision*.
191 See Koch, *Quest*, esp. pp. 49–67, for physiological description of neuronal analogues underpinning synthetic models of argument.
192 *EL*, p. 409.
193 As documented by Lears, *No Place of Grace*.
194 *EL*, p. 7.
195 *PR*, p. 119.
196 *CPP*, p. 816.
197 *SMW*, p. 149.
198 *CPP*, p. 665.
199 *PP*, p. 63.
200 Johnson, *Emergence*, p. 138.
201 *Ibid*, p. 140, quoting Weiner.
202 *EL*, p. 209.
203 *V*, p. 437.
204 *Ibid.*, pp. 440–1.
205 Stéphane Mallarmé, Preface to "Un Coup de dés," in *Oeuvres complètes*, ed. Henri Condor and G. Jean-Aubry (Paris: Bibliothèque de la Pléiade, 1945), p. 455.
206 Aviv Regev and Ehud Shapiro, "Cells as Computation," *Nature* 419 (September 26, 2002), 343. The work of Christine Skarda, *The Perceptual Form of Life*, elaborated as well by Walter J. Freeman most recently in *How Brains Make Up Their Minds*, is illuminating in this context and bears reflexively on Simone Weil's notion of *décréation*, important to Stevens.
207 *EL*, p. 22
208 *Ibid.*, p. 254.
209 *PP*, p. 682.
210 *PR*, p. 105.
211 Henry James, "The Art of Fiction," p. 52.

7 GERTRUDE STEIN, JAMES'S MELANCTHON/A

1 Gertrude Stein, *The Making of Americans* (Normal, IL: The Dalkey Archive Press, 1995 [1925]), p. 284; hereinafter references to this title will be indicated by *MA*.
2 Richard Powers, *The Gold Bug Variations* (New York: William Morrow & Co., 1991), p. 248, describes the genome in these terms. His novel provides, within its fiction, an account of the history of genetics leading to Watson and Crick's 1953 discovery of the structure of the double helix, as well as a lucid and accurate description of the nature and behavior of the coding mechanism of its protein molecules, brilliantly using as heuristic Bach's anticipation in his Goldberg Variations of this structure and process. I shall occasionally borrow from his text, hereinafter referred to as *GBV*, to illuminate points.

3 Gertrude Stein, *Three Lives* (New York: Penguin, 1990 [1909]), p. 75; hereinafter references to this title will be indicated by *TL*. I do not mean to suggest that the character Melanctha is to be identified with Stein; indeed, in the "story of the story" of "Melanctha," she is May Bookstaver and Stein is Jefferson Campbell. I am using Stein as James's Melancthon figuratively.

4 *MA*, p. 437.

5 Steven Meyer, *Irresistible Dictation: Gertrude Stein and the Correlations of Writing and Science* (Stanford: Stanford University Press, 2001), p. 228; hereinafter references to this title will be indicated by *ID*.

6 Emerson "Poetry and Imagination," p. 471.

7 Gertrude Stein, "I Came And Here I Am," in her *How Writing Is Written: Volume II of the Previously Uncollected Writings of Gertrude Stein*, ed. Robert Bartlett Haas (Los Angeles: Black Sparrow Press, 1974), p. 72, quoted in *ID*, p. 150.

8 Gertrude Stein, *Lectures in America* in *Writings 1932–1946*, ed. Catharine R. Stimpson and Harriet Chessman (New York: The Library of America, 1998), p. 294; hereinafter references to this title will be indicated by *LIA*.

9 Deep Jaitly, Paul Kearney, Guo-Hui Lin, and Bin Ma, "Methods for Reconstructing the History of Tandem Repeats and Their Application to the Human Genome," www.csd.uwo.ca/~bma/pub/jcss2.ps., p. 1.

10 Details regarding Stein's curriculum drawn from both *ID*, p. 55, and Richard Bridgman, *Gertrude Stein in Pieces* (Oxford: Oxford University Press, 1970), p. 36.

11 Gertrude Stein, *The Autobiography of Alice B. Toklas* in *Writings 1903–1932*, ed. Catharine R. Stimpson and Harriet Chessman (New York: The Library of America, 1998), p. 742; hereinafter references to this title will be indicated by *ABT*.

12 Bridgman, *Stein Pieces*, pp. 37–8.

13 William Bateson, "Historic Figures," www.bbc.co.uk/history/historic_figures/bateson_william.shtml, p. 1.

14 Bateson Family Papers, American Philosophical Society, www.amphilsoc.org/library/mole/b/batesonfam.htm, p. 2.

15 *ID*, p. 4.

16 *ABT*, p. 781.

17 Bateson, "Historic Figures," p. 1.

18 Bateson Family Papers, p. 3.

19 Bateson, "Historic Figures," p. 1.

20 *GBV*, p. 94.

21 Elinor Bluemel, *Florence Sabin: Colorado Woman of the Century* (Boulder, 1959), p. 44, quoted in Bridgman, *Stein Pieces*, p. 35.

22 Gertrude Stein, *Unpublished Writings of Gertrude Stein*, vol. VIII: *A Novel of Thank You* (New Haven: Yale University Press, 1958), p. 238; quoted in Ulla E. Dydo with William Rice, *Gertrude Stein: The Language That Rises, 1923–1934* (Evanston: Northwestern University Press, 2003), p. 127; references to Dydo/Rice are hereinafter indicated by *LR*.

23 *LR*, p. 55.

24 *Ibid.*, p. 57.

25 *Ibid.*, p. 18.

26 *LIA*, p. 314.

27 *LR*, p. 78.

28 *GBV*, p. 94.

29 *MA*, p. 539.

30 *LIA*, p. 331.

31 *GBV*, p. 90.

32 *LIA*, p. 292.

33 *Ibid.*, p. 293.

34 *Ibid.*, pp. 285–6, 322, 291–2, 298, 273, 275.

35 William James, "The Place of Affectional Facts in a World of Pure Experience," in *Writings 1902–1910*, ed. Bruce Kuklick (New York: The Library of America, 1987), pp. 1209–10; quoted in *ID*, p. 15.

36 *ID*, pp. 270, 261.

37 *LIA*, p. 244.

38 *ID*, p. 254.

39 *Ibid.*, p. 263.

40 *Ibid.*, p. 318.

41 *Ibid.*, p. 319.

42 *Ibid.*, p. 321.

43 *Ibid.*, p. 320.

44 Reuben Brower, "Reading in Slow Motion," his introduction to *In Defense of Reading*, the 1962 volume of essays by teachers of the Harvard course which he coedited with Richard Poirier (New York: E. P. Dutton), as noted by Meyer.

45 Gertrude Stein, *The Geographical History of America* in *Writings 1932–1946*, p. 429; hereinafter references to this title will be indicated by *GHA*.

46 *LIA*, p. 308.

47 *ABT*, p. 711; and p. 866, compared as well "to that of mathematicians."

48 *GBV*, pp. 72, 88, 54.

49 *LIA*, p. 309.

50 *Ibid.*, pp. 271–2.

51 Gertrude Stein, *Wars I Have Seen* (New York: Random House, 1945), p. 17.

52 *ID*, pp. 10–11; quotation from Gertrude Stein, *Picasso: The Complete Writings*, ed. Edward Burns (Boston: Beacon Press, 1970), p. 38.

53 Gertrude Stein, *Everybody's Autobiography* (Cambridge, MA: Exact Change, 1993 [1937]), p. 250, quoted also in *ID*, p. 10.

54 *LIA*, p. 294.

55 *TL*, p. 112.

56 Daylanne English, "Gertrude Stein and the Politics of Literary-Medical Experimentation," *Literature and Medicine* 16:2 (1997), 188–209.

57 *Ibid.*, pp. 190, 195.

58 I agree here with Steven Meyer who observed in a note to me that the implicit critique of genetic determinism in "Melanctha" prefigures the recent critique of such determinism in current genetics. I am grateful to him for directing me

to Scott Gilbert, John Opitz, and Rudolf Raff, "Resynthesizing Evolutionary and Developmental Biology," *Developmental Biology* 173 (1996), 357–72, where they explore the integration of developmental biology with genetics in a "new synthesis" that will move beyond the "modern synthesis" of genetics and evolution. See also Evelyn Fox Keller, *The Century of the Gene* (Cambridge, MA: Harvard University Press, 2000). In the same vein, Richard Lewontin, in arguing against reductive applications of Darwinian theory, emphasizes that the interactions among what he calls the "triple helix" of gene, organism and environment are too complex for such approaches; see especially his *The Triple Helix: Gene, Organism, and Environment* (Cambridge, MA: Harvard University Press, 2000). Most notably, the "new synthesis" recuperates the models of "morphogenetic fields" and "homologies of process" set aside in the "modern synthesis" but fully informing, *avant la lettre*, William James's conceptual models inherited by Stein. This point will be taken up in closing this chapter.

59 *TL*, pp. 59, 60, 62, 63, 72, 96, 76, 77, 78.
60 *ID*, p. 9.
61 Quoted in *LR*, p. 75.
62 Janet Malcolm, "Someone Says Yes To It: Gertrude Stein, Alice B. Toklas, and 'The Making of Americans,'" *New Yorker* (June 13 & 20, 2005), 150.
63 "Poetry and Imagination," pp. 460, 468, 441, 454–5.
64 *Ibid.*, p. 442.
65 *ID*, p. 12, and quoting from William James's *The Will to Believe*.
66 Meyer quoting Ralph Church, a young philosopher commenting in 1928 on the experience of reading Stein for the avant-garde journal *transition* (*ID*, p. 15).
67 Emerson, "Poetry and Imagination," p. 443.
68 *TL*, p. 112.
69 *ABT*, p. 741.
70 *Ibid.*, pp. 739–40.
71 *PP*, p. 266.
72 H. Allen Orr, "Turned On: A Revolution in the Field of Evolution?" *New Yorker* (October 24, 2005), 87.
73 *GHA*, p. 372.
74 *Ibid.*, p. 428.
75 *TL*, p. 60.
76 *GHA*, p. 377.
77 *V*, pp. 448–9.
78 *GHA*, p. 457.
79 *V*, p. 36.
80 *TL*, p. 95.
81 *GHA*, p. 442.
82 *Ibid.*, p. 414.
83 *Ibid.*, p. 380.
84 *TL*, p. 146.

85 *Ibid.*, p. 107.
86 Damasio, *Descartes' Error*, p. 128; cited in *ID*, p. 352.
87 Philip Lieberman, *Eve Spoke: Human Language and Human Evolution* (New York: W. W. Norton, 1998), p. 103; cited in *ID*, p. 352.
88 Joan Retallack, "The Difficulties of Gertrude Stein, I & II," in *The Poethical Wager* (Berkeley: University of California Press, 2003), p. 151.
89 *Ibid.*, p. 153.
90 *GBV*, p. 627.
91 *LIA*, p. 272.
92 *GHA*, p. 407.
93 Meyer similarly observes (*ID* p. 83): "the reader is obliged to reproduce the recursive act of reading which . . . was part and parcel of the original process of writing. Such *experimental reading*, as it were, is not a matter of reductively decoding Stein's writing word for word or phrase for phrase but of neuraesthetically reproducing her 'stud[ies] of the relations of words in meaning sound and volume' in ways specified by the compositions themselves."
94 *GHA*, p. 392.
95 Emerson, "Poetry and Imagination," p. 444.
96 *GHA*, p. 455.
97 *ID*, p. 12.
98 *GBV*, p. 257.
99 *MA*, p. 284.
100 *GBV*, pp. 113, 195, 204, 250–2.
101 *P*, p. 509.
102 *EL*, p. 471.
103 *GBV*, pp. 75–7.
104 *P*, p. 481.
105 *EL*, p. 555.
106 *LIA*, p. 272.
107 *P*, pp. 540, 522.
108 Martin Heidegger, *Sojourns, The Journey to Greece*, tr. John Panteleimon Manoussakis (Albany: State University of New York Press, 2005), p. 60.
109 *CPP*, p. 786.
110 Whitehead, *Adventures*, p. 24.
111 *ID*, pp. 325, 395.
112 *Ibid.*, p. 395; Gilbert *et al.*, "Resynthesizing," pp. 359–60.
113 *ID*, pp. 395–6.
114 Edmund Wilson, "Gertrude Stein," in *Axel's Castle: A Study in the Imaginative Literature of 1870–1930* (New York: Scribner's, 1969 [1931]), pp. 234–5.
115 Gertrude Stein, Notebook 14 (NB–14), p. 3, among unpublished notebooks in working notes for *MA* at the Beinecke Library, Yale University, as cited in an earlier draft of Meyer's *Irresistible Dictation*.

Bibliography

Abisdris, Gil, and Adele Casuga, "Neils Bohr and Robert Frost," www.nsta.org/
main/news/pdf/tst)109_58.pdf.

Anderson, Quentin, *The American Henry James* (New Brunswick: Rutgers University Press, 1957).

Baltrušaitis, Jurgis, *Anamorphoses ou Thaumaturgus opticus: Les perspectives dépravées
– II* (Paris: Flammarion, 1996).

Balzac, Honoré de, *Louis Lambert, Les Proscrits, Jésus-Christ en Flandre* (Paris:
Gallimard, 1980).

Barkow, Jerome H., Leda Cosmides, and John Tooby, eds., *The Adapted Mind:
Evolutionary Psychology and the Generation of Culture* (New York and Oxford:
Oxford University Press, 1995).

Barthes, Roland, *Mythologies* (New York: Vintage, 2000).

Barzun, Jacques, *A Stroll with William James* (Chicago: University of Chicago Press,
1983).

Bateson, William, "Historic Figures," www.bbc.co.uk/history/historic_figures/bat-
eson_william.shtml.

Bateson Family Papers, American Philosophical Society, www/amphilsoc.org/lib-
rary/mole/b/batesonfam.htm.

Bayley, John, "Silent Music," *New York Review of Books* (November 20, 2003),
46–8.

Beach, Joseph Warren, "Emerson and Evolution," *University of Toronto Quarterly*
3 (1934), 474–97.

Beer, Gillian, *Darwin's Plots: Evolutionary Narrative in Darwin, George Eliot and
Nineteenth-Century Fiction* (London and Boston: Ark / Routledge & Kegan
Paul, 1983).

  Open Fields: Studies in Cultural Encounter (Oxford: Clarendon / Oxford University Press, 1996).

  "Physics, Sound, and Substance: Later Woolf," in *Virginia Woolf: The Common
Ground* (Ann Arbor: University of Michigan Press, 1996), pp. 112–24.

Benjamin, Walter, *Reflections*, ed. Peter Demetz (New York: Harcourt Brace
Jovanovich, 1979).

Bluemel, Elinor, *Florence Sabin: Colorado Woman of the Century* (Boulder, 1959).

Bohr, Niels, *The Philosophical Writings of Niels Bohr*, vol. I: *Atomic Theory and the Description of Nature* (Woodbridge, CT: Ox Bow Press, 1987).

Bolla, Peter de, "In the Butcher's Shop," *London Review of Books* (September 23, 2004), 19.

Bridgman, Richard, *Gertrude Stein in Pieces* (Oxford: Oxford University Press, 1970).

Brower, Reuben, and Richard Poirier, eds., *In Defense of Reading* (New York: E. P. Dutton, 1962).

Brown, Lee Rust, *The Emerson Museum: Practical Romanticism and the Pursuit of The Whole* (Cambridge, MA: Harvard University Press, 1997).

Browne, Janet, *Charles Darwin: The Power of Place, Volume Two of a Biography* (Princeton: Princeton University Press, 2002).

Charles Darwin: Voyaging, A Biography (Princeton: Princeton University Press, 1995).

Buell, Lawrence, *Emerson* (Cambridge, MA: Harvard University Press, 2003).

"Thoreau and the Natural Environment," in *The Cambridge Companion to Henry David Thoreau*, ed. Joel Myerson (Cambridge: Cambridge University Press, 1996), pp. 171–94.

Bunn, James H., *Wave Forms: A Natural Syntax for Rhythmic Languages* (Stanford: Stanford University Press, 2002).

Cameron, Sharon, *Thinking in Henry James* (Chicago: University of Chicago Press, 1989).

Cavell, Stanley, *Conditions Handsome and Unhandsome: The Constitution of Emersonian Perfectionism* (Chicago: University of Chicago Press, 1990).

Emerson's Transcendental Etudes (Stanford: Stanford University Press, 2003).

The Senses of Walden, An Expanded Edition (San Francisco: North Point Press, 1981).

This New Yet Unapproachable America: Essays after Emerson after Wittgenstein (Albuquerque: Living Batch Books, 1989).

Clark, Andy, "Magic Words: How Language Augments Human Computation," in *Language and Thought: Interdisciplinary Themes*, ed. Peter Carruthers and Jill Boucher (Cambridge: Cambridge University Press, 2003), pp. 162–83.

Clarke, Bruce, "A Scientific Romance: Thermodynamics and the Fourth Dimension in Charles Howard Hinton's 'The Persian King,'" *Science, Technology & the Arts: Weber Studies, an Interdisciplinary Humanities Journal* 14:1 (Winter, 1997): www.altx.com/ebr

Clifford, James, *The Predicament of Culture: Twentieth-Century Ethnography, Literature, and Art* (Cambridge, MA: Harvard University Press, 1988).

Clifford, W. K., "Body and Mind," *Fortnightly Review* (1874), rpt. in *Lectures and Essays*, ed. L. Stephen and F. Pollock (London: Macmillan, 1879), pp. 31–70.

Collinson, Patrick, "Part of the Fun of being an English Protestant," *London Review of Books* (July 22, 2004), 22–3.

Crary, Jonathan, *Techniques of the Observer: On Vision and Modernity in the Nineteenth Century* (Cambridge, MA: MIT Press, 1991).

Crews, Frederick, "Saving Us from Darwin," *New York Review of Books* (October 4, 2001), 23–9.

Crick, Francis, and Christof Koch, "Consciousness and Neuroscience," *Cerebral Cortex* 8 (1998), 97–107.

"A Framework for Consciousness," *Nature "Neuroscience"* 6:2 (February, 2003), 119–26.

Croce, Paul Jerome, *Science and Religion in the Era of William James*, vol. I: *Eclipse of Certainty, 1820–1880* (Chapel Hill: University of North Carolina Press, 1995).

Damasio, Antonio, *Descartes' Error: Emotion, Reason, and the Human Brain* (New York: G. P. Putnam's Sons, 1994).

The Feeling of What Happens: Body and Emotion in the Making of Consciousness (New York: Harcourt, Brace and Co., 1999).

Daniel, Stephen H., *The Philosophy of Jonathan Edwards: A Study in Divine Semiotics* (Bloomington: Indiana University Press, 1994).

Danielewski, Mark Z., *House of Leaves* (New York: Pantheon, 2000).

Darwin, Charles, *Charles Darwin's "Beagle" Diary*, ed. R. D. Keynes (Cambridge: Cambridge University Press, 2001).

Charles Darwin's Notebooks, 1836–1844: Geology, Transmutation of Species, Metaphysical Enquiries, ed. Paul H. Barrett, Peter J. Gautrey, Sandra Herbert, David Kohn, and Sydney Smith (Ithaca: Cornell University Press, 1987).

The Descent of Man, and Selection in Relation to Sex (rpt. Princeton: Princeton University Press, 1981 [London, 1871]).

On the Origin of Species by Means of Natural Selection (London, 1859), ed. John Burrow from 1st edn. (Harmondsworth: Penguin, 1968).

The Variation of Plants and Animals under Domestication, 2 vols. (London: John Murray, 1868).

Davenport, Guy, *The Geography of the Imagination* (San Francisco: North Point Press, 1981).

Delbrück, Max, "A Physicist's Renewed Look at Biology – Twenty Years Later," Nobel Lecture, December 10, 1969, rpt. http://nobelprize.org/medicine/laureates/1969/delbruck-lecture.html.

Dennett, Daniel C. *Consciousness Explained* (Boston: Little, Brown & Co., 1991).

Freedom Evolves (New York: Penguin, 2004).

Dewey, John, *Art as Experience* (New York: Perigee, 1980).

Experience and Nature (La Salle, IL: Open Court, 1929).

Dydo, Ulla E., with William Rice, *Gertrude Stein: The Language That Rises, 1923–1934* (Evanston: Northwestern University Press, 2003).

Dyson, Freeman, "Clockwork Science," *New York Review of Books* (November 6, 2003), 41–7.

Eddington, Arthur, *The Nature of the Physical World* (London: J. M. Dent & Sons Ltd., 1938).

Edelman, Gerald M., *Bright Air, Brilliant Fire: On the Matter of the Mind* (New York: Basic Books, 1992).

Wider than the Sky: The Phenomenal Gift of Consciousness (New Haven: Yale University Press, 2004).

Edwards, Jonathan, *Images or Shadows of Divine Things*, ed. Perry Miller (New Haven and London: Yale University Press, 1948).

"The Mind," in *The Works of Jonathan Edwards*, vol. VI: *Scientific and Philosophical Writings*, ed. Wallace E. Anderson (New Haven and London: Yale University Press, 1980), pp. 311–98.

"Miscellany No. 782," in *The Works of Jonathan Edwards*, vol. XVIII: *The "Miscellanies" 501–832*, ed. Ava Chamberlain (New Haven and London: Yale University Press, 2000).

"Of Being," in *The Works of Jonathan Edwards*, vol. VI: *Scientific and Philosophical Writings*, ed. Wallace E. Anderson (New Haven and London: Yale University Press, 1980), pp. 202–7.

The Works of Jonathan Edwards, vol. II: *Religious Affections*, ed. John E. Smith (New Haven and London: Yale University Press, 1987).

The Works of Jonathan Edwards, vol. VIII: *Ethical Writings*, ed. Paul Ramsey (New Haven and London: Yale University Press, 1989).

The Works of Jonathan Edwards, vol. IX: *A History of the Work of Redemption*, ed. John F. Wilson (New Haven and London: Yale University Press, 1989).

The Works of Jonathan Edwards, vol. X: *Sermons and Discourses, 1720–1723*, ed. Wilson N. Kimnach (New Haven and London: Yale University Press, 1992).

The Works of Jonathan Edwards, vol. XI: *Typological Writings*, ed. Wallace E. Anderson and Mason Lowance, Jr., with David Watters (New Haven and London: Yale University Press, 1993).

Einstein, Albert, "Autobiographical Notes," in *Albert Einstein: Philosopher-Scientist*, ed. P. A. Schilpp, vol. I (London, 1970).

Emerson, Ralph Waldo, *The Early Lectures of Ralph Waldo Emerson*, 3 vols., ed. Stephen E. Whicher, Robert E. Spiller, and Wallace E. Williams (Cambridge, MA: Harvard University Press, 1959–72).

Essays and Lectures, ed. Joel Porte (New York: Library of America, 1983).

Journals of Ralph Waldo Emerson 1820–1872, vol. III (Boston and New York: Houghton Mifflin, 1910).

The Letters of Ralph Waldo Emerson, 6 vols., ed. Ralph L. Rusk (New York: Columbia University Press, 1966).

"Poetry and Imagination," in *Ralph Waldo Emerson*, ed. Richard Poirier (Oxford and New York: Oxford University Press, 1990), pp. 440–73.

English, Daylanne, "Gertrude Stein and the Politics of Literary-Medical Experimentation," *Literature and Medicine* 16:2 (1997), 188–209.

Estenssoro, Hugo, "Tell Laura I love her," *The Times Literary Supplement* (July 16, 2004), 13.

Farmelo, Graham, ed., *It Must Be Beautiful: Great Equations of Modern Science* (London and New York: Granta, 2002).

Feyerabend, Paul, *Against Method* (London: Verso, 1997).

Feynman, Richard, *QED: The Strange Theory of Light and Matter* (Princeton: Princeton University Press, 1988).

Fields, R. Douglas, "Making Memories Stick," *Scientific American* (February, 2005), 75–81.

Flannery, Tim, "A Bird's-Eye View of Evolution," *New York Review of Books* (June 27, 2002), 23–8.

Freeman, Walter J., *How Brains Make Up Their Minds* (New York: Columbia University Press, 1999).

    Societies of Brains: A Study in the Neuroscience of Love and Hate (Hillsdale, NJ: Lawrence Erlbaum, 1995).

Frye, Northrop, *Spiritus Mundi: Essays on Literature, Myth, and Society* (Bloomington: Indiana University Press, 1976).

Gamwell, Lynn, *Exploring the Invisible: Art, Science and the Spiritual* (Princeton: Princeton University Press, 2002).

Garbarini, Nicole, "Heartbeat Poetry: Verse Speaks to Matters of the Heart – Literally," *Scientific American* (October, 2004), 31–2.

Gargano, James W., "*The Ambassadors* and *Louis Lambert*," *Modern Language Notes* 75 (March, 1960), 211–13.

Gavin, William Joseph, *William James and the Reinstatement of the Vague* (Philadelphia: Temple University Press, 1992).

Gilbert, Scott, John Opitz, and Rudolf Raff, "Resynthesizing Evolutionary and Developmental Biology," *Developmental Biology* 173 (1996), 357–72.

Goodman, Russell B., *Wittgenstein and William James* (Cambridge: Cambridge University Press, 2002).

Grafton, Anthony, *The Footnote: A Curious History* (Cambridge, MA: Harvard University Press, 1999).

Greenblatt, Stephen, *Renaissance Self-Fashioning: From More to Shakespeare* (Chicago: University of Chicago Press, 1980).

Groddeck, Georg, *The Book of the It* (New York: International University Press, 1976).

Gunn, Giles, "Pragmatic Repossessions," in *Thinking Across the American Grain: Ideology, Intellect and the New Pragmatism* (Chicago: University of Chicago Press, 1992).

Habegger, Alfred, *The Father: A Life of Henry James, Sr.* (New York: Farrar, Straus and Giroux, 1994).

Hacking, Ian, *Historical Ontology* (Cambridge, MA: Harvard University Press, 2002).

    An Introduction to Probability and Inductive Logic (New York: Cambridge University Press, 2001).

    "Probability and Determinism, 1650–1900," in *Companion to the History of Modern Science*, ed. R. C. Olby, G. N. Cantor, *et al.* (London: Routledge, 1990).

Hadfield, Andrew, "Erasmus's errata slips," *The Times Literary Supplement* (March 14, 2003), 31.

Hammel, Bill, "An Essay on Patterns in Musical Composition Transformations, Mathematical Groups, and the Nature of Musical Substance," http://graham.main.nc.us/~bhammel/MUSIC/compose.html.

Haraway, Donna Jeanne, *Crystals, Fabrics, and Fields: Metaphors of Organicism in Twentieth-Century Developmental Biology* (New Haven and London: Yale University Press, 1976).

Heaney, Seamus, *Finders Keepers: Selected Prose, 1971–2001* (New York: Farrar, Straus and Giroux, 2002).

Heidegger, Martin, *Sojourns, The Journey to Greece*, tr. John Panteleimon Manousakis (Albany: State University of New York Press, 2005).

Heimert, Alan, "Afterword," in *The Puritans in America: A Narrative Anthology*, ed. Alan Heimert and Andrew Delbanco (Cambridge, MA: Harvard University Press, 1985), pp. 405–13.

Henderson, Linda Dalrymple, *The Fourth Dimension and Non-Euclidean Geometry in Modern Art* (Princeton: Princeton University Press, 1983).

Henry, Holly, *Virginia Woolf and the Discourse of Science: The Aesthetics of Astronomy* (Cambridge: Cambridge University Press, 2003).

Hervey, Mary F. S., *Holbein's Ambassadors, the Picture and the Men* (London: G. Bell and Sons, 1900).

Hocks, Richard A., *Henry James and Pragmatistic Thought: A Study in the Relationship between the Philosophy of William James and the Literary Art of Henry James* (Chapel Hill: University of North Carolina Press, 1974).

Howe, Susan, *The Midnight* (New York: New Directions, 2003).

Hutchison, Hazel, "The Other Lambert Strether: Henry James's *The Ambassadors*, Balzac's *Louis Lambert*, and J. H. Lambert," *Nineteenth-Century Literature* 58 (December, 2003), 230–58.

Jaitly, Deep, Paul Kearney, Guo-Hui Lin, and Bin Ma, "Methods for Reconstructing the History of Tandem Repeats and Their Application to the Human Genome," www.csd.uwo.ca/~bma/pub/jcss2.ps.

James, Henry, *The Ambassadors*, ed. S. P. Rosenbaum, Norton Critical Editions (New York: Norton, 1964).

The American Scene (Bloomington: Indiana University Press, 1969).

"The Art of Fiction," in Henry James, *Literary Criticism: Essays on Literature, American Writers, English Writers*, ed. Leon Edel (New York: The Library of America, 1984), pp. 44–65.

Autobiography, ed. Frederick W. Dupee (Princeton: Princeton University Press, 1983).

The Complete Notebooks of Henry James, ed. Leon Edel and Lyall H. Powers (Oxford: Oxford University Press, 1987).

"Honoré de Balzac," in Henry James, *Literary Criticism: French Writers, Other European Writers, The Prefaces to the New York Edition*, ed. Leon Edel (New York: The Library of America, 1984), pp. 31–151.

"John Tyndall," in Henry James, *Literary Criticism: Essays on Literature, American Writers, English Writers*, ed. Leon Edel (New York: The Library of America, 1984), pp. 1357–62.

Letters, vol. IV: *1895–1916*, ed. Leon Edel (Cambridge, MA, and London: The Belknap Press of Harvard University Press, 1984).

Literary Criticism: French Writers, Other European Writers, The Prefaces to the New York Edition, ed. Leon Edel (New York: The Library of America, 1984).

James, William, *The Correspondence of William James*, vol. I: *William and Henry, 1861–1884*, ed. Ignas K. Skrupskelis and Elizabeth M. Berkeley (Charlottesville: University Press of Virginia, 1992).

The Correspondence of William James, vol. II: *William and Henry, 1885–1896*, ed. Ignas K. Skrupskelis and Elizabeth M. Berkeley (Charlottesville: University Press of Virginia, 1993).

The Correspondence of William James, vol. III: *William and Henry, 1897–1910*, ed. Ignas K. Skrupskelis and Elizabeth M. Berkeley (Charlottesville: University Press of Virginia, 1994).

The Correspondence of William James, vol. IV: *1856–1877*, ed. Ignas K. Skrupskelis and Elizabeth M. Berkeley (Charlottesville: University Press of Virginia, 1995).

Essays in Philosophy, ed. Gerald E. Myers (Cambridge, MA: Harvard University Press, 1978).

"The Place of Affectional Facts in a World of Pure Experience," in *Writings 1902–1910*, ed. Bruce Kuklick (New York: The Library of America, 1987).

A Pluralistic Universe (Cambridge, MA: Harvard University Press, 1977).

Pragmatism, A New Name for Some Old Ways of Thinking in *Writings 1902–1910*, ed. Bruce Kuklick (New York: The Library of America, 1987).

The Principles of Psychology (rpt. Cambridge, MA: Harvard University Press, 1983 [1890]).

Psychology: Briefer Course in *Writings 1878–1899*, ed. Gerald E. Myers (New York: The Library of America, 1992).

"The Sentiment of Rationality," in *William James, Writings 1878–1899*, ed. Gerald E. Myers (New York: The Library of America, 1992), pp. 950–85.

The Varieties of Religious Experience in *Writings 1902–1910*, ed. Bruce Kuklick (New York: The Library of America, 1987).

"What Psychical Research Has Accomplished," in *Writings 1878–1899*, ed. Gerald E. Myers (New York: The Library of America, 1992), pp. 680–700.

The Writings of William James: A Comprehensive Edition, ed. John J. McDermott (Chicago and London: University of Chicago Press, 1977).

Joad, C. E. M., *Philosophical Aspects of Modern Science* (New York: Macmillan, 1932).

Johnson, Steven, *Emergence: The Connected Lives of Ants, Brains, Cities and Software* (New York: Simon & Schuster, 2002).

Keller, Evelyn Fox, *The Century of the Gene* (Cambridge, MA: Harvard University Press, 2000).

Kemp, Martin, "Spiritual Shapes: Ernst Haeckel's 'art forms in nature,'" *Nature* 413 (October 4, 2001), 460.

Kibbey, Ann, *The Interpretation of Material Shapes in Puritanism: A Study of Rhetoric, Prejudice, and Violence* (Cambridge: Cambridge University Press, 1986).

King, John Owen, *The Iron of Melancholy: Structures of Spiritual Conversion in America from the Puritan Conscience to Victorian Neurosis* (Middletown: Wesleyan University Press, 1983).

Knight, Janice, "Learning the Language of God: Jonathan Edwards and the Typology of Nature," *William and Mary Quarterly* 48:4 (1991), 531–51.

Koch, Christof, *The Quest for Consciousness: A Neurobiological Approach* (Englewood, CO: Roberts and Co., 2004).

Krook, Dorothea, *The Ordeal of Consciousness in Henry James* (Cambridge: Cambridge University Press, 1962).

Lambert, David, *William James and the Metaphysics of Experience* (Cambridge: Cambridge University Press, 1999).

Langer, Suzanne, *Philosophy in a New Key: A Study in the Symbolism of Reason, Rite, and Art* (Cambridge, MA: Harvard University Press, 1996 [1942]).

Lattig, Sharon, Project Statement for "The Orders of Time," unpublished paper (December, 2003).

Lears, T. J. Jackson, *No Place of Grace: Antimodernism and the Transformation of American Culture, 1880–1920* (New York: Pantheon, 1981).

Le Doux, Joseph, *The Emotional Brain* (New York: Simon and Schuster, 1996).
   Synaptic Self: How Our Brains Become Who We Are (New York: Penguin, 2003).

Levin, Jonathan, *The Poetics of Transition: Emerson, Pragmatism & American Literary Modernism* (Durham and London: Duke University Press, 1999).

Levinas, Emmanuel, *On Escape: De l'évasion*, tr. Bettina Bergo (Stanford: Stanford University Press, 2003).

Lewis, R. W. B., *The Jameses: A Family Narrative* (New York: Farrar, Straus and Giroux, 1991).

Lewontin, Richard, *The Triple Helix: Gene, Organism, and Environment* (Cambridge, MA: Harvard University Press, 2000).

Liddell and Scott's Greek–English Lexicon, new edition (Oxford: Clarendon / Oxford University Press, 1979).

Lieberman, Philip, *Eve Spoke: Human Language and Human Evolution* (New York: W. W. Norton, 1998).

Livio, Mario, *The Golden Ratio: The Story of Phi, The World's Most Astonishing Number* (New York: Broadway Books, 2002).

Locke, John, *An Essay Concerning Human Understanding*, ed. Peter H. Nidditch (Oxford: Clarendon / Oxford University Press, 1991).
   Two Treatises on Government (rpt. London: Routledge, 1884 [1680–90]).

Lodge, David, *Language of Fiction: Essays in Criticism and Verbal Analysis of the English Novel* (New York: Columbia University Press, 1967).

Loewinsohn, Ron, "Jonathan Edwards' Opticks: Images and Metaphors of Light in Some of his Major Works," *Early American Literature* 8 (1973), 20–32.

Lovejoy, Arthur O., "The Thirteen Pragmatisms," *Journal of Philosophy* 5 (1908), 1–42.

Lyell, Charles, *Principles of Geology*, 3 vols., ed. Martin Rudwick (Chicago: University of Chicago Press, 1990).

Lykken, Joseph D., "Disappearing Dimensions," *Nature* 412 (July 12, 2001), 130.

Malcolm, Janet, "Someone Says Yes To It: Gertrude Stein, Alice B. Toklas, and 'The Making of Americans,'" *New Yorker* (June 13 & 20, 2005), 147–65.

Mallarmé, Stéphane, *Oeuvres complètes*, ed. Henri Condor and G. Jean-Aubry (Paris: Bibliothèque de la Pléiade, 1945).

Manier, Edward, *The Young Darwin and his Cultural Circle* (Dordrecht, 1978).

Marsden, George M., *Jonathan Edwards: A Life* (New Haven and London: Yale University Press, 2003).

Matthiessen, F. O., *The James Family: A Group Biography* (New York: Vintage, 1980 [1947]).

Maturana, Humberto R., and Francisco Varela, *The Tree of Knowledge: The Biological Roots of Human Understanding*, rev. edition (Boston and London: Shambala, 1998).

McCrone, John, "Reasons to forget: scientists count the ways we get it wrong," *The Times Literary Supplement* (January 30, 2004), 3.

Mele, Alfred, "We have reasons to believe," *The Times Literary Supplement* (August 9, 2002), 24.

Menand, Louis, *The Metaphysical Club: A Story of Ideas in America* (New York: Farrar, Straus and Giroux, 2001).

Meyer, Steven, *Irresistible Dictation: Gertrude Stein and the Correlations of Writing and Science* (Stanford: Stanford University Press, 2001).

Miller, Perry, *Errand Into The Wilderness* (New York: Harper Torch Books, 1956).
Jonathan Edwards (New York: Meridian, 1959).
"Jonathan Edwards on 'The Sense of the Heart,'" *Harvard Theological Review* 41 (April 1948), 123–45.
The New England Mind: The Seventeenth Century (Cambridge, MA, and London: Harvard University Press, 1982 [1939]).
ed., *The Transcendentalists: An Anthology* (Cambridge, MA: Harvard University Press, 1950).

Momigliano, Arnaldo, *Alien Wisdom: The Limits of Hellenization* (Cambridge: Cambridge University Press, 1991).

Morrison, Philip, "Tales Behind the Tags," *Nature* 413 (October, 2001), 461.

Musser, George, "All Screwed Up: An Obscure Property of Light Puts a Spin on Astronomy," *Scientific American* (November, 2003), 22–5.

Myers, Gerald E., *William James: His Life and Thought* (New Haven: Yale University Press, 1986).

The New Oxford Annotated Bible, New Revised Standard Version, ed. Bruce M. Metzger and Roland Murphy (New York: Oxford University Press, 1989).

Newton, Isaac, *Opticks, or, A Treatise of the Reflections, Refractions, Inflections & Colors of Light* (based on the fourth edition, London, 1730 rpt. New York: Dover Publications, 1979).

Nicolson, Marjorie, *Newton Demands the Muse: Newton's "Opticks" and the Eighteenth-Century Poets* (Princeton: Princeton University Press, 1966).

Orr, H. Allen, "Turned On; A Revolution in the Field of Evolution?" *New Yorker* (October 24, 2005), 85–8.

Ospovat, Dov, *The Development of Darwin's Theory: Natural History, Natural Theology, and Natural Selection, 1838–1859* (Cambridge: Cambridge University Press, 1995).

Packer, Barbara, "Emerson and the Terrible Tabulations of the French," in *Transient and Permanent: The Transcendental Movement and Its Contexts*, ed. Charles Capper and Conrad E. Wright (Boston: Northeastern University Press, 1999), pp. 148–67.

Emerson's Fall: A New Interpretation of the Major Essays (New York: Continuum, 1982).

Peirce, Charles Sanders, *The Essential Peirce: Selected Philosophical Writings*, vol. I: *1867–1893*, ed. Nathan Houser and Christian Kloesel (Bloomington: Indiana University Press, 1992).

Perry, Ralph Barton, *The Thought and Character of William James, Briefer Version* (New York: Braziller, 1954).

Petruccioli, Sandro, *Atoms, Metaphors, and Paradoxes: Niels Bohr and the Construction of a New Physics* (Cambridge: Cambridge University Press, 1993).

Poirier, Richard, *Poetry and Pragmatism* (Cambridge, MA: Harvard University Press, 1992).

The Renewal of Literature: Emersonian Reflections (New York: Random House, 1987).

Robert Frost: The Work of Knowing (Stanford: Stanford University Press, 1990 [1977]).

"Why Do Pragmatists Want to Be Like Poets?" in *The Revival of Pragmatism: New Essays on Social Thought, Law, and Culture*, ed. Morris Dickstein (Durham: Duke University Press, 1998), pp. 347–61.

Posnock, Ross, *The Trial of Curiosity: Henry James, William James, and the Challenge of Modernity* (New York and Oxford: Oxford University Press, 1991).

Powers, Richard, *The Gold Bug Variations* (New York: William Morrow & Co., 1991).

Prickett, Stephen, *Narrative, Religion and Science: Fundamentalism Versus Irony, 1700–1999* (Cambridge: Cambridge University Press, 2002).

Ramachandran, V. S., *A Brief Tour of Human Consciousness* (New York: Pi Press, 2004).

Ransom, John Crowe, *The World's Body* (Baton Rouge: Louisiana State University Press, 1968).

Regev, Aviv, and Ehud Shapiro, "Cells as Computation," *Nature* 419 (September 26, 2002), 343.

Retallack, Joan, "The Difficulties of Gertrude Stein, I & II," in *The Poethical Wager* (Berkeley: University of California Press, 2003).

Richards, Robert J., *Darwin and the Emergence of Evolutionary Theories of Mind and Behavior* (Chicago: University of Chicago Press, 1987).

The Romantic Conception of Life: Science and Philosophy (Chicago: University of Chicago Press, 2002).

Richardson, Alan, *British Romanticism and the Science of Mind* (Cambridge: Cambridge University Press, 2001).

Richardson, Joan, "Emerson's Sound Effects," *Raritan* 16:3 (Winter, 1997), 83–101.
"A Reading of 'Sea Surface Full of Clouds,'" *Wallace Stevens Journal* 6:3 and 4 (Fall, 1982), 60–8.
Wallace Stevens: The Early Years, 1879–1923 (New York: Beech Tree Books / William Morrow, 1986).
Richardson, Robert D., Jr., *Emerson: The Mind on Fire* (Berkeley: University of California Press, 1995).
Ritterbush, Philip, *The Art of Organic Forms* (Washington: Smithsonian Institute Press, 1968).
Rorty, Richard, *Contingency, Irony and Solidarity* (Cambridge: Cambridge University Press, 1989).
"How Many Grains Make a Heap?" *London Review of Books* (January 20, 2005), 12–14.
Philosophy and the Mirror of Nature (Princeton: Princeton University Press).
Rossi, William, "Emerson, Nature, and the Natural Sciences," in *A Historical Guide to Ralph Waldo Emerson*, ed. Joel Myerson (New York: Oxford University Press, 2000), pp. 101–50.
Ruf, Frederick, *The Creation of Chaos: William James and the Stylistic Making of a Disorderly World* (Albany: State University of New York Press, 1991).
Sacks, Oliver, "In the River of Consciousness," *New York Review of Books* (January 15, 2004), 41–4.
"Speed: Aberrations of Time and Movement," *New Yorker* (August 23, 2004), 60–9.
Schlaepfer, Hansjorg, "Cosmic Rays," *Spatium* 11 (November, 2003), 2–15.
Schrödinger, Erwin, *Nature and the Greeks and Science and Humanism* (Cambridge: Cambridge University Press, 1996).
Seager, William, "Consciousness, Information and Panpsychism," http://members.aol.com/NeoNoetics/CONSC_INFO_PANPSY.html.
"Seeing Science," special issue, *Representations* 40 (Fall, 1992).
Sepper, Dennis L., *Newton's Optical Writings: A Guided Study* (New Brunswick: Rutgers University Press, 1994).
Shell, Alison, review of *Psalm Culture in Early Modern England*, *The Times Literary Supplement* (January 14, 2005), 28.
Shermer, Michael, "Demon-Haunted Brain," *Scientific American* (March, 2003), 47.
Shulevitz, Judith, "From God's Mouth to English," *New York Times Book Review* (October 17, 2004), 8.
Skarda, Christine, *The Perceptual Form of Life* (Cambridge, MA: MIT Press, 1999).
Smith, John E., Harry S. Stout, and Kenneth P. Minkema, eds., *A Jonathan Edwards Reader* (New Haven and London: Yale University Press, 1995).
Stafford, Barbara Maria, *Visual Analogy: Consciousness as the Art of Connecting* (Cambridge, MA: MIT Press, 1999).
Stein, Gertrude, *The Autobiography of Alice B. Toklas* in *Writings 1903–1932*, ed. Catharine R. Stimpson and Harriet Chessman (New York: The Library of America, 1998).

Everybody's Autobiography (Cambridge, MA: Exact Change, 1993 [1937]).

The Geographical History of America in *Writings 1932–1946*, ed. Catharine R. Stimpson and Harriet Chessman (New York: The Library of America, 1998).

"I Came And Here I Am," in *How Writing is Written: Volume II of the Previously Uncollected Writings of Gertrude Stein*, ed. Robert Bartlett Haas (Los Angeles: Black Sparrow Press, 1974).

Lectures in America in *Writings 1932–1946*, ed. Catharine R. Stimpson and Harriet Chessman (New York: The Library of America, 1998).

The Making of Americans (Normal, IL: The Dalkey Archive Press, 1995 [1925]).

"Patriarchal Poetry," in *Writings 1903–1932*, ed. Catharine R. Stimpson and Harriet Chessman (New York: The Library of America, 1998), pp. 567–607.

Picasso: The Complete Writings, ed. Edward Burns (Boston: Beacon Press, 1970).

Three Lives (New York: Penguin, 1990 [1909]).

Unpublished Writings of Gertrude Stein, vol. VIII: *A Novel of Thank You* (New Haven: Yale University Press, 1958).

Wars I Have Seen (New York: Random House, 1945).

Stevens, Wallace, *Collected Poetry and Prose*, ed. Frank Kermode and Joan Richardson (New York: The Library of America, 1997).

Letters of Wallace Stevens, ed. Holly Stevens (New York: Alfred A. Knopf, 1970).

Summers, David, *Real Spaces: World Art History and the Rise of Western Modernism* (London: Phaidon, 2004).

Swedenborg, Emanuel, *Apocalypse Revealed* (New York: The Swedenborg Foundation, 1981).

The Shorter Heaven and Hell (London: Seminar Books, 1993).

Taves, Ann, *Fits, Trances, & Visions: Experiencing Religion and Explaining Experience from Wesley to James* (Princeton: Princeton University Press, 1999).

Taylor, Eugene, "The Appearance of Swedenborg in the History of American Psychology," in *Swedenborg and His Influence*, ed. Erland J. Brock (Bryn Athyn, PA: The Academy of the New Church, 1988).

"Peirce and Swedenborg," *Studia Swedenborgiana* 6:1 (June, 1986), 42–56.

ed., *William James on Exceptional Mental States: The 1896 Lowell Lectures* (Amherst: University of Massachusetts Press, 1984).

Tegmark, Max, "Parallel Universes," *Scientific American* (May, 2003), 41–51.

Thoreau, Henry D., *Faith in a Seed: The Dispersion of Seeds and Other Late Natural History Writings*, ed. Bradley P. Dean (Washington, DC: Island Press, 1993).

Tiffany, Daniel, *Toy Medium: Materialism and the Modern Lyric* (Berkeley: University of California Press, 2000).

Tintner, Adeline R., *Henry James and the Lust of the Eyes: Thirteen Artists in His Work* (Baton Rouge and London: Louisiana State University Press, 1993).

"A Source for James's *The Ambassadors* in Holbein's 'The Ambassadors' (1533)," in *Leon Edel and Literary Art*, ed. Lyall H. Powers assisted by Clare Virginia Eby (Ann Arbor: UMI Research Press, 1988), pp. 135–50.

Tooby, John, and Leda Cosmides, eds., *The New Cognitive Neurosciences* (Cambridge, MA: MIT Press, 2000).

Toulmin, Stephen, and Jane Goodfield, *The Architecture of Matter* (Chicago: University of Chicago Press, 1982).

Transactions of The Connecticut Academy of Arts and Sciences 38 (December, 1949), rpt. www.biologie.uni-hamburg.de/b-online/snowbird/prefaces/essay_del-brueck.htm.

Tufts, James H., "Edwards and Newton," *Philosophical Review* 294 (November, 1940), 609–22.

Tyndall, John, "Scientific Use of Imagination," in *Fragments of Science: A Series of Detached Essays, Addresses, and Reviews*, 2 vols. (rpt. London: Gregg International Publishers Ltd., 1970 [Longman's, Green, 1892]).

Updike, John, "Silent Master," *New Yorker* (June 28, 2004), 98–101.

Vivas, Eliseo, "Henry and William: (Two Notes)," *Kenyon Review* 5 (1943), 580–94.

Walls, Laura Dassow, *Emerson's Life in Science: The Culture of Truth* (Ithaca and London: Cornell University Press, 2003).

Wedgwood, Hensleigh, "Grimm on the Indo-European Languages," *Quarterly Review* 50 (October, 1833), 169–89.

Weiner, Philip P., *Evolution and the Founders of Pragmatism* (New York: Harper & Row, 1965).

Whitehead, Alfred North, *Adventures of Ideas* (New York: The Free Press, 1967).

The Function of Reason (Boston: Beacon Press, 1948).

Process and Reality: An Essay in Cosmology, corrected edition, ed. David Ray Griffin and Donald W. Sherburne (New York: The Free Press, 1985).

Science and the Modern World (New York: The Free Press, 1967).

Whyte, Lancelot Law, "Kepler's Unsolved Problem and the *Facultas Formatrix*," in Johannes Kepler, *The Six-Cornered Snowflake: A New Year's Gift* (1611), tr. Colin Hardie (Oxford: Clarendon / Oxford University Press, 1966).

Williams, Raymond, *The Long Revolution* (Peterborough, Ontario: Broadview, 2001 [1961]).

Writing in Society (London and New York: Verso, 1983).

Williams, Rowan, "What shakes us?" *The Times Literary Supplement* (July 4, 2003), 10.

Wilson, Edmund, "Gertrude Stein," in *Axel's Castle: A Study in the Imaginative Literature of 1870–1930* (New York: Charles Scribner's Sons, 1969 [1931]), pp. 237–56.

Wilson, Eric, *Emerson's Sublime Science* (New York: St. Martin's Press, 1999).

Wolff, Cynthia Griffin, *Emily Dickinson* (New York: Alfred A. Knopf, 1986).

Yeazell, Ruth Bernard, *Language and Knowledge in the Late Novels of Henry James* (Chicago: University of Chicago Press, 1976).

Zeki, Semir, *Inner Vision: An Exploration of Art and the Brain* (Oxford: Oxford University Press, 1999).

Index

accretion
  and asymmetry, 76
  and crystal growth, 75
  and Emerson's style, 76, 78
  and Henry James's use of words, 152
  as mode of development, 17
  and William James's *Principles*, 163
  as vehicle of cognition (W. James), 222
action potentials, 107, 120
adaptation, 65, 95, 101, 220, 227
  and Darwin revising *Origin*, 6
  of Darwinian method by Peirce, 124
  and Emerson, 67, 76
  of rhetorical forms, 6
  syntactic, 19
  and thinking, 8
Adorno, Theodor (*Aesthetic*), 98
aesthetic, the / aesthetics, 98
  activity of, 264n.51
  American aesthetic into Pragmatism, 11, 12, 21
    (Stevens)
  and American style, 32
  as category of thought, 3
  centrality of for W. James, 100
  corruption of idea of, 256–7n.25
  and Edwards, 58
  emergence of as category of thought, 70, 85
  emergence of new, 226
  and Emerson, 71, 73
  etymology, 164
  experience of as religious, 152
  as feeling, sensation, 47
  and Kant, 69
  as morality (H. James), 174
  and pleasure (W. James and Fechner), 220
  and religious experience (W. James), 103, 121
  restoring balance, 135
  "science of" (Baumgarten), 188
  and Stein, 252
  and Stevens, 188
  structure of, 224

and W. James, 100
and W. James's "interest," 104
and Whitehead, 10
see also Edwards, Jonathan; Emerson, Ralph
  Waldo; James, Henry; James, William;
  Stein, Gertrude; Stevens, Wallace
affect, affection/s, 89
  and Edwards, 13, 37, 40, 41, 51–5
  and Emerson, 62
  of the mind (Emerson), 64
  and power of words (Emerson), 76
  and Stein, 246
Agassiz, Louis, 120, 121. *See also* James, William
The Ambassadors, *see* James, Henry
amplification
  and Edwards, 42, 53
  and Emerson, 43
  and H. James, 171
  and language as computational instrument,
    146
  as mode of argument, 1
  in Old Testament, 41
  by repetition and variation, 40
  and Stevens, 43, 194
  and style of Edwards and Emerson, 42
  and W. James (*Principles*), 163, 194
amplifier
  human body as (Whitehead), 126
analogy, 60
  Locke's use of, 4, 9
  as participatory performance, 61
  and probability, 120
  and Stein, 238
  See also crystals, crystallization,
    crystallography
anamorphosis, 4, 143, 256n.19, 289n.109
  in botany, 157
  definition of, 155
  and H. James, 18, 156
  and "historical drift of time," 154
  in Holbein and H. James, 154

Anderson, Wallace, 28, 33–4
appetite, appetition, 87, 220
　and Edwards, 55–6
　and Emerson's aesthetic choices, 15
　as exercise of imagination (Emerson), 14
　of language, 8, 10
　of language and thought, 6
　and satisfaction (Whitehead), 7
　of thought (Whitehead), 56, 67, 220
　and W. James, 7
Arensberg, Walter (Arensberg Circle), 20, 205
Aristotle (subject–predicate distinction), 3
asymmetry
　and crystal growth, polarity, 76, 202, 218
attention, 226
　and Edwards, 25, 31, 55
　to mind in thinking, 148
　optical (Helmholtz), 127
　and W. James, 107, 118 (habit of) 126, 127, 163 (as consciousness)
　see also Edwards, Jonathan; James, William,
aurora borealis, 130, 212

Bach, Johann Sebastian, 31, 201, 241, 262n.23
Bacon, Francis, 1, 2, 21, 26, 66, 89, 205
balance
　of belief, 40
　homeostasis and aesthetic function, 22, 103, 105, 119, 135, 191, 202
　and Stevens, 207
　and W. James, 99
Balzac, Honoré de, 19, 138
　Louis Lambert, 140, 166–71
Bancroft, George, 58
Barthes, Roland, 7
Bateson, William, 234, 235–6, 241
Baumgarten, Alexander, 188
Beach, Joseph Warren, 268n.5
Beer, Gillian, 83, 85, 125, 128, 214, 253n.6, 256n.24
　on language theory, 91–3
　on language used by scientists, 128–9
belief, 61, 115, 119, 160
　degrees of (Hacking), 215
　and habit, 42, 202
　neurological effects of (W. James), 190
　and sensation, thinking as basis of (H. James), 171
　and Stevens, 185, 188
　and W. James, 105, 106, 116
　See also Stevens, Wallace
Bell, Charles, 48. *See also* Emerson, Ralph Waldo: reading in common with Darwin
Benjamin, Walter, 133, 293n.92
Bernard, Claude (homeostasis), 114, 259n.64

Bible, 3, 28, 65, 99, 200. *See also* Book of Psalms; Book of Revelation
Bloom, Harold, 111
Bohr, Niels, 183, 214, 218
　on the atom, 205–6, 208–9
　on Einstein's achievement, 216
　and Lucretius, 186
　and Stevens, 22, 204–6, 208–9
　wave–particle duality as "irrational element," 204
Book of Psalms, 192, 199, 200–1, 204
Book of Revelation, 137, 165, 166
Boscovich, Roger, 207
brain,
　activity of (recursive), 31
　activity of (W. James), 31
　changes in as aurora borealis (W. James), 130, 212
　description of (Emerson), 66–7
　fractal neural networks of, 248
　mirror neurons in, 71
　model of (Stein), 248
　orientation association area (OAA), 56–7
　self-regulation of (feedback), 229
　soul in (Edwards), 57
　states of (W. James), 16, 130
Brinnin, John Malcolm, 242
Brower, Reuben, 240
Brown, Lee Rust, 80, 258n.49
Browne, Janet, 90
Browne, Thomas, 62, 88
Buell, Lawrence, 49, 64, 270n.40, 271n.66, 273n.112
Bunn, James H., 262n.24
Bunyan, John, 109, 111, 112

Cameron, Sharon, 145
Carlyle, Thomas, 85
Cavell, Stanley, 12, 110, 254n.9
Chamberlain, Ava, 39
Christ, Jesus, 65, 191–2, 195
Clark, Andy, 137, 140, 141, 143–5, 146, 147–8, 149, 228, 251, 256n.23
　on conversion of patterns in second-order cognitive dynamics, 152
　on second-order cognitive dynamics, 149–50
Coleridge, Samuel Taylor, 9, 48, 68, 90, 262n.24
continuity, law of, 1, 89, 120, 205
conversion
　directions for (Edwards), 39
　and Edwards, 25, 32, 37, 41, 55, 57
　and Emerson (secular), 14, 65, 75, 117, 244
　idea of (secular use and Emerson), 139
　of idea of subject (W. James), 105
　and language (Emerson), 230

conversion (*cont.*)
    light as model for (Edwards), 33
    and organic process (Emerson), 76
    of patterns (in second-order cognitive
      dynamics), 152
    and Stevens, 193, 197
    and W. James, 103–4, 108–11 (of Emerson's
      "Crossing" passage), 119, 194
Cotton, John, 6
Crary, Jonathan, 260n.9
Crick, Francis, 69, 159, 226, 250, 252, 290n.133
Croce, Paul Jerome, 100, 122, 124, 133
crystals, crystallization, crystallography, 84, 134,
    202, 207, 229
    aperiodic (genome), 232
    and asymmetry, 76, 202
    crystal analogy, 69, 81 (for Darwin and
      Emerson), 69, 96, 135 (Haraway), 252
    "crystal soul" (Haeckel), 200
    Delbrück on, 214
    and DNA molecule, 69
    and Emerson, 63
    and formation of snowflake, 211, 218
      (Fibonacci Series and spiralling)
    growth of by accretion, 152
    growth of by repetition, 72
    and lattice of space, 200
    and spiralling form, 31–2
    and Stevens, 201–2
    structure and behavior of, 75–6
    and Swedenborg, 17, 75–6
    see also Swedenborg, Emanuel,
cybernetics, 229, 259n.64

Damasio, Antonio, 247, 254–5n.12
Daniel, Stephen, 47–8
Danielewski, Mark Z., 257n.34
Dante Alighieri, 21, 74, 169
Darwin, Charles, 1, 48, 70, 78, 79, 90–5, 218,
    223, 224, 225, 235
    and adaptation and linguistic form, 6
    and Chauncey Wright, 122
    on common ancestry, 227
    on evolution, 63, 91
    on free will, 87, 119
    and language, 4, 81, 83
    and language theory, 90–3
    on mind as thought-secreting organ, 105
    and natural selection, 40
    on pleasure, 6–7, 87, 220
    reading in common with Emerson, 88
    reading *Paradise Lost*, 81–2
    and thinking as life form, 8
    on thought, 2
    and W. James, 103, 105, 114, 120, 126–7

*The Descent of Man, and Selection in Relation
    to Sex*, 105
On the Origin of Species, 1, 8, 40, 113; method
    of 127
    probability and, 120
    revision of, 4, 6, 81
    style of, mimetic of evolutionary process, 16
Davy, Humphry, 90
de Broglie, Louis, 180, 181
Delbrück, Max, 208–10, 214, 218
Descartes, René, 4, 9
Dewey, John, 140
Dickinson, Emily, 12, 257n.33, 272n.86
distortion, 40, 121, 220
    and Anne Hutchinson, 6
    and Edwards, 58
    Emerson on, 8
    of H. James's style, 19, 153, 156
    and Mercator projections, 4
    "more than rational," 3, 40, 58, 121, 143, 173,
      220
    rhetorical (Antinomian Crisis), 6
    in syntax and grammar, 10
    and Whitehead, 220
DNA (deoxyribonucleic acid), 15, 232, 248, 250
    and crystallization, 69
    and RNA information transfer, 31, 79, 115,
      202, 227, 248
Dydo, Ulla (and William Rice), 233, 237

Eddington, Sir Arthur, 171, 184
Edelman, Gerald M., 125, 238, 248
    theory of neuronal group selection (TNGS),
      125, 130
Edwards, Jonathan, 4, 94, 96
    and "actual ideas," 25, 27, 30, 31, 35, 37, 39, 47,
      55, 57
    and adaptation of traditional forms of
      expression, 6
    and affect, affection/s, 13, 37, 40, 41, 51–5
      (illustration of), 57
    amplification in style of, 40, 42, 53
    and appetite, appetition, 55
    "appetite of the mind," 56
    and attention, 31 (and will), 46, 55
    "attention to the mind in thinking," 25, 29,
      30, 35, 54
    and Bible, 28
    "Blank Bible," 42
    and breakdown of subject–predicate
      scheme, 9, 47
    and conversion, 25, 32, 33, 37 (experience of)
      39 (directions for), 41, 57
    and "delight," 13, 14, 35, 57, 59–60
    "dependence" for, 59–61

and Emerson, 63, 64–5, 118
and "excellence," "excellency," 45
and fact and feeling, 39
and feeling, 53, 55
and Great Awakening, 6
and habit, perceptual, 42
and habit as "natural . . . foundation for
    action," 34, 42
and habit of contemplating nature, 30
and light, 13–14, 29 (as language of God) 32,
    33 (as model of conversion), 33, 38, 44 (and
    God's grace), 47 (behavior of)
mutation of style, 39
mutations of utterance, 39
and Newton's *Opticks*, 5, 14, 24–5, 28, 35–7,
    45–6, 53, 60
and performance in/of language, 52, 59
"prehension" for, 55
and relation of God and nature, 39
and relation of matter to spirit, 38
and repetition, 35, 39, 41, 50, 52, 57, 58
and repetition as "creation," 38
"room of the idea," 4, 25, 29, 41, 47, 55
"sense of the heart," 9, 25, 29, 32, 33, 47, 48–50
    (definition), 194
"sensible knowledge," 25
"speculative knowledge," 25
on spiders and linguistic form, 14
spiralling use of words, 31, 34, 40
style of, 10, 39 (of preaching)
and typology, 27, 30, 32, 36, 47, 51, 52, 261n.14
and W. James, 102
and will, 31, 34
"Of Atoms," 33, 38
"Beauty of the World," 46
"Of Being," 34, 179
*The Distinguishing Marks of a Work of the
    Spirit of God*, 49
A History of the Work of Redemption, 39, 40,
    58
Images or Shadows of Divine Things, 27, 44, 214
Miscellany no. 782, "Ideas. Sense of the
    Heart. Spiritual Knowledge or Conviction.
    Faith," 24, 25, 61, 255n.17
"Natural History of the Mental World or of
    the Internal World" ("The Mind"), 31, 52,
    146
Personal Narrative, 13, 14, 35, 37, 56, 57, 58, 59
Religious Affections, 34, 102, 262n.34
"Things to be Considered an[d] Written fully
    about," 35, 38
*Thoughts on the Revival of Religion in New
    England*, 49
see also Emerson, Ralph Waldo
Einstein, Albert, 22, 118, 183, 184, 200, 213, 216

electromagnetism, 117
    language of, 126
Emerson, Ralph Waldo, 48, 98, 99, 112, 115, 121,
    139, 146, 156, 225, 229, 233, 252, 278n.49
and accretion as stylistic feature, 76, 78
and adaptation of voice, 76
and the aesthetic, 71, 73, 89
and amplification as stylistic feature, 42
"axis of vision," 14, 40–1, 65
and Coleridge, 68
and collapse of time, 169
conversion for, 14, 65, 75, 117, 139, 244
and crystal metaphor/analogy, 63
and Edwards, 63, 64, 65, 67, 71, 76, 79, 89
    facts for, 67
and Goethe (*Organismus*), 68
and imagination, 77
and indexing, 15, 43, 76, 79
and Jardin des Plantes, 14, 66, 85, 97
and language, 8, 68, 77 (as "organ"), 78, 80
    ("of facts"), 81, 93, 230 (*Nature*)
"Man Thinking," 162
mind for, 63, 67 (as "organic agent"), 104
    (action of)
natural historians, philosophers, scientists
    read by, 66
"natural history of the intellect," 15, 78
and *Naturphilosophie*, 68
"original relation to the universe," 62
and *Paradise Lost*, 86
on pleasure, 63, 244
and polarity, 65, 78
read by Stevens, 21, 187, 200
reading in common with Darwin, 88
on relation/s, 63, 64, 161
and repetition, 76
on spirit, 39, 67
and "stubborn fact," 275n.7
style of, 3, 79
style of and "imperfect replication," 14–15,
    111–12
and Swedenborg, 14, 66, 72–3, 75, 76, 134,
    150
and thinking as life form, 8
"to think," 143
and W. James, 109–10
and wave theory, 207
"Circles" ("the flying Perfect"), 174
"The Divinity School Address," 66, 102, 193,
    194–6, 197, 199
"Experience," 80, 250
"The Method of Nature," 11, 79
"A Natural History of the Intellect," 43
Nature (1836), 10, 42, 62, 63, 68, 87, 104
"Poetry and Imagination," 243–4, 261n.10

Emerson, Ralph Waldo (*cont.*)
  Representative Men, 62, 63, 66
  "Spiritual Laws," 137–8
  see also James, Henry; James, William; Stein,
    Gertrude; Stevens, Wallace
empiricism, radical, 1. *See also* James, William
English, Daylanne, 242
"errors of descent"
  and "imperfect replication" (Steve Jones), 40
An Essay concerning Human Understanding, see
  Locke, John
Euler, Leonhard, 207
evolution, evolutionary process, 8, 15, 39, 63, 84,
  121, 213, 250
  and modern evolutionary synthesis, 15, 40
  and music, 226
  and mutation, 40
  and *Origin* as mimetic of, 16
  and *Principles* as mimetic of, 16
  and probability, 120
  and Stein, 241
  and W. James, 101, 106

fact/s, 263n.41
  Darwinian, 101
  for Edwards, 39
  for Emerson, 67
  necessary redefinition of (Hacking), 215
  "stubborn fact/s" (Emerson, James, and
    Whitehead), 10, 202, 275n.7
  for W. James, 99, 163
  see also James, William
Faraday, Michael, 90, 108, 117, 207, 213
  and electromagnetism and polarity, 65
  and Helmholtz, 17
  and influence on W. James, 118
Fechner, G. T. (on pleasure and the aesthetic),
  220
feedback
  and brain self-regulation, 229
  feedback loops, 248
  and feedforward loops, 130
  mimetic and H. James, 157
  and recursive brain activity, 31
feeling/s
  as "actual idea," 47
  for Edwards, 53, 55
  and fact, 40
  "lures for" (Whitehead), 10
  "structure of" (Williams), 79, 220
  of time (Eddington), 171
  of time and Strether, 172–3
  as vectors, 126, 164 (Whitehead)
  and W. James, 7, 29 (and learning), 98, 101,
    164, 176, 177–8, 266n.76
  for Whitehead, 10

for words (Stevens), 198
  see also James, William
Feyerabend, Paul, 5, 49, 254n.8
Feynman, Richard, 213
Fibonacci Series, 31, 218
Fodor, Jerry, 256n.23
Foucault, Michel, 3
Freeman, Walter, 298n.206
Freud, Sigmund, 110–11, 116
  The Interpretation of Dreams, 21, 116
  and pleasure, 6
Frost, Robert, 12, 208
Frye, Northrop, 202

Galileo, Galilei, 86
Gavin, William Joseph, 279n.57
genetics, 40, 236
  and modern evolutionary synthesis, 15, 40
genome (human), 232, 233–4
  and word patterning in Stein, 240
God
  idea of, 11, 12
  language of (Edwards), 29
  as light, 60
  metaphor for mind of, 89
  mind of, 44
  "Spirit of" (Edwards), 30
  transformation of idea of, 89
Goethe, Johann Wolfgang von, 200
  and crystal analogy, 69
  and *Organismus*, 68, 189
Greenblatt, Stephen, 155, 158
Grimm, Jacob G.
  and language theory, 91–3

habit
  "of accurate thought" (Tyndall), 159
  as aspect of life of the mind and Pragmatism, 1
  of attention (Stein), 248
  of contemplating nature (Edwards), 30
  of cultivating attention (W. James), 118
  and language, 153
  as "natural foundation for action" (Edwards),
    34, 42
  and neuronal currents, 160
  perceptual (Edwards), 42
  shaping perception, 202
  of speech, 13
  W. James on, 8
Hacking, Ian, 95
  on emergence of probability and words in
    their sites, 214–16
  and "particulate fact," 226
Haeckel, Ernst, 200
  and crystal analogy, 69
  and "crystal soul," 200

Hamann, Georg, 95
Haraway, Donna, on metaphor and crystal
   analogy, 68–70, 135
Hazlitt, William, 218
Heaney, Seamus, 223
Heidegger, Martin, 251
Heimert, Alan, 260n.4
Heisenberg, Werner, 186
   and language and atoms, 206
   and set of relations, 207
   and Stevens, 22, 186
Hejinian, Lyn, 248
Helmholtz, Hermann von, 117, 130
   and "interest" (W. James), 156
   and physiological optics, 226
   and W. James, 17, 125–8
Herder, Johann Gottfried von, 95
Hindemith, Paul, 209
Hocks, Richard, 285n.10, 286n.37
Holbein, Hans the Younger, *The Ambassadors*,
   19, 142, 158, 256n.19. *See also* James, Henry
Holmes, Oliver Wendell, 268n.5, 268n.19
homeostasis, homeostatic balance, 107, 114, 191,
   259n.64
   and aesthetic function, 22
   described by N. Weiner, 229
   perceptual, 103
   as style, 40–1
Hooke, Robert (*Micrographia*), 26
Humboldt, Alexander von, 95, 111
Hume, David, 4, 215, 230
Hutchinson, Anne (Antinomian Crisis), 6

imagination
   activity of, 128
   for Emerson, 77
   for W. James and C. S. Peirce, 120
"interest"
   for W. and H. James, 67, 89, 156, 163
   for W. James, 6, 104 (and the aesthetic), 134,
   163

James, Henry, 89, 98, 99, 113, 124
   aesthetic as morality, 174
   and anamorphosis, 18, 143, 154, 156,
   157
   and Balzac (*Louis Lambert*), 166–71
   and consciousness, 145, 149, 152 ("double
   consciousness")
   and distortion, 156
   on experience and consciousness, 230–1
   and feeling, 164
   and "feeling of time" (Strether), 172–3
   and H.G. Wells, 154
   and Holbein (*The Ambassadors*), 19, 142–3,
   153, 154

and "interest," 156
language of, 132
navigation used as metaphor by, 143, 144, 145,
   146, 152, 161–3 (and reading pragmatically)
and performance of language, 151
and pleasure, 157
reading *Pragmatism*, 18, 140, 149
and Swedenborg, 138–9, 165
and time, 171
and "the vague," use of, 145, 159
and W. James, 140 (*Pragmatism*), 145
   (*Principles*)
The Ambassadors, 17, 18, 133, 140
   New York Edition (1907–9), 17, 143, 153
Notes of a Son and Brother, 158
A Small Boy and Others, 133, 159, 164,
   176
James, Henry, Sr., 98, 99, 110, 112, 113, 119
   and encouraging sons to debate, 18
   and Swedenborg, 112–13, 133
James, William, 51, 52, 61, 63, 89, 94, 141, 183,
   226, 252
   and the aesthetic (centrality of), 100
   aesthetic and "interest," 104
   aesthetic and religious experience 103, 105
   and Agassiz, 112, 114
   and amplification, 163, 193–4 (of "*there*")
   on attention, 107, 118, 126, 127
   and belief, 105, 106, 116, 190 (neurological
   effects of)
   on brain activity, 31, 47
   brain changes as aurora borealis, 212
   on "brain-states," 16, 130
   and Bunyan, 115, 116, 117
   "cash-value," 104, 105 (of conversion)
   cinematic sense of perception, 225
   and Claude Bernard, 114
   common sense for, 224
   and consciousness, 160, 162–3 (and attention),
   177–8 (and language), 207 (as wave
   function)
   conversion for, 103–4, 119
   conversion of Emerson "Crossing" passage,
   108–11, 194
   conversion of idea of subject, 105
   and Darwin, 103, 114
   and "darwinian facts," 101
   and Darwinian information, 121
   and Darwinian notion of chance production,
   229
   and Edwards, 102, 118
   and Emerson, 102, 107 ("the divine
   Emerson"), 109–10, 114, 117, 278n.49
   and evolution (theory of), 101, 106
   "experience" for, 99, 104
   on "fact/s," 99, 163

James, William (*cont.*)
  and Faraday, influence of, 118
  on feeling/s, 7, 98, 101, 111, 164, 176, 177–8,
    224 (and "relations")
  and free will, 104, 116, 117, 119, 126, 135
  on habit, 8
  and Helmholtz, 17, 125–8, 156
  "interest/s" for, 6, 104, 134, 156, 163
  and Kant, 116–17
  and language (performative function of), 122,
    131
  mind as *pragma*, 100
  and Mozart, 225
  nervous collapse of ("vastation"), 107, 108–9,
    113, 116, 117
  on nervous system, 107
  and neural wave activity, 129
  and neurology, 106
  and the *Odyssey*, 114
  and Peirce, 123–4, 129
  and pleasure, 220
  and Pragmatism and radical empiricism, 1
  radical empiricism of, 131, 233, 244, 264n.51,
    278n.41 ("doctrine of relations")
  and "relation/s," 101, 105 ("relation *in
    relation*"), 175–6 (senses of), 249
  on sound of words, 228
  and Stein, 19, 232, 234, 245
  and Stevens, 187, 218
  and "stubborn facts," 10, 99, 202
  style of, 106
  and Swedenborg, 17, 73, 173
  "*there*," 230
  on thinking/thought, 7, 8 (as life form), 17
    (processes of)
  "the vague," 17, 101, 108, 120, 125, 145, 207,
    276n.16, 279n.57
  and will, 151, 174–5
  Pragmatism, 17, 74, 96, 215, 251
  and H. James reading, 18, 140, 149
  The Principles of Psychology, 2 (and *Origin*), 16,
    17, 19, 28–9 (and neuronal paths in cortex)
    100, 101, 106, 125, 129, 131 (style of) 140,
    143, 146, 151, 154 ("Perception of Time")
    156, 162, 164, 190, 222
  "The Stream of Thought," 7, 94, 129, 160,
    255–6n.18
  The Varieties of Religious Experience, 17, 101–3,
    104, 106–7, 115, 119, 131 (style of) 190
  The Will to Believe, 151
  "A World of Pure Experience," 249
Jesus Christ, *see* Christ
Joad, C. E. M., 206
Johnson, Thomas Hope, 209, 210, 212, 213
Jones, Steve, 40

Kant, Immanuel, 69, 71, 72, 95, 116–17, 138
Kepler, Johannes, 217
Kibbey, Ann, 256n.22
Kimnach, Wilson, 33, 39, 49
Knight, Janice, 30, 38, 44, 51
Koch, Christof, 159, 226, 289n.85, 290n.133,
  298n.191
Krook, Dorothea, 286n.34
Kuhn, Thomas, 68

Langer, Suzanne, 13, 249
language
  and aesthetic function, 10
  appetition of, 8, 10
  as computational transformer, 143, 146,
    147–8
  and consciousness (W. James), 177–8
  corporeal aspects of (Carlyle), 85
  Darwinian, 83
  and Emerson, 8, 68, 78, 230
  evolution of, 218
  as fact, 10
  "of facts" (Emerson), 80
  fluency in and repetition, 27–8
  as fundamental power (Darwin and
    Emerson), 81
  and H. James, 132
  H. and W. James's understanding of
    (Emerson), 74
  and habit, 153
  inadequacy of, 19
  and Langer, 13
  as life form (H. and W. James), 140
  as matter, 48, 202
  mimetic forms of, 13
  as ministerial performance, 10–11
  occulting properties of, 19
  as organ (Emerson), 77
  as organic form, 6
  as performance, 3
  performative function of (W. James), 122
  as *pragma*, 208
  as prayer, 244
  and quantum theory (Bohr), 205–6
  and quantum theory (Heisenberg), 206
  relation to thinking, 96
  scientists, use of and sensible effects, 128–9
  sentences as "vibratory organisms"
    (Whitehead), 238
  Shakespearean, 2
  and Stevens, 21
  and thought (debate on), 256n.23
  used pragmatically, 141
  as vehicle of activity of consciousness (H. and
    W. James), 148

and W. James, 131
and wave behavior, 129
see also Edwards, Jonathan; Emerson, Ralph
Waldo; James, Henry; James, William;
Stein, Gertrude; Stevens, Wallace
language theory, 84, 90–3
Levin, Jonathan, 100
Lewontin, Richard, 256n.23, 301n.58
Lieberman, Philip, 247
light, 32
activating asymmetry and polarity, 218
descriptions of, 213
and Edwards, 13–14, 29, 32–4, 38
as God, 60
and spiritual energy, 137
and Stevens, 183–4
see also Edwards, Jonathan
Locke, John
use of analogy and breakdown of
subject–predicate scheme, 9
epistemology of as snow melting (Hazlitt), 218
and extension of Cartesian perceptions into
empiricism, 4
"furniture of the mind," 4, 69
imagination of, 60
language as fact, 10
"Presence-room," 25
and *semiotike*, 48, 50, 146
tabula rasa, 56
theory of language (Miller on), 9
on words and ideas, 8
An Essay concerning Human Understanding, 4,
5, 24, 47
Lodge, David, 286n.25
Loeb, Jacques, and free will and tropism, 135
Loewinsohn, Ron, 260n.4
Lovejoy, Arthur O., 295n.137
Lucretius, 66, 84, 186
Luther, Martin, 50
Lyell, Charles, 37, 83, 92, 95, 225, 263n.41

Malcolm, Janet, 233, 243
Mallarmé, Stéphane, 22, 229
Marsden, George, 32, 42, 261n.23
Marvell, Andrew, "The Garden," 177
Maxwell, James Clerk, 89, 117
Mayr, Ernst, "imperfect replication," 40
McDermott, John J., 278n.41
Menand, Louis, 121–2
Mendel, Gregor, 40, 236, 237
metaphor
of "critical opalescence," 211
and I. A. Richards and H. James, 157
for mind of God, 89
of navigation (H. James), 143–6, 152

as principle of organization in science, 68, 129,
135
of snow (Stevens), 216
Meyer, Steven, 233, 235, 238–41, 243, 247, 248,
249, 251
Milch, David, xii
Miller, Perry, 9, 24, 28, 32, 47, 51, 257n.39,
261n.14, 269n.39, 277n.22
Milton, John, *Paradise Lost*, 81–2, 84, 86,
87, 97
mimesis
and feedback, 157
and linguistic forms, 13, 86
of texts (Emerson), 80
"mimetic logic" (Posnock), 156
mind
activity of (Emerson), 63, 74, 79, 104, 202
(and Necker cube), 151 (stochastic), 262n.24
(as pleasure)
evolution of (W. James), 101
"feeling mind" (W. James), 115
as organ, 56
as "organic agent" (Emerson), 67
as photographic plate (Tyndall), 159
as *pragma* (W. James), 100
as "thought-secreting organ" (Darwin), 105
Moll, Elsie, 189, 191
Momigliano, Arnaldo, 271n.59
Montaigne, Michel de, 50
More, Henry, 33, 65
Munsterberg, Hugo, 19, 234
mutation, 201, 250
and Edwards's style, 39
and Emerson's style, 79
engine of evolution, 40
"Experience is in . . . ," 12
and "imperfect replication," 15
and poetic form (Stevens), 22
and thinking, 8
of thought (Hacking), 215
of utterance (Edwards), 39
Myers, Gerald, 100

natural selection, 40, 83, 96, 121, 241
ideational (Emerson), 67
Naturphilosophie, and Emerson, 68
Necker, L. A. (Necker cube), 202
Needham, Joseph, 252
neuroscience, 107
Newton, Sir Isaac, 72, 86, 108
"crucial experiment" of, 26
on light, 65, 76; hypothesizing wave–particle
property of 69
Opticks, 5, 14, 24–5, 35
see also Edwards, Jonathan

Nicolson, Marjorie, 32
Nietzsche, Friedrich, 98, 110

occasion
  and Edwards, 55
  and Whitehead, 10, 182, 202, 257n.35
Oegger, Guillaume, 268n.4
Opticks, see Newton, Sir Isaac
Organismus (Goethe)
  and Emerson, 68
  and Stevens, 189
Ospovat, Dov, 253n.6, 272n.81
Owen, Richard, 72, 252

Packer, Barbara, 258n.49
Pater, Walter, 129
Peirce, Charles Sanders, 63, 89, 120, 123–4, 125,
    129, 141, 151
  common sense for, 224
  and Darwin / Darwinian information, 121
  and Emerson, 120, 121
  "firstness" for, 71
  "metaboly" for, 226
  and "objective evasion of induction"
    (Hacking), 215
  reading *Origin*, 1–2
  reading Poe, 12
  and Stevens, 203–4
  and Swedenborg, 133
  and W. James, 15
  see also James, William
performance
  and Emerson, 73, 89
  and Edwards, 48, 52
  and H. James, 151
  language as, 3
  and ministerial function, 10–11
  participatory, as analogy, 61
  of reception (Emerson), 112
  of recursiveness, 43 (Stevens)
  of text (Edwards), 59
  verbal, and religious experience, 104
philology, comparative, 84, 90, 96
phototropism, 135
  of ideas (Emerson), 81
phyllotaxis, and spiralling forms, 32
Planck, Max, 22, 180
Plato, 66, 84, 181
  idealism of, 115
  "Cratylus," 227
  "Phaedrus," 169
pleasure, 89, 105, 112
  and appetite and aesthetic choices, 6–7
  and balancing (equations), 27
  and Darwin, 87

and Emerson, 63, 244
and H. James, 157
nature of, 225, 231
preparation for, 227
as prime motive of life (Darwin), 220
Poe, Edgar Allan, 12
Poirier, Richard, 12, 110, 141, 240, 254n.8, 279n.57
polarity, 89, 103
  and asymmetry and light, 218
  and crystal growth, 72, 76
  and Emerson, 65
  and Emerson's style, 78, 96
polarization, 117, 128
Posnock, Ross, 125, 132, 133, 140, 141, 156, 276n.16
Powers, Richard, 298n.2
pragma, 10, 96, 100, 208, 244
Pragmatism (Jamesian), 99, 107
  and the aesthetic, 12
  development of, 122
  as evolved from Puritan form of thinking, 1–2
  inflected by radical empiricism, 1
  master-plan of (Peirce), 124
  method of, 56, 127
  as moral activity, 149
  as "old wine in new bottles," 150
  as secular morality, 140
  as self-reflexive theorizing, 135
  and Stein, 245
  and Stevens, 21, 210
  and "Truth happens to an idea," 42
*Pragmatism, A New Name for Some Old Ways of
    Thinking,* 17. *See also* James, William
Prickett, Stephen, 41
The Principles of Geology, see Lyell, Charles
The Principles of Psychology, see James, William
probability
  emergence of (Hacking), 214
  and theory of evolution (Darwin), 120
psychology, and H. James, 159

quantum mechanics, 131
quantum theory, 184
  "new," 205–6
  and Stevens, 22
  and "vibrations," 214
Quetelet, Adolphe, 89

Ransom, John Crowe, 187
recursiveness, 40, 43, 135
Reed, Sampson, 269n.39
Reformation, The, 9, 11, 12, 50, 86, 112, 200, 249
  project of, 150
  religious debate surrounding and Holbein, 154
  and W. James, 251
  work of, 149

relation/s, 86, 95, 96
  between, 110, 225
  between fact and feeling, 2
  "between relations" (Clark), 147
  between words and perception (Locke), 9
  between work of God and nature (Edwards),
    39
  "doctrine of" (W. James), 278n.41
  and Edwards, 55
  and Emerson, 63, 64, 161
  of feeling, thinking, and desiring (Stevens),
    219
  and Heisenberg, 207
  of linguistic signs, 146
  of matter to spirit (Edwards), 38
  new, and external representation (Clark), 150
  new, between words (Hacking), 215
  "original relation to the universe" (Emerson),
    12
  of protein molecules and neurons, 238
  reciprocal, of perception and linguistic
    transcription, 233
  "stop nowhere" (H. James), 89
  of sun's light and elements, 45
  of thoughts and language (W. James), 177–8
  and W. James, 101, 105, 175–6 (sense of, as
    feeling, W. James), 249
  of whole to part as bodily event (Whitehead),
    228
  spatio-temporal and musical scale, 227
repetition
  in Bible, 42
  "continuous" (Stein), 249
  and crystal growth, 69
  and Edwards, 35, 38 (as "creation"), 41, 50, 52,
    57, 58
  and Emerson, 76
  and fluency in language, 27
  and inhibitory process of brain activity, 31
  and mapping, 227
  neuronal effects of (W. James), 27–9, 146
  and Stevens, 202
  and variation (Edwards), 39
  and variation (Stein), 248
  and variation (Stevens), 201
  and variation as motive of evolutionary
    change, 39
replication, imperfect, 15, 40, 43, 65, 112, 144,
    194, 202, 217
Retallack, Joan, 233, 247–8
Rice, William, 233
Richards, I. A., 157
Richardson, Alan, 266n.81
Richardson, Joan, 271n.66
Richardson, Robert, 80, 258n.49, 270n.40

Rizzolatti, Giacomo, 71
RNA (ribonucleic acid), and DNA information
    transfer, 31, 79, 115, 202, 227
"room of the idea," as conceptual/linguistic
    space, 4, 5
Rorty, Richard, 12, 257–8n.43, 265n.62, 277n.16
Rudwick, Martin, 83

Sacks, Oliver, 159, 288n.69
Saint-Hilaire, Geoffroy, 134
Sandeman, Robert, 118
Santayana, George, 132, 190
Schleiden, Matthias Jacob, 69
Schrödinger, Erwin, 206, 213
Sedgwick, Adam, 90
self-identity/imitation, law of and DNA–RNA
    information transfer, 115
Selfridge, Oliver, 87
semiotike, 52. *See also* Locke, John
"sense of the heart," *see* Edwards, Jonathan
Sepper, Dennis, 26
Shakespeare, William, 2, 65
Skarda, Christine, 298n.206
spiralling, as physical and aesthetic structuring
    principle, 31, 34, 40, 199–201, 218, 229
Stafford, Barbara Maria, 45
Stein, Gertrude
  and the aesthetic, 252
  and radical empiricism, 238
  and W. James, 19, 234, 245, 246
  Everybody's Autobiography, 243
  The Geographical History of America, 248
  *The Gradual Making of "The Making of
    Americans"*, 237
  The Making of Americans, 20, 232, 245
  "Patriarchal Poetry" 234
  Three Lives, 20, 242–3, 245, 246–7
Stein, Leo, 235
Stein, Michael, 234
Stevens, Garrett, Sr., 203–4
Stevens, Wallace, 43, 89
  and the aesthetic, 188
  and aurora borealis, 212
  and belief, 185
  and Bohr, 22, 204–6, 208–9
  conversion for, 193, 197
  and death of Satan, 169
  and Einstein's discoveries, 22, 183, 211
  and Elsie Moll, 189, 191
  and Emerson, 21, 187, 200
  and Emerson's "Divinity School Address,"
    193, 194–6, 197, 199
  and "facture," 182, 200, 208, 221
  "feeling for words," 198
  "fiction," 22

Stevens, Wallace (*cont.*)
  and Goethe, 200
  and Haeckel, 200
  and Heisenberg, 22, 186, 204
  "irrational element," 4
  and language, 21
  and light, 183–4
  and Mallarmé, 22, 229
  and musicality, 218–23
  and *Organismus*, 189
  and Peirce, 203–4
  and Planck, 22, 180, 204
  "poetry of the subject," 4, 5, 197
  and Psalms (Book of), 192, 199, 200–1, 204
  and quantum theory, 22, 206
  "satisfactions of belief," 188, 191, 199
  snow as metaphor for, 216, 217–18
  and Stein, 20
  style of, 201
  style of and spiralling, 199–201
  and thinking as evolving form, 21
  "true subject," 4, 5, 197
  and "vibration/s," 198, 211
  and W. James, 187, 190, 207, 218
  and Whitehead, 181, 182
  word use as "critical opalescence," 211
  "The Auroras of Autumn," 212
  "The Comedian as the Letter C," 21, 200
  The Irrational Element in Poetry, 196–9, 216
  "The Man with the Blue Guitar," 196
  "An Ordinary Evening in New Haven," 208,
    210–13
  "Peter Quince at the Clavier," 218–23, 227
  "The Snow Man," 217
  "Sunday Morning," 191, 192–3
style, 41, 58, 121
  common features in Edwards and Emerson,
    42
  of Edwards, 39
  as homeostatic adjustment, 40–1
  "new intellectual" necessary after *Origin*, 122
  "plain style," 257n.39
  of Stevens, 199–201
subject–predicate scheme, 3
  breakdown of, 4, 6, 8, 9, 47
superposition/s, 186, 211
  and wave activity of thinking, 131
Suzuki, D. T., 273n.112
Swedenborg, Emanuel, 93, 133, 137, 152, 218
  and Balzac, 19, 166, 168–9
  as "Buddha of the North" (*Louis Lambert*),
    167
  and crystal analogy, 72, 75–6
  and crystallography, 17
  and Emerson's reading of, 14, 72–3, 75–7
  and H. James, 165

  and H. James Sr., 112–13
  and W. James, 17, 73, 173
  Apocalypse Revealed, 165
  Heaven and Hell (and H. James), 138–9
  see also Emerson, Ralph Waldo; James, Henry,
    Sr.; James, Henry; James, William

Taves, Ann, 58, 264n.53, 276n.15
teleology, 12, 81, 226
theory of neuronal group selection (TNGS), 125.
  See also Edelman, Gerald M.
thinking
  evolution of, 6
  as evolving form (and Stevens), 21
  as life form, 8
  W. James on, 7, 17
Thoreau, Henry David, 12, 80
Three Lives, see Stein, Gertrude
Tiffany, Daniel, 216–17, 218
Tintner, Adeline, 19, 142–3
Tufts, James H., 260n.4
Tyndall, John, 82, 84, 126, 128–9, 159
typology, ix, 43, 86
  and Edwards, 27, 30, 32, 36, 47, 51, 52, 261n.14
  and Emerson, 43
  naturalized (Stevens), 214
  and Puritan thinking, 1–2
  and repetition, 28

Updike, John, 154

Van Vechten, Carl, 243
variation, 201, 226, 227
  and copying genetic information, 40
  of Edwards's words and phrases, 31
  rhythmic (Bateson), 235
  and speciation (and Stevens's style), 223
Varieties of Religious Experience, The, see James,
  William
vibration/s, 198, 211, 229
  and Bateson, 235
  "of organic deformation" (Whitehead), 182,
    229
  and stability in "new" quantum theory, 214
  and Stevens, 198, 211
  "vibratory organism" (Whitehead), 235
  "vibratory organisms" as sentences
    (Whitehead), 238
Vico, Giambattista, 217

Walls, Laura Dassow, 80, 258n.49
Watson, James, 69, 250, 252
wave activity, 117, 128
  and Emerson (Faraday), 65
  and language, 129
  neural (W. James), 129

wave forms (Whitehead), 182
wave motion, 89
wave packets, 108, 120
wave–particle duality, 181, 210, 226
  as "irrational element" (Bohr), 204
  Newton's anticipation of, 69
wave theory, 118
  and Emerson, 207
waves
  firing and neural connections, 127
  as superpositions, 131
Wedgwood, Hensleigh, 90–3
Weil, Simone, 298n.206
Weiner, Norbert, 87, 229, 259n.64
Wells., H. G., 154
Whewell, William, 70
Whitehead, Alfred North, 94, 96, 100, 110, 126,
    144, 225, 235
  and "actual entities," 7, 10
  and "appetition and satisfaction," 7
  and "appetition of thought," 56, 67, 220
  on constitution of self in relation to
    environment, 6
  continuing work of W. James, 7
  on embodiment, 9
  on emotional energy, 47
  "event" for, 263n.41
  on feeling/s, 10
  on feelings as "vectors," 164
  "identity philosophy" of, 75
  and "the 'idea' idea," 257–8n.43
  "lures for feeling," 10

"occasion" for, 10, 202, 257n.35 (definition)
and *Paradise Lost*, 84
philosophy of organism, 56, 67, 71, 253n.4
and "prehension," 37, 75, 249, 263n.41
  (definition)
relation of whole to part ("bodily event"),
  228
and Stevens, 181
and "stubborn fact," 10, 202–3, 275n.7
on subject–predicate scheme shift, 4, 8
"vector feeling-tone," 227
vibration – "vibratory organism/s," 235, 238
and wave forms, 182
The Function of Reason, 254n.11
Process and Reality, 1, 220, 255n.14
Science and the Modern World, 181
Whitman, Walt, 12
will
  and brain activity, 31
  Chauncey Wright on, 122
  and Edwards, 31, 34, 60
  free (Jacques Loeb), 135
  in *Louis Lambert*, 168
  and W. James, 151, 174–5
Williams, Raymond, 79, 220
Williams, William Carlos, 205, 242
Wilson, Edmund, 232, 243
Wilson, Eric, 258n.49
Wilson, John F., 41, 58, 263n.49
Wright, Chauncey, 17, 122

Zeki, Semir, 226